THE NIKONIAN CHRONICLE

From the Beginning to the Year 1132

(Volume One)

Edited, Introduced and Annotated

by

Serge A. Zenkovsky

Translated

by

Serge A. and Betty Jean Zenkovsky

THE KINGSTON PRESS, INC.
Princeton, New Jersey 08542

Copyright © 1984 by Serge A. Zenkovsky and Betty Jean Zenkovsky. All rights reserved.

ISBN 0-940670-00-3

Printed in the United States of America
Published by
The Kingston Press, Inc.
P.O. Box 1456
Princeton, NJ 08542

The preparation of this volume and costs associated with its publication were supported by the Translations and Publications Programs of the National Endowment for the Humanities, an independent federal agency.

CONTENTS

Preface ix
Introduction: The Nikonian Chronicle, its Problems and its Era xiii
    Manuscripts and Redactions of *The Nikonian Chronicle* xx
    Editors and Compilers of *The Nikonian Chronicle* xxvii
    Sources of *The Nikonian Chronicle* xxxi
    Information Found only in *The Nikonian Chronicle* xxxv
    Puzzles of the Calendar and of the Chronology xxxvii
    Transliteration xl
    Proper and Geographic Names; Titles xli
    Structure and Language of *The Nikonian Chronicle* xliii
List of Titles of Entries in Volume One of *The Nikonian Chronicle* xlvi
Foreword to Volume One of *The Nikonian Chronicle* liii
List of Abbreviations lxv
Glossary of Russian and Byzantine Terminology lxviii
Genealogical Tables of the First Russian Dynasty lxx
Text of *The Nikonian Chronicle* to the year 1132 1

PREFACE

In publishing this English edition of *The Nikonian Chronicle*, the latest and largest in scope of medieval Russian historical works, its translators hope usefully to serve the purposes of studies of Russian history. *The Nikonian Chronicle* was last published in its Russian edition in Volumes xi—xiii of *Polnoe sobranie russkikh letopisei (Complete Collection of Russian Chronicles)*, St. Petersburg, 1862-1904. Photographically reproduced in the 1960s by the Academy of Sciences of the U.S.S.R., Moscow, in a very limited number of copies, it became a rare item—which, moreover, is not easily read by persons untrained in Old Russian and not well-acquainted with medieval Russian history.

Compiled in the sixteenth century on the basis of more ancient manuscripts, of which some are no longer extant, the original text of *The Nikonian Chronicle* presents a number of problems which arose during its original compilation. Indeed, the writers and editors of *The Nikonian Chronicle* worked on the basis of already ancient, often ill-preserved manuscript materials. They were confronted with missing pages—as can be seen in the text of *The Nikonian Chronicle* (further abbreviated, "*Nik.*")—as well as difficulty in reading damaged pages and paragraphs, errors made by the previous scribes, the misspelling of some names or unclear annual entries. Therefore, in preparing this English text, the present editor and his co-translator were frequently obliged to check the text of *Nik.* against the earlier available sources and to make appropriate corrections, explanations and annotations on the basis of the extant, more ancient Russian and foreign materials, as well as contemporary research.

As many Russian chronicles, *Nik.* is not merely a record of historical events, but also a kind of encyclopedia of the history of Russia and, to some extent, of the Eastern Christian world. Consequently, besides a description of occurrences, there also appear inserted documents and stories which were not directly related to the Russian past. In this edition the translators have reproduced the actual text dealing with Russian history, as it was published, in its entirety; however, in view of the monumental size of this chronicle—over 1,500 printed pages, *in quarto*, in the published Russian edition—they have taken the liberty of omitting some stories and theological discussions solely of Byzantine or South Slavic origin which do not contain any information on Russia, *per se*. Indeed, the compilers and redactors of *The Nikonian Chroncile* and of one of its immediate antecedents, the so-called *Khronograficheskii spisok piatoi novgorodskoi letopisi (Chronographic Redaction of the Fifth Novgorodian Chronicle)*, added most liberally a large number of Byzantine and Balkan narratives or historical-theological material to their other early Russian sources; therefore, *Nik.* abounds in interpolations which do not have any direct bearing on an understanding of Russia's past. Still, several of these digressive addenda—which provide insight into what Russians could learn from Byzantine history—have intentionally been retained by the present translators, particularly in the early part of the *Chronicle*.

This work, being of considerable magnitude, could not have been accomplished without the assistance of several organizations and a great many of our friends and colleagues in the academic world. First of all, we must mention the National Endowment for the Humanities, whose financial support enabled us to labor several years on the preparation of this English edition. Thanks to a grant from the National Endowment for the Humanities, we could cover all resources available in the United States and devote the preponderant part of our time to the translation and interpretation of this chronicle. Here, we would like to express our particular gratitude to the administration of the National Endowment for the Humanities, and, especially to Dr. Susan Mango, who, on many occasions, gave her time most cordially to problems of our project and our relations with the Endowment.

A research and travel grant of the American Council of Learned Societies permitted the translators to travel to Russia in 1979, to work there in libraries and archives and, most importantly, to discuss with Russian specialists in the history of medieval Russian and Russian chronicle writing a number of questions pertaining to problems encounted in *Nik*. Among these specialists we must, first of all, mention researchers in Old Russian literature and history in Leningrad and, especially, friends and colleagues in the Sector of Old Russian Literature of the Academy of Sciences. The head of this

Sector, member of the Academy of Sciences of the U.S.S.R., Dr. Dmitrii S. Likhachev, gave his whole-hearted support to our work and was most friendly and helpful in permitting the editor to work in the library and offices of the Sector. He was of great aid in elucidating a number of questions connected with Russian chronicle writing. We would also like to mention here Dr. Likhachev's *Russkie letopisi* (Moscow-Leningrad, 1947) and his commentaries to *Povest' vremennykh let* (Moscow-Leningrad, 1950) which were of great help in clarifying many puzzles of *Nik*. Among Professor Likhachev's colleagues in the Sector of Old Russian Literature with whom the editor held a number of useful discussions, there should also be mentioned L.A. Dmitriev; his wife, R.P. Dmitrieva—whose *Bibliografiia russkogo letopisaniia* (Moscow-Leningrad, 1962) is invaluable for all those who work with Russian chronicle writing; O.V. Tvorogov; O.A. Belobrova, and G.M. Prokhorov. N.S. Demkova, R.G. Skrynnikov of the University of Leningrad, and V.P. Budaragin of the Drevnekhranilishche (Depository of Old Russian Handwritten Books and Manuscripts in the Pushkinskii Dom of the Academy of Sciences) were often of great assistance in furnishing information, materials and suggestions.

In Moscow the editor had the privilege of meeting several members of the Institute of History of the Academy of Sciences, among whom must be mentioned, first of all, the late A.A. Zimin, the outstanding historian of the Russian sixteenth century, who—despite his grave illness—most graciously granted this editor a number of hours in which matters of sixteenth-century Russian history and Russian historical writings were discussed. Another member of the Institute of History of the Academy of Sciences in Moscow, Dr. Boris Kloss—who is a leading specialist on *The Nikonian Chronicle* and is the author of *Nikonovskii svod i russkie letopisi xvi-xvii vekov* (Moscow, 1980)—was most helpful to this editor in discussing the sources and writers of *Nik*. His book has become a "must" for everyone who deals with late Russian chronicle writing.

There is not space enough to list all the persons in various libraries who assisted the editor and his associate in their research. We would like, particularly, to mention the most friendly personnel of the Slavic Division and General Reading Room of the Library of Congress, those of the New York Public Library, the Library of Vanderbilt University—where this project was conceived—and of the University of North Carolina in Chapel Hill. In Russia, we wish to acknowledge the understanding aid of the staff of the Public Library of M.E. Saltykov-Shchedrin (the former Imperial Public Library), of the Library of the Academy of Sciences, and of the Library of Pushkinskii Dom, all in Leningrad; the staff of the Lenin Library and the Central State Archives of Ancient Documents (TsGADA) in Moscow. Thanks to the kindness of the personnel of all these institutions, the editor was able not only to locate important items in their rich book collections but, also, to work with some original *ms.* redactions of *Nik*.

Our former colleagues at Vanderbilt University, in particular, Dr. Josef Rysan, the editor's departmental chairman there—and, after the editor's retirement, Dean Robert Chauvin of Stetson University—assisted us in many ways by facilitating our academic and scholarly endeavors.

My debt to Betty Jean, my wife, research associate and co-translator, remains the greatest of all. This debt is not only for her most invaluable and patient collaboration throughout all phases of the work on *The Nikonian Chronicle*, but also for her sound judgment and inspiration, which permitted the editor to bring this bulky project to its final stage of publication.

Serge A. Zenkovsky
Professor Emeritus, Vanderbilt University

INTRODUCTION

The Nikonian Chronicle
Its Era
And Its Problems

The so-called *Nikonian*—or *Nikon's*—*Chronicle* was the last, official and most complete historical work of the Russian Middle Ages.[1] As used here, the word, "official," designates those chronicles written in the office of either a reigning prince or, as in this case, of a prince's bishop. Indeed, *The Nikonian Chronicle* was produced initially in the office of the Metropolitan of Moscow, and then in the offices of Ivan IV. It covers Russia's past from the foundation of the Russian state in the ninth century to the second half of the sixteenth. No other Russian chronicle embraces such a long period of time, takes into account so many events, or draws upon such a variety of historical sources. The compilers' simultaneous use of a large number of no longer extant chronicles from the different principalities, each with a varying point of view, provides a many-faceted and often impartial picture of the development of the Russian state and the deeds of the Russian princes, while preserving invaluable data on Russia's past.

It can justly be said that, appearing, as it did, toward the end of the era of Russian chronicle-writing, *The Nikonian Chronicle*[2] has

---

1. The gigantic *Litsevoi letopisnyi svod (Illuminated Codex of Chronicles)* was produced later, in the third quarter of the sixteenth century, but for the most part it follows the *Nikonian* text. Its volumes dealing with Russian history begin only in the year 1114. *The Voskresenskaia Chronicle*, also written in the early sixteenth century, is primarily an extension of the earlier, strictly Muscovite work.

2. Further abbreviated as *Nik.*

the same importance as *The Primary Chronicle* did at its beginning. While *Nik.* was certainly not the final, it was the last major Russian chronicle. *The Primary Chronicle*, although not the very first, nevertheless became the cornerstone for all subsequent Russian chronicle-writing. Both of these chronicles strongly reflect the mentalities, political situation and cultural environment of their times.

In order better to understand *The Nikonian Chronicle* and its compilers' modes of thought, it is worthwhile to view it against the background of Russian cultural evolution at that time—that is, the sixteenth century, since *Nik's.* first part was written in the 1520s-1530s and its second part was completed in the 1550s.

Historians differ markedly in evaluating sixteenth-century Russian evolution. Nineteenth-century scholars of the sixteenth century largely disregarded cultural events, being concerned primarily with the dramatic political and social events of that time: Russia's spectacular territorial growth from the Grand Duchy of Moscow into an imperial power, the unification of all the eastern Russian lands, the conquest of Kazan' and of the territories east of the middle and lower Volga, and penetration into the Urals and even western Siberia. It was also the century of the tragic reign of Ivan IV, of the enserfment of the peasants, and the end of the dynasty, so it is understandable that historians' interest was concentrated on the political and social changes. Also, nineteenth-century historians had few materials by which to judge sixteenth-century Russian culture. Only in the early twentieth century has the Russian icon been rediscovered and studied systematically. Only since World War II have the sixteenth century changes in music been revealed and investigated; and just recently art historians have taken a closer look at the sixteenth-century Russian churches, secular architecture and medieval sculpture and embroidery. The known polemical and hagiographic literature, similarly, have only lately undergone more careful scrutiny and analysis.

Regrettably, debate over the "progressive" impact of the fifteenth- and sixteenth-century heretical movements has strongly obscured from the sight of their modern defenders the very fact that the victory of those religious dissenters, with their simplistic, one-sided rejection of iconography and of the sacred arts, would most likely have brought about the wholesale destruction of the most beautiful achievements of Old Russian visual arts. Now we might only have known the names of Theophan the Greek, Rublev and Dionysius but we would have been deprived of the joy of viewing and admiring their works. There is no doubt whatsoever that the followers of Kuritsyn and Bashkin would have demolished the sacred arts just as fanatically as the supporters of the Reformation destroyed the ecclesiastic arts of Germany, Scandinavia and England.

The profound impact of Byzantium's betrayal of Orthodoxy in Florence in 1439, and of the fall of Constantinople in 1453, on all facets of Russian culture in the fifteenth and sixteenth centuries often have not been taken into account. The loss of her spiritual and aesthetic mentor of the preceding half-millennium forced Russia to seek out new patterns for aesthetic and intellectual inspiration and to solve by herself problems which had previously been resolved for her by Constantinople. This sudden disappearance of the source of its cultural inspiration, however, was quickly overcome by two new trends: the influence of the West and that of Russian national folk culture.

Taking to wife Sophia Paleologue, niece to the last Byzantine emperor, Ivan III in reality was marrying not a Greek princess but an Italian aristocrat who, instead of strengthening the Byzantine spiritual tradition in Russia, helped to introduce there Italian technicians, architects and craftsmen, thus opening the door to the first wave of Western influence in Russia. Milanese architectural forms appeared in the Kremlin and its Granovitaia Palata (the official reception hall of the Kremlin); Venetian decorative details adorned the Cathedral of Archangel Michael there; Western Renaissance artistic influence penetrated even late fifteenth- and sixteenth-century manuscripts, as well as the ornamentation of the earliest Russian printed books.[3] *D'iak* I.M. Viskovatyi, guardian of the state seal, one of the most outstanding statesmen under Ivan IV and, most probably, also one of the editors of *Litsevoi svod*, complained as early as the 1550s that it was possible to perceive even in Russian icons the "Latin heretical sophistication." Viskovatyi

---

3. *U istokov russkogo knigopechataniia*, edited by M.M. Tikhomirov, Moscow, 1959, pp. 31, 116, 144.

obviously was referring to the fundamental changes in Russian arts and to a basic movement away from the earlier Byzantine and Russo-Byzantine cultural patterns.[4]

Russian literature of the sixteenth century is usually described as "polemical" and "encyclopaedic"—features which were, certainly, new to Russian letters. Polemical works appeared at that time out of the necessity to protect Orthodoxy—*i.e.,* as reflected in the writings of Josef Volotskii, Metropolitan Daniel and Zinovii Otenskii—and to protect or defend the state—as in the works of Ivan IV, himself, or of Peresvetov—from the new tendencies in thought and society. In the sixteenth century, there being no longer a Byzantium whose Patriarch could furnish the necessary directives for attitudes and arguments against the heretics as there had been before the Council of Florence and the fall of Constantinople, Russia had to counter them alone or rely on other guides. Interestingly enough, it was the Dalmatian Dominican monk Benjamin who, in Novgorod, provided the argumentation against secularizing trends, while, in 1490, the Imperial ambassador, George De La Torre, supplied Novgorod's Archbishop Gennadius with exact instructions on how the Catholic Inquisition dealt with heretics.[5] Later, in the sixteenth century, Maxim the Greek—a former monk in Florence's Monastery of Saint Mark, from which Savanarola preached—likewise most energetically advised the Russian rulers to exterminate heretics.[6]

The second source of new inspiration, purely national, was the influence of folk culture, its aesthetic ideas and motifs on "official," upper class and church culture. Its most striking and significant effect could be seen in the new architectural style of Russian churches. The building of the *shatrovaia*—a tent-shaped church in Kolomenskoe in 1534 in which the tent, or spire-like roof replaced the traditional cupola—constituted the earliest manifestation of Russian national forms, particularly of wooden constructions, in the sphere of church architecture. The recently deciphered sixteenth-century Russian musical scores were perhaps less spec-

---

4. "Rozysk o... strokakh... I.M. Viskovatogo," *Chteniia v moskovskom obshchestve istorii i drevnostei rosiiskikh,* 1888, v. 2, s. III, p. 11.

5. Sedel'nikov, A. "Rasskaz 1490 goda o Inkvizitsii," in *TODRL* Vo. I, AN, Leningrad, 1932, pp. 33-37.

6. See Zenkovsky, S., *Russia's Old Believers,* Munich, 1970, p. 61.

tacular, but still of tremendous consequence for the development of Russian musical culture. In his suburban residence, Aleksandrovskaia sloboda, Ivan IV, himself—not only a talented polemicist but also a connoisseur of church music, as well as a composer—brought together several innovationist church choirmasters and composers whose works, as well as Ivan IV's own compositions, have, fortunately, been preserved. In their creations the old homophonous Byzantine church chant becomes more and more influenced by purely Russian folksongs, and the first elements of polyphonic melodies appear in the performances and compositions of such talented musicians and hymnologists as the brothers Rogov, Fedor Krestianin, Markel Bezborodyi, *et al.*[7] In Russian literature, together with the ornamentalism and monumentalism of the "official" encyclopaedic or polemic works, one can find new elements of realism and fiction.[8]

The motifs and themes of oral folklore fiction constantly penetrated these "official" letters of the upper classes and ecclesiastical writers. The dragon made its appearance in the historical work, *Story of Kazan'*, and the hagiographic *Story of Peter and Fevroniia*; folk lamentations were introduced in the same *Story of Kazan'*, in the *Novgorodian Fifth Chronicle* and in *Licevoj svod*[9] while the names of the bogatyrs[10] can be found in the chronicles.[11] *The Story of Peter and Fevroniia*, written by a well-known religious and social writer, Ermolai-Erazm, is of particular interest because this

---

7. Uspenskii, N.D., *Drevne-russkoe pevcheskoe iskusstvo*, Moscow, 1971; and especially Brazhnikov, M.V., *Drevne-russkaia teoriia muzyki*, Moscow, 1972; and also his *Fedor Krestianin–stikhiry*, Moscow, 1974.

8. These elements of realism and fiction are emphasized by D.S. Likhachev, who termed depictions of everyday life as elements of *"byt."* (Byt: way of life.) See his *Razvitie russkoi literatury X-XVII vekov*, Leningrad, 1973, pp. 130-133; and Dmitriev, L.A., *Zhiteinye povesti russkogo severa kak pamiatniki literatury XVII-ogo veka*, Leningrad, 1973, pp. 269-270.

9. The lamentations of the widow of the Khan of Kazan' over her late husband and of Princess Evdokiia over the body of Dmitrii Donskoi.

10. The heroes of historical epics, the defenders of Russia and her people.

11. Moiseeva, G., *Kazanskaia istoriia*, Moscow-Leningrad, 1954, pp. 47, 101; Dmitrieva, P.P., *Povest' o Petre i Fevronii*, Leningrad, 1979; for the chronicles, see the following pages.

moralistic vita is saturated with phantastic motifs from fairy tales, riddles and other kinds of oral fiction.

Simultaneously with the growth of new literary expression, the aforementioned encyclopaedic works, such as the *Chetii minei (Monthly Readings)*, organize and codify the heritage of vanished Byzantium and the literary achievements of disappearing pre-Muscovite Russia. The monumental *Litsevoi svod (Illuminated Codex of Chronicles)* was likewise an encyclopaedia of Biblical, Roman, Byzantine and Russian history.

Remaining the last independent Orthodox nation, Russia inevitably felt it necessary to strengthen the state's and church's ideological positions so as to withstand the Moslems, the Latins and the heretical movements whose successes could have resulted in the utter annihilation of Russia's spiritual, intellectual and artistic heritage. Having experienced just the beginnings of its own Reformation, the country moved rapidly toward a Counter Reformation, and in sixteenth-century Russian culture there clearly appear such contrasting features as to remind us of those which can be perceived in later Western Europe. It would hardly be an exaggeration to say that from its pre-Renaissance period—a term suggested by D.S. Likhachev for the Russian cultural evolution of the fifteenth century—Russia actually bypassed the Renaissance, itself, and moved into a new cultural era of a *sui generis* early Muscovite sixteenth-century Baroque of a rather limited Russian Counter Reformation. This very specific Russian phenomenon preceded the West European Baroque, which was later quite differently reflected in seventeenth- and eighteenth-century Russia. It can be seen that sixteenth-century Russian culture, just as the later Western Baroque, is characterized by two contrasting manifestations: on the one hand, penetration of new Western or folk cultural tendencies into the "official" culture; and, on the other hand, concomitantly, a certain revival of the Byzantine cultural heritage, the latter being reinterpreted and adapted to the requirements and needs of the time.[12] Such, for example, was the case of the so-called "theological" icons and frescoes illustrating Biblical events and teachings created in the sixteenth century *ad*

---

12. Let us remember that in the West "Baroque" reflected both the medieval spiritual heritage and the artistic achievements of the Renaissance.

majorem gloriam Dei, as well as theological works of the late fifteenth- and sixteenth-century writers.

The Nikonian Chronicle—which, itself, was a monumental encyclopaedia of Russian history, since its editors brought together in one work all the preserved chronicles from the formerly independent principalities, as well as other important materials—also reflects these two trends: namely, innovations and preservation of the old heritage. Besides covering all of Russian history, it contains a multitude of documents and historical, hagiographical and ecclesiastic narratives. It is true that ever since *The Primary Chronicle* Russian historical writing always included some documents in the chronicles—the earliest example being the text of Oleg's treaty with Byzantium—as well as extended narratives, as in the stories about the Kievan Cave Monastery and the dramatic narrative of the blinding of Vasil'ko. *The Nikonian Chronicle*, however, surpasses all earlier Russian historical writings in the amount of such assembled material. Thanks to *Nik.*, the now-vanished chronicles and other literary works have been at least partially preserved for posterity. But *Nik.* is also an ideological work. By introducing stories from Byzantine and Balkan history, it aimed at connecting the Russian past with that of these Orthodox countries, pointed to their fall under the blows of the infidel Turks, and demonstrated Russia's unique position as the last defender of the Orthodox faith and culture. It is also, to some extent, a polemical work since its editor undertook a strong defense of the institutions of the Church, of the authority of the head of the Russian church, and, especially, of ecclesiastic possessions, particularly the ownership of land. In order to prove his point, the editor depicted preceding heads of the Russian church as defenders of ecclesiastic landholdings—sometimes only stressing their "possessionist" views, at other times embellishing their real or imagined speech. Fortunately, this editing of historical events is limited almost solely to ecclesiastic matters and does not affect the bulk of the original texts of its sources.

It can be surmised that in compiling *The Nikonian Chronicle,* its authors and editors intended to create a new type of historical work. They managed not only to collect all available Russian sources but to add new data even to the earliest decades of Russian history. Such, for instance, are the items concerning the earliest Christianization of the Russian princes in A.D. 870, some new material on Sviatoslav's campaign in the Balkans, A.D. 970, new information about relations between Russia and the Turkish nomads, mention of the first heretical movements (A.D. 1004), and many other additional features. The compilers of *Nik.* did not hestiate to mention for the first time in Russian chronicle-writing the heroes of the historical epics *(byliny)*—the *bogatyrs*, Aleksandr Popovich (A.D. 1000, 1216, 1225); Demian Kudenich (A.D. 1148); Ian Usmoshvets (A.D. 1001); Dobrynia Riazanich-Zlatoi Poias (A.D. 1016, 1225). Occasionally, they even did not hesitate to use colloquial speech and phraseology of the time to provide greater emphatic expressiveness to their narration.

This complexity of sources, the reflection of diverse trends, and, consequently, often complex texts found in *Nik.* all have necessitated constant supplemental commentary and textual explanation by the present editor and his associate translator of this English edition. Likewise, the existence of *Nik.* in numerous *ms.* copies, different versions and even different redactions sometimes required a discussion of them, as well as a clarification of their interrelationships.

I. MANUSCRIPTS AND REDACTIONS OF *THE NIKONIAN CHRONICLE*

Only a few Russian chronicles were named after their compilers, writers or scribes. To such a category belong *The Laurentian Chronicle,* which was so-named for the supervisor of its writing, Monk Laurentius, who completed supervising its compilation in 1377; *The Primary Chronicle,* whose main part is often called *"Nestor's" Chronicle;* the West Russian *Chronicle of Avraamka*; *The Chronicle of Bishop Paul,* and a few others.

The great majority of Russian chronicles were named after the city or place where they were written—as, for instance, the *Chronicles of Novgorod, Pskov, Moscow, Galicia-Volynia, Tver', Riazan', Suzdal', Vladimir, Ustiug,* etc. Then, quite a few received their names from their place of preservation—for instance, the early fifteenth-century *Hypatian Chronicle* (from the Monastery of St. Hypatius near Kostroma, where it was found); *The Königsberg Chronicle* (also, often called "Radziwill's") because it was preserved in the Königsberg Library; the *Muzeinyi Spisok, Arkhivskii Spisok,* etc.

Finally, some were named for their last or most outstanding

owner—such as the *Ioasaf, Osterman, Radziwill, Shumilov,* etc., *Chronicles* or *mss.* To this last category, also, belongs the name, "Nikonian." (The most important chronicles are hereinafter further abbreviated, as follows: *Nikonian–Nik.; Laurentian–Laur.; Hypatian–Hyp.)* Indeed, the first *ms.* copy of *Nik.* to be discovered by a modern historian—in this case, by V.N. Tatishchev in the first half of the eighteenth century—once belonged to Patriarch Nikon (1652-1658), whose name was written on the *ms.* This *ms.* discovered by Tatishchev was published for the first time under the title, *Russkaia letopis' po Nikonovu spisku* (SPB, 1767-1782). When, later, it was published on the basis of the earliest original *ms.*, it still preserved its name, "Nikonian", in *PSRL (Complete Collection of Russian Chronicles).* Its latest and most accurate edition has the name, *Patriarshaia ili Nikonovskaia letopis'*. The *ms.* found by Tatishchev was not the original but merely a seventeenth-century copy of the original sixteenth-century text. Since that time a considerable number of *ms.* copies of this so-called *Nikonian Chronicle* have been found, and it is quite probable that several more may still be discovered in some archive or private collection. Most of these manuscripts are, themselves, just handwritten copies of earlier ones, and few are of significance to historians, or to the translators of the present work.

The most important—especially, in its first and more ancient portion up to the year 1520—of all the aforementioned manuscripts is the *Obolenskii ms.,* so-named after its nineteenth-century owner, Prince M.A. Obolensky (further abbreviated in this text as "Obol."). It is an impressive, handwritten work of 1,209 sheets *in folio.* We write here "sheets" or "folios," rather than "pages," because the number is found only on the first page of each sheet. Presently *Obol.* is preserved in Moscow in the Central State Archives of Ancient Documents (TsGADA), under Cipher 201, no. 163. It consists of three parts, unequal in historical value.

Of these three parts of *Obol.*, the first—the longest and most important—contains folios 1-939 and begins with the Biblical narrative of the partition of the earth among the sons of Noah, followed by an account of the migration of the Slavs and, especially, of the Eastern Slavs. Then it commences Russian history with the story about the three brothers, Kii, Shchek and Khoriv, who, according to the *Primary Chronicle,* laid the foundation of the city of

Kiev. It then treats the history of Russia, bringing it up to the year 1520.

The first part of *Obol.* was written in the offices of the Metropolitan of Moscow in the late 1520's and very early 1530's, and it is the earliest and original *ms.* text of the *Nikonian Chronicle.*

The second part of *Nik.*, Folios 940-1166, containing entries for the years 1521-1556, is considerably shorter than the first. It is not an original work, as is the text of the first part, and it was written in the 1550s in the government offices. To a large extent it follows the text for the same years of the so-called *Patriarshaia Letopis'* (hereinafter abbreviated, "*Patr.*"). The remaining folios of the *Nik. ms.* fol. 1166-1209 are no longer part of the *Chronicle* and consist of an assortment of heterogeneous materials of little historical importance; therefore it was left out of the English edition.

Patr., also sometimes called *Akademicheskaia XIV* because it is preserved in the Library of the Academy of Sciences in Leningrad, is a magnificently produced volume in full folio, likewise written in the 1550s in the government offices. It is 875 folios *in toto*, beginning with a list of the Russian metropolitans and bishops. The next folios, 44-731, reproduce the text of *Nik.* very exactly, up to the year 1520. Thus, *Nik.* is original up to 1520 and then adheres largely to *Patr.*, while *Patr.* follows *Nik.* to the year 1520 and is original for the years 1520-1566.[13]

Albeit, as regards the years 1520-1541, *Nik.* differs from *Patr.* in that it follows the text of the so-called *Voskresenskaia Letopis'* (hereinafter abbreviated, "Vosk."), which *Patr.* follows only for the years 1520-1533.[14] The remaining, final, part of *Patr.*, the years 1533-1566, contains another distinct and original historical work, the so-called *Letopisets nachala tsarstva Tsaria Velikovo Kniazia Ivana Vasilievicha (Chronicle of the Beginning of the Reign of Tsar and Grand Prince Ivan Vasilievich,* hereinafter abbreviated, "*Let. nach.*"). This is an earlier version of *Let. nach.*, to the year 1552, also published

---

13. Zimin, A.A., Introduction to *Ioasafovskaia letopis'*, Moscow, 1957, p. 5; and Kloss, pp. 190-195.

14. Published in *PSRL*, Vols. VII-VIII, *Voskresenkaia letopis'* was primarily an extension of *Moskovskii svod* 1479, published in *PSRL*, Vol. XXV. It does not include all the variety and wealth of information from the local, "provincial" chronicles as does *Nik.*

separately in *PSRL,* Vol. xxix. *Obol.* follows this text of *Let. nach.* in the entries for the years 1541-1551, while for 1533-1541 the authors of *Obol.* used, as stated above, the *Vosk.* version of *Let. nach.* The latter—*Let. nach. tsarvstva (Obol.,* years 1541-1556; *Patr.*, 1533-1556) —apparently was written under the supervision of Aleksei Adashev, Ivan IV's closest and most influential adviser and statesman in the 1540s and 1550s.[15]

Beginning with the year 1520, the style and organization of *Nik.* differ to some extent from the earlier, original, part. Since its writer dealt with events of the sixteenth century only, the language is more uniform. The years 1533-1537 are divided not only into annual entries, but also into chapters. (Chapters 59-70 follow the text of *Vosk.*). But, as in the original part of the chronicle up to the year 1520, the entries for 1520-1556 contain a number of documents and narratives while the subtitles are more frequent than in the first original part of *Nik.*

Patr. is preserved in Leningrad in the Library of the Academy of Sciences (BAN) under Cipher 32.14.8. The name, *Patriarshii,* or *Patriarhalis*, was given to this *ms.* by the eighteenth-century historian, A.L. Schloezer. *Patr.* is of great importance for reading the text of the first part of *Nik.* because in the *Obol. ms.* some words, even pages, are no longer well-enough preserved or clear. *Patr.* is only a quarter-century younger than *Obol.* and is very distinctly penned and much more carefully produced than *Obol.*[16] N.P. Likhachev was the first to ascertain the correct relationship between *Obol.* and *Patr.* S.F. Platonov determined the relationship between the second part of both of these *mss.*; and the same conclusion was reached by the recent and latest investigator of *Nik.*, B.M. Kloss.[17] Quite certainly, it was used by Ivan IV and his leading statesmen as a kind of handbook and archival compendium in discussions and decisions of important state matters.

The most monumental *ms.* in terms of size and illustrations, and third in importance, of all the extant "Nikonian" *mss.*, is the so-called

---

15. Zimin, A.A., *I.S. Peresvetov i ego sovremenniki*, Moscow, 1958, pp. 29-41.

16. Likhachev, N.P., *Paleograficheskoe znachenie bumazhnykh vodianykh znakov*, St. Petersburg, 1899, Vol. I, pp. 319-393. Platonov, S.F., "K voprosu o Nikonovskom svode," *IORIaS*, SPB, 1902, v. vii, book 3, pp. 24-33.

17. See S.F. Platonov, *op. cit.*; Kloss, p. 190 ff.

Litsevoi letopisnyi svod (Illuminated Codex of Chronicles). Indeed, this is a ten-volume, really monumental work some 9,000 pages long, illustrated with 16,000 illuminations or miniatures. A.E. Presniakov pointedly called *Litsevoi svod* a "Muscovite sixteenth-century encyclopaedia of history." Its three first volumes are devoted to Biblical and general history. The other seven deal with Russian history from 1114 to 1567. Most likely there existed another, now lost, volume covering Russian history prior to 1114, roughly the period treated by the *Primary Chronicle*. The first three volumes of *Litsevoi svod*, dealing with Biblical and general history, are usually called "Chronographs," with the addition of the name of the place where they are located. The remaining seven dealing with Russian history are named mostly after their last owners, before these volumes were deposited in state libraries.

These seven volumes of *Litsevoi svod* treating Russian history have not been preserved in good order. Probably, the folios of these *mss.* were either not bound immediately after being written or the pages have been taken out of their bindings for the purpose of making corrections or additions. It is also possible that their bindings deteriorated so much that the sheets were kept for a certain time just in piles. In any case, the order of the folios in the new binding is completely wrong. For instance, the first two volumes dealing with Russian history—the first, so-called *Golitsynskii ms.*—which in its 1035 folios contains material for the years 1114 to 1472—and the second one, the so-called *Laptevskii ms.* (1005 folios), containing material from 1116 to 1252—probably used to form just one single volume. Indeed, chronologically, the pages of these two volumes interpolate and should be arranged chronologically in the following way: *Gol.*, pp. 1 to 18; then *Lapt.*, p. 1; then *Gol.*, pp. 58, 19-57, 79-118, 60-78, *etc.*; then *Lapt.*, pp. 2-98; then *Gol.*, pp. 200-219; then *Lapt.*, pp. 99-332, etc.[18] Moreover, many entries for the years 1235-1424 are also found in yet another *ms.*, the so-called *Ostermannovskii*, bound in two volumes.

The eighth, or fifth dealing with Russian history, is the *Shumilovskii ms.*, which has been preserved in a more orderly manner and covers the years 1472-1533.

The so-called *Sinodal'nyi ms.* and the *Tsarstvennaia Kniga* are the

---

18. See the introduction to Vol. IX of *PSRL*.

last two volumes of *Litsvoi svod*, and were left unbound; although their folios were sewn together later, their chronological order was also not observed. The confusing condition of folios of *Litsevoi svod* was a stumbling block for its reading, publication and comprehensibility regarding its relationship to the earlier ms. copies of *Nik*.

The entire complex of *Litsevoi svod* is usually divided into three distinct groups: the first one, the so-called *Chronographs*—which, as mentioned above, deal with Biblical and ancient history; the second, the *Chronicle of Ancient Years*, from A.D. 114 to 1533—which covers the period ending with the death of Vasilii III; and, finally, the third—the *Chronicle of Recent Years,* 1533-1567, dealing with the first thirty-four years of the reign of Ivan IV. The location of each individual volume and its contents are as follows:

1. *Chronograph I,* GIM, also called *Muzeiskii Sbornik*, Moscow, (GIM—Gosudarstvennyi istoricheskii muzei—The State Historical Museum in Moscow), Cipher *Muz.* 358.

2. *Chronograph II,* BAN, Leningrad (BAN—Biblioteka Akademii Nauk, in Leningrad), new Cipher 17.17.9.

3. *Chronograph III,* GPB, Leningrad (GPB—Gosudarstvennaia publichnaia biblioteka im. M.E. Saltykova-Shchedrina, the former Imperial Public library), Cipher F.IV.151 in 1979; now probably, reclassified.

4. *Golitsynskii ms.*, years 1114-1472, Leningrad, GPB, F.IV.225. Its earliest publication in 1772 was called *Tsarstvennyi letopisets.*

5. *Laptevskii ms.* (used to be part of *Golitsynskii*, no. 4 above), Leningrad, GPB, Cipher F.IV.233. (Years 1116-1251).

6.-7. Two volumes of *Ostermannovskii ms.*, dealing with 1235-1424. Leningrad, BAN, Cipher 31.7.30. Also known as *Drevnii letopisets*, they fill the gap in *Golitsynskii ms.*, between folios 381 and 383.

8. *Shumilovskii ms.*, years 1472-1533, Leningrad, GPB, Cipher F.IV.232.

9. *Sinodal'nyi ms.*, abbreviated *Sin.*, covers the years 1535-1542 and 1553-1567. The years 1558-1587, however, are not in *Nik*. It is located in Moscow, GIM. *Sin.* 962 (also known as *Nikonovskaia letopis' s risunkami*).

10. *Tsarstvennaia kniga* (abbreviated, *Tsarst.*) covers the years 1533-1553. Moscow, GIM. *Sin.* 149.

These two last *mss.* used to be one single volume, but some folios which are now in *Tsarst.* were removed from *Sin.* in the 1570's in order to make some far-reaching corrections of a political nature. Several folios from both *Sin.* and *Tsarst.* are missing, but the text can be reconstructed from later *ms.* copies of them. These copies are known as *Lebedevskaia letopis'* and *Aleksandro-Nevskaia letopis'*. (Actually, both of these were also a single work.) These last two manuscripts—*Leb.* and *Al.-Nev.*—were published in *PSRL*, Vol. xxix.

Thus, *mss.* 5-8 fill the gap in *Golitsynskii ms.* (no. 4), while *Tsarst.*, with the addition of the missing folios from *Leb.* and *Al.-Nev.*, fill the gap in *Sin.*[19]

As O.I. Podobedova surmises, the *Chronographs*, vols. 1, 2 and 3, dealing with Biblical and general history, were probably begun between 1547 and 1552 in the scribes' office of Metropolitan Macarius. The next five volumes, all dealing with Russian history to 1533, were probably prepared before 1564 under the supervision of the Chosen Council (*Izbrannaia Rada*), a board of close advisers to Ivan IV in the 1550s, and especially, under the active editorship of Aleksei Adashev in the Sovereign Workshop of Scribes. The remaining last two volumes (9 and 10, *Sin.* and *Tsarst.*) were likewise compiled in the Sovereign's Workshop of Scribes under the supervision of Ivan IV's other senior official, the most influential in those years, D'iak I.M. Viskovatyi. The oft-mentioned B.M. Kloss, the latest and most thorough investigator of the entire set of the *Nikonian mss.*, including *Litsevoi svod*, comes to the conclusion that work on the basic text of *Litsevoi svod*—excluding later corrections—was, however, done between 1568 and 1576, while the final corrections were made between January, 1574, and November, 1581.[20] The *Litsevoi svod* redaction of *Nik.* often provides more extensive descriptions of important historical events, and quite frequently

---

19. The corrections in *Tsarst.* were probably made either by D'iak Viskovatyi or by Ivan IV himself. See Al'shits, S.D., "Ivan Groznyi ili D'iak I. Viskovatyi," in *TODRL*, Vol. XVI. Al'shits points out the similarity of style of these corrections with Ivan IV's letters to Kurbsky. Kloss, pp. 226-231, assumes that *Sin.* and *Tsarst.* used to be one single volume.

20. Podobedova, O.I., *Miniatiury russkikh istoricheskikh rukopisei*, Moscow, 1965; and her article in *Voprosy istochnikovedeniia*, Vol. IX (1961), pp. 304-315; Kloss, pp. 245, 249 and 223.

adds new data not found in *Obol.* or *Patriarshii.* Its compilers and editors obviously had some historical sources other than *Nik.* and quite often edited portions of the original *Nik.* text. Moreover, in the mid-sixteenth century the political situation and power structure were changing, and so the officials who edited *Litsevoi svod* obviously considered it judicious in some cases to make appropriate reinterpretations of the historical material.

The several dozen other *ms.* copies of *Nik.* sometimes assist in reading less well-preserved parts of the more important aforementioned *mss.*; but none provide new information or contribute to the study of Russian history, so they are not discussed here.

The Nikonian Chronicle was published in the *Complete Collection of Russian Chronicles (PSRL—Polnoe sobranie russkikh letopisei,* Vols. IX-XIII, 1862-1904), on the basis of these three basic *ms.* texts: *Patriarshii, Obolenskii* and *Litsevoi svod*—while some other manuscripts were used to fill lacunae in them or to provide a correct reading.

The present English language edition of *The Nikonian Chronicle* follows the above-mentioned publication in *PSRL* and is based primarily on the texts of the *Obolenskii* and *Patriarshii* manuscripts. Occasionally, where the texts of these *mss.* are incomplete due to missing pages either in them or in their earlier source materials, the translators used the corresponding passages from the text of *Litsevoi svod.* Sometimes, defective passages of *Nik.* were corrected according to the *Laurentian, Hypatian, Novgorodian, Late Fifteenth-century* (so-called *1479) Muscovite,* or some other earlier chronicles. Finally, when the text of *Litsevoi svod* was more detailed and seemed historically more interesting than the corresponding texts in *Obol.* and *Patr.*, the translators followed the former. All these instances are indicated in footnotes.

II. EDITORS AND COMPILERS OF *THE NIKONIAN CHRONICLE*

Some seventy years ago A.A. Shakhmatov, the most perceptive and brilliant scholar of Russian chronicle writing, discussing the *Nikonian Chronicle,* pointed out that it was certainly the work of an ecclesiastic writer who edited the *Chronicle* with the purpose of glorifying the Russian church and, especially, of providing greater prestige to the Metropolitan See of all Russia. A more recent student of the same problem, the late A.A. Zimin, in his introduction to

Ioasafovskaia (Op. cit., pp. 12 ff.) determined that the writing of this chronicle was completed at the beginning of the 1520's, very soon after the appointment of Metropolitan Daniel to the Muscovite See. He stresses the similarity in ideology and texts of the *Nikonian* and *Ioasafovskaia* chronicles. Following A.E. Presniakov's studies, he confirms that from the years 1461 to 1520 both chronicles are very close in their texts and interpretations of the historical happenings. When, in August, 1979, the present editor had the privilege of discussing the *Nikonian Chronicle* with A.A. Zimin, that eminent Russian historian emphasized that already in the 1960's he became persuaded that Metropolitan Daniel was the writer or editor of *Nik.* A.N. Nasonov also stressed the role of Metropolitan Barlaam and Daniel in Russian chronicle writing of the late fifteenth and early sixteenth centuries, when *Nik.* was produced.[21] B.M. Kloss, himself formerly a student of Zimin's, recently published the most exacting and exhausting study of *Nik.* In it he came to the conclusion that, indeed, Metropolitan Daniel was not only the initiator but also the editor, or the writer, of *Nik.* Kloss' main observations and deductions are extremely persuasive and convincing. First of all, he compared the texts of the earlier sources used by the compilers and editors of *Nik.* with *Nik.*, itself. He determined all additional sentences, new Biblical quotations, some new phraseological expressions introduced by the compilers into the *Nik.* text, fed them into a computer, and then compared them with similar quotations and stylistic manners of nearly all sixteenth-century writers. The result was most gratifying. Out of some twenty-five Russian writers of that time, Metropolitan Daniel uses much more often than anyone else these new additional quotations and phrases in *Nik.* taken from the *Gospel*, the *Old Testament*, the early Church Fathers, and even Daniel's own writings. It indicates that he was at least one, and probably the main, editor of *Nik.*

For instance, Kloss found that out of a hundred and five quotations from the *Bible* and early Church Fathers encountered in *The Nikonian Chronicle*, seventy-two are the same as those used by Daniel in his own works. Checking, however, the list of these Biblical quotations which Kloss considered to have been added to the earlier texts by Daniel, against *Laur.* or *Hyp.* up to 1157, the present editor

21. Nasonov, A.N., *Istoriia russkogo letopisaniia*, AN SSSR, M., 1969, pp. 374 ff.

found that several of them were, in reality, not added but were already present in either *Laur.* or *Hyp.*, which were indirect sources for *Nik.*

The next after Daniel in frequency of the use of these Biblical quotations were Maxim the Greek and Joseph of Volotsk, with thirty-two and thirty-one quotations—and who, by the way could not have participated in the writing of *Nik.* because Joseph of Volotsk had died by the time *Nik.* was compiled and Maxim the Greek dealt primarily with the translation of some Greek theological and canonical works, and did not participate in writing the chronicles. Thus, there is no doubt that it was Daniel who, as in the above cited opinion of A.A. Shakhmatov, most persistently re-edited the characterizations of the Metropolitans of Russia with the purpose of glorifying them.[22] Daniel, according to Kloss' conclusions, also added moralistic and theological digressions to the original texts.

B. Kloss also ascribes to Metropolitan Daniel some pro-Muscovite bias in presenting Moscow's relations with the Kazan' Tatars and Lithuania. This opinion of Kloss' is rather debatable because he disregards numerous other rather strongly anti-Muscovite presentations of the rivalry between Moscow, Tver', Novgorod and other Russian lands as they appear in *Nik.*, and even some rather unflattering (for Muscovite armies and princes) descriptions of wars with Lithuania and Kazan'. If Daniel were really a careful pro-Muscovite editor of *Nik.* in its entirety, he would certainly have eliminated these interpretations of events which were damaging to numerous Muscovite princes—as, for instance, Ivan Kalita's treatment of Prince Mikhail of Tver'. He could easily have edited or eliminated them even when they were taken from the chronicles of Novgorod, Tver' and other principalities. It seems to the present writer that Daniel's role in editing *Nik.* was limited to a reinterpretation of a limited number of passages and additions of quotations and to his own interpolations, in which the role and importance of the Metropolitan See and of the Church, in general, was described. He would, however, hardly be the man who wrote the main text dealing with purely political and cultural developments of Russian history.

22. See Shakhmatov, A.A., *Otzyv o sochinenii S.K. Shambinago: Povesti o Mamaevom poboishche*, St. Petersburg, 1910, p. 85.

Most probably, there was another editor, or more, who were in charge of the selection of sources for the *Obolenskij ms.* redaction of *Nik.* up to the year 1520. Indeed, we know that in the chronicle's workshop of Muscovite See there were produced in the late fifteenth and early sixteenth centuries several chronicles besides *Nik.*—namely, the *Ioasafovskaia, Novgorodian 5th Chronographic, a.o*—which required a considerable staff of experienced and trained chroniclers. It may be that one, or several, of these still anonymous other editors likewise introduced into the chronicle elements of folklore—as, for instance, mention of the *bylina* heroes, Alesha—or Aleksandr—Popovich and Dobrynia Nikitich, some humorous expressions in depicting battles between the Novgorodians and Suzdalians, as well as the preserved description of the rude manners of the defenders of Moscow on the city walls during the invasion by Khan Tokhtamysh in 1382. These features, combined with quite numerous unflattering details of the Muscovite princes' attitudes toward other principalities and even toward foreign powers, confirm the impression that Daniel's editorial and, especially, compilatory role was most likely limited only to such passages in which either church problems were treated, or moralistic and laudatory descriptions of metropolitans, princes, and some other historical personalities were introduced.

Indeed, Daniel, being occupied as head of the Russian church and, himself, a prolific ecclesiastic writer, could hardly have found the time to select the sources which form the main historical fabric of the first part of *Nik.*—that up to 1520. Obviously, there should have been in the metropolitan chancery a man or men well-trained historically who was or were responsible for selecting the historical sources for writing the annals of Russia's past. It was also probably he—or they—specialists in chronicle writing, well-versed in Russian history and with excellent knowledge of source materials, and not Metropolitan Daniel, who introduced into *Nik.* occasional ribald stories and anecdotes about the Byzantine courts taken from the so-called *Chronograph*, which was compiled partially in Byzantium and in the Balkans, and partially in Russia. These anecdotes about the adultery of the Empresses, murders of Emperors and members of their families, military upheavals and deceits all contrast strikingly with the moralistic quotations and theological discussions scattered throughout *Nik.* by Daniel in places appropriate for the edification of readers and the glorification of the Metropolitan See, or for defense of the Church's holdings. Even if some of these Byzantine court stories had been introduced in any of *Nik's* sources, Daniel, as a "professional" indefatigable moralist, would have eliminated at least some of them from the *Chronicle*. Thus, it is undeniable that, most probably, Daniel gave his blessing to the compilation of *Nik.* and edited several of its passages; but, also, it can hardly be doubted that other editors, no less than Daniel, contributed in selection of the sources and in the compilation of the long text of the *Chronicle*. This selection, which reflects the points of view of various Russian lands, often provides *Nik.* with extremely valuable objectivity, and its editors did not hesitate to point it out when the grand princes of Muscovy were cruel, broke their pledges or annexed the territories of other princes to their realms.

III. SOURCES OF *THE NIKONIAN CHRONICLE*

Although studies of *The Nikonian Chronicle* began in the eighteenth century when some of its later *mss.* were discovered, only at the beginning of the twentieth did its sources become seriously investigated. A.A. Shakhmatov—whose ingenious scholarly mind, similar to our modern computers, was able to retain the various texts of the scores of chronicles simultaneously—was the first to provide a nearly complete picture of the source materials used by the compilers of *Nik.* He pointed to the great wealth of these sources and to the extremely complex structure of *Nik.* The basic source—from *Nik.*'s very beginning up to the mid-fifteenth century—was the so-called *Chronographic Redaction of the Fifth Novgorodian Chronicle*.[23] This chronicle—as well as other materials in the richest *ms.* collection of GIM (Gosudarstvennyi istoricheskii muzei)—remained off limits, at least during my visit to Russia in 1979, to foreign and, sometimes, even native Russian historians who are not from Moscow. So the present editor, unfortunately, could not have recourse to it.

Another important source for the writing of *Nik.* was *Ioasafovskaia letopis'* (further abbreviated, *Ioasaf.*), which was discovered by Shakhmatov and named after its sixteenth-century

---

23. Further abbreviated as *Chron. red. 5th Novg.* Researchers of the early twentieth century used to call it *Chronographic Fourth Novgorodian* because the *Fourth* was its main source.

owner, Metropolitan Ioasaf.[24] *Ioasaf.* covers the years 1437 to 1520. Beginning with the year 1454, *Nik.* follows almost the entire *Ioasaf.* text.[25]

Yet another chronicle, likewise discovered by Shakhmatov, himself, was the *Simeonovskaia*.[26] *Simeon.* was of prime importance for work on *Nik.* embracing the period, 1177-1493. According to Shakhmatov and to *Nik.*'s later scholars, the *Simeon.* is very close to the *Troitskaia Chronicle* (further abbreviated, "*Troits.*"), which burned in 1812 during Napoleon's invasion of Moscow and whose text has been partially preserved in N. Karamzin's *History of the Russian State*. Together with *Ioasaf.* and *Chron. red. 5th Novg., Simeon.* became one of *Nik.*'s basic sources.[27]

The remaining sources for *Nik.*, according to Shakhmatov, were the so-called *Russian Chronograph of 1512* and several other chronicles, including late fifteenth-century Muscovite ones.

A.N. Nasonov in his *Istoriia russkogo letopisaniia* (Moscow, 1969, pp. 407-8) added the chronicles of Tver' to the above sources of *Nik.*, while A.G. Kuz'min both proved that now inextant chronicles of Riazan' likewise became reflected in *Nik.* and confirmed that *Simeon.* was one of its important sources.[28]

The latest and most thorough research on *Nik.* is that of Boris Kloss, who quite recently published his *Nikonovskii svod i russkie letopisi XVI-XVII vekov* (Moscow, 1980). He agrees with most of Shakhmatov's findings, as well as Priselkov's, Nasonov's, Kuz'min's and other specialists' in Russian chronicle writing, regarding the sources of *Nik.*; but he goes farther into the depth of *Nik.*'s sources, providing more proof of their interrelations, and makes quite a number of important original conclusions. Confirming that the main sources of *Nik.* were *Chron. red. 5th Novg, Ioasaf., Simeon.*, the

---

24. See A.A. Zimin's introduction to *Ioasafovskaia letopis'*, Moscow, 1957.

25. See *op. cit.*, introduction, p. 7 ff.

26. Published in *PSRL*, Vol. XVIII; it was an important source for *Nik.* See the introduction to *Simeonovskaia letopis'*, *PSRL*, Vol. XVIII. Further abbreviated as *Simeon.*

27. See M. Priselkov's introduction to the reconstructed text of *Troitskaia letopis'*, Moscow, 1950. *Troits.* together with *Laur.*, *Hyp.* and the oldest redaction of *Novg.* was one of the four oldest chronicles.

28. Kuz'min, A.G.., *Riazanskoe letopisanie*, Moscow, 1965, pp. 14-34, 116-199.

Russian Chronograph of 1512, the writings of Tver' and no longer extant chronicles of Rostov and Riazan', Kloss adds to them a now vanished South Russian chronicle which preceded *Laur.* and *Troits.* He says that this now-vanished chronicle, and not *Laur.* and *Troits.,* themselves, as thought by Shakhmatov, furnished the important material for the first parts of *Nik.*'s text, specifically, for events in South Russia in the period from the ninth to the thirteenth centuries.[29] He also shows that another preserved chronicle, the so-called *Vladimirskii letopisets* (further abbreviated, *Vlad.,* published in *PSRL,* Vol. xxx), which covers the years 1177-1523, likewise furnished important material for *Nik.*

Similarly to the *Ioasaf.* and *Simeon.,* the *Vlad.* was written about the same time as *Nik.* Kloss proves that up to the year 1177 when the *Simeon.* begins, the *Vlad.,* together with *Chron. red. 5th Novg.,* were the main sources of information for the compilers of *Nik.*[30]

The influence of the chronicle of Tver' is reflected in similarities of *Nik.'s* text with such of Tver's preserved writings as *Rogozhskii letopisets* and *Tverskoi sbornik* (both published in Vol. xv of *PSRL*). Simultaneous use of material from Tver' with that of the Muscovite chronicles (produced in the office of the Grand Prince of Moscow and compiled in the last decades of the fifteenth century) contributed to a more balanced and multifaceted presentation of the rivalry between Moscow and Tver', both of which struggled for leadership over all northeastern Russia.

Strangely enough, although these late fifteenth-century Muscovite chronicles are very rich in information, it was rather *Chron. red. 5th Novg.* and *Ioasaf.* that influenced the writers of *Nik.* The former is especially strongly reflected in *Nik.* from *Nik.*'s very first pages up to the middle of the fifteenth century (1454), when *Nik.*'s compilers switched over to the text of *Ioasaf.*[31] and *Simeon.* To a certain extent these three main sources for *Nik.,* all written in the offices of the Metropolitan See, may be considered either probable prototypes for *Nik.,* or an intermediate stage in the gathering of material which thereafter was enriched by yet other sources, for instance, the *First Novgorodian Chronicle, Senior Redaction,* the oldest

29. Kloss, p. 185 ff.
30. Kloss, p. 145.
31. *Ioasaf.,* p. 7.

preserved Russian chronicle and which was used to supplement the text of *Chron. red. Fifth Novg*. Not all of these other sources can always be identified, however. The additional identified, but not preserved ones are the chronicles of Rostov, Riazan', Suzdal', Nizhnii Novgorod and some western Russian works.

Finally, as mentioned in the Foreword, *Nik.* abounds in stories and historical reports about Byzantium and the Orthodox Southern Slavs. The main part of this very liberally interpolated material is taken from *Russian Chronograph 1512*, or an early version of the *West Russian Chronograph* (likewise, early sixteenth-century). Since most of these stories and historical events have little or nothing to do with Russia, the translators, as stated in the Preface, have omitted a considerable number of them. In order, however, to provide the flavor of sixteenth-century Russian knowledge of Byzantium and, especially, of the Byzantine court, we have preserved a certain number of these stories. We should not forget that Byzantine history, especially before the taking of Constantinople by the Crusaders in 1204, was to a considerable extent one of palace upheavals. Indeed, in 1058 years of Byzantine history, out of 109 emperors, sixty-five were assassinated, twelve died in monasteries or prison, three died of hunger and eighteen were castrated or blinded. R. Guerdan in his *Byzantium* (New York, 1962, p. 135) put it quite appropriately—that Byzantium "was an absolute monarchy tempered by assassination." Thus it was hardly an example of a very moral government; but it was familiar to the Russian sovereigns and upper strata and may have been unintentionally imitated by some of them.

The readers of *Nik.* will notice the frequent lengthy genealogical references introduced after the names of the princes. For instance, under the year 6786/1278 the chronicler specifies that "Grand Prince Boris Vasil'kovich of Rostov was the grandson of Konstantin, gr. grandson of Vsevolod, gr. gr. grandson of Iurii Dolgorukii, gr. gr. gr. grandson of Vladimir Monomakh, gr. gr. gr. gr. grandson of Vsevolod, gr. gr. gr. gr. grandson of Iaroslav, gr. gr. gr. gr. gr. grandson of Great Vladimir." These genealogies are also found in *Voskresenskaia chronicle* (*PSRL,* Vol. VII) and in a manuscript volume devoted to this sort of genealogical data on Lithuanian and Russian princes.[32] In Kloss' opinion, these

---

32. Kloss, p. 178.

genealogies were introduced in order to increase the prestige and demonstrate the superior ancestry of the Muscovite princes. The above example of the ancestry of Grand Prince Boris Vasil'kovich of Rostov and genealogical lineages of innumerable other non-Muscovite princes, however, casts doubt on such an assumption. By the end of the fifteenth century the genealogy of the Russian princes became so long and involved, especially in view of a certain repetitious monotony in their names, that the chroniclers apparently decided it was necessary to clarify to which line of the dynasty the particular princes belonged. Thus, the purpose of these references was for general information and not necessarily aimed at extolling the Muscovite princes, as Kloss thinks. And, indeed, for us, now, these genealogical delineations, although often repetitious and annoyingly long, nonetheless serve the useful purpose of identifying the princes enumerated—who frequently have not only the same first name but also the same patronymic.

IV. INFORMATION FOUND ONLY IN *THE NIKONIAN CHRONCILE*

Nik. is particularly valuable for the information contained in its folios which is not to be found in any other extant chronicle or document. These items to be found exclusively in *Nik.* are of a most varied nature. They deal with the deeds and deaths of princes; activities of the bishops and metropolitans; raids by nomads; and deaths and occasional baptisms of the nomadic rulers—Pechenegs, Polovets, Torks, and, finally, Tatars of the Golden Horde. We can not always be certain what the sources were for these entries. The ones dealing with the histories of principalities other than Moscow, Tver' and Novgorod came, almost certainly, from the vanished chronicles written in these princes' or bishops' courts: for instance, we find in *Nik.* quite abundant material on Riazan',[33] Nizhnii Novgorod, Suzdal' and Rostov, all of which, as mentioned above, was incorporated into *Nik.* from the local historical writings.

Numerous details of Russia's relations with the Golden Horde from the year 6798/1290 to 6921/1413, most certainly, have their origin in the archives of the bishop of Sarai, capital of the Golden

---

33. See Kuz'min, A.G., *Riazanskoe letopisanie*, Moscow, 1965, pp. 14-21, 36, 119-198, *a.o.*

Horde. These bishops cared not only for the religious needs of the Orthodox population and visitors to Sarai, but also were, *de facto*, Moscow's permanent diplomatic residents in that outpost.

Also, probably, from ecclesiastic archives—primarily, of the Metropolitan of Russia—come the numerous scattered data about the administration of the Russian Church, the journeys of the metropolitans and bishops, the first Russian heresies (6512/1004 and 6631/1123), the earliest baptism of the Russian princes, the names of the first heads of the Russian church, as well as other events within the Russian church. Some historians surmise that under Metropolitan Cyprian the archives of the Metropolitan See were moved from Kiev to Moscow, but it is only a suggestion, not confirmed by any known facts.[34]

Of particular interest are the entries dealing with the period treated in the *Nik.* redaction of *The Primary Chronicle*. We were able to find some fifty items unique to *Nik.* and have indicated them in our annotations. B.A. Rybakov expressed the opinion that the writers of *Nik.* had at their disposal some South Russian sources concerning the ninth to twelfth centuries which were not included in *The Primary Chronicle mss.*[35] Kloss, too, believes in the existence in the sixteenth century of such South Russian chronicle sources.[36] Nonetheless, he expresses doubt as to the authenticity of some items of this period in *Nik.* Certainly, mention of Gostomysl as the first known Novgorodian leader—although also mentioned in *Nov. Kom.*—and the revolt against Riurik by the people of Novgorod under the leadership of Vadim, sound very much like later folkloristic memories. Let us not forget, however, that such folkloristic recollections in many lands, including Russia and Scandinavia (its sagas) often actually did reflect historical facts. It is obvious, for instance, from any text of *The Primary Chronicle*, that a considerable amount of information about the past came to the writer from Vyshata and Jan Vyshatich, who told the chronicler about quite a number of important historical events.[37] Both spoke not only about

---

34. See the Foreword to this first volume of *The Nikonian Chronicle*.

35. Rybakov, B.A., *Drevniaia Rus'*, Moscow, 1963, pp. 162-173 and 182-187.

36. Kloss, pp. 185, 187.

37. See D.S. Likhachev's edition of *Povest' vremennykh let*, Moscow, 1959, Vol. II, pp. 14-20; and Kuz'min, *op. cit.*, 8a, 159-162, 364-367.

their participation in events but also about the deeds of their fathers. Similar recollections could have been preserved by other persons and recorded in the vanished chronicles. And here one can reasonably wonder why a chronicler, in the era of the centralization of northeastern Russia, would invent a story in *Novg. Kom.* about Gostomysl (repeated in *Nik.*) and, in *Nik.*, about a Novgorodian revolt against a legendary ancestor of the Muscovite princes? In any case, such epic recollections could hardly have been introduced by the strongly pro-government Metropolitan Daniel.

Most of these unique items of *Nik.*, both in the ninth-century entries and later, do not have any political or ecclesiastical coloration and hardly were motivated by a bias on the part of *Nik.*'s writers. See, for instance, under 6373/865, Askol'd's and Dir's campaign against Polotsk; under 6616/1108, the exact date being March 9, of the building—rather, the founding or completion—apparently in Kiev, of the Church of St. Michael. To the same category belong the name of Pecheneg and Polovetsian rulers, similarly found only in *Nik.* Indeed, it is hardly possible to doubt that the office of the Metropolitan See had at its disposal in the early sixteenth century some additional, no longer extant, historical materials—probably some now unknown versions of the chronicle of Kiev or Pereiaslavl',[38] from which they obtained many data now specific strictly to *Nik.* At least one of these, the baptism of Askol'd and Dir in the 860's, is confirmed by Byzantine sources. As already mentioned above, this event will be discussed *in extenso* with some other information on Russian history in the Foreword to this first volume and in the annotations. Since some of these unique entries in *Nik.* are of an ecclesiastic nature they have not been discussed very much by recent Soviet Russian historians. Nonetheless, they are of considerable importance in comprehending the earliest period of Russia's past.

V. PUZZLES OF THE CALENDAR AND OF CHRONOLOGY

The Russian medieval calendar and chronology, as practically

---

38. The frequent use of the Ultra-March year—see section five of this introduction—suggests that the *Chronicle of Pereiaslavl' Russkii* was one of *Nik.*'s important sources.

all calendars and chronologies of that time, require explanation, for they quite often present real problems and difficulties in the correct dating of events. When the Russians accepted Christianity from Byzantium, they also accepted the Byzantine chronology, which commenced with the beginning of the world—an event which took place in 5508 B.C., according to their chronological system of the tenth century. The Byzantine year began not on January 1, as we begin it now, but on September 1. The Eastern Slavs, however, continued to start their calendar year not on September 1 but on March 1 (six months *later* than the Byzantine New Year). Only in the fifteenth century did Russia switch entirely to the Byzantine New Year on September 1, while under Peter I Russia accepted the contemporary Western chronological system which begins the year with January 1. The "March" New Year—which, as stated above, began six months *after* the Byzantine "September" New Year—was used almost consistently until the beginning of the twelfth century. Thus, the Russian *Primary Chronicle* up to the year 1110 permits in most cases a rather easy conversion of the Russian chronology into the contemporary one. In the twelfth century, though, for reasons still unknown, Russian chroniclers began, simultaneously with the March year, to use the so-called "Ultra-March year," which began *not six months after* the Byzantine year but *six months earlier* than the Byzantine one. Through the twelfth century to the beginning of the fifteenth, this "Ultra March" year was often used simultaneously with the "March year" and, in some rare cases, with the "September year"—thereby creating, during these three or three and a half centuries, great complications for any exact conversion of Russian chronicle chronology into a modern one. This "Ultra March" chronology was not used, however, in all Russian cities but only in certain ones: for instance, Pereiaslavl'-Russkii used the "Ultra March" calendar, while in Kiev the "March calendar" was used.

Russia was not an exception in this complexity of medieval chronology. In southern Italy in the twelfth to fourteenth centuries Italians began the New Year on September 1; in Milan, Genoa and many other cities, on March 1; in Florence, on March 25 (the Day of Annunciation); and still others started the New Year before January 1, or sometimes and in some cities after January 1—just as the Russians did, with the "March" and "Ultra March" year. No less complex and diverse were the chronologies in medieval Germany,

France and other West European countries.

As an illustration of Russian chronology in the twelfth to fourteenth centuries, the following example may be given: the year 1175 A.D. corresponds to January-August of the year 6683 and September-December of 6684 in Byzantine chronology. In Russia, however, the same year would be recorded, in the case of the March system, as January-February of 6682 and March-December of 6683; or, in the case of the Ultra March system, as January-February, 6683 and March-December, 6684. Thus, when the compiler of a new chronicle was using previous material with two or three different calendar styles, and if he was not aware of the exact date and month of the given event, he had to choose among three different dates—the years 6682, 6683 or 6684. Sometimes, in order to avoid making a choice of a date, in *Nik.* he would repeat the same event under different dates; or, in other cases, he would use the date which seemed to him the most judicious. Therefore not infrequently we find such instances in *Nik.* of the use of double dating for a given historical event.[39]

The foregoing description of the September, March and Ultra March calendars has not yet brought us to a complete understanding of the dating of events by medieval chroniclers—primarily, by the Eastern Orthodox and medieval Russian historians. Of importance, also, is an understanding of the *era* system—that is, of the calculation of the period between the Biblical version of the creation of the world and the date of the birth of Christ. In tenth- to fifteenth-century Byzantium this period was estimated at 5508: thus, the year 1012 would be, accordingly, 6520; but at least until the tenth century the "Old Byzantine era" of 5505 between the world's creation and Christ's birth was also used. Thus, 1012 could be 6517. In Antioch and the Near East the Antiochian era was used, which allocated only 5500 years to this same period: thus, 1012 became 6512; while in Egypt the Alexandrian system was applied—with only 5493, or even 5492 years for the calculation of Christ's birth after the creation of the world. In this system, 1012 becomes 6505 or even 6504. Consequently, we derive four different systems of calculating dates, with up to sixteen years' difference: 6520 and 6504, for the

---

39. An extended discussion of this problem can be found in N.G. Berezhkov, *Khronologiia russkogo letopisaniia*, Moscow, 1963, especially pp. 9-17; and Kuz'min, *op. cit.*, pp. 226 ff., 247.

year 1012.⁴⁰ Conversely, 6520 could designate 1028, 1027, 1020, 1017 and 1012. In Bulgaria, through which and from which the earliest historical works came to Russia, in the late ninth century the Old Byzantine (5505) and Antiochan (5500) systems were used for the calculation of historical dates, and some Bulgarian writers even used the so-called "Hyppolit era," with 5504 years before Christ as the date for the creation of the world. In the medieval Christian world there were at least several dozen other "eras" of determining historical dates. These coexisting calendar systems and eras all resulted in considerable confusion when Russians started dating their own historical writings after their all-national conversion to Christianity under Vladimir.⁴¹

The problem of medieval Russian chronology has not yet been entirely solved. In the present translation the editor has not tried to resolve these problems of chronology, whose solution would require years of devoted concentration on elucidating the chronologies used by diverse Russian chronicle writers in various regions. He has felt it his duty, though, to forewarn readers of this complexity, which is too often disregarded both by Russian and by Western historians. In the present translation the editor adheres to the system of the Russian printed edition of *Nik.* in *PSRL*, wherein 5508 years are always automatically deducted from the date given by the chronicler. When, in certain cases, however, the chronology is obviously unclear or doubtful and can be corrected through correlation with other Russian or foreign sources, the present editor so indicates in footnotes. Likewise, similar comments are made in most of the instances when *Nik.*'s dating disagrees with that of other earlier chronicles. In some cases when an annual entry mentions an eclipse of the sun, the editor was able to verify its date on the basis of historical astronomical calendars. He expresses his gratitude for the assistance of Professor Robert Hardie of Vanderbilt University.

VI. TRANSLITERATION

No generally accepted and consistent English transliteration system exists for Russian words. Practically every translator and

---

40. Kuz'min, *op. cit.*, 223-229.
41. See Kuz'min, *op. cit.*, pp. 221-226.

writer of books on Russia uses his own manner of transliterating. The Library of Congress transliteration is quite convenient for bibliographical purposes and it is used here in the footnotes for bibliographic references, and in the Bibliography at the end of the work. Though it is not totally precise in rendering the sounds and letters of Russian, the Library of Congress system was also used within the text for the sake of consistency.

VII. PROPER AND GEOGRAPHIC NAMES: TITLES

In the *Nikonian Chronicle*, as in most medieval manuscripts, the orthography of nouns is rarely consistent. For instance, Andrei or Ondrei, Vasilii or Vasilei are the same name. Fedor sometimes appears as Feodor, Akinf as Okinf. For the sake of uniformity and an easier identification of historical personages, modern Russian transliteration of proper and geographic names serves as the base. Still, the earlier abbreviated form of the patronymic is used: i.e., Iaroslavich, Monomashich in place of modern Iaroslavovich or Monomakhovich—when they appear in *Nik.*; and Danilo, the common Russian form of that name before the nineteenth century, in place of Daniil.

It must also be mentioned that quite often the same person can be found in the chronicle under different designations. For instance, Prince Ivan Vasilievich Obolenskii-Striga is mentioned as "Prince Ivan," "Striga," "Prince Ivan Vasilievich," *etc.* So, for easier identification, the complete name has been given, where possible, in this translation: i.e., "Prince Ivan Vasilievich Obolenskii-Striga." As long as a prince is an appanage (independent or semi-independent) ruler, he is called "Prince of the appanage:" *i.e.*, "Prince of Mozhaisk" or "Prince of Serpukhov." When, however, the same person or his children become service princes of the grand prince or lose their appanage, then they are mentioned as "Prince Mozhaiskii" or "Prince Serpukhovskii," the former title having become a family name. For the names of saints and the clergy, the English equivalent (*i.e.*, "Nicholas," "Alexander," "Basil") or the original Biblical names—*i.e.*, "Abraham" instead of "Avraamii," "Theognostos" instead of "Feognost," are given. It should not be forgotten that most Orthodox saints originally had Greek names, while among the clergy—especially, among bishops and metropolitans—there actually was a large number of Greeks, and they are identified by their Greek names.

As far as foreign names are concerned, either personal or geographic, when they can be identified, their original foreign form and not the Russian one is used. The transliteration of the Turkic—Pecheneg, Polovetsian and Tatar—names is very complicated. In *Nik.* these names are often rendered in a transliteration very different from the one now used in historical works dealing with the nomads and, especially, the Islamic world. This problem is complicated by the fact that these numerous nomadic tribes, themselves, often used a very different form for the same basic name. Thus, Ottoman Turkic pronunciation would be very different from Kazan' Tatar. The present editor, not being a specialized Turkologist and in order to bring some uniformity into the rendering of these names, has applied predominantly the transcription of G.V. Vernadsky, as used in his *A History of Russia*, Vol. III: *The Mongols and Russia* (New Haven, 1953), slightly modified according to the editor's system of transliteration. In many cases when the Turkic names found in *Nik.* do not appear in Vernadsky's work, the present translators have been obliged to use their own judgment and their own meager knowledge of Turkic linguistics and the Islamic world.

The Old Russian system of titles differs very considerably from the Western. Therefore the translators have adapted it to standard American terminology found in the most reputable historical works. For the Russian title, "kniaz'," thus, they use "prince" and not "duke;" and for "velikii kniaz'," "grand prince" and not "grand duke," the latter being reserved in Russia only from the eighteenth century on for members of the Imperial family. The chronicle writers used the term, "tsar'," indiscriminately for the heads of large empires or for the Russian ruler. For instance, they called Byzantine emperors, the rulers of Muscovy and khans of the Golden Horde all "tsar'." In this translation, "tsar'" is reserved for the Russian tsars, beginning with Ivan IV. For the Byzantine rulers, as well as the heads of the Holy Roman Empire of the German nation, the standard title, "emperor," is used here. The Tatar rulers are called "khan," while the lesser Tatar nobility are designated as "lords" or "prince," usually with the word, "Tatar," added in order to distinguish them from the Russian ones. The very common rank or title, *"boiarskie deti,"* is translated "junior boyars," since very often in place of *"boiarskie deti,"* the chronicle writer used the expression, *"mladshie boiare."* The *"dvoriane"* is translated as "service nobility." Finally, the Russian "voevoda"—which may be either the commander of a modest troop or of an army, or a governor—is not translated but used as it is. The same method is applied for "namestnik," who can be a minor administrative official in the fourteenth century and governor of a large region in the sixteenth. Some other ranks and terms are practically untranslatable and are likewise used in the Russian form, with explanations in footnotes and glossary.

VIII. STRUCTURE AND LANGUAGE OF *THE NIKONIAN CHRONICLE*

In the first part of *The Nikonian Chronicle,* up to the year 1520, the text is organized along the system of yearly entries. It begins, however, with undated narrative, a general biblical introduction followed by the story of the migration of the Slavs, and some events from Russian and Byzantine history. The first dated entry is in the year 6367/859.[42] With a very few exceptions, the remaining text is strictly divided into annual entries following the traditional Russian chronicle writing which began with *The Primary Chronicle* in *Laur.* and *Hyp.* versions. In view of the scarcity and high cost of parchment and, later, of paper, the chronicles were not divided into paragraphs, even when the entry was sometimes several dozens of pages in length. Still, even in *The Primary Chronicle* in the *Laur.* and *Hyp.* versions and, later, in others—especially in *Nik.*—the text of the entry sometimes includes a title of a story or of a document. For example, in *The Primary Chronicle* (*Laur.* and *Hyp.*) under the years 907 and 912 the text of Oleg's treaty with Byzantium is singled out, although without any title. Then, under the year 946, one finds the title, "The Beginning of the Reign of Sviatoslav, Son of Igor'." Later, more such titles are found—i.e., "About the Murder of Boris" (1015); "The Beginning of Yaroslav's Reign in Kiev;" *a.o.* Such titles in both the *Laur.* and *Hyp.* texts of *The Primary Chronicle* are exceptional, though.

The structure of the text of *The Primary Chronicle* and later en-

---

42. *Laur.* and *Hyp.* begin with the year 6360/852 but, similar to *Nik.*, speak of the Varangians only in the year 6367/859.

tries in *Nik.* differ very considerably from these earliest versions of *Prim. Chron.* The number of titles is large, and sometimes even a short recording of an event is preceded by a title, beginning on the same line where the previous sentence ends. For instance, under the year 6629/1121 the title and the annual entry read, "Metropolitan Nicephorus Passed Away. In the year 6629 in the month of April, Nicephorus, Metropolitan of all Russia, passed away."

The present translators have singled out in separate paragraphs such titled passages but since the *Chronicle* is not consistent within its own system of titles, the translation furnishes additional titles in brackets. For instance, in the case of the wars between Grand Prince Iziaslav of Kiev and Iurii Dolgorukii, the description is many dozens of pages in length, even in the printed Russian text, and the editor added some titles.

The present translation likewise breaks into separate paragraphs lengthy descriptions or entries which treat a number of disparate events.

It must be added that the original divisions into annual entries were not always observed in the *Chronicle.* Such is the case of Ol'ga's revenges, of Vladimir's baptism and the discussions which preceded it, *vitae* and stories about the Kievan Cave Monastery. Several other descriptions of events take up not one but several years, yet formed the same topic, and are recorded in one entry.

The objective of this translation was to present an easily understandable text which yet preserves, as far as possible, the flavor of its Russian original. The style of the *Nikonian Chronicle* is uneven because the scribes of the manuscripts endeavored in most cases to preserve the orthography and stylistics of the earlier materials they used to compile *Nik.* Therefore there can be found in *Nik.* sometimes nearly classic Church Slavonic—especially in the earlier entries or in religious texts—and a language often quite colloquial deriving from the business Russian of the era, as in some entries of the fifteenth and sixteenth centuries, and even earlier.

The original writers of the chronicles, whether in the eleventh or sixteenth centuries, dealt with events and persons which or who, presumably, were well known and could be easily identified by their contemporaries; consequently, many sentences in the *Chronicle* abound in pronouns, terse, laconic presentation and omissions. Rendering such sentences into readable literary English presents considerable difficulties. If the Old Russian sentences are rendered into modern English, readers will be unable to comprehend the slightest idea of the style of medieval chroniclers. Therefore the present translators decided to compromise. They have attempted to preserve the chronicle's style but, to make it more readily comprehensible, sometimes have added, in brackets, additional words to facilitate reading the sometimes ponderous sentence structure.

For easier identification of persons and sites, such supplemental words as "prince," "voevoda," "river" or "city" have been added, sometimes in brackets.

There are, also, some other problems which arose during the original compilation of *Nik*. Its compilers and editors, working on the basis of more ancient, often ill-preserved manuscripts, were sometimes confronted with missing or barely legible pages—which is reflected in *Nik.*, itself. Often they had totally damaged paragraphs or pages, with errors made by earlier chroniclers; and, at times, incorrectly written names—all of which resulted in unclear texts or omissions of annual entries in *Nik.*, itself. Sometimes, unable to decipher a name or sentence exactly, they unavoidably repeated the errors of an earlier scribe.

Consequently, in preparing this English text the present editor was frequently obliged to check *Nik.*'s text against the earlier available sources and to make appropriate corrections and annotations on the basis of the Russian and foreign original materials, more ancient than *Nik.*, as well as to consult contemporary research.

LIST OF TITLES OF ENTRIES OF VOLUME ONE OF
THE NIKONIAN CHRONICLE
(TO A.D. 1132)

[The titles in brackets were added by the editor.
The other titles are as they appear in *Nik.*]

Introductory Part
[Partition of the Earth among Noah's Sons] 1
After the Destruction of the Tower [The Slavs] 3
The River Route 4
The Apostle Andrew's Prophecy
  Concerning the City of Kiev 5
The Beginning of the City of Kiev 6
About the Slavs 8
About the Avars 8
About the Polians 8
About the Christianization of Bulgaria 11
About the Other Bulgarian Prince 12
About the Campaign of the Russians
  against Constantinople 12
Portent 13
About the Murder of Caesar Bardas 13
About the Ascendance of Basil the Macedonian to Emperor .. 14
About the Campaign of the Sons of Hagar
  against Constantinople 15
About the Varangians 15
About the Khazars 15

The Ninth Century
First Annual Entry [A.D. 859] 15
About the Russian Princes Riurik, Sineus and Truvor [862] .. 16

Portent 18
About the Emperor's Horse Stables [869] 18
About the Broken Mirror [876] 19
About the Assassination of Emperor Michael [876] 19
The 87th Reign: That of Basil the Macedonian [867-886] ... 20
The Earthquake 21
About the Russian Prince Askol'd; [His Baptism] [876] 24
About the Death of Emperor Basil [886] 26
The Reign of Leo the Philosopher, Son of Basil [887] 26
Punishment 28
The Reign of Oleg [881] 29
About the Hungarians [898] 31
The Mission [of Cyril and Methodius] [898] 32
The Pope of Rome [898] 33
About the Translation of the Scriptures
    from Greek into Slavic [898] 34

The Tenth Century
About the Same from Another Chronicle 34
About Oleg [907] 35
Portent [911] 38
About the Horse. Oleg's End [912] 42
About the Magicians [912] 43
The Reign of the Greek Emperors, Alexander, Brother of Leo,
    and of Constantine, Son of the Latter [912] 45
The Reign of the Greek Emperor Constantine VII
    Porphyrogenitus, Son of Leo [913] 46
About the Russian Prince Igor' [913-945] 49
About the Bulgarian Tsar 49
The Reign of Romanus Lecapenus, Emperor of the Greeks . 50
About the Council of Reconciliation 50
About the Transfer to Constantinople of the Icon
    Not Made by Human Hands 50
About the Russian Prince Igor' 52
Beginning of the Reign of Sviatoslav [946-973] 52
The Second Reign of Constantine Porphyrogenitus,
    Son of Leo, and the Reign Lasted Fifteen Years 53
In the Reign of Romanus, Son of Constantine
    Porphyrogentitus [959-963] 53

About the Baptism of Ol'ga [955] 55
Prince Sviatoslav 57
The Reign of the Greek Emperor Nicephorus Phocas [966] . 58
About the Russian Prince Sviatoslav [967]................ 62
From the Greek Chronicle: The Reign
    of the Greek Emperor John Tzimisces [970] 65
About Sviatoslav [970] 66
About the Russian Princes [970] 67
The Beginning of the Reign of Iaropolk [973] 72
Portent [979].. 73
The Reign of Vladimir in Novgorod
    [and the War with Iaropolk] [980] 74
The Beginning of the Reign of Vladimir in Kiev [980-1015]. 76
How Many Women did Solomon Have? [980] 77
Saracens [986] 79
Germans [986] 79
Khazar Jews [986] 80
Greeks [986] 80
[The Speech of the Philosopher
    About the Christian Faith] [986] 81
About the Ark 84
[Prince Vladimir's Conversion
    to Christianity] [987-988].............................. 97
[*The Sermon*] [988] 102
About the Councils [988]................................. 103
About the Latins [988] 104
About Peter the Stammerer [988] 105
Metropolitan Michael of Kiev and all Russia [988-992] 106
Leontius, Metropolitan of Kiev and all Russia [992]......... 112
Metropolitan Leontius of Kiev and all Russia
    Appoints Bishops to the Cities [992].................... 112
Robbers [998] 116

The Eleventh Century
Bogatyrs [1001] 118
The Passing of Pious Grand Prince Vladimir [1015] 121
About the Hungarians [1015]............................. 122
[Martyrdom and *Encomium* of St. Boris
    and St. Gleb] [1015] 123

The Murder of Boris 124
The Burial of Boris 125
The Murder of Gleb 125
The Burial of Gleb and Boris 128
Encomium to the Saintly Passion Martyrs Boris and Gleb 128
[War Between Sviatopolk and Iaroslav] [1015] 129
The Murder of Sviatoslav [1015] 129
The Rule of Sviatopolk [1015] 129
About Prince Iaroslav [1015] 129
The Rule of Iaroslav in Kiev [1017] 131
[The Reign of Iaroslav the Wise] [1017-1059] 135
About the Search for the Bodies of the Holy Passion Martyrs 135
About the Magicians [1024] 137
[Portent] [1028] 139
The Passing of Bishop Joachim [1030] 139
The Death of Mstislav [1033] 140
Establishment of the Metropolia [1037] 141
Metropolitan Theotemptus [1039] 143
The Reign of the Greek Emperor Constantine,
  Brother of Basil [1025-1028] 143
The Reign of the Greek Emperor Romanus
  Argiropulos [1028-1034] 144
Iaroslav Sent his Son, Vladimir, to Campaign
  Against Constantinople [1043] 145
The Greek Emperor Monomachus 146
Founding of the Church of Holy Sophia [1045] 147
Election of the Metropolitan [Ilarion] of Russia
  by the Russian Bishops [1051] 148
Beginning of the Cave Monastery and the Narrative,
  Why the Monastery was Called
  Monastery of "The Cave" [1051] 148
About the Rules of Studion [1051] 150
The Passing of Iaroslav [1054] 151
The Reign of Iziaslav in Kiev [1055-1078] 153
Consecration of Bishop Stephen [1060] 154
About the Horrifying Portent [1065] 155
Homily on Divine Punishment [1068] 158
[Kievan Revolt Against Iziaslav] [1068] 160
[Iziaslav Flees to Poland] [1068] 160

Introduction

[Vseslav, Prince of Kiev] [1068] 161
The Death of Bishop Stephen [1068] 161
[Iziaslav's First Return to Kiev] [1069] 162
About the Diviners [1071] 163
About the Diviners [1071] 166
About Simon the Magician [1071] 167
A Diviner Appeared [1071] 167
[Death of St. Theodosius; Caloyer of the
  Monastery of the Caves] [1074] 170
Sviatoslav Comes with his Son, Gleb [1074] 172
Death of Sviatoslav, Son of Iaroslav [1076] 180
[Third Reign of Iziaslav in Kiev] [1077] 180
[Oleg's Sedition. Death and *Encomium*
  of Prince Iziaslav] 180
Death of Boris; Death of Iziaslav; *Encomium* [1078] 182
The Reign of Vsevolod Iaroslavovich in Kiev [1078-1094] ... 184
[Iaropolk's Death and *Encomium*] [1086] 185
Death of Metropolitan John of Kiev and all Russia [1089] ... 188
Ephraim, Metropolitan of Kiev and all Russia [1091] 188
[Transfer of the Relics of
  St. Theodosius; *Encomium*] [1092] 189
Portents [1092] 193
The Death of Prince Vsevolod [1094] 194
The Reign of Sviatopolk [The Second]
  in Kiev [1094-1114] 195
[Homily] [1094] 198
Locusts [1094] 202
Bishop Stephen's Death [1095] 202
Death of Bishop German [1095] 204
[Struggle between Vladimir Monomakh and Oleg] [1096] ... 205
[Boniak Attacks Kiev] [1096] 206
[The Background of the Polovetss] [1096] 207
[The Walled People of the Northern Urals] 208
[New Conflict between Mistislav Monomashich
  and Oleg Sviatoslavich] [1096] 209
Metropolitan Ephraim 211
[Struggle in Suzdalia between Mstislav and Oleg] [1096] 211
[Vasilii's Story of the Blinding of Vasil'ko
  and the Ensuing Feuds] [1097] 213

[The Princes' Convention in Liubech] [1097] 213
[Prince Davyd of Vladimir in Volynia Plots against
    Prince Vasil'ko of Terebovl'] [1097] 213
The Blinding of Vasil'ko [1097] 216
Vladimir [Monomakh] Vsevolodich Summons
    Davyd Sviatoslavich and Oleg Sviatoslavich [1097] 217
[Vasil'ko and Volodar' War against
    Davyd Igorevich [1097] 220
[Sviatopolk's Campaign in Volynia] [1097] 221

The Twelfth Century
The Reign of Emperor John Porphyrogenitus
    [of Byzantium] [1100] 226
[Novgorodians Want Mstislav to be their Prince] [1102] 227
Portents [1102] 227
[Joint Campaign of the Russian Princes against
    the Polovetss] [1103] 228
Arrival of Metropolitan Nicephorus [1104] 231
Portent [1104] 231
Metropolitan Nicephorus Consecrated Three Bishops
    to the Cities [1105] 231
The Death of Bishop Nicetas 233
The Consecration of Bishop John 233
Portent 235
Conflagrations [1112] 236
Consecration of Bishop Theoktistus [1113] 237
Portent [1114] 237
The Passing of Grand Prince Sviatopolk [1114] 237
Consecration of Bishop Daniel 237
Consecration of Bishop Cyril 238
The Reign of the Byzantine Emperor Manuel
    Porphyrogenitus [1114] 238
The Reign in Kiev of Grand Prince Vladimir Vsevolodich
    Monomakh, Iaroslav's Grandson [1114-1125] 238
Death of Bishop Lazar' 242
Consecration of Bishop Sylvester [1118] 242
Death of Metropolitan Nicephorus [1121] 243
Portent 243
Death of Bishop Daniel 243

Metropolitan Nicetas 243
Death of Bishop Amphilopheus [1122] 244
The Death of Bishop Sylvester 244
Consecration of Bishop Simeon 244
Iaroslavets Campaigns against the City of
   Vladimir [1123]; His Death 244
A Church Collapses [1123] 245
Conflagration [1124] 246
Portent [1124] 246
The Passing of Grand Prince Vladimir Monomakh [1125] ... 246
The Reign of Mstislav [The Great] [1125-1132] 247
Iaropolk Defeats the Polovetss [1125] 248
The Storm of Hail [1125] 248
Metropolitan Nicetas Dies [1126] 249
[Mistislav's Campaign against the Krivichs
   and Polotsk] [1127] 250
The Legend of Polotsk [About the Descendants of Rogvold,
   Rogneda, Iziaslav and Vseslav] [1128] 252
Consecration of Bishop Niphont [1130] 254
[Passing of Grand Prince Mstislav of Kiev] [1132] 255

FOREWORD TO VOLUME I OF THE ENGLISH EDITION OF *THE NIKONIAN CHRONICLE*

This first volume of the English edition of *The Nikonian Chronicle* covers the earliest period of Russian history up to the year 1132, the year of the death of Mstislav, Vladimir Monomakh's senior son and successor to the Kievan throne. Until Mstislav's death, despite some sporadic outbursts of violence among the members of the ruling dynasty, it was still a time of relative peace and unity for Russia. After his death, however, there begins an intense struggle not only among the various branches of the dynasty but even within these branches, themselves. Moreover, the same year—1132—we may observe the intervention in southern Russia—and, specifically, Kievan—affairs by Monomakh's younger son, Iurii Dolgorukii, who was prince in the most remote reaches of the country at that time—the territory along the upper courses of the Volga and Oka rivers. This territory soon became known as Suzdalian Russia. Dolgorukii's intervention in southern Russian affairs signifies the decline generally of south-central Russia and the rising power of Suzdalian Russia, better protected from the nomads and a more strictly organized domain. One-third of a century later Dolgorukii's son, Andrei Bogoliubskii, following his father's path, also conquers Kiev; but he is no longer interested in residing in declining Kievan Russia, he does not even assume the title, "Grand Prince of Kiev," so long sought by his father. Bogoliubskii's lack of interest in Kiev's throne reflected the political and economic reality of the time, as well as the profound changes which were taking place throughout all the nation. Novgorod, Smolensk, Galich, Chernigov and Vladimir in Suzdalia had become nearly as powerful and wealthy as Kiev, while this oldest Russian capital was suffering more and more from declining trade with Byzantium, from raids by the Polovets, and from the ceaseless princely internecine feuds.

This earliest period of the history of recently Christianized Russia witnesses a rather spontaneous first blossoming of Russian culture. The architectural monuments of Kiev, Chernigov, Novgorod, Ladoga and other cities, such writings as *The Primary Chronicle*, the *Lives of Boris and Gleb*, and the historico-philosophical *Sermon* by Hilarion, examples of the sanctity and spirituality revealed in the *Lives* of Saints Anthony and Theodosius, and of the above-mentioned Boris and Gleb, demonstrate the very rapid and significant cultural development which long influenced Russian history and the Russian mind throughout subsequent centuries.

While it is rather easy to determine and explain the end of this early Russian era in the year 1132, it is considerably more difficult to discern its beginning. Historians' speculations as to the origin of the Russian state are far from conclusive. We know definitely that Oleg and Igor' were its first historical rulers. We have some earlier Russian and foreign information about Kiev and the activities of the "Rus'"—or, as the Greeks used to call them, the "Rhos"—in the ninth century. Finally, we have substantial archeological evidence of the existence in the middle of the first millennium A.D. of an urban settlement where the later city of Kiev arose. Some explanation of this now obscure time, though, is necessary.

Archeologists point out that toward the middle of the first millennium A.D.[43] Kiev was already a populated site with tradesmen and craftsmen, and that on the so-called "Old Kievan Hill," or mountain, a fortified mansion was built—apparently the local ruler's. Old memories repeated by the writer of *The Primary Chronicle* ascribed the founding of the city to Kii, a chieftain of the Polian tribe, and to his brothers Shchek (Shchok, in *Nik.*) and Khoriv; but *The Primary Chronicle* is silent about the date of the city's founding. The chronicler dismisses a later rumor that Kii was just a ferryman and adds that, as such, he would not have been received by the Byzantine emperor or have built a fortress town on the river Danube. Then, the story goes, Kii became the founder of the local ruling family—which many historians presume ruled there into the middle of the ninth century, when Askol'd and Dir seized Kiev.

When did this Kii live? Some indirect foreign sources permit us to believe that he lived in the sixth or seventh century. For instance,

---

43. *Istoriia Kieva*, Uk. AN, Kiev, 1953, Vol. I, pp. 32-39.

The History of Taron, an Armenian chronicle attributed to Zenob Glak and written shortly after A.D. 700[44], tells us that in the land of the Poluni (Polians) a certain Kuar (Kii) and his brothers, Metei and Khorean (Khoriv), founded three cities and named them after their own names—Kuar (Kiev), Metei and Khorean. Since this story is narrated just before a discussion of events during the reign of Emperor Mauritius, A.D. 582-602, it is usually considered that Kuar (Kii) lived before or around A.D. 600.

Procopius of Caesarea, in his *War with the Goths,*[45] reports that in the time of Justinian, 527-565, a certain Hilbudius, chieftain of the Ants,[46] was given the task of building a fortress on the Danube and of guarding the Danube frontier. Discovery of a tombstone near Constantinople in 1902 by the Bulgarian archeologist, Iordan Ivanov, permits us to associate this Hilbudius with Kiev and, eventually, with Kii. On this tombstone it was written, "Here is buried Hilbudius, son of Sambatas, who died in the month of November of the seventh Indiction."[47] We know that "Sambatas" was another Byzantine name for Kiev, or for the Kievan fortress. Emperor Constantine Porphyrogenitus, 944-958, who was host to the Russian Princess Ol'ga, says in his famous *De administrando imperio* that before undertaking their journey to Constantinople the Russian boats would gather at the Kievan fortress of Sambatas. The appearance of the name, "Sambatas," in Constantine's treatise and on the tombstone permits us to surmise that Hilbudius—mentioned by Procopius, buried near Constantinople and one who built a fortress on the Danube—was Kii, who likewise built a fortress there and was received by the emperor, according to *The Primary Chronicle.*

The spreading of direct and indirect information about Kii (Hilbudius) from Armenia to the Balkans would not be astonishing in view of the situation in the Eurasian prairie in the sixth and early seventh centuries. At that time the Turks, or Turkots, built up a vast

---

44. See Abeg'ian, M., *Istoriia armiankskoi literatury*, Erevan, 1948, pp. 346-348.

45. Procopius of Caesarea, *Voina s gotami*, Russian translation, Moscow, 1950, pp. 293-298.

46. "Ants" is usually considered to be an early Byzantine name for the southeastern Slavs.

47. Ivanov dates this tomb with the year 529, but it could be half a century or more older.

empire stretching from the confines of China to the Black Sea and the Caucasus. This first Turkic empire was at war with Iran, so the China-Europe trade, primarily in silk, had to seek out a new northern route which bypassed the Caspian Sea from the north and then went either by way of the Black Sea or the Volga, Don and Dnieper.[48] In this way the region of Kiev was drawn into this trade, as well as its local tribal leaders who controlled the ferry on the Dnieper river—a convenient shelter protected by forest from the nomads. This propitious location of Kiev at the intersection of the Oriental-European trade route with that from Scandinavia to Byzantium in the next century became the main factor in the rise of this city. In his *Istoriia Khazar*,[49] M.I. Artamonov quotes the Byzantine historian, Menander, who wrote that in 568 the Central Asian Indo-European-speaking Sogdian silk merchants, unhappy over the war of the Turks with Iran, sent an embassy to Constantinople via the Caucasus in order to find direct contact with Byzantium. The Byzantines reciprocated, sending an embassy on their part to the Turks. On their way back they were obliged to bypass the Caspian Sea from the north, then journeyed to the Kuban valley and from there went north across the prairie through the land of the Alans—also Indo-European-speaking nomads—reaching the Black Sea and Constantinople. Such journeys involved Central Asia, the Caucasus, the prairie north of the Black Sea, and Byzantium, and word could easily have reached Armenia about Kiev's growth as a stopover before setting out down the Dnieper and Black Sea to Constantinople. One can only surmise about these historical and archeological data and events though not be quite certain that they are connected with Kii of *The Primary Chronicle* and the earliest appearance of Kiev in history.

The next problem of Russian history is the so-called "Norman" or "Varangian" question, which we do not intend here to ponder at length. We agree basically with N. Riasanovsky, who clearly summarizes the most recent historical and archeological data: there is definite proof of the presence of Normans in ninth-century Russia, but their cultural and organizational impact was rather

---

48. About the early Central Asian Turkic empire, see Grouset, G., *Empires des Steppes*, Paris, 1960; or Gumilev, L., *Drevnie tiurki*, Moscow, 1967.

49. Artamonov, M.I., *Istoriia Khazar*, Leningrad, 1952, p. 135.

insignificant, especially by comparison with the enormous Byzantine and very considerable Oriental Turkic influence on Old Russian culture and society. He adds that no historical Russian sources anterior to the twelfth century knew of Riurik, and that the chonicler who wrote *The Primary Chronicle* mentioned Riurik "for a definite dynastic purpose."[50] It is useful to remember that Metropolitan Hilarion in his famous *Sermon* in the 1050's mentions Vladimir's father, Sviatoslav, and his grandfather, "Old Igor'"—both pagans—but that there is no word of any Riurik.

The stories about Kii and, later, the Varangians and Riurik, are common to all texts of *The Primary Chronicle*, including *Laur.*, *Hyp.*, *Nov. Kom.* and many others. Unique to *Nik.*, however, among the other chronicles, is a short narrative in the annual entry for 6384/876, in which the chronicler says that after Askol'd's and Dir's unsuccessful attack on Constantinople—which is to be read in all versions of *Prim. Chron.*—both these Russian rulers of Kiev embraced Byzantine Christianity. According to a Byzantine source discovered by F.R. Cumont, this attack, however, occurred not in 876 but June 18, 860.[51]

Most Russian historians have disregarded this earlier conversion to Christianity by Russians, and only a few specialists on early Russia or in the history of the Russian church have discussed it. S.M. Soloviev, for instance, barely speaks about it in his *Istoriia Rossii* (Vol. I, p. 137); Kliuchevskii does not even mention it. Both were interested in the political, not cultural and spiritual, history of Russia. *The Primary Chronicle*, as well as subsequent chronicles—which ascribe the introduction of Christianity in Russia to Prince Vladimir—obviously do not mention Askol'd and Dir's conversion in order to maintain Vladimir's prestige as the first Christian leader and founder of the Russian so-called "Riurikid" dynasty. In some preserved redactions of the *Charter* of Vladimir, himself, however, given to the "Tithe" Church—*Desiatinnaia Tserkov'*—in Kiev, it is mentioned that Patriarch Photius of Constantinople, who was patriarch twice (858-867 and 877-886), sent a bishop named Michael to Prince Vladimir, who ruled

50. Riasanovsky, N., *A History of Russia*, Oxford University Press, 2nd ed., 1969, pp. 25-30.

51. See Cumont, F.R., *Anecdota Bruxellernsia. Recueil des Travaux publiés par la Faculté des Lettres*, Bruxelles, 1860, fasc. 9, p. 33.

980-1015!⁵² The same information is found in *Rogozhskii Sbornik* (*PSRL*, Vol. 15) under the year 988, and in several other fifteenth-century historical writings.

Despite a certain state of confusion, it may be supposed that the sending of a bishop to Russia by Photius (between 858 and 886) was still vividly recalled in Vladimir's time over a century later; but the scribe who recopied the text of Vladimir's *Charter* was so impressed by Vladimir's Christianization of Russia that he ascribed this dispatching of a bishop to Vladimir's reign, whereas Vladimir actually lived and reigned more than a hundred years after Askol'd and Dir. In any case, the fact of the Christianization of the early Russian princes and the sending of a bishop to Russia by Patriarch Photius is undeniable. Photius, himself, in his *Epistle* of 866-867, in which he lauds the Christianization of Bulgaria, says, "Not only did this nation [Bulgaria] give up its former unfaithfulness for the faith of Christ, but so did even the Russ [in Greek, "Rhos"], well-known for their cruelty and horrible slaughter which leave all similar events far behind, and who attacked everyone who lived around them and who, in their vainglory, raised their hands against the Roman Empire. Now they have changed their pagan [Photius writes "Hellenistic," meaning "pre-Christian"] impure faith, to which they used to belong, for the pure and true Christian faith. In this way they have placed themselves in the ranks of our [spiritual] subjects and our friends. And they have given up sacking us, and also their boldness, which they turned against us quite recently. Their desires and attachments to the faith have become so burning that they have accepted a bishop and shepherd, and with great fervor and diligence they have embraced the beliefs of Christians."⁵³ John Zonara's *Paralipomen*, completed around 1118 by this Byzantine historian, also speaks of the Christianization of the Russian princes in the time of Photius. Zonara's *Paralipomen* was translated into Old Slavonic in Bulgaria and was brought to Russia in the late fifteenth or beginning

---

52. For the text of Vladimir's *Charter*, *Ustav kniazia Vladimira*, see *Pamiatniki drevnerusskogo kanonicheskogo prava*, Part II, fasc. 1, *Russkaia istoricheskaia biblioteka*, Vol. 36, Petrograd, 1920, pp. 4-7. For a recent discussion, see Shchapov, Ia.N. *Kniazheskie ustavy i tserkov' v drevnei Rusi*, XI-XIV v., Moscow, 1972, p. 73.

53. See Photius' *Epistle* in Migne, J.P., *Patrologiae cursus completus. Patres Graeca*, Paris, 1860, Vol. 102, pp. 735-738.

of the sixteenth century. Via *Chronograph 1512* it came into the hands of the compiler of *The Nikonian Chronicle*.[54]

Besides Zonara's testimony, the content of Photius' *Epistle* is confirmed by other Byzantine historians: by Nicetas Paphlagonis in his *Vita Ignatii*[55] and by Emperor Constantine Porphyrogenitus in his biography of Emperor Basil the Macedonian. Constantine Porphyrogenitus provides the story, subsequently repeated by Zonara and *Nik.*'s compilers, telling how the Russians embraced Christianity only after the bishop threw the Gospel into a bonfire and the Gospel was miraculously preserved.[56] Paphlagonis and Constantine differ from Photius and *Nik.*: according to the former, the bishop was sent to Russia by Patriarch Ignatius, who took over the See after the dethronement of Photius. Most probably, Photius initiated the mission to Russia, while the mission actually arrived there during Ignatius' rule. In any case, these historians confirm the fact that the Rhos (Russian) rulers did accept Christianity. In *Prim. Chron.* we find (both in *Nik.* and in *Laur.* versions) another direct affirmation of these events: under the year 6390/882 the author of *Prim. Chron.* states without explaining that after their murder by Oleg, "the bodies of Askol'd and Dir were taken to the so-called 'Hungarian Hill' in Kiev, where now is the estate of Ol'ma, and they were buried there. Ol'ma [probably a Kievan boyar] erected a church over Askol'd's grave, dedicated to St. Nicholas [possibly the patron saint of the baptised Askol'd]; and Dir's grave is near the Church of St. Irene." With the death of Askol'd and Dir and the ensuing reign of the pagan princes, Oleg and Igor', Kiev's Christianization probably slowed in its development for a century; nevertheless, the nucleus of Kievan Christians kept alive their memory of it. Ol'ma probably erected the above-mentioned churches only after Vladimir's Christianization of Russia, and thus preserved the earlier Russian Christian tradition of veneration of these two Russian Christian princes killed by the pagan invader,

---

54. See Popov, A.N., *Obzor khronografov russkoi redaktsii*, Vol. II, Moscow, 1866, pp. iii-iii and 4-5; as well as Tvorogov, O.V., *Drevnie russkie khronografy*, Moscow, 1975, p. 183.

55. Nicetas Paphlagonis, *Vita Ignatii*, in Migne, *op. cit.*, Vol. 105, p. 516.

56. See Theophanes Continuatus, *Theophili Michaelis f. Imperium Chronographia*, Bonn, 1838, v. 4, p. 196.

Oleg. Before Vladimir's Christinizationn, the Church of St. Elias in Kiev was apparently the only place where Christians congregated.

Whom did Photius or Ignatius send to Russia? Most probably, Bishop Michael, mentioned in *Nik.* as head of the church and as Vladimir's contemporary. Not accidentally is he named in the above-mentioned *Charter* of the "Tithe" Church, and his name is always connected with that of Photius. The authors of the fifteenth-century chronicles, as well as of *Nik.*, endowed Michael with a number of standard ecclesiastical virtues, but these are commonplace in the later era, not in that of *Prim. Chron.* itself.

The early and rapid development of Russian letters and Christian arts, already in the last decade of the tenth century, produced the *Sermon*, or *Speech, of the Philosopher*, addressed to Vladimir;[57] then, in the initial decades after Christianization by Vladimir, Metropolitan Hilarion's masterly *Sermon on Law and Grace*; and such works as the earliest versions of the *Passion of Boris and Gleb*, Luka Zhidiata's *Homily*, and the first chronicles, which preceded *Prim. Chron.* These early literary works cannot be explained without keeping in mind the previous Christian roots in Russian soil. A small but apparently staunch community of Christian confessors obviously survived the pagan resurgence of the late ninth and most of the tenth centuries, bringing up a generation which aided Vladimir in consolidating Christian culture in Russia. Vladimir's grandmother, Ol'ga, probably also became Christian in the 950's under the influence of this original Russian Orthodox community in Kiev.

The Primary Chroncle's bias in ecclesiastic matters is seen not only in the case of Michael, head of the shortlived Russian church hierarchy in the time of Askol'd and Dir; it is equally silent concerning the first fifty years of church leadership—from 988/9, when Vladimir Christianized all of Russia and made Eastern Christianity the faith of the Russian people—to 1039. Only in the annual entry for the year 1039—the time of Iaroslav—does *Prim. Chron. (Laur., a.o.)* mention for the first time, and somewhat casually, that "Church of the Holy Theotokos built by Vladimir, father of Iaroslav, was consecrated by Metropolitan Theotemptus..."

---

57. See the early version of the *Speech of the Philosopher in Laur.*; and Likhachev, D.S., *Velikoe nasledie*, Moscow, 1975, p. 19.

obviously, a Greek. The Russian church, however, like any other Orthodox one, could not have existed without bishops, and the silence of *Prim. Chron. (Laur.)* here can be explained neither by the actual absence of a hierarchy nor by insufficient information on the part of the writer. Apparently, he preferred, or was forced by the Greek Metropolitans, not to speak of the hierarchy of the Russian church during the first half-century of its existence before the Greek Theotemptus came. Why? There can only be one answer: during these fifty years the Russian church remained not under the jurisdiction of Constantinople but of another church—most probably under the autocephalous western Bulgarian Archbishopric of Ohrid.

Under 989 and 996 *Prim. Chron. (Laur.)* and *Nik.* both state that Anastas, who helped Vladimir conquer Chersonesus, with other priests from there accompanied Vladimir to Russia, where this Anastas was appointed chief of the clergy of the "Tithe" Church (the Church of the Theotokos, mentioned above). Since the "Tithe" Church received its exclusive privilege from Vladimir, including the tithe, it was most certainly the cathedral church of the Kievan diocese, and Anastas was the first local bishop there. Not accidentally, this Anastas is mentioned in several annual entries—the last time in 1018 *(Laur., Nik., a.o.)* and each time in connection with the "Tithe" Church. It may be asked whether Anastas aided Vladimir in Chersonesus and was so honored in Russia because he was not Greek but Bulgarian and resented the Greek conquest of Bulgaria.

In the later chronicles (especially, *Novg. Kom.*, under 989; the *Second, Fourth, a.o., Novg.* and some others) we read that when Vladimir was baptised and Christianized all of Russia he assigned a metropolitan to Kiev, and bishops, priests and deacons to the other cities. "... And so Archbishop Joachim, a man from Chersonesus, came to Novgorod..." Thus, since the first Russian clergy and hierarchy was primarily from Chersonesus and not directly from Constantinople, it would seem that the priests, at least, probably were able to celebrate the church services and to preach in the Slavic tongue—most likely, Bulgarian, which at that time was very similar to Old Russian—and that they were of Bulgarian origin. As a matter of fact, Byzantium at that time was in the process of conquering Bulgaria, using the most cruel means, and the emigration from

Bulgaria first to the Crimea, and then directly to Russia, should have been very sizable.

In 1913 a Russian historian, M.D. Priselkov, came out with a very persuasive explanation of the early condition of the Russian church—a theory which, since then, has been accepted generally by historians interested in the past of Russian Christianity: fearing Byzantine imperialism, Vladimir placed the Russian church under the jurisdiction of the autocephalous western Bulgarian archbishop of Ohrid, the capital of Bulgaria until 1018. Even after 1018, when the Greeks conquered it, the bishop of Ohrid remained autocephalous, or independent from Constantinople, until the 1030s. The names of the first heads of the Russian church—Leontius, mentioned in *Nik.* in 6500/992 to 6512/1004; and John, mentioned in 6516/1008—were also the names of historically well-known archbishops of Ohrid. Both Leontius (also named Leon, Leont, Lev) and John are likewise mentioned in a large number of Russian chronicles written in the fifteenth and sixteenth centuries. They are also included in the list of bishops provided in *Novg. Kom.*,[58] in *Tver'. Sbornik, a.o.* In the eleventh-century *Chtenie* and in *Skazanie* about Boris and Gleb, significantly, John is not called "Metropolitan of Russia" but just "Archbishop" (as head of the Ohrid church and "shepherd of Christ's flock.")[59]

Let us also remember that Vladimir's sons, Boris and Gleb, were children of his Bulgarian Christian wife, the last before his marriage to the Greek Princess Anna, and that she might have influenced Vladimir to embrace Christianity. Vladimir even attempted to support the West Bulgarian state of Samuil (980-1014), but because of pressure by Turkic nomads in the south Russian prairie, he was obliged to give up this attempt and to stabilize the Russian-Byzantine border along the Danube.[60]

All these historical mentions and use by the Russians, from the very beginning of their Christianization, of Bulgarian-translated or -created liturgical and other religious and historical books, point very strongly to the cultural dependence of early Russia on

58. See pp. 473, 478, 480.
59. See *Zhitiia sv. muchenikov Borisa i Gleba i sluzhby im*, ed. by D.I. Abramovich, Petrograd, 1916, pp. 17-19, 53, 56, 136.
60. Pashuto, p. 90.

Bulgaria, and probably to the early ties between the Russian church and the Bulgarian Patriarchate, later Archbishopric, of Ohrid.

When, in 1037, however, Constantinople placed a Greek in charge of the Ohrid church, the reason for Russia's connection with it disappeared. In that year Iaroslav built the new cathedral church of Holy Sophia (Wisdom of God), imitating Constantinople, where the Church of Holy Sophia was the patriarchal church; and he, apparently, asked then the patriarch of Constantinople to assume shepherding of the Russian church. Thus, there appears in Kiev Metropolitan Theotemptus, who, as mentioned above, in 1039 consecrated the apparently rebuilt "Tithe" Church there.[61]

With the Greek assumption of the administration of the Russian church, there came as well the appointment not only of Greek metropolitans to Russia, but also of many bishops. Doubtless, the Greeks did their best to eradicate from all writings any memory of the Russians' ecclesiastic independence from them. That they also cared little—in contrast to the West European, Roman Catholic, missionaries—for any enlightenment of the Slavs is demonstrated by the fact that they neither established any school in Russia nor were concerned to teach Greek there, the original language of the *Gospel* and of old Greek culture.

Such is the only plausible explanation, suggested by Priselkov, why no heads of the Russian church are mentioned in *The Primary Chronicle* from 988/9 to 1039. But there still remained vague recollections of these hierarchs, and after Russia's proclamation of its ecclesiastic independence from Constantinople in 1441 the names of the first metropolitans of Russia began to reappear, although the details of their activities and exact dates by then had been forgotten, having never been recorded in the early annals of Russian history.

We conclude here our discussion of these selected obscure passages in the first volume of *The Nikonian Chronicle*. This rather lengthy consideration of the beginnings of the Russian church seems to this editor unavoidable for an understanding of early Russian cultural history. The church was the main vehicle of Russian intellectual and artistic development, and lacking some

---

61. Kartashev, Vol. I, pp. 163-165; Priselkov, M.D., *Ocherki po tserkovno-politicheskoi istorii Kievskoi Rusi*, SPB, 1913.

comprehension of its initial role in Russia, it is difficult to grasp the earliest cultural evolution and rapid successes of Christianity in Russia—as, for instance, is demonstrated in the cases of Boris and Gleb, of Hilarion, of Antonius and Theodosius, and the early blossoming of Russian letters and arts.

A clarification of the earliest stages of Christianity and of the church of Russia seem especially pertinent now, since these questions have rarely been discussed in the last few decades by Russian historians. The work on *The Nikonian Chronicle*, with its mention of the Christianized Askol'd and Dir, and the names of the first heads of the Russian church hierarchy, in our mind stimulates the need for a review of these problems.[62]

---

62. There are some comparatively recent contributions in English to the history of early Russia's Christianization and the early Russian church. See Vasiliev, A., *The Russian Attack on Constantinople in 868*, Cambridge, Mass., 1960; Ericsson, K., "The earliest Conversion of Rus' to Christianity," *Slavonic and East European Review*, Vol. 44, No. 102, London, 1966; Obolensky, D., *The Byzantine Commonwealth, Eastern Europe*, London, 1971; Dvornik, F., *Byzantine Mission Among the Slavs*, New Brunswick, 1970. In Russian, the above-mentioned works by Priselkov and Kartashev remain the most detailed studies of the same period. Some of these works agree, some disagree, with the above presentation of this problem.

LIST OF ABBREVIATIONS (I)
(Bibliographical)

(This is not a complete Bibliography. The latter will appear in the last volume of this English edition of *The Nikonian Chronicle*. Additional bibliographical information can be found in the footnotes.)

Artamonov	Artamonov, M. I., *Istoriia Khazar*, The Hermitage, Leningrad, 1952
Abramovich	Abramovich, D. I., Ed., *Zhitiia sv. muchenikov Borisa i Gleba i sluzhby im*, Petrograd, 1916
Bréhier	Bréhier, L., *La vie et la mort de Byzance*, Albin Michel, Paris, 1969
Dmitriev	Dmitriev, L. A., *Zhiteinye povesti russkogo severa*, AN, Leningrad, 1973
Dmitrieva	Dmitrieva, R., *Bibliografiia russkogo letopisaniia*, AN, Moscow-Leningrad, 1962
Hyp.	*Ipatevskaja letopis'*, *PSRL*, Vol. 2
Ioasaf. Chr.	*Ioasafovskaia letopis'*, Moscow, 1950
Kartashev	Kartashev, A. V., *Ocherki po istorii russkoi tserkvi*, Paris, 1959, Vols. I and II.
Kloss	Kloss, B. N., *Nikonovskii Svod i russkoe letopisanie XVI-XVII v.*, Nauka, Moscow, 1980.
Chronograph	*Khronograf 1512*, *PSRL*, Vol. 22
Kuz'min	Kuz'min, A. N., *Nachal'nye etapy drevne russkogo letopisaniia*, Izdat. Moskow, 1977
Laur.	*Lavrentievskaia letopis'*, *PSRL*, Vol. 1
Likhachev	Likhachev, D. S., edit. and com., *Povest' vremennykh let*, AN, Moscow, 1950, Vols. 1-2
Likhachev, *Letopisi*	Likhachev, D. S., *Russkoe letopisanie*, AN, Moscow-Leningrad, 1957
Likhachev, *Nasledie*	Likhachev, D. S., *Velikoe nasledie*, Sovremennik, Moscow, 1975
Migne	Migne, J. P., *Patrologiae cursus completus*, Series Graeca, Paris, 1860, Vols. 102, 105
Musc. Late 15th C.	*Moskovskii letopisnyi svod kontsa piatnadtsatogo veka*, *PSRL*, Vol. 25

Musc. Late 15th C. Abbr.	Sokrashchennye moskovskie letopisnye svody kontsa piatnadtsatogo veka, PSRL, Vol. 27
Nasonov	Nasonov, A. N., Istoriia russkogo letopisaniia, Moscow, 1969
Nik.	Patriarshaia ili Nikonovskaia letopis, PSRL, Vols. 9-13
Novg. Kom. and Novg. Syn.	Novgorodskaia pervaia letopis' starshego i mladshego izvodov, Moscow-Leningrad, 1950
Novg. Chr.	Novgorodskaia letopis' in PSRL, Vols. 3-4
Pashuto	Pashuto, V. T., Vneshniaia politika Drevnei Rusi, Nauka, Moscow, 1968
Prim. Chr.	The Primary Chronicle; see Likhachev
PSRL	Polnoe sobranie russkikh letopisei (Complete Collection of the Russian Chronicles), 1841—, AN Moscow, Vols. 1-34
Rogozh. Let.	Rogoszhskaia letopis, publ. in PSRL, Vol. 15
Simeon. Chr.	Simeonovskaia letopis', PSRL, Vol. 18
Sof.	Sofiiskaia letopis', PSRL, Vols. 5-6
Soloviev	Soloviev, S. M., Istoriia Rossii s drevneishikh vremen, Moscow, 1959-1966, Vols. 1-30
TODRL	Trudy otdela drevnerusskoi literatury, AN SSSR, Vols. 1-34, Leningrad, 1932-1980.
Tvorogov	Tvorogov, O. B., Drevnerusskie khronografy, AN, Leningrad, 1975
Tver'. Sbornik	Tver'skoi Sbornik in PSRL, Vol. 15
Ustiuzh. Ch.	Ustiuzhskii letopisnyi svod, AN Moscow, 1950
Vasiliev, A. A.	History of the Byzantine Empire, Univ. of Wisconsin Press, 1958, Vols. 1-2
Vernadsky	Vernadsky, G., and M. Karpovich, History of Russia, Vols. 1-2, New Haven, Yale Univ. Press, 1953
Vladimir. Let.	Vladimirskii letopisets, PSRL, Vol. 30
Zenkovsky	Zenkovsky, S., Medieval Russia's Epics, Chronicles and Tales, 2nd rev. ed., E. P. Dutton and Co., New York, 1969
Zimin	Zimin, A. A., Introduction to the Ioasafovskaia letopis', see above

LIST OF ABBREVIATIONS (II)
(Libraries and Manuscripts)
(For the location of *mss.*, see Introduction)

AN	Akademiia Nauk (Academy of Sciences, USSR).
BAN	Biblioteka Akademii Nauk (Library of the Academy of Sciences of the USSR), Leningrad.
Chron. red. 5 Novg.	*Chronographic* redaction of the *Fifth Novgorodian Chronicle*, in *ms.* only, in GIM.
GIM	Gosudarstvennyi istoricheskii Muzei (State Historical Museum), Moscow.
GBIL	Gosudarstvennaia biblioteka imeni Lenina (Lenin State Library), Moscow.
Obol.	*Obolenskii ms.* redaction of the *Nikonian Chronicle*. See Ch. I of Introduction.
Patr.	*Patriarshii ms.* redaction of the *Nikonian Chronicle*. See Ch. I of Introduction.
Radzivill Chr.	*Radzivillovskaia letopis'* in *ms.* only BAN.

GLOSSARY OF RUSSIAN AND BYZANTINE TERMINOLOGY

BASKAK	Mongol Tatar official, mostly a tax collector in Russia.
BOYARIN, BOYAR	Noble of high rank. Since the 13th century they formed an exclusive group out of which were chosen the Prince's councillors and high officials.
DENGA	Basic monetary unit since the 14th century (from Mongol *Tamga*—seal). A ruble contained usually 100 Novgorod or 200 Moscow dengas.
DRUZHINA	A prince's retinue or bodyguard; permanent nucleus of a prince's armed force.
GRIVNA	A unit of weight of about 410 grams. A grivna of silver a monetary unit.
INDICTION	Byzantine unit of chronology: a fifteen-year period. Year beginning September 1.
KAZAK	Originally Turkic nomads, not connected with a tribe; frontiersmen; later, free Russian settlers along the rivers of the prairie. Raiding was one of their main activities.
KUNA	Marten fur; it was a monetary unit in ancient Russia.
LOGOTHET	In Russian, *Logofet:* High Byzantine office, primarily in charge of financial matters.
METROPOLIA	Large bishopric. In Russia the entire territory and administration of the church.
METROPOLITAN	Metropolitan bishop, head of the Russian church.
NAMESTNIK	Local administrator and judge, appointed by the Grand Prince.
NOGATA	A monetary unit of kuna (see above) system; usually equal to $2\frac{1}{2}$ rezana, or $\frac{1}{20}$ grivna kun.
NOMOCANON	Byzantine codex of ecclesiastic law and, partially, civil law.
PARAKIMOMEN	In Byzantium only; palace eunuch supposed to sleep at the door of the imperial bedchamber; as emperor's closest servant, often exercised considerable influence.

POPRISHTE	A measure of distance usually equivalent of one versta.
POSADNIK	An elected high official, commissioner. In Novgorod, elected chief administrator. In Kievan Russia, an official appointed by the Prince.
PUD	Measure of weight. Since the eighteenth century, equivalent of forty pounds.
REZANA	In early Kievan times one grivna kun was the equivalent of fifty rezana. A small monetary unit.
RUBLE	Basic unit of Russian monetary system since the fourteenth century. Equivalent of 100 Novgorod or 200 Muscovite kuna. (Since the sixteenth century, 200 and 100 kopeks.)
SAZHEN'	Linear unit equivalent of three arshins or seven feet.
SCHEMA	Second and highest monastic tonsure. Very strict rules.
SLUGA	A servitor in medieval Russia; in the army, equal to a squire.
STOLNIK	A court official who aids the prince at table. Later, a high official just beneath a boyar.
TYSIATSKII	Literally, commander of a troop of a thousand men. In all the major cities tysiatskii commanded city soldiers and militia.
VECHE	A town meeting. After the thirteenth century it disappeared, except in Novgorod and Pskov, where the veche became a kind of citizens' diet, meeting on the main city square.
VERSTA	Unit of distance about ⅔ of a mile, or 1,063 km.
VOEVODA	Appointed by the Prince, a high official. May be an army or detachment commander, or the chief military, administrative and judicial officer, or governor of a territory.
USHKUINIK	From *ushkui*, a river boat: Novgorodian adventurers or freebooters who raided along the rivers of Northern Russia and the Volga.

GENEALOGICAL TABLES OF THE RUSSIAN REIGNING
DYNASTY
IN THE IX-XII CENTURIES

CONTENTS

Table 1—General overview of the first seven generations.

Table 2-9—Lineages of the sons of Iaroslav the Wise, son of St. Vladimir.
   2—of Vladimir (no patrimony, later Galich)
   3—of Iziaslav (mostly Western Russia, sometimes Kiev)
   4—of Sviatoslav, and specifically his son, Oleg (Chernigov and sometimes Kiev)
   5—of Sviatoslav, and specifically his grandson, Sviatoslav Ol'govich (Seversk land)
   6—of Sviatoslav, and specifically his son, Davyd (Chernigov and Murom)
   7—of Sviatoslav, and specifically his son, Iaroslav (Murom and Chernigov)
   8—of Vladimir Monomakh, and specifically his son, Mstislav (Kiev, Volynia, Pereiaslavl', Suzdalia)
   9—of Vladimir Monomakh, and specifically his son Rostislav (Smolensk)

Table 10—Lineage of Iziaslav, son of St. Vladimir (Iziaslav, Prince of Polotsk and of the Krivichs)

The data for these tables are taken from *Nik., Laur., Hyp.* and *Novg. I,* as well as from the following works:
   1. D. S. Likhachev, Ed., *Povest' vremennykh let*, M-L 1950, v. 2.
   2. M. S. Solov'ev, *Istoriia Rossii*, M-L 1959 edition, Vol. I.
   3. N. de Baumgarten, *Généalogie des Rurikides russes et mariages oxidentaux du X au XII s.*, Rome, Orientalia Christiana, 1927.

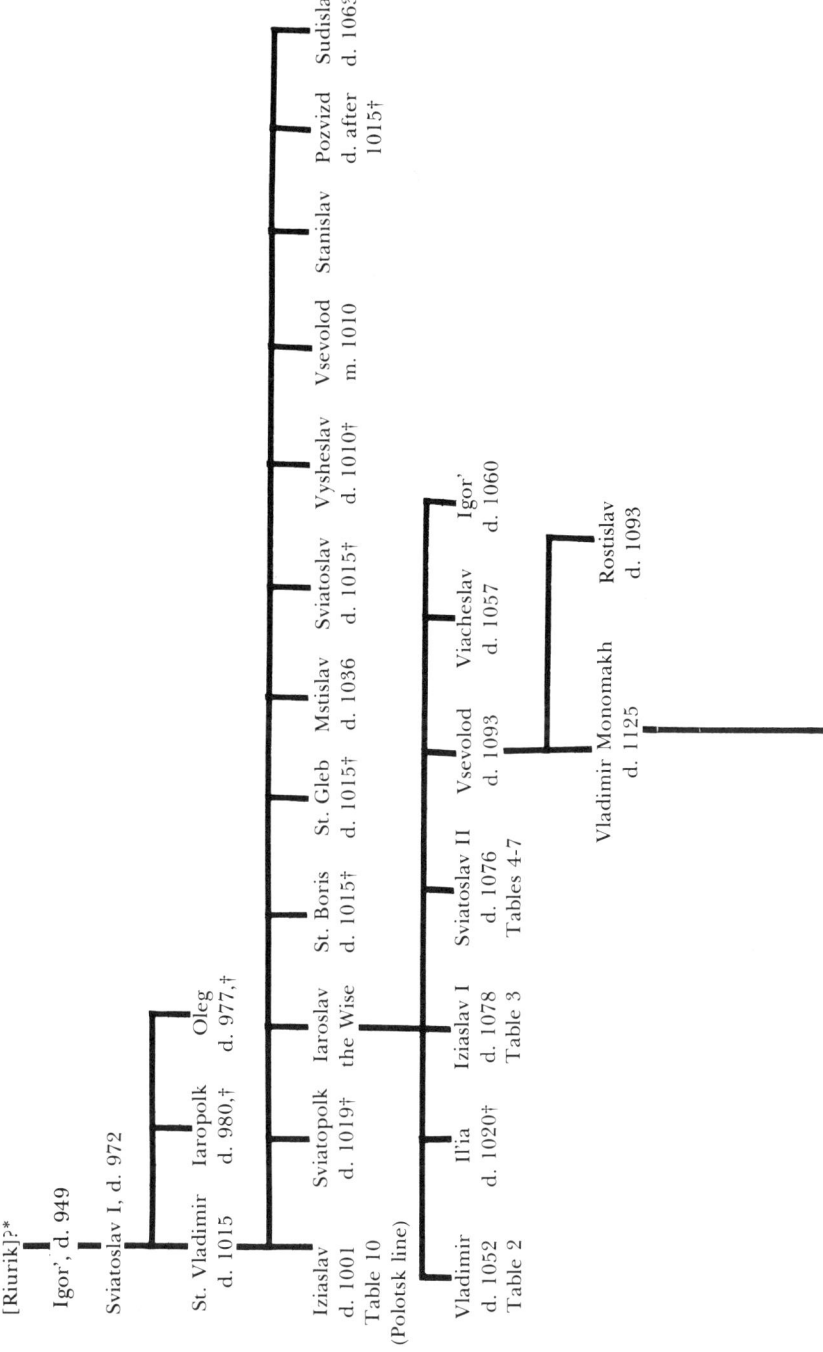

GENEALOGY OF THE RUSSIAN PRINCES, IX-XII CENTURIES
Table 1.
The Main Line: of Iaroslav the Wise and then of Vladimir Monomakh

lxxii   Introduction

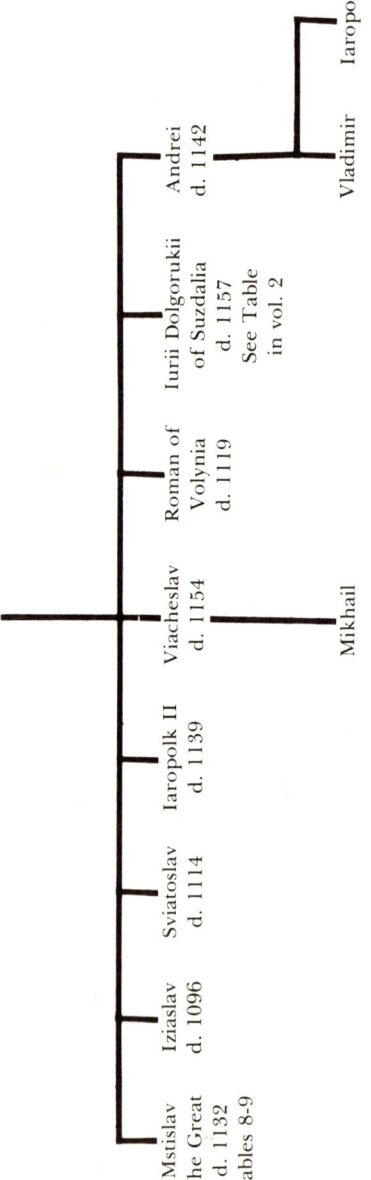

*The mythical Riurik, who was "invited" in 862 to a not yet existing Novgorod, is a legendary personality who cannot definitely be called Igor's father.

NOTE: In the above and following Tables "d" denotes "died;" "m" indicates "mentioned" (not married"); and the sign, † indicates "without issue."

The seniority of some princes is in several cases unclear.

GENEALOGY OF THE RUSSIAN PRINCES, IX-XII CENTURIES
Table 2.
Lineage of Vladimir, son of Iaroslav the Wise (Princes mostly of Tmutarakan' and Galich Land)

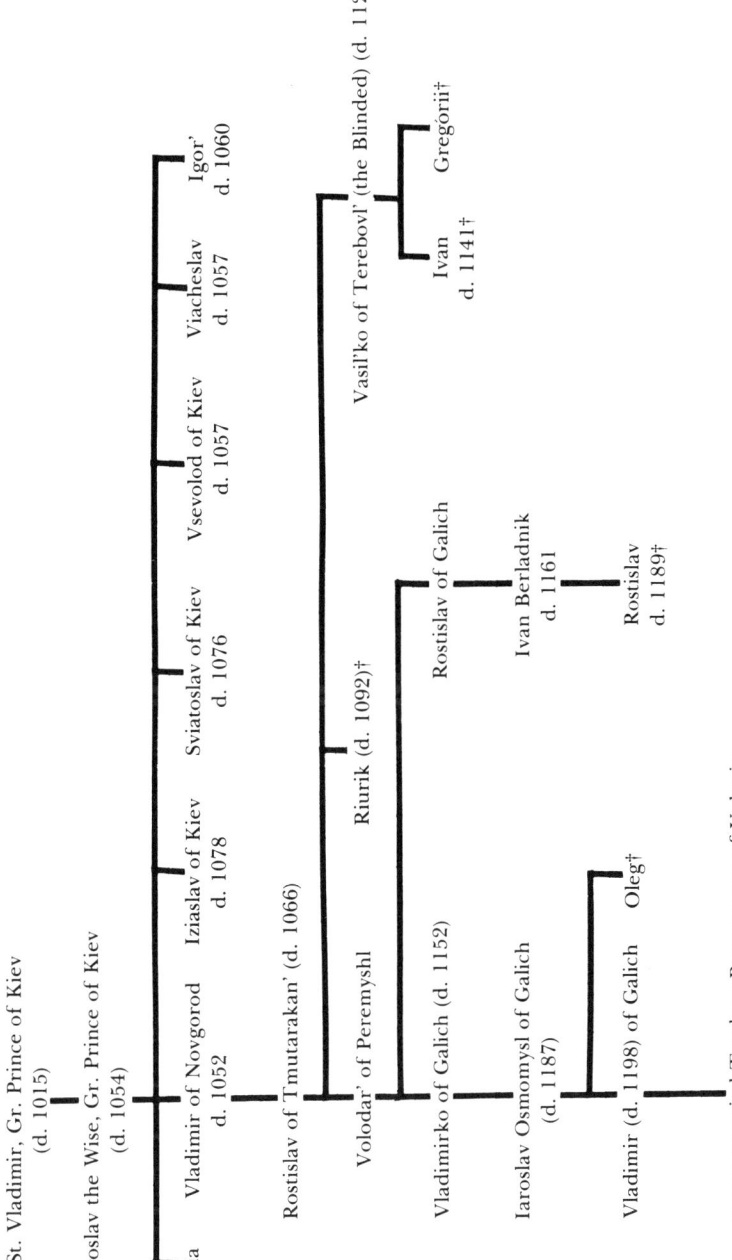

Introduction

GENEALOGY OF THE RUSSIAN PRINCES, IX-XII CENTURIES
Table 3.
Lineage of Iziaslav, son of Iaroslav the Wise, princes of Kiev, Volynia, Polotsk and Pinsk

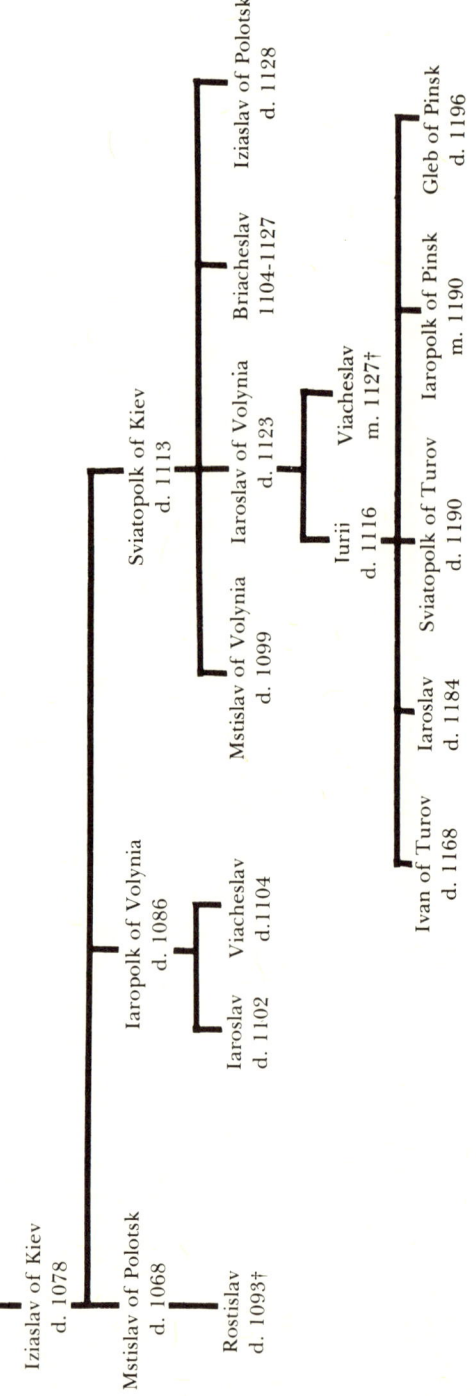

Princes of Pinsk, of unknown lineage

Vladimir Aleksandr of Dubrov Rostislav
m. 1204   m. 1224   m. 1228

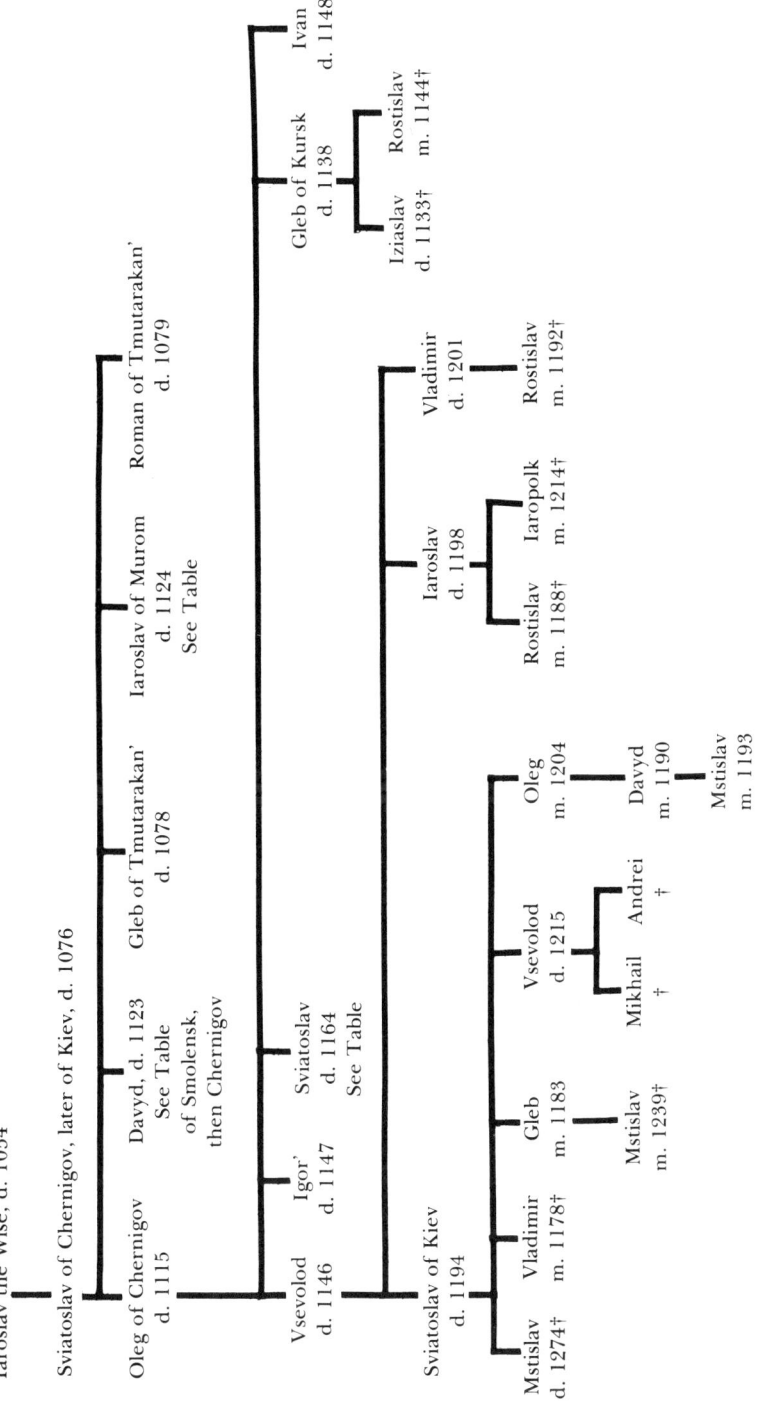

GENEALOGY OF THE RUSSIAN PRINCES, IX-XII CENTURIES
Table 4.
Lineage of Sviatoslav, son of Iaroslav the Wise, and, specifically, Sviatoslav's son, Oleg
[The Olgovichs of Chernigov and sometimes Kiev; Tmutarakan'; Smolensk]

lxxvi *Introduction*

GENEALOGY OF THE RUSSIAN PRINCES, X-XII CENTURIES
Table 5.
Lineage of Sviatoslav Ol'govich, Grandson of Sviatoslav, Son of Iaroslav the Wise

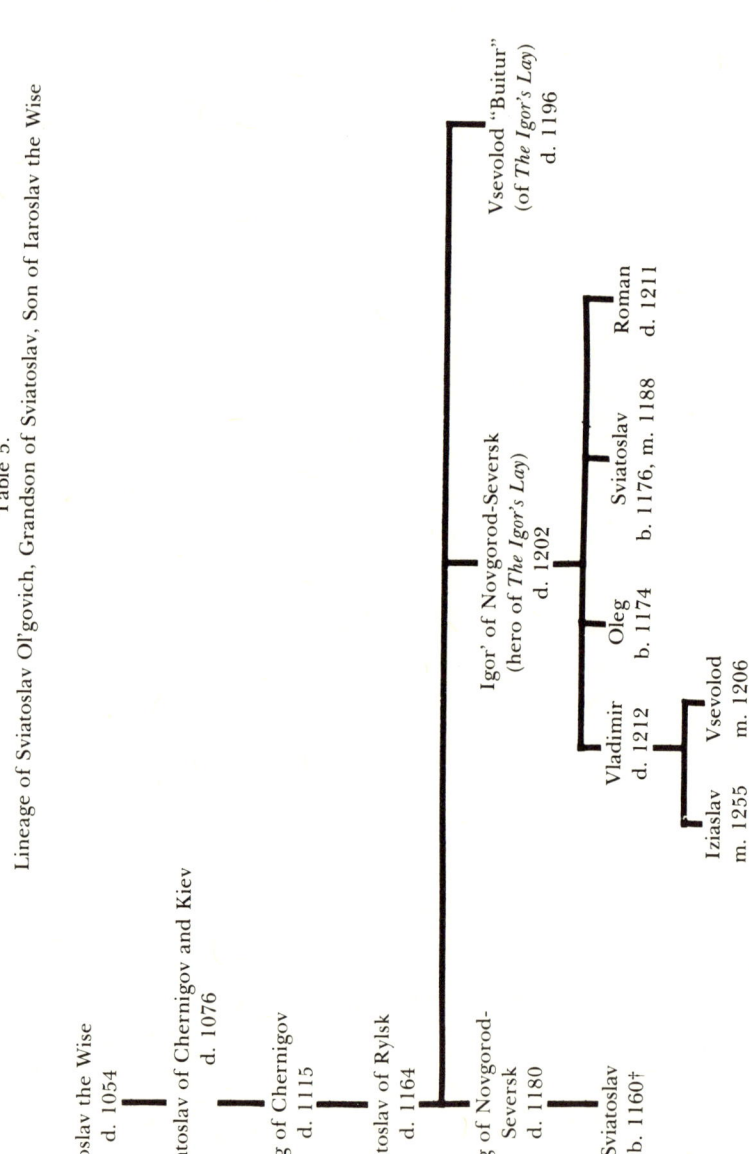

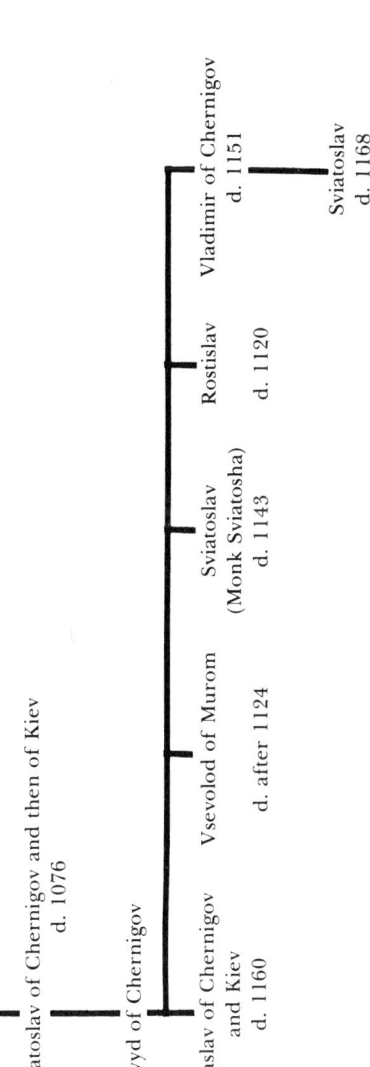

GENEALOGY OF THE RUSSIAN PRINCES, X-XII CENTURIES
Table 6.
Lineage of Davyd Sviatoslavich, Grandson of Iaroslav the Wise
("Davydovichs" of Chernigov and Murom; sometimes of Kiev)

lxxviii   Introduction

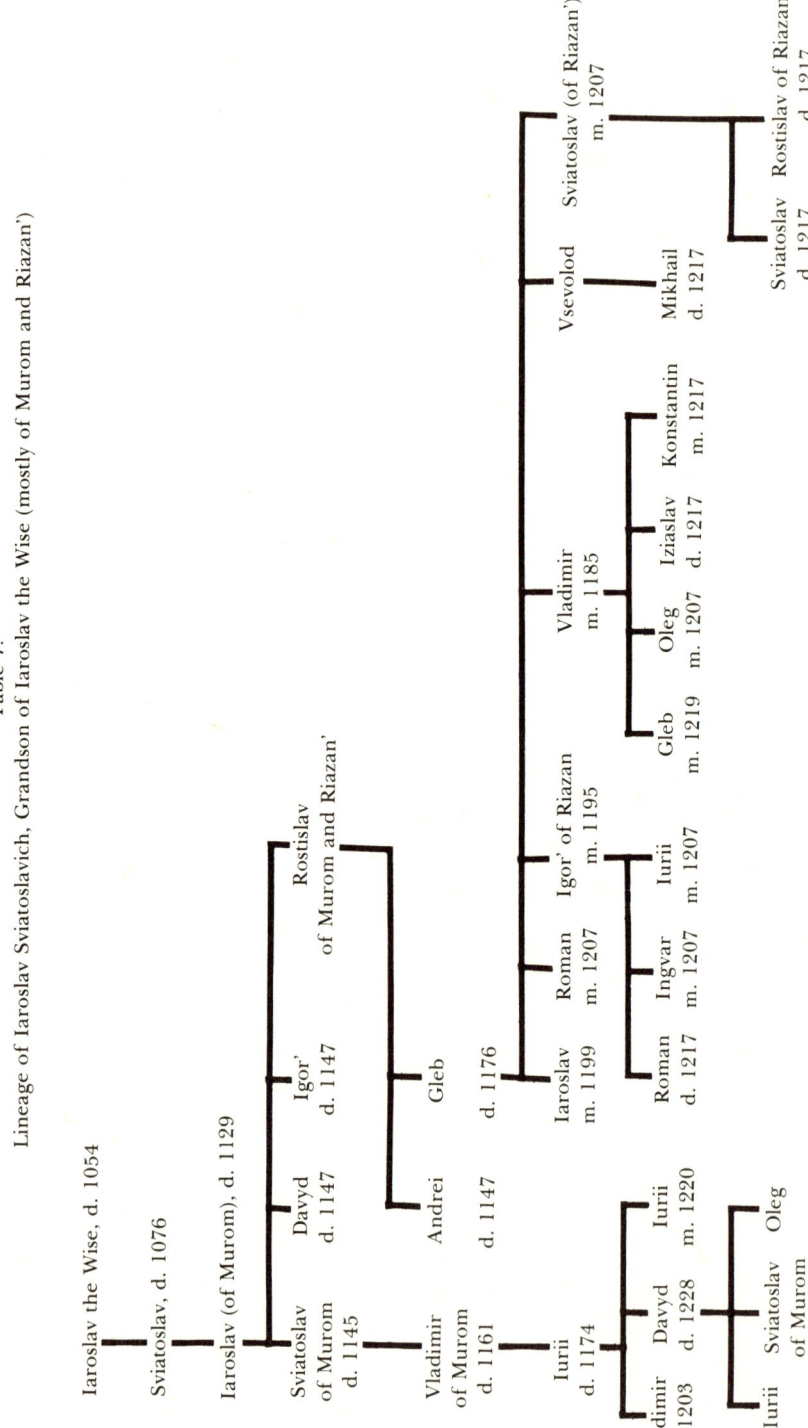

GENEALOGY OF THE RUSSIAN PRINCES, X-XII CENTURIES
Table 7.
Lineage of Iaroslav Sviatoslavich, Grandson of Iaroslav the Wise (mostly of Murom and Riazan')

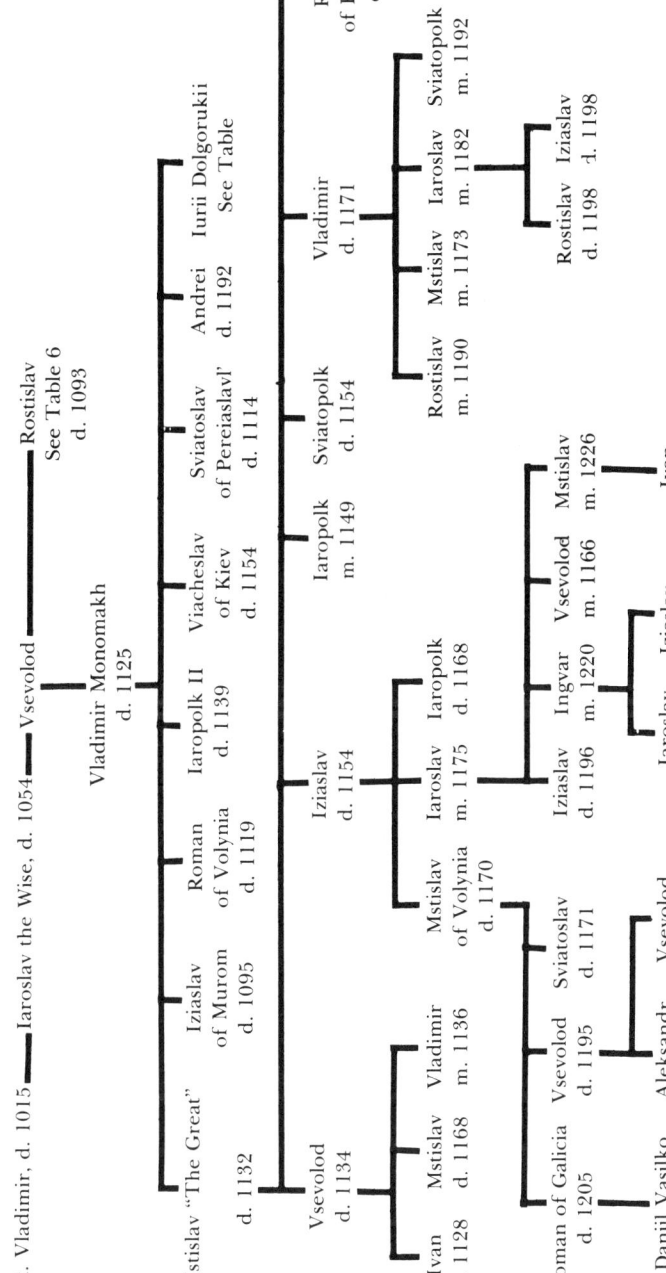

GENEALOGY OF THE RUSSIAN PRINCES, X-XII CENTURIES
Table 8.
Lineage of Mstislav the Great, Son of Vladimir Monomakh
[Monomashichs of Kiev, Pereiaslavl', Volynia, Murom, and other lands]

GENEALOGY OF THE RUSSIAN PRINCES, X-XII CENTURIES
Table 9.
Lineage of Rostislav Mstislavich, Grandson of Vladimir Monomakh
(primarily Smolensk or Toropets)

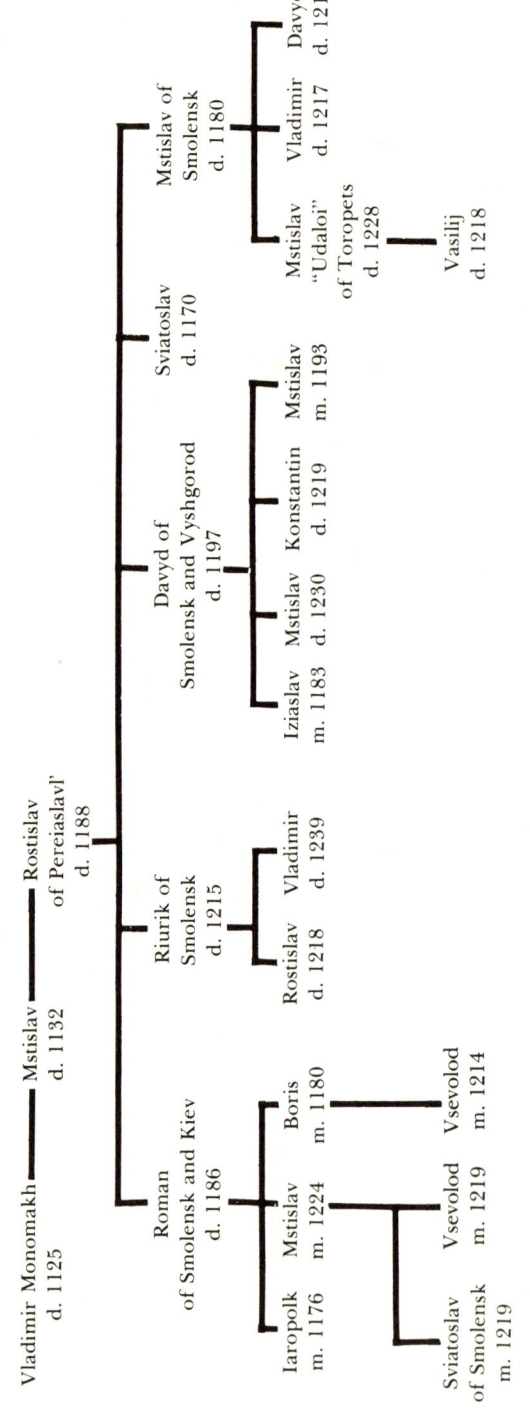

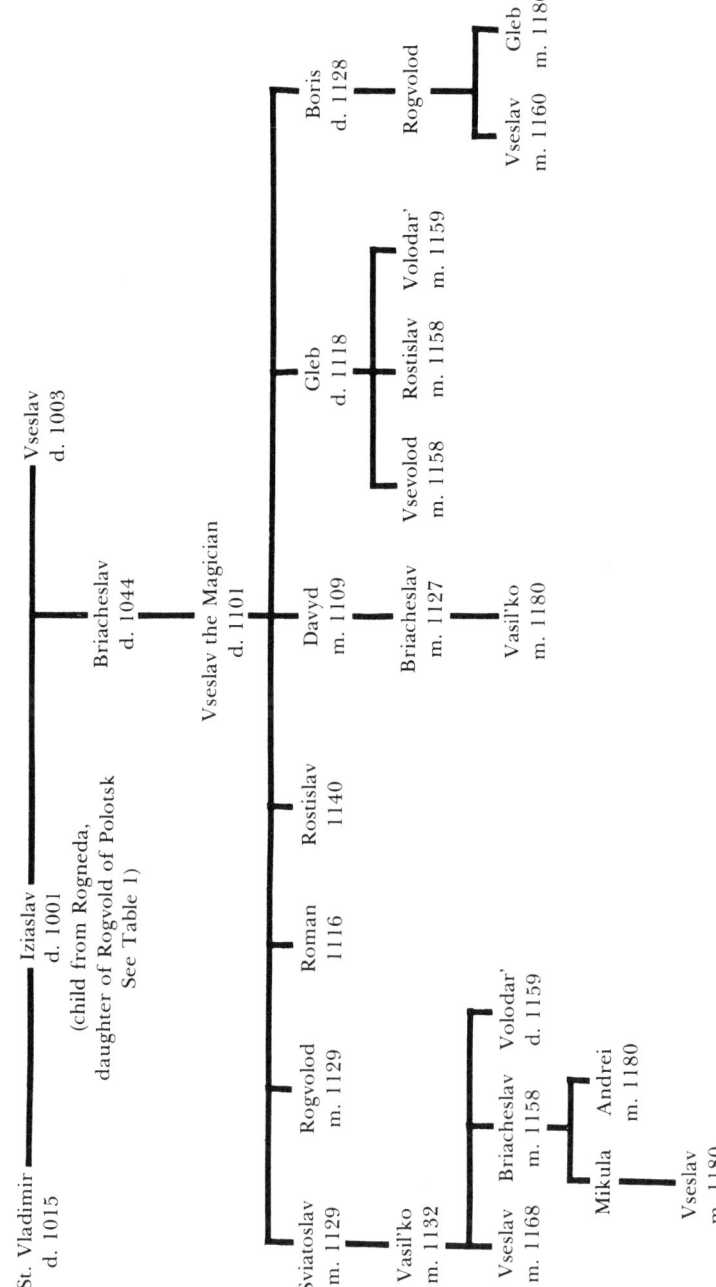

GENEALOGY OF THE RUSSIAN PRINCES, X-XII CENTURIES
Table 10.
Lineage of Iziaslav, Son of St. Vladimir
(Princes of the Land of Polotsk and Krivichs)

THE NIKONIAN CHRONICLE

[PARTITION OF THE EARTH AMONG NOAH'S SONS][1]

We begin this narrative about the following: from whence the Russian land arose, who began to rule in it, and what the origin of the Russian land was.

After the flood, Noah's three sons—Shem, Ham and Japheth—partitioned the earth [among themselves] [*Gen.* 10:32]:[2] Shem's part [was] the eastern lands: Persia, Bactria and even India, in length. In width, it extended as far as Rhinokurur,[3] and then, so to say, from the East and as far South [as] Syria, Media, the [valley of the] Euphrates river, Babylon, Corduena,[4] Assyria, Mesopotamia, Arabia the Ancient, Elymais, India, Arabia the Strong, Coelesyria, Commagene and all Phoenicia.

---

1. The text of *Nik.* from the beginning to the year 1118 is close to that in *Laur.* The description of the division of the earth among Noah's sons was taken by the writer of *The Primary Chronicle* from the Greek chronicle by Georgios Harmatolos. From the same chronicle also were taken the shorter items dealing with Byzantium. The longer anecdotes about the Byzantine emperors follow the text of the *Chronograph* (Byzantine, South Slavic and Russian name for books of general and Russian history in which the divisions into years, as in the Russian chronicles, did not exist). The dates of the Byzantine events are not always exact. The sources of other items, unique to *Nik.*, are not always identifiable.

2. The following names of these lands were taken by the writer of the *Prim. Chron.* from Harmatolos. When identified, they are given in their standard English forms. Unidentifiable cities and lands are marked with "?."

3. Rhinokurur: a city between Egypt and Palestine.

4. Corduena: unclear. Probably, Corduena, on the upper Tigris in southern Armenia (as in Harmatolos). In *Nik.* this name reads "Korodunia." Here and further the names in *Nik.* are corrected on the basis of *Prim. Chr.* (ed., D.S. Likhachev) and Harmatolos. See *Prim. Chr.*, Vol., 2, 206-214.

Ham's [part]: to him fell the Southern lands: Egypt, Ethiopia[5] which is close to India, the other Ethiopia, in which the red Ethiopian river which flows toward the East originates, the Thebaid, Libia—which extends as far as Cyrene—Marmaria,[6] Syrtis, the other Libia, Numidia, Massyris [and] Mauritania across from Cadiz.[7] And those which are in the East are Cilicia, Pamphilia, Pysidia, Mysia, Lycaonia, Phrygia, Camara, Lycia, Caria, Lydia, the other Moesia, Troya, Phrygia, Camalia, Solidia, Bethamia and Phrygia the Ancient.[8] Islands: all the [following] belong to it: Sardinia, Crete, Cyprus and the river Gihon [also] called the Nile.

Japhet's part: to him fell the Northern and Western lands: Media, Albania [present Azerbaijan], Little and Great Armenia, Cappadocia, Paphlagonia, Galatia, Colchis, Bosporus, Maeotis, Devria, Sarmatia, Tauria, Scythia, Thrace, Macedonia, Dalmatia, Molossia, Thessalia, Locris, Pellepe, which is also called Peloponnese, Arcadia, Epirus, Illyria, the Slavs, Lychnitis, Adriaca and the sea of Adria.[9] Islands: also to him belong the islands Britannia, Sicilia, Eubea, Rhodes, Chios, Lesbos, Cythera, Zacynthos, Cephallonia, Ithaca, Corcyra, and a part of another [island's] land called Ionia. Rivers: the [valley of the] Tigris river, which flows between Medes and Babylon; [rivers flowing] to the Pontus [Black Sea] from the northern lands are the river Danube, the Dniester river with the Carpathian mountains, which are also called Hungarian, and from thence as far as [the river] Dnieper. And other rivers are the Desna, Pripet', Volkhov and Volga, which flows from the East into Shem's part.[10]

And in Japheth's part dwell: Russia, Chud' and the following tongues: Meria, Muroma, Ves', Mordva, Chud' beyond the Portages, Perm', Pechora, Jam, Ugra [Finnic tribes], Lithuania, Samogitia [also a Lithuanian tribe], Kors' and Chud along the shores

---

5. Ethiopia: Byzantines used to call "Ethiopia" the lands south of Egypt and even some in southeast Asia. In this case, it is Asian Ethiopia.

6. Marmaria: the land between Egypt and Cyrenaica.

7. All these lands are in North Africa.

8. This second group of Ham's lands is in Asia Minor.

9. Japhet's lands include the Caucasus, part of Asia Minor, the land north of the Black Sea, and the Balkans.

10. Some names of Russian rivers, as well as of Slavic and Finno-Ugric tribes, were added by the author of *Prim. Chr.* to Harmatolos' text.

of the Varangian [Baltic] Sea. And along this sea farther to the east, as far as the part of Shem, live the [Varangians] further west along this sea as far as the English and the French lands. Also to the tribes of Japheth belong the Varangians, Swedes, Normans, Goths, Russians, English, Galicians [of Spain], Poles, Vlakhs [Rumanians], Romans, Germans, Carolingians, Venetians, Italians and others. Toward the northwest they are neighbors of the tribes of Ham.

Shem, Ham and Japheth, after dividing the earth and casting lots, [agreed] not to trespass into their brothers' lots, and each lived in his part. And one language and people multiplied after the flood, and in the days of Jokton and Peleg [*Gen.* 10:25-26] they conceived the idea of building a tower as high as heaven, itself. They gathered in a place [called] Shinar and decided to build a tower that would reach unto heaven, as well as the city of Babylon around it. And they worked on the tower for forty years but could not complete it. The Lord saw the city and the tower and said, "They are one people and one language." And God confounded the tongue and divided them into seventy and two tongues and scattered them all over the earth. After having confounded the tongues, God destroyed the tower with a powerful storm and its ruins are till now between Assyria and Babylon; and it is 1000 and 800 and 60 and 6 yards high, and of the same width, and it has been preserved for many years. [*Gen.* 11:1-9]

AFTER THE DESTRUCTION OF THE TOWER. [THE SLAVS]

After the destruction of the tower and the divisions of the tongues, the sons of Shem occupied the eastern lands; the sons of Ham, the southern lands; and those of Japheth took the western and northern lands. And from these seventy-two tongues came the Slavic tongues, from a tribe of Japhetus, which is called Norics, and those are the Slavs.

Many years later the Slavs settled on both sides of the Danube [river], where the Hungarian land and the Bulgarian one are. And from thence the Slavs scattered all over the land, taking their names from the places where they settled: those who settled along the river Morava called themselves Moravians; others, Czechs; and others, White Croatians; and others, Serbs; and others, Karintians; and some, Danubians. And when the Romans[11] met the Slavs on the

---

11. Actually, Germans of the so-called Roman Empire of the German Nation founded by Charlemagne; they encountered Slavs around A.D. 800.

Danube, they settled themselves there and oppressed them. Those Slavs who came to the river Wisla took the name of Liakhs, and some of these Liakhs called themselves Poles; and some other Liakhs [called themselves] Lusatians; and some, Mazovians; and some, Pomorians. In the same manner, these Slavs came to [the river] Dnieper and took the name of Polians;[12] and some, because they settled in the forest, Drevlians.[13] And others settled between the [rivers] Pripet' and Dvina and were named Dregovichs [Dregovichi]; and some, Polochians [Polochane] because of the river Polota, which is a tributary of the river Dvina.

[Other] Slavs who came from the [river] Danube settled around Lake Il'men and [continued] to call themselves by their name [Slovens]. They built a city and called it Novgorod, and appointed Gostomysl[14] as their elder. And others settled on [the rivers] Seim and Sula and took the name, Severs.[15] And in such a way the Slavic tongue spread; and therefore their writing is called Slavic.

THE RIVER ROUTE.

The Polians lived apart, on the hills [of the shore of the Dnieper] and the way from the Varangians to the Greeks was there. From the Greeks up [the river] Dnieper and from the upper Dnieper portage [Volok] to the river Lovat', along the Lovat' to great Lake Il'men, and from it flows the [river] Volkhov, which flows into the big lake Neva;[16] and the delta of the Neva enters the Varangian [Baltic] Sea. On this sea one can go to Rome, and from Rome to Constantinople. From Constantinople it is possible to go to the Pontus[17] into which the river Dnieper flows. The Dnieper originates in the Oka forest[18] and flows southward; the Dvina begins in the same forest and its

---

12. *Poliane:* from *pole*, "prairie."

13. *Drevliane:* from *drevo, derevo,* "wood."

14. The name Gostomysl is not in *Laur.* or *Hyp.*, but is found in *Novg. Kom.*, year 988/9 and in the lists of posadniks, pp. 164, 471, as well as the *Sofiiskaia, Voznesenskaia, Chronograph,* and other chronicles.

15. *Severiane:* those of the north.

16. Actually, to the Ladoga and then the Neva river.

17. *Pontus Euxinus:* the Greek name for the Black Sea.

18. Oka forest: formerly, a dense forest between the upper course and tributaries of the Dnieper, the West Dvina, the Oka and Volga rivers.

course is northward, and it flows into the Varangian Sea. The Volga [river] also originates in the same forest. Its course is eastward and its delta is at the Khvalis [Caspian] Sea and has seventy mouths.

This way one can go along the Volga from Russia to the Bulgars and to the Khvalis Sea.[19] Going further east, one can enter the lands of Shem: by the river Dvina one can go to the Varangians, from the Varangians to Rome, and from Rome into the lands of Ham. The Dnieper's delta at Pontus [the Black Sea] has three mouths. This sea is known as the Russian one, and along its [shores] the Apostle Andrew, Peter's brother, is said to have travelled and to have taught.

When Apostle Andrew taught in Sinop and [from thence] went to Korsun'[20] he learned that he was in the vicinity of the delta of the Dnieper and wanted to go [by way of the Dnieper] to Rome; and he came to the delta of the Dnieper and ascended the river Dnieper.

THE APOSTLE ANDREW'S PROPHECY CONCERNING THE CITY OF KIEV

Journeying up to the curve of the river, the holy Apostle Andrew came [to the place where Kiev is now located] and stopped on the hills of the shore. When he arose the next morning he told his pupils who were with him, "Do you see these hills? Divine grace will shine upon these hills and here will arise a great city which God will have built here, and there will be many churches [here.]" He ascended those hills and blessed them and erected a cross there, praying to God. And then he descended [to the shore] and many years later the city of Kiev was built there.

[Then] Apostle Andrew went up the Dnieper river and arrived at [the tribe] of Slavs living where the city of Novgorod now is and he saw the people there and their customs, and he was astounded to see how they bathe in steambaths. He went further to the Varangians, came to Rome and told how he had preached and what he had seen.

19. Volga Bulgars: a tribe speaking an archaic Turkic tongue which lived south and west of the present city of Kazan'. Most of them became converted to Islam in the ninth/tenth centuries and formed the northernmost outpost of Islamic civilization. These Islamized Bulgars became a component of the Kazan' Tatar Khanate. Some, apparently those who were not converted to Islam, preserved their tongue and are known now under the name "Chuvash."

20. Korsun': Chersonesus, a Greek colony in the Crimea, in about the same place as the port and city of Sevastopol'.

And he said, "I saw wooden steambaths and there they have large stones. They heat these stones till they become red and then they splash themselves with a fermented drink[21] and then they lash themselves with young branches till they are barely alive; and then they pour cold water on themselves and in such a way, revive. And they do this, tormenting themselves thus, every day." The Romans heard this and marvelled. After remaining for some time in Rome, Andrew returned to the land of Sinop.[22]

THE BEGINNING OF THE CITY OF KIEV

The Polians [Poliane] lived in separate tribes which were ruled in each place by their kinfolk. There were three brothers: one of them had for his name, Kii; another, Shchok;[23] and the third, Khoriv: and they had a sister, Lybed'. Kii lived on the hill where now is the road to Borichev. His brother, Shchok, lived on the other side of the hill which is now called Shchokovitsa; and Khoriv lived on a third hill which is named Khorivitsa after him. And they laid the foundation of a town which they named for their elder brother, giving it the name, Kiev. Near the city of Kiev there was a big pine wood where they used to hunt wild animals. There were wise and intelligent men and they were called Polians; and their descendants, the Polians, live there to the present. Some well-informed people say that Kii was a ferryman [across the Dnieper river]. But this is wrong: Kii had a ferryman on the other side of the Dnieper and therefore they called him a ferryman, himself. If he were just a ferryman, he would not have been able to campaign against Constantinople with a strong army. But Kii was the prince of his clan and campaigned in many lands. He also lived in peace and brotherly relations with the emperor of Constantinople, and he was honored by him and

---

21. *Kvas:* a fermented drink made of bread, berries or fruit.

22. Eusebius: a fourth-century Christian historian, possibly referring to earlier sources of the second century, wrote of the Apostle Andrew's mission in Scythia, present southern Russia, most probably then Greek colonies of the Black Sea shore. Later, Byzantine historians, as well as the author of the Russian *Primary Chronicle*, add more details to this information, though by no means authentic ones. In any case, the theme of the Apostle Andrew preaching in Scythia, later Russia, became very popular among medieval Russian writers.

23. In the Russian *Primary Chronicle (Laur.)* his name is Shchek.

everyone else. He went with his warriors to campaign against the Bulgarians [on the Danube]. When he arrived at the Danube he liked a place there and built a town there, and wanted to settle there with his kinsfolk; but they [the Bulgarians] did not let him stay there and continually fought against him. There is, however, a town [built] there until now, and the people of the Danube who live there call it Kievets. He also campaigned against the Bulgars of the Volga and Kama, defeated them, returned to his town of Kiev and remained there till the end of his life. His brothers, Shchok and Khoriv, and their sister, Lybed', also died there.[24]

After them their family continued to rule over the Polians. And the Drevlians had their own principality; and the Dregovichs, theirs; and the Slavs in Novgorod, their own; and the others, their own on the [river] Polota: these [people are called]Polochians. Next to them are the Krivichs—they inhabit the upper Volga, the upper Dvina and the upper Dnieper, and Smolensk is their town. There the Krivichs live, and the Severs live next to them. And around Beloozero live the [Finic tribe of] Ves'; and on lake Rostov live the [Finnic tribe of] Meria, as well as the Merias on lake Kleschino.

Along the Oka, which flows into the Volga, live [the Finnic tribes of] Muroma, who have their own tribe; the Meshchera, who also [have] their own; the Mordva, also having their own; and the Cheremisa, who also have theirs.

And the Slavic language is spoken in Russia [by the following tribes]; Polians, Drevlians, Novgorodians, Polochians; Dregovichs; Severs; Buzhans, because they live on the Bug river and who later have been called Volynians. And these are the tribes which pay tribute to the Russians: Chud', Meria, Ves', Muroma, Cheremisa, Mordva, Perm', Pechora, Iam [all Finnic tribes]; Lithuanians, Samogitians, Korsa [Kur—Lithuanians], Norova, Livs—all of them have their tribes, and are the descendents of Japheth because they live in the Northern lands.

---

24. An eighth-century Armenian historian, Zenob Glak, in his *History of Taron,* writes that in the land of Polani (Polians) three brothers, Kuar (Kii), Meltei (*Shchek; Shchek* and *Meltei,* according to N. Marr, both mean "snake," "serpent") and Khorean (Khoriv) founded the city of Kuar (Kiev). It happened around A.D. 600. *Istoriia SSSR,* izd. AN, Vol. II-IX centuries, M., 1958, pp. 779-780; for more details see the Foreword to this volume.

ABOUT THE SLAVS

Certain Bulgars came to the Slavic tribes, who lived on the Danube; they came from the land of the Scythians, also called Khazars. And they settled along the Danube among the Slavs. After them came the White Hungarians, who occupied the Slavic lands. These Hungarians appeared in the time of Emperor Heraclius, who fought with the Persian King Khozroy.[25]

ABOUT THE AVARS

At that time there were also Avars who made raids against Emperor Heraclius,[26] and almost took him prisoner. These Avars campaigned against the Slavs and were violent with the Duleb women: when an Avar would go on a journey, then each Avar would harness to his wagon five or six Duleb women, and they were proud that [they used] them for riding and offended the Slavs. Those Avars had powerful bodies and were extremely strong, and because no one could resist them they were therefore proud; but God annihilated them and they all disappeared because [they incited] God's wrath. To this day there is a saying in Russia: "They vanished like the Avars," and not one remains of their people, and nothing remains after them.

ABOUT THE POLIANS

As we said, the Polians originated from the Slavs and they lived apart; and the Drevlians also were from the Slavs but called themselves Drevlians. The Radimichs and the Viatichs, however, were of Polish origin. There were two brothers among the Poles: Radim and another, Viatko. And coming [into their present habitat], Radim settled on the [river] Sozh, and [his descendants] called themselves Radimichs. But Viatko settled with his tribe on the [river] Oka, and because of him they are called Viatichs to the present day. And they [all] lived in peace; the Polians, the Drevlians, the Severs, the Radimichs, the Viatichs, and Khorvats and the Dulebs, who lived

---

25. The chroniclers apparently confused these White Huns (Ugry) either with Bulgars or with the Avars. See following paragraph.

26. *Avars:* a federation of Mongol tribes which came from eastern Mongolia to Europe in the seventh century. They were defeated and their realms were destroyed by Charlemagne around A.D. 800. Heraclius: Byzantine emperor, A.D. 610-641.

on the southern Bug [river], where the Volynians now live. But the Liutichs and the Tiveretss settled on the Danube [river] and on the Dniester [river], and there were a great many of them—as far as the [Black] Sea, and there their cities are to the present day, and their [land] is called "Great Scythia" by the Greeks.

All of them had their own customs, the law of their forefathers, and traditions, and all of them had their own mores. Following the mores of their forefathers, the Polians are peaceful, quiet and respectful; they respect greatly their parents and their people, and have wedding ceremonies. The Drevlians [to the contrary] are beastly and live like animals. They would kill each other; they eat impure food; they do not have any wedding; and they kidnap girls to have for wives. The Radimichs, the Viatichs and the Severs have the same mores: they are like any other beasts in the forest, eat impure food, speak obscenely in the presence of their parents and have no respect for their tribe. They do not have wedding ceremonies but just festivals in their towns, and all assemble for these festivals and do all manner of devilish dances; and during [these festivals and dances] they carry off wives for themselves, and they do it after an earlier prearrangement with them; they would have two or even three wives [apiece]. When one of them dies, they would have a feast over the corpse and they would build a great pyre on which the dead would be laid and burned. And then they would gather his bones, put them into a small receptacle and place it on a pole at the crossroad; and they do so to the present day. The Krivichs practice the same customs, as well as the other pagan [Slavs] because without the knowledge of divine law they create their own law. Georgios Harmatolos says in his chronicle, "There are people who have a written law. Others have customs which come from their ancestors, which are considered law because they have no written law. Among the first are the Syrians, who live at the end of the world and who have for law the customs of their forefathers. They have the law not to commit adultery, not to steal, not to bear false witness, not to kill, not to commit any other crimes. There is the law among the Baktrians[27] who are also called Brahmins, or 'Islanders',[28] who,

---

27. In *Nik.* the transliteration is incorrect: "Ktiriiaks."

28. Bactrians or Rahmans (Brahmins), a legendary ideal people hardly related to the Bactrians of Persian Central Asia and India.

according to the instructions and piety of their forefathers, do not eat any meat, do not drink wine, do not commit any lechery because they are afraid [to trespass the law]. They do no evil to anyone, although those next to them are different and follow another law; they do all manner of misdeeds and are very wrathful—beyond the nature [of man]. They live in the inner part of the land and eat people and kill travellers and eat in the manner of dogs. The law of the Chaldeans and Babylonians is different: they marry their own mothers, they commit carnal sin with their brothers' children, they kill and commit all manner of shameless deeds. The Geleans [?][29] have another custom: their women plough, build temples, do all manner of men's deeds and make tools. And they commit adultery as much as they want [because] they are not restrained by their husbands. Their women are very courageous; they hunt strong beasts and command over their husbands. In Britannia many men sleep with the same woman and many women sleep with the same man, and they follow their lawless law of their forefathers without any restraint or jealousy. The Amazonians have no husbands but are like dumb animals. They are filled with carnal desires: and only once every year, in spring, they have intercourse with neighboring men because at that time they have some sort of festival or great celebration. And when they conceive from them a child in their wombs, they run away from thence. When the time comes to give birth to the child, and if they give birth to a male child, they kill him, but if it is a female child, they bring it up very carefully."[30]

And in the same way in our time now the Polovetss keep the law of their forefathers.[31] They shed blood and boast of it. They eat dead animals and all manner of impure food—hamsters and marmots. And they marry their mothers-in-law and their sisters-in-law, and also commit other bad customs following their forefathers. We, Christians, however, who are in so many lands, we believe in the Holy Trinity, in one baptism, in one faith, and have one law [for us all] because we all believe in Christ, are baptized into Christ and we have put on Christ.

29. In *Primary Chronicle,* Teleans."
30. End of the quotation from Harmatolos, *Prim. Chr.,* II, p. 228.
31. Here should be "Pechenegs," not "Polovetss." The fact that the chronicle writer mentions the Polovetss here indicates that this part of *Nik.'s* initial sources was written at least in the mid-eleventh century, when the Polovetss, or Cumans, appeared in the south Russian prairie.

After these years and after the death of those brothers [Kii, Shchek and Khoriv], the Polians were oppressed by the Drevlians and by their other neighbors; and then the Khazars[32] found them [the Polians] dwelling in these mountains and in the forest, and they came upon them and the Khazars said, "Give us tribute." And the Polians agreed to give them a sword from each household, and the Khazars carried them to their prince and to their elders, saying, "We have received new tribute." But the others said, "From whence?" And they replied, "In the forest on the hill along the Dnieper river." And they said, "What did they give you?" And they showed them the swords. And then the Khazar elders said, "Prince, this tribute is not good. We have conquered them with a weapon having one edge, which is called the 'saber;' but their weapon has two edges and is called 'sword,' and [later] they will have tribute from us and from other countries." And this happened not because they spoke according to their mind but it occurred according to the will of God. It happened in the same way as under the Pharoah, king of Egypt: When Moses was brought before Pharoah, the elders of Egypt said to the Pharoah, "Oh, King, this one wants to submit the land of Egypt." And so it happened, and the Egyptians were destroyed by Moses. In the same way these Khazars ruled over the Polians but thereafter the latter began to rule over the Khazars, and the Russians rule over the Khazars to the present day.

ABOUT THE CHRISTIANIZATION OF BULGARIA

Once when there was war the sister of the Bulgarian prince was taken prisoner by the Greeks, and she was baptized, and at the [Byzantine] Emperor's court she was taught Books; and it happened under Emperor Michael.[33] Thereafter she became the wife of a boyar named Theodore Kiphar, and she taught her brother everything about Christianity. At that time diseases of the plague occurred among the Bulgarians and many died, and then he [the ruler of the Bulgarians] accepted the teaching and faith of his sister, and from that time the disease of the plague stopped. And he sent [an envoy] to Constantinople, asking that a bishop come to baptise

---

32. The Khazars were a Turkic confederation whose state was located on the lower Volga and in the northern Caucusus.

33. Emperor Michael III, 842-867.

them. When the Bulgarians learned of this they conspired to kill him. He bestirred himself, however, and fought them, pledging on the Cross, and he defeated them, pledging on the Cross, and he defeated them with the Cross, which he carried before them. And in this way they accepted baptism with love.[34]

ABOUT THE OTHER BULGARIAN PRINCE

The Bulgarian Prince Boris came to Constantinople asking for the holy baptism of his entire principality. And by divine Grace he was permitted to accept it. And he received baptism from [the Byzantine] Emperor Michael[35] and in baptism he was [also] named Michael after the latter [Emperor].[36]

ABOUT THE CAMPAIGN OF THE RUSSIANS AGAINST CONSTANTINOPLE

At one time the Russian princes Askol'd and Dir came against Constantinople: this happened in the first week of Lent during the reign of Emperor Michael and his mother, Theodora[37] who taught about veneration of the holy icons. They [Askol'd and Dir] committed many murders. Emperor Michael and Patriarch Photius celebrated a service throughout the entire night in the Church of the Holy Mother of God of Blachernae. This place is called Blachernae because a Scythian prince named Blachernae was killed there. They [Emperor, Patriarch and clergy], chanting, carried the vestments of

---

34. Prince Boris embraced Christianity in 864. This item, different in the *Primary Chronicle*, was taken from the *Chronograph*.

35. The Byzantine Emperor Michael III—born IX/1/840, became emperor in 842; died in 867—usually known under his nickname, "The Drunkard." He was from the Amorean dynasty, which originated in Phrygia and Asia Minor and was of partially hellenized, perhaps even Jewish, background. His mother, Theodora, was instrumental in the final restoration in 843 of veneration of the icons in the Orthodox church. She was forced by her son to become a nun but her brother, Bardas, who received the highest rank—of *Curopalate*, a title equal to the Roman Caesar—was most influential in state affairs from 856 to 865. The Byzantine emperor—Basileos—used to give the rank of *Caesar* to his co-rulers. Later they would even receive the title of Basileos. In 866 Basil the Macedonian became Michael III's co-ruler.

36. This item, taken from the *Chronograph*, is different from the *Primary Chronicle*.

37. See above footnote.

the Holy Mother of God and dipped the edge of them into the sea, whereupon a storm started up at once and the boats of the godless Russians were cast ashore, and they were all killed.[38]

PORTENT

A short time thereafter, ashes fell from the skies, looking like blood, and stones were to be seen [thereafter] on the road, while the vineyards became red as blood.

ABOUT THE MURDER OF CAESAR BARDAS

Basil the Macedonian[39] bore false witness about Bardas to Emperor Michael: he said, "Bardas is thinking of killing you." He [the Emperor], however, did not believe this. Then Basil instructed the *logothet*[40] who was Bardas' son-in-law, and he had given him an oath, saying to him, "The Emperor loves you but because of your father-in-law [Bardas] he does not give you the title of 'Caesar.' But if you talk under oath about him to the Emperor, the latter will decide to kill Bardas and I will intercede with the Emperor, and he will give you the title, 'Caesar.'" The *logothet* was tempted by Basil, and under oath told the Emperor about Bardas, "He wants to kill you." Then the Emperor believed it and became inimical toward Bardas. When this happened, Leo the Philosopher [Basil's son] instructed Bardas to defend himself against the intention of the Emperor. There were portents about the death of the Caesar [Bardas]. Then an apparition appeared of two caesars standing on a pillar in the church of St. Anne. It started shaking and the smaller apparition collapsed. Leo the Philosopher, son of Basil, interpreted this portent [in the following way]: the second caesar [Bardas] would die at the hands of the first one. And Empress Theodora, Bardas' sister, sent Bardas a

---

38. See similar information under the year 866 and 876. This attack took place in 860; in *Hyp.*, under 866.

39. Basil, a peasant from Macedonia, became a Byzantine general and favorite of Emperor Michael. He became Michael's co-ruler in 866 after the assassination of Bardas, and then, in 867, he killed Michael III, proclaimed himself Emperor of Byzantium, and laid the foundation of the most successful Byzantine dynasty, usually called "Macedonian," 867-1057. He died August 29, 886.

40. *Logothet:* a very high official in Byzantine bureacracy whose function changed from time to time.

vestment which was two measures shorter [than it should have been], and it was shiny with golden embroidery on it. She was asked, "Why did you send a short one?" [She answered] "I suggest that the shining of the gold symbolizes his short days." Emperor Michael took counsel with Caesar Bardas and with Basil the Macedonian, the *parakimomen*,[41] whether they should start a war [for the island of Crete]. Leo the Philosopher besought Bardas not to go with them. He said, "You will not return." On the holiday of Easter the Emperor went with a small army to the Thracian land. [A certain] John the Chaldean, having learned of the conspiracy against [Caesar] Bardas, came to his tent in the evening and told his servant, "In the morning your lord will be cut to pieces." He informed the Caesar but the latter did not believe him. Bardas did not sleep the whole night. In the morning he donned his gold embroidered vestments, mounted his horse and went to the Emperor's tent. Basil took the Caesar by hand, led him to the Emperor and [Bardas] sat down with the Emperor. Basil approached him from behind and struck the Caesar [Bardas] with his sword, and his courtsmen attacked along with him, cutting [Bardas] to pieces, while Emperor Michael just watched silently. When, the next morning, the Emperor and Basil returned to Constantinople, a certain monk shouted, "You have campaigned well, Emperor! You have killed your mother's brother, your own uncle, and you have reddened your right hand with the blood of your relative."[42]

ABOUT THE ASCENDANCE OF BASIL THE MACEDONIAN TO EMPEROR

In the morning of Holy Pentecost the Emperor came to the cathedral, ascended the ambo with Patriarch Photius, who was with him, and commanded that the boyars be told, "Caesar Bardas intended to kill me. If it were not for the intervention of *parakimonen* Basil and those accompanying him, who saved me, I would not now be alive. Therefore I want Basil to become Caesar because he is a faithful protector of my empire, and everyone should glorify him as Caesar." Caesar [Basil] was standing nearby and shedding many

---

41. *Parakimomen:* chief eunuch, or courtier, in the palace, supposed to guard the door of the imperial bedchamber.

42. This occurred in A.D. 865. This item is from the *Chronograph*; it is not in the *Primary Chronicle* or in *Laur*.

tears. He [the Emperor] ordered Patriarch Photius to put on him the **859**
vestments of Caesar, and the crown. And Basil bowed to the feet of
the Emperor.

ABOUT THE CAMPAIGN OF THE SONS OF HAGAR AGAINST CONSTANTINOPLE

A great many sons of Hagar came to Constantinople [to attack it], doing so on several occasions.[43] When the Princes of Kiev, Askol'd and Dir, learned of this they campaigned against Constantinople and committed many bad deeds.

ABOUT THE VARANGIANS

The Varangians came from beyond the sea and imposed tribute on the Slovens [Slavs] of Novgorod, and said to the Novgorodians and to the people of Meshchera, and to the Krivichs, that every man should pay tribute of one hare skin and one squirrel fur.

ABOUT THE KHAZARS

The Khazars levied a tribute from the Polians, from the Severs and from the Viatichs, of one hare skin from each household.[44]

[Here begin the annual entries.]

In the year 6367/859.[45] The Slovens, who were called Novgorodians, the Merias and the Krivichs rebelled against the Varangians and drove them beyond the sea, refusing to pay them any tribute; and they began to rule themselves and to build a fortress. And there was no justice among them. One clan fought another, and they warred and captured, and there was endless bloodshed. Thereafter they assembled and decided, "Let us look who from among us might be our prince and might rule us. Let us look for such a one and establish him either from among us or from the Khazars or from the Polians or from the people of the Danube or from the Varangians." And there was great discussion about it.

---

43. The Greeks called only nomads "sons of Hagar;" in this case, they meant the Arabs.

44. In *Laur.*, in the year 6367/859.

45. This first entry of the annals begins with some chronological confusion. In the previous passage were mentioned the Christianization of Bulgaria, A.D. 865, and the assassination of Caesar Bardas, A.D. 865. Now comes the year 859 in *Nik.*; in *Laur.* 6370/862.

859 Some wanted one; others, another. And so, after taking counsel, they sent to the Varangians.

In the year 6367/859.

In the year 6368/860.

In the year 6369/861. In the time of Emperors Michael and Basil, and of Patriarch Photius, the Slovens, who were called Novgorodians, the Merias and the Krivichs went to the Varangians and said, "our land is large and abundant. Come to rule over us."[46] The latter were afraid of their bestial customs and mores, and with difficulty selected three brothers.[47]

ABOUT THE RUSSIAN PRINCES, RIURIK, SINEUS AND TRUVOR

In the year 6370/862. From the German land[48] three brothers came with their entire clans: Riurik, Sineus and Truvor. And Riurik became head of Novgorod. Sineus became head of Beloozero; and Truvor, in Izborsk. And from these Varangian newcomers [*nakhodniki*] came the word, "Russia" ["*Rus*'"], and since that time it is known as the Russian land because the people of Novgorod are called in such a way to the present time. And before they were called "Slovens" (or Slavs), but now they became named "Russians" because of these Varangians, since these Varangians were called *"Rus'."*[49]

In the year 6371/863. Emperor Michael and Caesar Bardas went campaigning against the Bulgars. At that time there was famine in Bulgaria. The Bulgarians became frightened and asked to be Christianized. Their prince and boyars came to Constantinople and

---

46. The text of the *Laurentian* and *Hypatian* chronicles reads: "Said the Russians [*Rus'*], the Chud', the Slovens and the Krivichs and all: 'Our land is large and abundant but there is no order in it. Come to be princes and rule over us.' And the brothers made the choice, together with their clans, and took with them the entire Rus', and came to the Slovens."

47. Error in chronology: in 861 Basil was not yet emperor; in *Laur.* in the year 6370/862.

48. By the word "Germans," ("*Nemtsy*") the Russians meant all Germanic-speaking countries, including Scandinavia.

49. See the Foreword concerning the origin of the words *"Rus"* and "Russia," and the legendary Riurik. According to archeological evidence Novgorod did not exist as a city or even a village before the beginning of the tenth century. Karger, M.K., *Novgorod Velikii*, Leningrad-Moscow, 1966, p. 11.

they Christianized him; and his godfather was Emperor Michael, who gave him the name of Simeon. And all the boyars accepted baptism, and they were released home with great honor. And in this way the entire Bulgarian people accepted holy baptism.[50]

864

In the year 6372/864. The son of Askol'd [of Kiev] was killed by the Bulgars. The same year the Novgorodians took offense and said, "Why should we be servants [of the Varangians]? We suffer much evil from Riurik and from his clan." The same year Riurik killed Vadim the brave, and he also killed many other Novgorodians who were the latter's supporters.[51]

In the year 6373/865. Sineus and Truvor died childless, and Riurik took over the reigns of both brothers and began to rule alone. And he distributed the towns to the men of his clan. One received Polotsk; one Rostov; another, Beloozero. The same year a son was born to Riurik, and he was named Igor'. The same year Askol'd and Dir fought against the people of Polotsk and performed many misdeeds.[52]

In the year 6374/866. The princes of Kiev—Askol'd and Dir—campaigned against the Greeks. At that time Emperors Michael and Basil were away campaigning against the Arabs. And when they came to the Black Sea, they received an envoy from the *eparch* [governor], who said that the Russians were advancing toward Constantinople with 200 and more boats. They returned, and as soon as they entered the city they went with Patriarch Photius to the Church of the Holy Mother of God of Blachernae, and they carried out the vestments of the Most Pure Mother of God, weeping and shedding many tears; and they dipped its edge into the sea. At that time the sea was very quiet but when they put the vestments into the sea, a tremendous storm arose which destroyed many boats and drowned the godless Russians.[53]

In the year 6375/867. Askol'd and Dir returned from Constantinople with a very small retinue, and there were many tears in Kiev. The same year there was a famine in Russia. The same year

---

50. Chronological error: this campaign took place in 859; in 858 in *Laur.*

51. Not in *Hyp., Laur.* or *Novg. Kom.*

52. Not in *Laur.*

53. Chronological error: this attack took place on June 16, 860. See similar item in the preceding undated entries, and under the year 876.

868 Askol'd and Dir killed a great many Pechenegs. The same year many Novgorodian men escaped from Riurik in Novgorod and fled to Kiev.⁵⁴

In the year 6376/868. Basil the Macedonian began to reign, and he reigned for eighteen years and eleven months.⁵⁵

In the year 6377/869.

PORTENT

The land in Constantinople shook for forty days, and a great many fortresses and houses fell apart. The same year Empress Theodora gave some Byzantine land to the Bulgarians and named it *"Zagorie."* [*"Zagorie"* means "land beyond the mountains."] And that is the reason the Bulgarian rulers are called thus.⁵⁷

ABOUT THE EMPEROR'S HORSE STABLES

Emperor Michael built stables for his horses and adorned them with marble, and put a water pipe there. Then he said to magister Peter, "See what an immortal monument I have created for myself." The other said, "Emperor Justinian demonstrated the most natural deed in building the divine church, and he exhausted all his treasury for its adornment, yet he is not very often remembered; but you, Emperor, have built a place for the preservation of dung. And you say that for this reason you will be remembered!"

In the year 6378/870.
In the year 6379/871.
In the year 6380/872.
In the year 6381/873.
In the year 6382/874.
In the year 6383/875.

In the year 6384/876. [Emperor] Michael reigned twenty and four years, when the Great Indiction ended.⁵⁷

---

54. For chronology, see the previous entry.

55. Basil started reigning alone in 867.

56. Wrong chronology: Theodora could not have done this in 868 when Basil I reigned.

57. Chronological errors: the XIIth Indiction (a cycle of fifteen years which was used in Byzantine chronology) actually ended in 6384 (876), but this was no longer the reign of Michael III, who was killed in 867—rather, it was the reign of Basil the Macedonian.

ABOUT THE BROKEN MIRROR

876

Emperor Michael exhausted the entire state treasury with his playmates. He wasted it not only on golden griffins but also on a golden poplar made with great craftsmanship—otherwise to say, a tree on which all manner of golden birds sat and sang their songs as if they were alive. And those who listened to it were greatly impressed, marvelling at this new invention. And [now] I duly weep and shed tears, and must say a word, and I speak of this, sighing deeply: Leo, the most clever among the philosophers, made for his father and Caesar, Basil the Macedonian, an unusual artifice, a mirror, in which at any hour, while living in the Imperial palace [in Constantinople], he could view whatever might be happening [in other places, *i.e.*] in Arabia or Syria. Once when [Emperor]Michael organized chariot races he was informed by someone [who was operating the mirror] that the Syrian army was moving with strong forces and was advancing rapidly. When Emperor Michael heard of this, he became afraid that the people, learning of it, would become upset and would destroy his arena; and [therefore] he ordered that this mirror be broken. "Oh, woe to his temptation! Oh, woe to the evil-mindeness! Woe, woe! How much of the Greek treasury did this man of evil life waste, this drunkard and offender! But that is enough tears to weep over this story!"[58]

ABOUT THE ASSASSINATION OF EMPEROR MICHAEL

Emperor Michael had neither son nor daughter. A wise man said that his seed did not have the natural quality—or, so to say, the possibility of conceiving children because he was addicted to a wrong manner in the deeds of Aphrodite [sexual life]—or, so to say, perverse lechery. Michael always enjoyed all manner of devil's games and he participated personally in chariot races. Once when he drove very well in a chariot of four horses, he was praised by someone named Basilisk. And he decided to reward this one who had praised him neither with gems nor with pearls but by elevating him to the rank of Caesar—taking that rank of Caesar from Basil [the Macedonian] and giving it to this one. Realizing that [Michael] always changed his mind suddenly, Basil became afraid, seeing him [Michael] indulging in perverse lechery and revelry. And he [also]

---

58. An item from the *Chronograph,* not in *Laur.*

876 realized that he [Michael] had exhausted the Byzantine treasury with his playmates. [So] he organized a conspiracy with some other people to kill Michael. Theodora, his [Emperor Michael's] mother, sent a missile to him in which she cautioned him concerning Basil's conspiracy against him, but he did not believe it. [Once] in the evening when Emperor Michael was very drunk, Basil arrived unbeknownst to anyone because [being *parakimomen*] he could open the [imperial] bedchamber with a key. And when Emperor Micharl arose from supper Basil conducted him by the arm into his bedchamber. Kissing his hand, Basil departed. [Meanwhile] Michael ordered Basilisk, whom he wished to make Caesar, to [sleep in his bedchamber] and guard him.

When Emperor Michael, greatly intoxicated, was asleep, Basil approached, bringing some others with him. [One of them] Peter the Bulgarian rushed at the Emperor but those who were with the Emperor resisted and awakened the Emperor. But John the Chaldean struck the Emperor with his sword, cutting off both his hands. And then Jacob the Syrian killed Basilisk with his sword. One who saw that both of the Emperor's hands had been severed wept bitterly; however, a certain Leo, who had a merciless heart, plunged his sword into Michael's heart and slit his belly. Then Basil walked into the Imperial palace and sent Paul the *chitonite*.[60] to accompany Michael to the grave. He was wrapped and put in a carriage, and it could be seen that his intestines spilled onto the ground. Everyone wept, and the mother and sister of this accursed one wailed. He was taken in a boat and was buried in the monastery of Christopolis.[61]

THE 87TH REIGN: THAT OF BASIL THE MACEDONIAN

Basil reigned with Michael one year and four months, and after Michael another nineteen years [867-886]. Although Michael passed his life in evil, only God can judge and take vengeance against those. Those who participated with Basil in his assassination were struck by God's vengeance, and they ended their lives with evil deaths. Jacob the Persian fell from his horse but his foot remained in the stirrup and he was trampled by his horse, dying badly hurt. John the

---

60. *Chitonites:* a eunuch attached to the imperial bedchamber.

61. Christopolis, now Kavalla, is a port on the Aegean Sea, east of Saloniki; an item from the *Chronograph*, not in *Laur.*

Chaldean was killed by a lance while commanding an army. Leo, son **876** of Emperor Basil's brother, was slashed to pieces by the knives of his own slaves. The daring Jacob, called "the Persian,"[62] was eaten by worms. Constantine was hacked with swords. Marian, brother of the Emperor [Basil] was thrown off his horse, broke his leg and died in great agony because of the worms that developed [in the wound]. See what manner of judgment strikes those who venture [to raise their hand] against such [as an Emperor] in hatred and envy and do not anticipate God's vengeance. It is written, " 'Vengeance is mine!' saith the Lord to evildoers." [*Rom.* 12:19][63]

THE EARTHQUAKE

There was an earthquake, and for forty days the earth shook and the church of the Holy Mother of God in Sygma collapsed. [Before this happened] Leo the Philosopher [Basil's son] ordered everyone to leave the church but they paid him no heed and all were killed.

When Emperor Basil came to the church [after the assassination of Emperor Michael], wanting to have communion with the Honorable Body and Blood of Our Lord Jesus Christ, Patriarch Photius drove him away from the Divine Communion, calling him "manslayer" and "robber" and unworthy of the Sacrament. Basil became angry and brought a bishop from Rome with a charter from the Pope, and Photius was driven out of his See as having wrongly accepted it.[64] When Alexander, son of the Emperor, was born [November 23, 871] Emperor Basil wanted to distribute his treasury to the people and he ordered that the places where the gold was kept be investigated. At the beginning [of Emperor Michael III's reign] great wealth had been accumulated but now he saw that all [the coffers] were empty, and he grieved and grew sad because he could not do [what he wanted]. Indeed, an Emperor who does not have a rich treasury is like a very old and weary eagle which has neither feathers nor claws nor beak; therefore Basil was very sad that Emperor Michael had squandered everything with his playmates. And the Byzantine honor was hurt, and they [the people of Byzantium] were in difficulties, ready to prostrate themselves before

---

62. "Syrian," in an earlier story.
63. Item from the *Chronograph*, not in *Laur*.

876 the accursed [late Emperor Michael] because they were, so to say, at the very end and could scarcely breathe. But the [new] Emperor [Basil] endeavored to renew and restore [the Empire's power] with his Imperial wisdom. And those who earlier had been in opposition and had departed the Imperial City again turned to him [for help]. Thereafter there was great effort and grief, and [everywhere] a shield on the arm, armour, helmets, lances, and the ever vigilant eye which would not rest in sleep in order to be alert for fighting and bloodletting. [Now] the barbarians learned that Basil was like an awakening animal—which arises courageous against those who offend him, and thereupon they ran, trembling, away from him. And he [Basil] returned the [lost] territories to the Greeks and made of an aged and worn-out woman a young and beautiful virgin.[65] And he strengthened the scepter of the Greeks against their enemies. The Emperor converted many Jews to Christianity, giving them ranks and greatly honoring them. And [liking] Nicholas Mansionarius, to whom the Holy Martyr Diomedius appeared and who prophesied the reign of Basil, he raised this Nicholas [to *syncellus*] of the great church.[66] And he honored the latter's brothers, John and Paul, with very high rank. And he appointed Constantine *genic* and *logothet*.[67]

His Holiness [Patriarch] Ignatius left the storms of life and passed away to God, to His good and great shelter.[68] In the meantime extremely clever Photius, who steadily desired the See and to rule the church, conceived a deeply complicated and evil idea. First, he approached the Emperor's sons and wife, telling them one

---

64. Photius was deposed September 25, 867, and Patriarch Ignatius was made patriarch for the second time on November 23 of the same year. This patriarchal dethronement divided the Byzantine church into two antagonistic parties, one of which represented more conservative trends and the other more reformist. Photius, patriarch of Constantinople from 858 to 867 and from 877 to 886, was a great humanist and an erudite writer. He was responsible to a considerable degree for the break between the Eastern and Western churches. He achieved sizable success in the conversion of the Slavs to Christianity.

65. Here is meant he made of old Byzantium a new Byzantium.

66. *Syncellus:* senior advisor or heir of the patriarch.

67. *Genic, logothet:* high officials.

68. Patriarch Ignatius died Oct. 22, 877.

or two stories, inventing an anecdote for them, and then interpreted them like a genuine wise man, intervening on behalf of some actions and creating [real] interest. And thanks to all of this, he was considered by the Emperor as a man of great wisdom; and he, the most eager, attained the [Patriarchal] See.[69]

The mind of those born on earth is inevitably faulty, and some mores are inborn in human nature. Therefore Emperor Basil came under the influence of some serpent-like people who knew how to concoct flattery, construct intrigue and sow discord among beloved ones: between a father and his children, a mother and daughter, a bride and her bridegroom. Such was Theodore Santabaren, a mean and devilish person who was Metropolitan of Euchaitus: because of Photius' influence [Emperor] Basil liked him [Santabaren] and considered him saintly, sagacious and a wonderworker while [in reality] he was a sorcerer and a magician. [Emperor] Basil [however] held him in great honor as a saintly man. [At that time] the Emperor grieved deeply after the death of his son, Constantine; and Santabaren told him, "I will show you your son alive." Once when the Emperor was coming out of the vineyards he saw a phantom horseman dressed in a gold-embroidered vestment and resembling his deceased son, Constantine. The Emperor saw him with his own eyes, embraced him, and was told that it was his late son. Because of this [apparition] the Emperor built a church and a monastery on that spot, and his faith in Santabaren grew still stronger; but Basil's son, Leo, called him a sorcerer and magician.[70] Leo married Theophano, daughter of Martinak, and his father made him Caesar [Co-Emperor].[71] Santabaren, who disliked Leo, continued conspiring to cause the father to hate the son; consequently, he approached Leo with flattery, taught him and said, "Oh, you are young, my Caesar! You should have a big dagger with you. When you are hunting with your father you may encounter a wild beast, and the dagger will be of great help; and in case there should be some gossip about your father, pull out the dagger and frighten these evil gossipers." The latter did not understand [Santabaren's]

---

69. Photius became patriarch for the second time in 877.

70. Santabaren was apparently an intriguer practiced in magic and necromancy.

71. Basil made Leo Caesar and Co-Emperor on January 6, 870.

flattery and trusted him. He put a dagger into his boot and began carrying it. [Thereupon] Santabaren told his [Leo's] father, "Emperor, Your Majesty should know that your son, Leo, has an evil thought concerning you: in case you want to verify whether I am telling the truth, order [your people] to observe whether he does not carry a dagger hidden in his boot."

The Emperor went to the hunt, and with him was his son, Leo; and when he was searched they found the dagger hidden in the boot. And so Santabaren seemed to have told the truth. When Leo told [the Emperor] about Santabaren's plot, the Emperor did not believe him and became very angry, and ordered him imprisoned in the jail of the palace, where he remained a long time.[72]

The Emperor greatly revered [Prophet] Elias, and on the day when the Prophet's memory is celebrated he held a banquet with his princess. In that palace was hanging [in a cage] a bird called *"fittakas"*—or, as some others call it, "parrot," which imitated with its voice the words it heard from people. Once it heard a man weeping and saying, "Leo *mou!* Leo *mou!*"[73] [During the banquet] this [bird] started speaking clearly and distinctly: "Leo! Leo!" Hearing this, the princess began to weep and beseeched [the Emperor] tearfully on behalf of Leo, saying, "Oh, Emperor! This animal [actually, bird] which [hangs] above us is speechless, yet it implores and seeks its master, while we humans, able to speak, do not even remember him since he has been so long jailed." The Emperor was touched by these words, forgave his son and made him Caesar again as he had been before.[74]

ABOUT THE RUSSIAN PRINCE ASKOL'D

In the year 6384/876, continued. There were people who were called "Russians" and "Cumans" who lived at the Pontus Euxinus and who began to campaign in the Roman land, wanting to march

---

72. Basil very much liked his elder son, Constantine, who died young, and he cared little for Leo, whom he, as well as most Byzantine writers, considered the natural son of his wife and Emperor Michael III. During Leo's imprisonment he even intended to blind him. Brehier, p. 110.

73. "Oh, my Leo!" in Greek.

74. Caesar Leo was imprisoned in April, 885, and was released from Prison July 19th of the same year.

against Constantinople.⁷⁵ High Providence forbade it them because they were struck by the wrath of God, and their princes, Askol'd and Dir, were obliged to return home unsuccessful. [The Emperor] Basil at that time was waging war against the sons of Hagar⁷⁶ and the Manicheans.⁷⁷ He made a peace treaty with the afore-mentioned Russians and persuaded them toward Christianity. They promised to accept baptism and requested a bishop. And the Emperor sent them one. When they decided to be baptized they lost courage [at the last minute] and told the bishop, "Until we see a miraculous portent from you we do not want to become Christian." And the bishop said, "Ask what you want." And they told him, "We want you to throw the Holy Gospel, which teaches the words of Christ, into the fire. If It does not burn we will become Christian. And whatever you teach us, we will preserve and will not trespass [the law]." And the bishop said, "Since you wish it, it will be as you desire." And he ordered that a large bonfire be lit and the bishop raised his hand toward Heaven, saying, "Christ-God, glorify Thy Name!" And he put the Holy Gospel into the fire and it remained in it a long time but the fire did not touch it. The Russians saw this, marvelled at the power of Christ, and all of them became Christian.⁷⁸

876

75. "Pontus Euxinus," meaning "Hospital Sea," was the Greek name for the Black Sea. By "Roman land" the chronicle writers meant to designate the "Byzantine Empire." Mention here of the Cumans, whom the Russians called "Polovets," indicates that this part of the annual entry was written after 1054, when the Polovetss are first mentioned in the Russian chronicles and, probably, had just appeared at that time in the south Russian prairie. It may be, however, that this name was applied to some other nomadic Turkic tribes, probably Pechenegs, roaming north of the Black Sea.

76. "Sons of Hagar" is the usual name for the nomads—in this case, the Arabs.

77. The Paulician or Manichean heretics in Asia Minor and, especially, in Armenia, later became known in the Balkans as Bogomils, and in Western Europe under the name "Cathars" or "Albigensians." All these religious sects shared the common teaching that Good and Evil are equal in power and while Good is supreme in the Heavens, Evil rules on the earth.

78. The first part of this item is a repetition of the earlier stories about Askol'd's and Dir's attack on Constantinople, and can be found in *Hyp.* and *Laur. mss.* under the year 6374/866. In the *Nik.* it was already mentioned: first, in the undated introductory part (after the story of the conversion of Bulgaria), and then under the year 6374/866. The second part, dealing with the Christianization of the Russians (*Ros—Rus'*—apparently Varangians

877 ABOUT THE DEATH OF EMPEROR BASIL

Once Emperor Basil went hunting and encountered a very large elk. The Emperor raised his sword against it in order to strike the elk, but the elk caught the Emperor with his antlers by the belt, and the Emperor remained hanging on the antlers. Then someone came and cut the belt with his knife, and in this manner the Emperor was saved. But instead of thanking this man, he ordered him beheaded, saying, "How might he raise a sword against his Emperor?" Because of this wound caused by the elk's antlers, the Emperor developed an internal infection and after a short time he died.[79]

THE REIGN OF LEO THE PHILOSOPHER, SON OF BASIL

In the year 6385/877.[80] After Basil's death his son, Leo, reigned for twenty years and four months.[81] He removed Photius from the Patriarchal See because of his support of Santabaren, and he put his own brother, Stephanus [in his place as Patriarch]. [Then] he sent [his agents] to Euchaitus and let them bring Santabaren, and then he let them beat and blind him; [then] he was jailed in Athens. Once when the Emperor attended the Church of the Saint Martyr Mocius, a certain criminal of very mean appearance, looking as a man possessed, attacked the Emperor with a staff and hit him in the head. Had he not been caught on a chandelier, he would have killed him.[82] He was seized and tortured to confess who his accomplice was but he said nothing, since he was like one possessed.

---

and Slavs) and the conversion of Askol'd and Dir, was probably borrowed later from Byzantine sources. Both Patriarch Photius, in his epistle of 866-867, and Constantine Porphirogenitus, in his *De Administrando Imperio*, wrote after this attack in 860 that the *Ros* (Russians) became Christians and were given a bishop. This is the earliest information about the propagation of Christianity in Russia. See the commentaries in the Foreword to this Vol. Not in *Hyp.* or *Laur.*

79. Basil I died August 29, 886. Item from *Chronograph*, not in *Laur.*

80. In *Nik.* printed text, *PSRL*, Vol. IX, p. 14, probably an error: 6395 and 887, should be 6385 and 877.

81. Actually, Leo VI, the Philosopher or the Wise, reigned not twenty years but twenty-six years, from 886 to 912.

82. Erroneous chronology. This attempted assassination took place on April 21, 902.

[At that time] there lived a certain Marcus, a man of saintly life, **877** inspired by Divine Spirit and adorned with virtue, who saw that the Emperor was in low spirits because he harmed the man who had attempted [to kill him]; and this monk came to heal the Emperor with good words. And he propheised with his well-meaning lips: "Oh, Emperor! Do not have in your mind any thoughts about your passing and do not grieve about [possible] death. By the Supreme Hand you are granted ten more years of life and reign." Having said this, [Marcus] fell silent but the Emperor was delivered from wound and grief. Then the Emperor requested that Marcus compile the quadruple chant [on the occasion of the holiday of] Holy Easter, and write [additional] chants for the prayer book.

The first wife of this Emperor Leo was Empress Theophano. She was still alive when the Emperor took [as a second wife] Zoe, daughter of the *curopalate*,[83] and started living with her, which Empress Theophano ignored. At that time she [Theophano] remained continually in the convent of Saint Mary of Blachernae, practicing [spiritual] exercises of prayer, and there she passed to God, pleasing Him, and was thereafter considered to be a wondermaker. This happened after she had been Empress for only two years.[84] A priest blessed [the marriage of] the Emperor and Zoe but [thereafter this priest] was interdicted from officiating. Zoe lived with the Emperor for one year and died.[85] [The Emperor] wanted to place her body in a marble sarcophagus but he found attached to it a writing [which said], "The accursed daughter of Babylon." Patriarch Stephanus, Emperor Leo's brother, passed away and Nicholas was made Patriarch.[86] And the Emperor took a third wife, named Eudoxia. She, however, [also] soon died childless.[87] Then the Emperor decided to marry for the fourth time, also a Zoe.[88] [He did this] not because he was obsessed with passion but because he wanted an heir, and to see children of his aging blood.[89] This fourth and last

83. *Curopalate*: head of the Palace, a position equal to Major Domus.
84. Theophano died December 16, 894.
85. Zōe died in August, 896.
86. Patriarch Stephanus died in 889. Nicholas became Patriarch in 896.
87. Eudoxia died in 897.
88. Since the Orthodox church permits only three legal marriages, Emperor Leo's fourth marriage was considered uncanonical.
89. In *Nik.*, "body."

877 one [wife of Emperor Leo] gave birth to a son born to the purple who was named Constantine.[90] It is not dignified when the servants of God do whatever is desired by the Emperor and defile the imperishable and immaculate Church. The bride of Christ celebrating a fourth marriage![91]

[Patriarch] Nicholas was Primate at that time, the first in the Church, and he made the ruling from the See of the city of Constantinople. And without fear or trembling he said this boldly to the Emperor,[92] and following the words of the Prophets he spoke the words of God before the Emperor about this prohibition [of a fourth marriage]: "Fear of God drives away fear of those men who may sentence you and who rule." Therefore Patriarch Nicholas was expelled [by the Emperor] from his flock and See and was condemned to deportation. In his place a certain Euthemius was appointed, who lived in Olympus.[93] It is said that he strictly observed divine rule and from the earliest age[94] accepted the divine yoke of monastic life. He shone with virtues and [had the gift of being able to] forecast the future.

PUNISHMENT

Fear and trembling came upon Emperor Leo. He moaned and shook. [Apparently because of an earthquake, a part of the city was destroyed and many palaces fell to pieces.][95]

In the year 6385/877.

In the year 6386/878.

In the year 6387/879. After seventeen years of reign, Prince Riurik died and transferred the rule to Oleg, who was of the same family as he. And he turned into his hands his son, Igor', because Igor' was a very young child. And from the first year of the reign of

---

90. *Porphyrogenitus:* "born in purple." The birth of a child to a ruling emperor was a very important and ceremonial event. All linen and bedding of the birth were to be made of purple cloth.

91. Here, "bride of Christ" means the Church.

92. That the fourth marriage is forbidden by church law.

93. Patriarch Nicholas was deposed and Euthemius made Patriarch February 1, 908. Actually, this entry under the year 887 discussed the entire twenty-six years of Emperor Leo's reign.

94. *"Ot molodykh nogtei."*

95. Item from *Chronograph*, not in *Laur.* or *Hyp.*

Emperor Michael I to the first year of reign of Oleg were twenty-nine years.[96]

In the year 6388/880.

THE REIGN OF OLEG

In the year 6389/881.[97] Oleg marched from Novgorod, taking Igor' with him. He came to Smolensk and took the city, appointing his own officials there. From thence he went down along the Dnieper and came to the Kievan hills; and Oleg learned that Askol'd and Dir ruled in Kiev. Igor' and Oleg, feigning that they were just passing by, hid themselves in the boats and told some of their retinue to go ashore, telling them secretly what to do. And they themselves, feigning illness, lay down in the boat. And he sent [his envoys] to Askol'd and Dir, saying, "I am a merchant from the land near Hungary and I am travelling to the Greeks from Prince Oleg and the young Prince Igor'. And now I am ill and have a great many large and precious pearls and all manner of jewelry. And I have to go to you and speak these words from mouth to mouth: 'You should come to them without delay.'" They [Askol'd and Dir] came with a very small retinue and went into the boat to see the ill merchant, and the latter told them, "I am Prince Oleg and here is the young Prince Igor', son of Riurik." And at once he killed Askol'd and Dir and ordered that they be taken to the mountain; and they buried them there [in this mountain] which is now called the Hungarian one, and now the homestead of Olma is there.[98] And on that grave Olma built a church to St. Nicholas, and the grave of Dir is behind [the church to] St. Irene. And Oleg began to rule in Kiev, saying, "This will be the mother of all Russian cities." And he came into possession of the entire Russian land. And he had with him the Varangian men and the Slavic men, and that is the reason why they are all called

---

96. These calculations by the chronicler are obviously mistaken, even if Riurik ever existed. Michael III was crowned co-ruler by his father, Theophilus, in 840. He began to reign together with his mother, Theodora, in 842, and he became the sole ruler of the Byzantine Empire in 856.

97. The first *Novgorodskaia letopis'*, ed. 1950, p. 107, calls Oleg not the prince but the *voevoda* of Prince Igor'. This information seems to predate the entry of the *Primary Chronicle* and *Nik*. In any case, Oleg and Igor' seem to be the first historically known, and not mythological—as Riurik—Rusian rulers.

98. Olma was apparently a Kievan eleventh century boyar.

883 Russians. And this Oleg began to build fortresses and introduced tribute over the entire Russian land.[99] The Slovens, the Krivichs and the Meria had to pay tribute to the Varangians. And from Novgorod, three hundred grivnas.[100] [And they pay it] every year up to now in order to preserve the peace. And he included many other countries in the Russian land and imposed a tribute on them.[101]

In the year 6391/883. Oleg campaigned against the Drevlians and Severs and imposed a tribute on them of one black *kuna*.[102]

In the year 6395/887. Leo,[103] son of Basil, became Emperor together with his brother, Alexander, and they reigned together for twenty-five years.

Altogether, these years [of the reign of Oleg and Igor'] are calculated in the following manner: from the year of the beginning of the reign of Oleg in Kiev to the first year of the reign of Igor'—thirty-one years. And he reigned after the death of Oleg for thirty-three years. And he used to be with Oleg and Oleg brought him a wife from Pskov named Ol'ga, who was ten [*sic*!] years old. And Igor' lived forty-three years with Ol'ga. And from the first year of Igor' to the first year of the reign of Svjatoslav are thirty-three years.[104] And from the first year of Sviatoslav's reign to the first year of Iaropolk's reign are twenty-eight years. And Iaropolk reigned for eight years. And Vladimir reigned for thirty-seven years. And from the beginning of the reign of [Emperor] Michael to the

---

99. In these sentences, which were taken from the earliest eleventh-century Russian chronicles, is an additional indication that the word *Rus'* originally designated the land of present Russia and its Slavic inhabitants, as well as, probably, Varangian immigrants and warriors.

100. *Grivna*: a piece of silver which was used as common coin in early Russia. At that time it contained about sixty grams of silver; later it went up to 200 grams.

101. In this entry of *Nik.* may be found details showing that it adheres to the text of work earlier than the *Primary Chronicle* (as in *Hyp.* and *Laur.*) and which can be found in the *First Novgorodian Chronicle*. Likhachev, II, 250-255.

102. *Kuna:* the fur of the marten. *Kuna* was also a monetary unit. Twenty-five furs, later fifty, of the *kuna* (marten) amounted to one *grivna*.

103. Leo VI, the Philosopher or the Wise, 886-912.

104. All these data, recorded some hundred years after Igor's death, are obviously not very exact.

Christianization of the Bulgarian land was seventeen years.[105] And **898**
from Christianization until translation of the Books [Gospel and
liturgical books into Church Slavonic], twenty-nine years. And from
the translation of the books till Christianization of the Russian land,
ninety-two years. And the Russian land was Christianized in the
ninth year of the reign of Vladimir. And from the Christianization of
Russia till the death of Vladimir and till the martyrdom of Boris and
Gleb [1015], and till the transfer of their relics—fifty-seven years.
And the first year of the transfer to the second transfer of the relics
and to the taking of Kiev, eighty-seven years.[106] And from the taking
[of Kiev] to the battle of Kalka [1224], twenty years [sic!]. And
Sviatopolk the Accursed reigned for three years and fought with his
brother, Iaroslav. And Iaroslav reigned for forty years. And
Vladimir Iaroslavich[107] reigned for four years.

ABOUT THE HUNGARIANS

In the year 6406/898. The Hungarians passed Kiev on the route
of the hill which is now called the Hungarian one. And they arrived
at the Dnieper and put up their tents there because they roamed
in the same manner as the Polovetss. The came from the east
and moved across the high mountains which are now called the
Hungarian mountains, and they conquered those who lived
there.[108] And before the Slavs used to live there.[109] And the Vlakhs
[Rumanians] also moved into the land of the Slavs but thereafter the
Hungarians chased the Vlakhs and settled in that land together with
the Slavs. And they submitted them. And since that time that land is
called Hungary. And the Hungarians started fighting with the
Greeks and occupied the Thracian land in Macedonia as far as
Salonika. And they started campaigning in Moravia and Bohemia.

105. Michael III started reigning in 842; Bulgaria was Christianized twenty-five years later, in 866/867.

106. Probably, here is meant the taking of Kiev by Prince Andrei Bogoliubskii, although it happened in 1169 and not in 1159.

107. Vladimir Iaroslavich, son of Iaroslav the Wise, died 1052. He ruled in Novgorod, *Novg.* p. 161, 470.

108. "Hungarian mountains," are now called the "Carpathian Mountains."

109. Hungarians settled in Pannonia, present Hungary, destroying the Slavic state of Great Moravia.

898   Once it was one single Slavic language and the Slavs lived on the Danube. And they were conquered there by Hungarians; there were also the Moravians, Czechs, Liakhs [Poles] and the Polians, who are now called Rus', living in those lands. And first the [Slavic] Books [Scriptures] were translated in Pannonia[110] in the city of Morava, which is in Illyria.[111] And therefore the [alphabet] is called the Slavic alphabet. And the same alphabet is in Russia and among the Bulgarians of the Danube.

THE MISSION

The Slavs already lived as Christians and their princes, Rostislav, Sviatopolk and Kochel, sent [envoys] to Emperor Michael, saying, "Our land is already baptized but we have no teachers who would teach and instruct us and interpret the Holy Books because we do not know either the Greek language or Latin. Some teach in one way and others in a different way, but we do not understand the mind or their literary meaning. Therefore, send us some teachers who can explain us the word of the Books and their meaning."[112] When Emperor Michael heard this he summoned all his learned men and told them of the Slavic prince's request. And the learned men said, "In Salonika there is a man by the name of Leo, and he has two verily intelligent and learned sons who know the Slavic tongue." When Emperor Michael heard this he sent for them to Leo in Salonika, telling him, "Send us your children, Methodius and Constantine, as soon as possible." Leo sent his sons forthwith and they came to the Emperor, who told them, "I was requested by the Slavic land, and they ask that I send them [a teacher] who will be able to interpret the Holy Books for them, because they want this." And they were persuaded by the Emperor and he sent them to the Slavic land, to Rostislav, Sviatopolk and Kochel.[113] When they arrived

110. In *Nik.*, "Spania," but it is Pannonia.

111. Morava is a river, and Moravia was a realm, part of present Czechoslovakia. Part of the territories of Great Moravia used to be in the Roman province of Illyricum or Illyria.

112. Rostislav, Sviatopolk and Kochel were princes of Great Moravia, which included present Czechoslovakia, Hungary and parts of Germany and Austria, but it was only Rostislav who sent, in 862, his envoy to Constantinople asking Emperor Michael III to send him missionaries with a command of the Slavic tongue.

113. Actually, only to Rostislav.

there they began to create the letters of a Slavic alphabet, and they **898** translated the [Epistles of the] Apostles and the Gospel. And the Slavs were happy when they heard about God's majesty in their own land, and thereafter they translated the Psalter, the *Ochtoichos*[114] and the other books. But some[115] started maligning the Slavic books, saying, "No peoples deserve to have an alphabet in their language with the exception of Hebrew, Greek and Latin, according to the writings of Pilatus, which he wrote on the Cross of the Lord."

THE POPE OF ROME

The Pope of Rome, learning of this, censured those who complained about the Slavic [liturgical] books, saying, "Let the words of Scripture be fulfilled: 'that all nations shall praise God'[116] and likewise: 'that all nations in various [tongues] shall proclaim the Divine Majesty as Holy Spirit gave them utterance.'[117] And whoever maligns the Slavic letters shall be excommunicated from the Church until he repents. For they are wolves and not sheep from whom it is fitting to learn and to preserve the fruit of that [knowledge]; but you, children of God, hearken unto His teaching and reject not the instruction of the Church as you were taught by your leader, Methodius." Constantine returned home and went to instruct the Bulgarian people but Methodius remained in Moravia.[118]

---

114. *Ochtoichos* is the book of church hymns organized in eight (*Ochto*) different musical scores.

115. "Some:" the German Catholic missionaries, who used Latin in the church services.

116. *Ps.* 72:17: "All nations shall call Him Blessed."

117. *Acts* 2:4.

118. This item about the Slavic mission of Sts. Cyril (whose lay name was Constantine) and Methodius is based on facts known from the *Lives* of St. Cyril and St. Methodius. Pope Hadrian II really authorized Constantine (Cyril) and Methodius to celebrate the church service in Slavonic. The information about the mission of Cyril to Bulgaria is contradictory. In any case, he died in Rome, while Methodius became the first bishop of Great Moravia; soon after, however, German missionaries succeeded in convincing the Moravian princes to accept Latin as their liturgical language, and Church Slavonic rapidly disappeared in the Moravian and Czech churches.

898 ABOUT THE TRANSLATION OF THE SCRIPTURES FROM GREEK INTO SLAVIC.

In the twelfth year of the reign [of the Byzantine Emperor] Leo the Wise, the Scriptures were translated.[119] There were 6414 years from Adam to the translation of the Scriptures, and eighty-two years from the seventh Oecumenic Council and thirty years from the Christianization of Bulgaria. Constantine the Philosopher and his brother, Methodius, translated the Scriptures from the Greek into Slavic. Bulgarians, Serbs, Albanians, Bosnians and Russians all speak the same language.[120] Holy Constantine the Philosopher translated many books and went to teach and to give the aforementioned nations the Holy Writ in their own languages. His brother, Saint Methodius, was appointed Bishop of Pannonia by Prince Kochel[121] in the city of Morava, which is in the province of Illyricum, where Apostle Paul travelled before him, preaching Christ.[122] He translated many books while there.

ABOUT THE SAME FROM ANOTHER CHRONICLE.

Thereafter Prince Kochel appointed Methodius to be Bishop of Pannonia,[123] to the See of the Holy Apostle Adronicus, one of the Seventy and disciple of the Holy Apostle Paul. Methodius assigned two priests who wrote very fast and then translated all the Scriptures and completed the translation from the Greek language into the Slavic within six months. They began in the month of March and finished on the 26th day of the month of October. Completing this, they gave due thanks and praise to God, who provided Bishop Methodius, the successor to Andronicus, with such grace. Apostle Andronicus taught in the Slavic language. Apostle Paul also

---

119. That is, in 898; actually, since the death of Methodius in 885, the activities of the Slavic mission were already curtailed in Great Moravia.

120. Although the Albanians used Church Slavonic as their liturgical language, they are not Slavs. Their language apparently belongs to the Illyric group of Indo-European tongues.

121. In the *Nik.* text we find once more "Spania" in place of "Pannonia," but it was obviously Pannonia, present Hungary, which in the ninth century was part of the realm of Great Moravia.

122. See Cyril and Methodius' mission to Great Moravia in the beginning of the story.

123. Again, in the *Nik.* text "Spania" appears.

travelled and taught in Moravia [which] is one part of Illyria, up to which Apostle Paul travelled. And there the Slavs were first. Paul taught the same Slavic people, and of the same people are we, the Russians. Therefore it may be said that Apostle Paul preached among the Russians and appointed Apostle Andronicus as his successor to [Christianize] the Slavic people.[124] The Slavic language and Russian are the same, although they are called Russians because of the Varangians, but originally they were Slavs. They are also called Polians, but their language is Slavic. They are called Polians because they live in the prairie.[125] But their Slavic language is the same. Let us return [now] to the previous [narrative].

In the year 6411/903. Emperor Leo incited the Hungarians against the Bulgarians, and the Hungarians invaded the Bulgarian land, occupying it. When [the Bulgarian ruler] Simeon learned of this he turned against the Hungarians, but the Hungarians withstood him and defeated the Bulgarians. Simeon escaped with difficulty to Silistria.[1]

In the year 6412/904. When Igor' grew up he followed Oleg and obeyed him. [The latter] brought him a wife from Pskov named Ol'ga. Thereafter Igor' and Oleg armed many warriors and [built] an endless number of ships.

ABOUT OLEG.

In the year 6415/907. Oleg started campaigning against the Greeks, leaving Igor' in Kiev. He took with him a great many Varangians, Slovens,[2] Chud', Krivichs, Meria, Polians, Severs, Drevlians, Radimichs and Viatichs, and Croatians and Dulebs and Tiveretss, who are interpreters[3] and whose [land] the Greeks call Great Scythia. And Oleg campaigned with all of them on horseback and in ships, and the number of ships was two thousand. When they arrived at Constantinople, the Greeks closed the Golden Horn and

---

124. This information is to a large extent legendary.

125. *"Pol'e"* in Old Russian meant not only "field" but also "steppe" or "prairie."

1. Here there is an error in dating. The Hungarians campaigned against Bulgaria in 893 and not in 903.

2. Slovens—Slavs from the region of Novgorod.

3. The Tiveretss apparently were used as interpreters because they lived in the vicinity of Greek colonies on the northern shore of the Black Sea.

907 the gates of the city.⁴ And they closed the gates of the city. Oleg left the boats and ordered the boats be pulled ashore, and he campaigned around the city, killing many Greeks, destroying and burning many buildings and churches. And of those prisoners whom he took, some he massacred, some he tortured and some he shot; others he ordered thrown into the sea. And the Russians caused much [harm] to the Greeks, as warriors usually do. Then Oleg ordered his warriors to make wheels and to put the boats on wheels. And when the wind was in the right direction they raised the sails and went in the boats on wheels over the land [in order to reach the Golden Horn].

When the Greeks saw this they became frightened and sent [their envoys] from the city to tell Oleg, "Do not destroy the city. We will give you whatever tribute you want." Oleg stopped his warriors, and the Greeks brought him food and wine from the city but he did not accept it because it was prepared with poison. And the Greeks took fright and said, "It is not Oleg but Holy Demetrius who is sent against us by God." And Oleg demanded that tribute be given for two thousand boats, twelve grivna for a man. And there were forty men in each boat.⁵ And the Greeks agreed to this and began to ask for peace so that he would not campaign in the Greek land. Oleg retreated slightly from the city and began discussing peace with the Greek Emperors, Leo and Alexander.⁶ He sent [his officials] Karl, Farulf, Velimede, Hrollaf and Stamede to them in the city, saying, "Get me this tribute." And the Greeks said, "We will give you what you want." And Oleg ordered that they give the warriors for two thousand boats twelve *grivna* for each rowlock, and then to pay tribute to the Russian cities: first, to Kiev; then to Chernigov; then to Pereiaslavl'; then to Rostov; then to Liubech'; and to other cities,

---

4. Golden Horn: a bay dividing Constantinople into eastern and western sides. The Greeks used to close it off by means of a complicated system of chains in order to prevent enemy attacks from its shores.

5. This payment of ransom of twelve *grivnas* per warrior was about normal for that era, but the number of ships (two thousand) and warriors (eighty thousand), to the contrary, seems exaggerated. Thus, not 960,000 *grivnas* of silver but a smaller ransom was most probably paid.

6. At that time in Byzantium two emperors reigned, the heirs of Basil I. They reigned from August 29, 889, together, until Leo's death May 11, 912. Alexander died in 913.

because the princess of those cities were under Oleg.[7] [Oleg suggested] the following conditions for the treaty: "Those [Russians] who come here will have as much food as they want, and if a merchant comes he must have a monthly allotment for six months: bread and wine and meat and fish and vegetables. And there must be steambaths prepared for them, as much as they want.[8] And when the Russians go home they should receive from your Emperor food, anchors, cordage and sails in the amount they require."

And the Greeks accepted, and all their lords said, "In case the Russians come without merchandise, they will not receive the monthly supplies. The prince should forbid his people from coming from Russia to cause evil in our villages and land. And those Russians who come should stay in St. Mamas' [section]. And our administration will send [agents] to record their names and then they can get their monthly allotments: first, [those] from the city of Kiev; and then from Chernigov; [and then] from Pereiaslavl'; and [then from] the other cities. And they must enter the city through the same gate without weapons, no more than fifty men. And they can proceed to buy what they need without paying any taxes."

The Emperors Leo and Alexander concluded peace with Oleg, giving their pledge on the Cross, while Oleg and his men pledged according to the Russian custom, on their weapons and in the name of Volos, god of cattle.[9] And they confirmed the peace. And Oleg said, "Make silken sails for the Russians and make linen ones for the Slovens.[10] And so it was done. And he [Oleg] hung his shield on the gate [of Constantinople], thus demonstrating his victory; and he withdrew from Constantinople. And the Russians unfurled their silken sails and the Slovens their linen ones, but the wind destroyed

907

---

7. Apparently besides Oleg and Igor', there were other most probably Slavic princes. In the treaty between Igor' and Byzantium of 945, some of them are definitely Slavic: Sviatoslav, Volodislav, Predislav, *a. o. Prim. Chr.*, vol. I, p. 34.

8. This word ("steambaths") is omitted in the *Nik.* but is to be found in the text of the *Laur.* chronicle.

9. It is worthwhile to note that Oleg and his men pledged in the name of the Russian Slavic god, Volos, and (in the text of the *Primary Chronicle*) also Perun, and not in the name of Scandinavian deities.

10. Probably Novgorodians. They are mentioned as "Slovens" at the beginning of this entry.

911 them, and the Slovens said, "Let us have our canvas ones. Those are not made for the Slovens." And Oleg returned to Kiev to his Prince Igor', bringing gold, brocade, fruit, wine and all manner of jewelry. And Oleg received the name, "The Magician,"[11] because the people were pagan and not Christianized.

PORTENT.

In the year 6419/911. A great star in the form of a lance appeared in the west.[12]

In the year 6420/912.[13] Oleg sent his officers to Constantinople to make peace and draw up an agreement between the Greeks and Russia. And sending them for this other consultation which took place in the reign of Emperors Leo and Alexander, he said [that they should make the following agreement]:

"We of the Russian people—Karl, Ingiald, Farulf, Throand, Leithulf, Fast and Steinritn—sent by Oleg,[14] Grand Prince of Russia, and all the serene princes and boyars under his sway, unto you, Leo, Alexander and Constantine[15]—great autocrats by the will of God, emperors of the Greeks—for the preservation and proclamation of long-lasting unity between the Christians [that is, the Greeks] and the Russians; and [this is done] in agreement with the intentions of our princes and according to the instructions of all those Russians who are under his [Oleg's] sway. Our serenity above all is willing to preserve with God's help and proclaim such friendly relations as now exist between Christians and Russians, and on many occasions considered it proper to proclaim and confirm this amity not only

---

11. *Prim. Chr.* II, pp. 270-271.

12. Possibly it was the comet of Galillee; it passed on June 11, 912. The early chronology of *Prim. Chr.* differs in some cases.

13. Since Oleg's campaign against Constantinople is described under the year of 907 and the treaty under 912 (actually, 911, since September 2, 6420, was in 911, the Byzantine year beginning with Sept. 1) it is believed by many scholars that the chronicle writer accidentally, or for some reason unknown, divided the story about the campaign and the treaty into two different entries. This is the opinion of Sergeevich, Shakhmatov, Obnorskii, Likhachev, Presniakov, *a.o.*

14. The names in *Laur.* and *Nik.* are not correctly spelled. In this translation the Scandinavian spelling is provided.

15. Constantine Porphyrogenitus: Emperor of Byzantium, 912-959, was Leo's son.

verbally but also in writing and by oath. And we pledge on our weapons to announce this friendship and to confirm it according to our faith and customs.

"The terms of this agreement which we have concluded for Divine peace and friendship are the following:

"First statement: let us conclude peace with you Greeks and with all our hearts and minds abide in friendship with each other; we will prevent the subjects of our serene princes from committing any evil or trespassing; and we will endeavor as far as possible to preserve irrevocable and unshakeable friendship in the years to come with you Greeks; it is expressed in [this] writing and [confirmed] by oath. Also, you Greeks should keep for all years to come the same irrevocable and unshakeable friendship toward our serene princes.

"We agree to the following as far as possible trespasses are concerned: in case there is obvious proof of a crime, we shall consider it definitive proof; but in case the proof is not certain, the party which claims that the proof is uncertain shall take oath according to his religion to this effect. And after the oath, if the crime is confirmed, punishment will be imposed according to the crime. In case a Russian kills a Christian [Greek] or a Christian kills a Russian, he shall die on the spot of the murder. If the man who committed the crime escapes and he is wealthy, the nearest relatives of the victim should receive a legal portion of his [criminal] wealth. His [wife][16] shall keep what is due to her according to the law. In case the perpetrator is without means and escapes, he shall remain under sentence until he is found, and then he will be put to death.

"If any man strikes another with a sword or attacks him with any other weapon, according to the Russian law[17] he shall pay five pounds of silver; if he who commits [such offense] does not have any property, he shall pay as much as he can, even the very clothes he wears may be taken from him. He also has to declare under oath that he can not receive any help from anyone else, and he will remain responsible for it until the entire [fine] is repaid. He must also swear that he is unable to receive any help from anyone else.

"In case a Russian steals from a Greek, whatever it may be, or a Greek from a Russian, and he is caught at once by the victim, when

---

16. Word added according to *Laur.*
17. "Russian" in *Laur.* and *Hyp.*; *Nik.* incorrectly says "Roman."

912 he has committed this crime—or in case he prepares such a crime—he may be killed by his victim; and neither Greek nor Russian will be responsible for his death. And he who was his victim can get back whatever was taken from him. But in case he surrenders himself, then he shall be arrested by the one from whom he stole and he will be bound; he must repay thrice as much as he stole. And in case a Russian hurts a Greek, or a Greek a Russian, or attempts [to steal] and his act is violent, then anything taken from the victim must be repaid thrice over [whatsoever he stole or attempted to steal].

"In case [a Greek] ship is driven by the wind upon a foreign shore and there in the vicinity is someone from among us Russians, and he [the shipowner] wants to forward his goods further into the Greek land, in such case he must be piloted through dangerous places. In case such a ship in the vicinity of the Greek land is prevented [from reaching its Greek port] by a storm or wind, or is disabled and unable to return home, then we, the Russians, will help the Greek [sailors] of this ship and will accompany it and their goods to safety.

"But in case some accident occurs to a Russian ship, and we [Greeks] pilot it to the Russian land, they may sell the goods of their ship if they have such an opportunity, while the ship will be taken back to Russia.

"And when we [Russians] travel to the Greek land either on a mission to your [Byzantine] emperor or for the purpose of trade, then we [Greeks] will let them sell their goods with honor. In case one of us Russians of such a ship is killed or some [of their goods] is stolen, the person who did this to the Russian will be punished for this crime according to the law.

"His [the killed person's] nearest relative will care for the killed person and will have the right [to do justice to] the murderer according to the law unless the perpetrator of the murder escapes from them.[18]

"In case a prisoner of either side is kept either by the Russians or by the Greeks, or is sold in one of those countries, and if he really is Russian or Greek, he must be ransomed, and the ransomed person must be returned to his own land. And the one who pays the ransom

---

18. This paragraph is not in the text of either *Laur.* or *Hyp.*

will be reimbursed, or must be offered the price of a *cheliadin*.[19]

"In the case someone is captured during war by those Greeks, he should be returned to his land and ransom money should be paid, as mentioned above, as if he were sold.

"If there should be a conscription [into the Byzantine army] and some [Russian] should wish to honor your emperor, he can do so if he is willing [to serve the emperor]. Those [Greeks] taken prisoner by the Russians or sold [to Russia] from another country, as well as those prisoners who came from those lands, must be sold for twenty gold coins and returned to Greece.

"ABOUT THE FOLLOWING: In case a Russian *cheliadin* is kidnapped, escapes or is sold by force and the Russians complain thereof, they have to prove it, and he should be returned to Russia. But if the [Greek] merchants also lose a *cheliadin* and complain, then they must search for this *cheliadin* until he is found. When they find him they may get him back. And in case someone interferes with the search, he will lose all his rights.[20]

"Those Russians who work among the Greeks [in the land] of the Christian emperor and who die without having left a will of their property—their property should go to their relatives in Russia. But in the case he leaves a will, the one mentioned as legatee of the property will receive his inheritance.

"In the case a criminal does not return to Russia, the Russians should complain to the emperor and he will be forced to return against his will to Russia. Russians should proceed with the Greeks in the same way in the case of a similar occurrence.[21]

"As confirmation and an inviolable pledge of peace, which should exist between the Greeks and the Russians, this treaty was written in duplicate on parchment by John and was attested by the hand of our emperor before the Most Revered Cross and the Holy and Indivisible Trinity, Our True God. And we, the emperors, inform you, Russians, of this and transmit this to your envoys.

"We [the Russians] have given our pledge to your emperor, who by the grace of God rules over God's creatures. [We do this]

---

19. A *cheliadin* may be a servant, serf or slave: the opinion of historians differs as to the exact definition of this term.

20. That is, the rights to contest or to keep the *cheliadin*.

21. In *Nik.*: this sentence is unclearly phrased; text is given after *Laur.*

912 according to the laws of our people—that neither we nor anyone else from our land will transgress the terms of this [agreement of] peace and amity, and we will submit the document to your emperor for ratification so that this agreement will become valid. And we will certify the conclusion of peace between us. The second of the month of September, the fifth of the Indiction, in the year 6420 [912] from the creation of the world."

Emperor Leo plied the Russian envoys with great honor and presented them with gold, brocade and precious cloth. And he attached to them his officials, who should conduct them to show them the beauty of the churches, the golden palaces and the treasuries contained therein: the vast amounts of gold, of brocade and of gems. And they showed them the relics of the [Passion] of Christ, [His] crown, the nails [used to crucify Him] and [His] purple robe, and the relics of the saints. They also taught them about their Greek faith and explained them the true religion. And so they let them go to their land with great honor. When Oleg's envoys came to him they related the speeches of the two emperors, and how they had concluded peace, and what provisions had been made between the Byzantine and the Russian lands, and that the oath should not be transgressed either by the Greeks or by the Russians. And Oleg lived in peace with all countries and ruled in Kiev.

ABOUT THE HORSE.
OLEG'S END.

Autumn arrived and Oleg remembered his horse, which he had ordered to be well fed and which he had not ridden. Once he asked the magicians and soothsayers, "From what shall I die?" And one magician told him, "Prince, you have a horse which you love and ride. You will die from it." Oleg kept this in mind and said, "I will never ride it, I will not see it again." And he ordered that it be fed but not brought to him, and so he remained for several years without seeing it, until he went against the Greeks.

When he came from the Greeks to Kiev, where he stayed for four years, in the fifth year he remembered his horse, from which he had been told by the magicians that he would meet his death. And he summoned the senior stableman, telling him, "Where is my horse which I gave you to be fed and cared for, and which I said I would not ride and that it should not be brought to me?" The latter answered, "The horse died." Oleg laughed and reproached the magicians, saying, "How wrong are magicians' words. All this is a lie. The horse died but I am alive." And he ordered [another] horse be saddled for him. "I want to see his bones." And he rode and walked to the place where the horse's bare bones and bare skull lay. And he dismounted his horse and laughed, saying, "Can I receive death from this skull?" And he put his foot on the skull and a snake crawled out of the skull and struck his foot. And from this he became ill and died. And all the people wept over him, lamenting greatly, and carried him and buried him on the mountain called Shchekovitsa, where his grave is to this day, and it is known as the grave of Oleg; and altogether his rule lasted thirty-three years.

ABOUT THE MAGICIANS.[22]

It is not astonishing what manner of magic can be achieved through witchcraft. And so it was in the reign of Domitian. [Roman Emperor Domitian, A.D. 81-96] At that time a magician was known named Apollonius of Tyana, who travelled throughout cities and villages performing his devil's magic.[23] He came from Rome to Byzantium, where he was besought by the inhabitants to perform the following: to drive away a multitude of snakes and scorpions so that they would stop hurting the people. There he also tamed a violent horse in the presence of a crowd of nobles. He also came to Antiochia[24] and was besought by them, the Antiochians, who were suffering from scorpions and mosquitoes. So he made a copper scorpion and buried it in the ground, and placed a small marble pillar above it. [Then] he ordered the people to walk through the city holding a stick in their hands, and to shake the stick, crying, "The city should be without mosquitoes!" And in this way the mosquitoes and scorpions disappeared from the city. And he was also asked about a possible earthquake but he only sighed and wrote on a

---

22. The following story was taken by the compiler of the *Prim. Chron.* from the chronicle of Georgios Harmatolos. In all preserved Russian *mss.* the text is not quite clear. The unclear passages in the Russian text are replaced by the original ones from Harmatolos' text. See *Prim. Chr.* Vol. II, year 912.

23. Apollonius of Tyana was a rather well-known philosopher of the Pythagoran school in the first century, A.D.

24. At that time Antiochia was the capital of Syria.

912 wooden table, "Alas, for thee, unfortunate city! The earth will shake thee and fire will burn thee! And then thou wilt be bewailed by the city on the shore of Orontes."

The great Anastasius of the city of God [Jerusalem] said of him, "In some places the magic performed by Apollonius remains effective to the present day. Some of it was performed to chase away the quadrupeds and birds which might have injured human beings; some to stop the river currents which overflowed from their shore and flooded. But some [of the magic he performed] destroyed or harmed living people in order to control [them] for violence. [The devils] performed such deeds on his [Apollonius'] behalf during his lifetime but even after his death they would still perform such marvels near his grave in order to seduce sinful people and submit them to the devils' temptation."

And so, what can be said about those who perform such magic deeds? Indeed, this one [Apollonius] was very adept in performing such deeds of witchcraft, albeit no one realized that he had become involved in such philosophical artfulness because of his insanity.[25] He should, however, have performed his magic which he wanted to do solely by means of words and not by means of actions. All this could happen because of divine will and the devils' actions. Through such happenings our Orthodox faith is tested, and we should be strong and staunch. [And we should remain] with God and not be turned away through false magic and deeds of Satan performed by the devil, himself, and the servants of his hatred.

It happens, however, that some people prophesy in the name of the Lord—as, for instance, Balaam [*Num.* 22-25.] and Saul did, and Caiaphus; and some people even managed to exorcise devils, as for instance, Judah and the sons of Sceva. [*Acts* 19:14-15.] Even the unworthy ones on many occasions received the grace of God, from which they profited. Balaam, himself, was a stranger to the good life and faith; but still the grace given him by God was evident, as other people witnessed it and were convinced. And the Pharoah was of the same nature for even he could foresee the future. Nabuchadnezzar also trespassed the law but [the Lord] revealed to him what would happen after many later generations. Thus it was witnessed that

---

25. "Philosophical" here means smart, clever.

before the arrival of Christ many [persons] of wrong mind performed wonders to deceive people who did not understand what is good. Such were Simon the Magician, Menander, and many others about whom it was truly said, "Do not be seduced by marvels."

And Oleg died.

In the year 6420/912.[26] Leo, wisest of emperors, suffered from a very evil disease, and seeing death approaching, he set on the throne of the empire his brother, Alexander, and his own son, Constantine, born from his fourth wife. At his last breath he told his brother, Emperor Alexander, "Oh, my beloved brother! I see that it will be hard for you to rule the empire." And it happened thus as he said.

THE REIGN OF THE GREEK EMPERORS, ALEXANDER, BROTHER OF LEO, AND OF CONSTANTINE, SON OF THE LATTER.[27]

After Leo the Wise, his brother, Alexander, reigned together with Constantine, son of Leo, for one year and one month. And he brought Nicholas back to the throne of the patriarch; [Nicholas was] deposed by Leo because he forbade him to attend church after his [the Emperor's] fourth marriage. And Euthemius, who was put [on the Patriarchal throne by Leo] in place of Nicholas, was deposed. Alexander indulged in excessive fondness for food, drink, dogs, birds and vain games, and by no means cared properly for power but spent his time practicing at the hippodrome and continually attended the hunt. And in addition to this, the worst was added: he took from the churches the hangings and chandeliers which belonged to God and adorned the hippodrome with them. And what was supposed to honor God was used for the [embellishment of] speechless [animals] and indecencies. For these reasons God soon removed honor from him. Once while dining he became drunk and went to see newborn puppies, and took one from the bitch. But [this bitch] became the weapon of God sent against him. He was bitten, and in two days he lost so much blood that he died, after having reigned for thirteen months.

26. Repetition of the year in *Nik*.
27. The compiler of *Nik*. took this story from *The Chronograph*.

912 THE REIGN OF THE GREEK EMPEROR
CONSTANTINE VII PORPHYROGENITUS, SON OF LEO

Constantine, son of Leo, reigned one year together with Alexander and then was left to rule alone, being only seven years of age. Therefore his mother, Zoë, assumed the rule of the empire and he reigned with her for seven years; and with Romanus, twenty-six years; and thereafter he reigned alone for fifteen years.[28] As it is said, Constantine was very young and this youth was the reason for many evils. Therefore the Emperor had to drink much grief, and even during his good years there were difficulties. [He was] like a young growing and newly planted tree which can barely withstand either a freeze or a strong wind, heavy rain or wearisome heat, or conquest of the city. Therefore there were injuries during his youth. And from all sides there were attempts to destroy its roots. Therefore it required great skill to escape evil-breathing disturbances; but people also say that a garden which grows in the wind develops much sturdier structure. So he, Constantine Porphyrogenitus, son of Leo, an emperor little in age, after many long movements of the sun and after many evil occurrences and many evil temptations, greatly increased his reason and wisdom. And he, as a skillful pilot, finally brought [the ship] under his command into a quiet port.

This was the first trial for the young Emperor: a certain Constantine, said to be the son of [a well-known general], Andronicus Ducas, gathered a large army led by good commanders and attempted to attack Constantine Porphyrogenitus without any regard for the latter's youth; but even an error may lead to salvation,

---

28. Zoe was Constantine's co-ruler from 912 to 920. During these years she had to fight with the powerful and ambitious Patriarch, Nicholas "Mystikus," so-called because he was the private, unofficial aid ("*mystik*" in Greek) of Emperor Leo. In 920 after a struggle with Leo Phocas, the government was seized by Romanus Lecapenus, the able and ambitious commander of the fleet, who forced Constantine to crown him co-emperor. The same year Romanus Lecapenus made his sons, Constantine and Stephen, his co-emperors, as well. In 944 his sons removed him (Romanus) from power and forced him to become a monk but in 945 Constantine VII Porphyrogenitus eliminated them, and for fourteen years was the sole ruler of Byzantium. When, from 912 to 944, he was practically removed from power, he nonetheless legally remained Emperor. He was one of the most learned men of his time.

as David sang: Constantine Ducas was ambitious, cruel and fast as a **912** horse but his own horse threw him and his own weapon tasted his body and became crimson with his blood.

As soon as this severe winter passed, another winter and storm arrived which was much worse than the first. Phocas the Magister [commander], whose first name was Leo, a man of imposing stature and smart in using his strength, was in command of all the Greek armed forces. Seeing that Romanus Lecapenus, commander of the fleet, was held in honor by the Emperor, Leo Phocas decided first to bide his time, preparing his possible escape. Concealing his intentions until some more propitious opportunity, he attempted to win over the Empire for himself. When the opportunity arrived, he began spreading evil rumors which he, himself, had fabricated and which were as the creation of a viper; and he claimed that he found some guilt in Romanus. This he did because he did not want to reveal his intentions, and pretended that he would fight Romanus because he cared for the Emperor and this would be in the latter's interest. Thus he followed the example of the evil-doing fox, because he wanted to be secure in the case of unfavorable developments. Through slyness he won over the military and built up a powerful army, gathering troops from everywhere: from Lycia, from Thrace, from Colchis, from Iveria, from Pamphilia, and he gathered as many regiments as there is sand in the sea.[29] These warriors were courageous, well-armed and strong, experienced in battle. With them he marched from Chrysopolis[30] against Constantinople, and one would not sin to call it a heavenly city.

The fields were crowded with brave men, and throughout the entire country there were the flashing of lances, shining of helmets, sparkling of light on shields, and the gleam of javelins in the air. There were soldiers with gold-encrusted shields, men with quivers, experienced horsemen, warriors in armour, and everyone could [well] be frightened by such an army. The old man, Romanus Lecapenus, commander of the navy, saw that the nation was fluctuating back and forth, and was as badly agitated as the sea or

---

29. Lycia and Pamphilia: regions in southern Asia Minor; Colchis (now Abkhazia) and Iveria (now Georgia): lands in the southwestern Caucasus. Thrace: a region in the Balkans northwest of Constantinople.

30. Chrysopolis: a city on the Asian shore of the Bosphorus, across from Constantinople, now called Skutari.

912 like a rudderless ship, because it was steered by the hand of a child. He cajoled the Emperor and won him over. Masters of intrigue and conspiracy who feigned to be friends of the autocrat provided him [the Emperor] with evil suggestions, advised him and plotted all manner of schemes and evil deeds.

The Emperor finally heeded those advisers who sought to gain him, accepted Romanus Lecapenus as a friend and appointed him guardian over his reign. [This guardian] was more eager [to assume the power] than anyone else. When Leo Phocas learned that the Emperor was in the hands of Romanus, he gathered many troops under the pretext that he was hurrying to the Emperor's aid, and he did his best to win over the people of the empire. God, however, aware of the perfidy and secret intentions of Leo Phocas, changed the direction of events.

And so Leo Phocas, this eager wolf, was not in the least able to succeed. Emperor Constantine, following the advice of Romanus Lecapenus, promulgated a *chrysobull*[31] directed at the troops under Leo Phocas' command, in which he condemned the latter's plot and praised the goodminded Romanus Lecapenus.

This resulted in confusion and rumors among the troops since the equivocal attitude of Leo Phocas was exposed. Because of the Imperial *chrysobull*, the entire military multitude developed doubts [concerning Phocas' intentions] and everyone abandoned him, leaving this accursed one alone. Thereafter, Phocas was arrested and his sight extinguished, and the light of his eyes was destroyed, for he was blinded.

[Beginning from this time] Romanus Lecapenus started guiding and restructuring the whole [government]. It could have happened that the young man [the Emperor] might have acquired another mother in him [in Romanus Lecapenus] but in place of this he became an evil stepmother, and not a well-minded mother. And so the saying was fulfilled: "Chasing away the wolves, he, himself, caught and hurt the lamb."

Emperor Constantine was forced to be well-minded toward the "benefactor" of his life and "guardian" of his dominion, and he honored him with the highest rank of "magister" in the emperor's hierarchy. Then, to this honor he had to add another, even better

---

31. *Chrysobull:* a solemn imperial decree confirmed by the church.

one, that of "father and guardian of his empire." Then, a still greater one; and so he became tied to Romanus. The latter gave him [the Emperor] his daughter in marriage; and after the wedding, in order to be still closer to his father-in-law, [Constantine] crowned Romanus as co-emperor, becoming still more bound to him.³²

ABOUT THE RUSSIAN PRINCE IGOR'.

In the year 6421/913. During the reign of Emperor Constantine, son of Leo the Wise, son-in-law of Romanus, Oleg died and Igor', son of Ruirik, began to reign in Russia. And the Drevlians started a war against Igor' after Oleg's death.

In the year 6422/914. Igor' marched against the Drevlians, defeated them and imposed on them a heavier tribute than there had been under Oleg. And he had a *voevoda* named Svenel'd.³³

And he subdued the Ugliches under his power; and Igor' imposed tribute on them and gave it to Svenel'd. One city, however, named Peresechen, did not surrender to Igor' and he remained by it for three years, taking it with difficulty. The Ugliches lived along the lower course of the Dnieper, and then moved to the region between the Bug and Dniestr [rivers], settling there; and the Drevlians' tribute was given to Svenel'd. And they had to pay a black *kuna* from each household.³⁴ But Igor's retinue said, "He gave too much to one single man; but we will discuss this later."³⁵

ABOUT THE BULGARIAN TSAR

During the reign of Constantine, Emperor of the Greeks, Simeon, Tsar of Bulgaria, made peace and went to Constantinople.

---

32. Constantine VII reigned 912-959.

33. "Svenel'd": in *Nik.* this name is transliterated as "Sventeld." In *Laur.* it appears as "Svenel'd" or "Svenal'd"; in *Hyp.* as "Svineld" and "Svengeld"; and in *Novg. KOM.*, "Svendeld." In the present translation, the spelling "Sventeld," has been corrected to "Svenel'd" as in the *Prim. Chr., Laur.* version.

34. *Kuna:* the fur of a marten, it is used to be a currency unit in ancient Russia.

35. The events described in the last paragraph can be found only in *First Novgorodian Chronicle,* p. 109; they are unavailable in the *Hypatian* and *Laurentian* chronicles. Correction made by the translator following the text of the *First Novgorodian Chronicle* (Com).

914 And he received a blessing from the Patriarch and dined with the Emperor, but when he left the city he began capturing [people], and there was a war and the Greeks succeeded in defeating him. Although the Bulgarians became Christianized they did not stop fighting [Byzantium].

THE REIGN OF ROMANUS LECAPENUS, EMPEROR OF THE GREEKS.

Romanus Lecapenus received the crown of Emperor from his son-in-law, Emperor Constantine Porphyrogenitus, son of Leo the Wise, grandson of Basil the Macedonian. This Romanus was loved by Emperor Constantine because of his [Romanus'] daughter and his friendship. And so there were two emperors, Romanus and Constantine, over the Greeks, and there was great agreement and tranquility among the people.

ABOUT THE COUNCIL OF RECONCILIATION

During the reign of these emperors, Romanus and Constantine, there was a Council of Union. This happened under Patriarch Nicholas, who had been deposed because of [Leo VI's] fourth marriage. He [the Patriarch] had condemned it and had written new rules.[36]

ABOUT THE TRANSFER TO CONSTANTINOPLE OF THE ICON NOT MADE BY HUMAN HANDS.

This happened when Emperor Romanus and his warriors besieged the city of Edessa. The latter's inhabitants wanted peace because no one came to help them. Therefore they gave him [Romanus] the Icon of Our Lord Jesus Christ Not Made by Human Hands.[37] Emperor Constantine and the Patriarch met it with great joy and placed it in the palace on August 16.

Emperor Constantine made Romanus Emperor and called him his "father" in order to be in great amity with him. The very clever

---

36. This Council of Union brought to an end the struggle between factions of the Byzantine Church which had started under Patriarch Photius. See the entry concerning Emperor Basil the Macedonian under the year 876.

37. According to tradition, Christ, Himself, left the imprint of His face on a purificator (towel). This is an eastern version of the Veronica Image of Christ.

Romanus plotted cautiously and strengthened his power, **914** [practically] removing his son-in-law, Constantine, from power—him, who was Porphyrogenitus and of the imperial line through his father and grandfather. And he [Romanus], himself, seized the scepter and was called "Emperor" by all peoples. And Constantine became no one because his power was overclouded in the same way as the stars are covered by a cloud. Romanus gorged more and more power and brought his mind's ambition to such a point that he took entirely someone else's bread, and fed with power not only himself but also fed his family. And the one—I mean Constantine—who owned the bread remained hungry. He made his senior son, Christophor, and the latter's son, emperors. And he made him autocrat and stressed everywhere that he and his children were the main emperors. And the saddest and most evil thing was that in charters sent to other [rulers] from Constantinople, Romanus' children and grandchildren were in the first place [and not Constantine]. But when the power of Romanus seemed to be completely established, in the way of the pillar of Klalan [sic.] then he was defeated and this accursed one suffered and lost power. This happened when Emperor Constantine became older, when his wisdom began to shine as the dawn, when he acquired the best advisers, men of good morals. Then he was able to cut the heads of the snakes: I mean here, the children of Romanus, and he took over the scepter of the dominion. He chased away the heavy cloud and began to shine with powerful rays. Romanus was then very aged because he had spent a long time in power. He was Emperor for twenty-six years and gave many gifts to everyone, and those to whom he gave gifts and did good deeds—that is, his sons—drove him from the throne. And his hair, which was previously adorned with a crown, was tonsured. And so it happens when old roots begin to decline.

Under this Emperor Romanus, Tsar Simeon [of Bulgaria] on several occasions occupied the land up to Constantinople, itself. He burned the Imperial palace and became ruler of Adrianople, where he died. The Bulgarian Tsar Peter had for a wife the granddaughter of this Romanus.[38]

---

38. This part of the story of Emperor Constantine was also taken from the *Chronograph*.

945 ABOUT THE RUSSIAN PRINCE IGOR'.

Under this Emperor Romanus, Igor' campaigned against the Greeks with a great many warriors. And when he [the Emperor] heard about it he gave him a tribute which was greater than that given to Oleg.[39]

In the year 6453/945.[40] The Drevlians killed Igor' near the city of Korosten' [the Drevlians' capital]. And after him his son, Sviatoslav, remained; he was very young; and his *voevoda* was Svenel'd. Ol'ga [Igor's wife, Sviatoslav's mother] threw twenty live Drevlians into a pit. They had come to ask her to be the wife of their prince. Thereafter [their prince] sent her fifty men and Ol'ga ordered that they be put in a steambath and burned. And then she, herself, marched to them, desiring revenge for her husband, and she killed five thousand of them.[41]

BEGINNING OF THE REIGN OF SVIATOSLAV

In the year 6454/946. During the last reign of Constantine Porphyrogenitus, Sviatoslav became the Prince of Russia and Ol'ga went with her son and with all their forces against the Drevlians, defeating them, and took all their cities. But she stayed [besieging] the city of Korosten' the whole summer, and so she decided to require from them a tribute of three doves and three sparrows from each household. They gave her this tribute. And in the evening Ol'ga ordered that some sulphur be put in a cloth and attached to the doves and sparrows, and fire set to it; and released [the birds to their homes]; and in such a way the entire city burned.[42]

---

39. This story was taken from *The Chonograph.*

40. In *Nik.* there are no entries for the years 915-944. In *Laur.*, however, under the years 941 and 944 are found the story of Igor's campaign against Constantinople and the text of the treaty between Igor' and Byzantium. Several historians have pointed out that the *Laur.* narrative is based on Harmatolos Continuatus and the *Vita of Basil the New.* In Greek sources Igor's name is not mentioned but the date of his attack is given as the year 941. It is possible that Igor's name was added by the writer of *Prim. Chron.* (some hundred or more years after the attack) on the basis of Russian historical epics and memories of Igor's campaign. This was quite usual at that time.

41. This text differs considerably from *Laur.* and *Hyp.*

42. This text differs considerably from *Laur.* and *Hyp.*

THE SECOND REIGN OF CONSTANTINE PORPHYROGENITUS, SON OF LEO, AND THE REIGN LASTED FIFTEEN YEARS.

946

Constantine Porphyrogenitus arrested the evil-minded children of Romanus Lecapenus, deported them and made them islanders or, better to say, sent them to the islands. And Bardas Phocas was appointed army commander—or, as the Greeks called it, the "domestic of *scholes*."[43] The eunuch Basil, the only castrated [son] of Romanus Lecapenus and who was born from a slave, was appointed *parakimomen*, guard of the imperial bedchambers. And since Bardas had lost his flame in battle and age had taken quite a bit of his striking power, the command of the army was offered to Nicephorus Phocas—as someone said, "From the lion to that puppy."

Constantine finally could see the son of his own loins, who was born of Helen, daughter of Romanus, and he was [also] called Romanus. Since with age he had become very attached to his wife, he preferred him [Romanus] to his [elder] son, Basil, who was great in victory, and he would carry this infant in his arms; and so he decided to forget the natural ties [to Basil] and he appointed his [second] son, Romanus [b. 957], to be co-emperor of the Greeks.

St. John of Rylo lived in the time of Emperor Constantine and the Bulgarian Tsar Peter.[44]

IN THE REIGN OF ROMANUS, SON OF CONSTANTINE PORPHYROGENITUS

After Constantine Porphyrogenitus, his son, Romanus, reigned in Constantinople for three years and three months. This one turned all his rule and all his power over to weakminded eunuchs, while he, himself, cared only for hunting and was devilishly fond of running the dogs. At that time the evil-minded Arabs, the sons of Hagar, conquered Crete and made it their stronghold. And from thence they constantly harassed the people on the continent. Nicephorus Phocas, eager in fighting and a skilled campaigner, had strong arms and distinguished himself as army com-

---

43. "Domestic of *scholes*" was the commander of the Imperial personal guard, composed of *skoli*, young pages to the Emperor.

44. St. John of Rylo was a Bulgarian saint.

947 mander, and filled the sea with excellent ships. Against these animals of water and land—that is, against the Arabs—he sent a strong army, defeated the enemies and destroyed the thievish strongholds of the Arabs. He also captured these robbers' chief, a daring man with long arms. He returned from thence with glorious victories, and was very much respected for these deeds. At that time the beautiful city of Antiochia, the most noble and refined city which was as adorned as a bride, was taken by the arms of the murderous Ishmaelites [Arabs], who dishonored it like a slave or a lecherous whore. And then the most courageous Phocas took up arms and campaigned against the enemies for the sake of his blood-related countrymen, and he defeated the foreigners and gave back to Constantinople [Byzantium] the city of Antiochia, just as a virgin with beautiful eyes is returned to a virtuous mother. When Phocas was campaigning, death took Emperor Romanus [III], who left the power to his wife, Theophano, as well as her small children. When Phocas learned of this he returned from where he campaigned, to the great city. He was met by a high official who required him to take a solemn oath that he would not be an enemy to Romanus' children, and he was sent back to Syria.

During the reign of Emperor Romanus there lived Michael Malein, who had been a pupil of Athanasius of Mt. Athos. Also during this reign, Tsar Peter of Bulgaria died, and his children, Boris and Roman, who were kept in Constantinople as hostages, were returned to their country.[45]

In the year 6455/947. Ol'ga left her son in Kiev and went to Novgorod and started organizing market places along the river Msta, and imposing tribute. In Luga she imposed tribute and duties. Her hunting places to this day are in the entire Russian and Novgorodian land, and also there are her towns and her market places, while her sledges remain in Pskov until now. Along the Dnieper and the Desna rivers were her market places and towns, and she also had a town near the city of Kiev. It is on the river Desna and it is called Ol'gino to the present day. Having organized all this and having personally inspected everything with her own eyes, she returned to her son, Sviatoslav, to Kiev, where she reigned with him in great concord.

45. This story was taken from *The Chonograph.*

ABOUT THE BAPTISM OF OL'GA

955

In the year 6463/955.[46] Ol'ga went to the Greek land and arrived in Constantinople. At that time there was the emperor named Tzimisces. And they told the Emperor of her arrival, and the Emperor asked her to come to him; and she went to him without delay. When the Emperor saw her, very beautiful in face and very intelligent in mind, he was astonished at her wisdom; and he talked with her, telling her, "You deserve to rule with me in this city." She understood this speech and said to the Emperor, "I am pagan, and if you want to baptise me, you should be my godfather. If you do not want to do so, I will not be baptised." The Emperor obeyed her words and subsequently he and the Patriarch baptised her. When she became enlightened, she rejoiced with her soul and body, and when the Patriarch taught her the faith, he said to her, "You are blessed among Russian women because you have abandoned darkness and love the light. And you will be blessed by the sons of Russia, until the last days of your grandchildren and of their descendants." And he told her about the rules of the Church, about prayer, about Lent, about alms and about keeping the body in purity. And she bowed her head and absorbed teaching as a sponge, and she bowed to the Patriarch, saying, "I will be protected by your prayers, most honorable lord, from the snares of evil."

In baptism she was named Helen in the same way as the ancient empress, mother of great Constantine. The Patriarch blessed her and let her go. After baptism she was invited by the Emperor, who told her, "I want to marry you." And she answered, How can you marry me, since you have become my godfather and call me your [god] daughter? There is not such a law among the Christians and you, Emperor, know so, yourself." And the Emperor told

---

46. Constantine Porphyrogenitus in his *De ceremoniis Aulae byzantinae* (Bonn, 1819, pp. 594-98) and Jugie, M., *Le Schisme byzantin,* Paris, 1941, p. 174, state that Ol'ga visited Constantinople in 957 during his, not Tzimisces', reign. She was received by Emperor Constantine on September 9 and October 18. According to Constantine's book, she was already baptised and was accompanied by an Orthodox priest. Therefore the story in the *Prim. Chron.*, repeated by *Nik.*, hardly provides a very exact report of her talks with the Emperor, or of the circumstances of her sojourn in Constantinople. (See also Kartashev, I. 97-104.)

955 the courtesans who were standing around, "Ol'ga outwitted me with her speech," because Ol'ga was very wise in speech. The Emperor, after hearing her words, gave her many gifts, gold and silver and brocade and various vases, and let her go, having called her his daughter. Ol'ga also wanted to return to her land but she went to the Patriarch and asked a blessing for her homeland, telling him, "My people are pagan and my son is also pagan. [I ask this blessing] in order to be preserved by God from all manner of evil." And the Patriarch told her, "Oh, faithful child! You were baptised into Christ and you accepted Christ and Christ will have you under His protection. It was the same when He protected Enoch and his [the latter's] descendants; and then Noah in his ark; and Abraham and Avimelech; and Lot from the people of Sodom; and Moses from the Pharoah; and David from Saul; and the three youths in the furnace; and Daniel from the beasts. In the same way God will protect you from evil and from its nets." The Patriarch, together with the entire Oecumenical Council, blessed her and let her go in peace to her land. And she returned to Kiev after having received holy baptism and the divine gifts in the Imperial City from the Most Honorable Patriarch. And so it happened, as it happened in the time of King Solomon. The Ethiopian queen came to Solomon because she wanted to hear Solomon's wisdom and see portents. Just as blessed Ol'ga, she was looking for good and the wisdom of God, and for imperishable glory, because there is the human and there is the divine. It is written, "Those who look for Me will find Wisdom." [*Prov.* 1:22; text is slightly changed.]

Blessed Helen [Ol'ga], when she was in Kiev, received an envoy of the Emperor, who told her, "I [the Emperor] have given you many gifts and you told me that when you return to Russia you will also send me gifts, slaves, wax, fur of squirrels, and warriors to help me." And Ol'ga answered and said to the envoy, "You have come from the Emperor. Tell him the following: 'If you would remember and wait for me in Pochaina, just as long as I waited [for you] at the Golden Horn only then will you receive something from me.'"[47] And thereafter she spoke at length with him and then

---

47. The meaning is simple: "You have to wait as long as I waited for you in Constantiople." Golden Horn: a bay which divides Constantinople into Eastern and Western parts. Pochaina: a river near Kiev, where Ol'ga's suburban residence was probably located.

she let the Emperor's envoy return home.

Ol'ga lived with her son, Sviatoslav, and the mother tried to persuade him to be baptised but he paid no attention to her words. He did not forbid baptism for those who desired it but he refused it himself. The Christian faith is an unusual thing for unbelievers. They do not understand it. They do not realize that they walk in darkness and do not see the glory of God. Ol'ga often used to tell Sviatoslav, "My son, I have learned about God and enjoy it; and if you learn about God, you will also enjoy it." But he did not heed this and said, "How can I accept another faith? My warriors will laugh at it and be angry." But Ol'ga told him, "My son, when you become baptised, they also will do the same." But he did not listen to his mother, following the pagan customs, because he was not aware that those who do not obey their mothers will have misfortune. It is written, "He who does not obey his father or mother will die the death." [*Exod.* 21:17] But this one, besides all, was angry with his mother. Solomon said, "One who teaches an unrighteous man has only disappointment." And again, "Rebuke not an evil man lest he hate thee." [*Prov.* 9:7-8] But Ol'ga loved her son, Sviatoslav, and, weeping, told him, "The will of God be done. If God wants to be Merciful to my people and to the Russian land, He will turn their hearts to Him, just as God has granted me to do." And saying this, she prayed to God every day for the people and for her son, and cared for him until he grew up and became an adult man.

963

PRINCE SVIATOSLAV.

In the year 6471/963. When Prince Sviatoslav grew up and became adult he began to assemble many brave warriors. He, himself, was very courageous and marched readily, like a leopard. He campaigned in many wars. When he marched he was not accompanied by carts or kettles and would not boil any meat, but would cut it in thin slices, whether horse meat or that of wild animals or some other, and he would bake it on coals. He never had any tent and as a bed he used his saddle-blanket, and his saddle as a pillow, and so did all his warriors. Before a campaign he would announce it to the other country, saying, "I intend to march against you." And so he went to the Oka and Volga rivers and found the Viatichs there,

965 and he asked them, "To whom do you pay tribute?" They answered, "We pay the Khazars a *shlag* from a plow."⁴⁸

In the year 6473/965. Sviatoslav went against the Khazars. Hearing of this, the Khazars went out against him with their prince, Kagan.⁴⁹ They started the battle, and there was a battle, and Sviatoslav defeated the Khazars, taking their city of Belovezh. He also defeated the Ias and Kasogs.⁵⁰ And he brought them [captive] to Kiev.

In the year 6474/966. Sviatoslav defeated the Viatichs and imposed tribute on them.

THE REIGN OF THE GREEK NICEPHORUS PHOCAS

After Romanus [II], son of Constantine Porphyrogenitus, Nicephorus Phocas reigned for six years and six months.⁵¹ It happened in the following way. When Nicephorus was campaigning in Syria, a ferocious beast like a heart-eating boar, who was the worst among all land animals, started struggling against him. It was a certain eunuch⁵² who had an important office in the empire and who, eager to have the power, hated the general [Phocas] because he could not stand the latter's successes and glory. He wrote a secret letter to Tzimisces, whose name was John from childhood and who

---

48. *Shlag*: Polish, *szelag*—shilling, a small coin hardly known in tenth-century Russia.

49. *Kagan*: actually, the title of the Khazar ruler.

50. The *Ias* (s. and *pl.*) were a people of the Iranian branch of the Indoeuropean linguistic group, usually called "Alans," presently known as Ossetians. They used to occupy a considerable part of the Russian prairie but now live only in the northern Caucasus. The Kasogs, presently called "Cherkess," were a Caucasian people living in the northwestern Caucasus.

51. Romanus II, 959-963, left two sons: Basil II, who was three years old, and Constantine VIII, who was two years old, and both of them became emperors. They reigned from 963 to 1025, but the actual power remained for some time in the hands of their mother, Empress Theophano, and the *parakimomen*, the eunuch Joseph Bringas. Soon thereafter, however, on April 16, 963, Nicephorus Phocas, commander of the army in Asia, was proclaimed emperor, occupied Constantinople and married the dowager. Theophano. On December 12, 969, he was assassinated by his general, John Tzimisces, who proclaimed himself Emperor and married Theodora, daughter of Romanus II. Brehier, pp. 157, 163-164. This story taken from *The Chronograph*.

52. Joseph Bringas, the *parakimomen*.

campaigned together with Nicephorus. In this letter he suggested that Tzimisces kill Nicephorus, come to Constantinople and become Emperor and ruler of the Greeks. Tzimisces received the letter and perceived the plotting [of the eunuch]. Tzimisces was a man with a well-educated mind who hated evil. He showed the letter to Nicephorus, advising him, "Expose and defeat the eunuch's murderous plot." This Tzimisces was a good man, handsome, patient and brave in heart, well-minded, an invincible warrior and magnanimous advisor. He would not bear hatred toward anyone or conceal any evil in his heart. It behooves great people to set the example for lesser ones. Paradise is a place of the spirit which preserves a blessed garden: it is a garden fed with many waters of divine blessing. And so was Tzimisces: great in bravery, taught how to use his lance and how to tighten his bow, and how to hit the infidels with his arrows. At that time he was waging war side by side with Nicephorus Phocas and had warriors entrusted to him under his command. He was a relative of Phocas, a man of the same blood.[53]

966

Holding that letter in his hand, he understood the murderous intentions contained in it, and the general [Tzimisces] exposed all this [to Nicephorus Phocas]. "Oh, woe to Greek honor!" said John Tzimisces to Phocas. "How long will the ship of empire be ruled by eunuchs with women's minds, whose intentions are all wicked, who are filled with evil, and of whom all are evildoers? They [the eunuchs] are versed in cunning and are inspirers of abominable malevolence."

When Phocas heard this his indignation burst like a violent flame, so mightily that a lion which was hiding and sleeping in the mountains opened his eyes and roared, and fright passed over the mountains and valleys.

Nicephorus was proclaimed Emperor, marched to Constantinople, entered it without difficulty, was seen there and everyone rejoiced, and all awaited him in the imperial palaces; and he shone with his serenity to slaves and to freemen alike. The [dowager] Empress was the first, with the clergy, to receive this man with open arms, and by unanimous decision Nicephorus became Emperor.

53. Both were of aristocratic Armenian descent.

966   He was a great warrior, daring in good deeds, strongarmed, tireless in work, hardened against diseases, and he married Theophano, the widow of Emperor Romanus, and demonstrated fatherly love toward her children. [Emperor] Phocas showed his bravery, daring and fervor in battle. He had a noble soul. He was strong and passionate in his deeds and could see a cunning horseman from afar; and he preserved a warm heart, just as a burning log holds fire amidst the ashes. When the time for action came, everything happened according to passing nature; but he, himself, kept the well-armed chariots of the empire firmly under his command. Phocas would strike like lightning and encircle the tribes of barbarian people like fire. As it is said, he went through the valley of many trees, driven by his spirit, and would destroy gardens and burn fire into the hills [of the enemy]. He was feared by the Arabs and Syria bowed to him, and Cilicia surrendered and Phoenicia obeyed, and all former Greek lands returned to the Greeks.

This Phocas was invincible against the enemy and a virtuous halo crowned this man. He was well-enlightened and was adorned with virtue. He had strength, was daring of mind and was a man of firm chastity. But no one born on earth is perfectly virtuous, even if he avoids sin, even if he strives to achieve the pinnacle of virtue. This well-crowned Phocas had so many wonderful qualities of body; he had a soul which shone as one of a newly-adorned bride; he cared so much about beauty of soul that he mortified his flesh and always wore a hair shirt. He avoided meals of meat and in every other respect shone as a light. Nonetheless, having earthly and human flesh, he still had some darker spots on the pure cloth of his soul.

The first of these spots was that although by sacrament [of marriage] he was the spouse of the Empress, yet he avoided having carnal relations with her, the widow of Romanus, whom he married.

The second was that although he was Emperor, he had the habit of using evil words, was too parsimonious and was somewhat indifferent toward the aristocrats and common people.[54]

And so unattractive and harmful features began to appear in him. All his body darkened and he was constantly morose because

---

54. Nicephorus Phocas spent all the empire's resources on the army because Byzantium had constantly to oppose enemy attacks in Europe and Asia.

there is no joy in aging, and his roots were wearing out.

966

I have to speak despite my poor mind. People were dying from horrible starvation and wept because they were ill from hunger. A single measure of grain was sold for a piece of gold. Phocas was informed of this and he heard about this grief but he did not want to cure this evil. He commanded that the empire's granary be emptied and the grain sold for gold. This Phocas was not wise enough to comprehend this problem. He had well-stocked granaries with many supplies, which were filled with wheat, but he did not follow the example of well-minded Emperor Basil the Macedonian [who distributed grain to the people]. He [Phocas] saw that the people in Byzantium were suffering from hunger and he did not want to fight this new punishment, so to say, hunger.

But the brave fought the brave, and evil defeated this man of great gifts. He ordered that one measure of wheat from the granaries [barns] be sold for twelve pieces of gold. Everyone has his own intentions but they are not always blessed ones.

Phocas was badly hurt by the outrage inflicted on him by the Empress, who initiated carnal relations with Tzimisces, with whom she committed adultery. He also noticed that Tzimisces had developed a warm desire for power in the empire; therefore he deprived him of all command and ordered him to go into exile. The Empress, however, was so possessed by passion and suffered so much, not seeing Tzimisces in the Imperial palace, that she insisted that Phocas bring Tzimisces back and return him to his former position. The latter [Tzimisces] returned, deeply hurt, resenting the affront done him. He knew, however, how to hide his feelings, and it seemed he had returned without a grudge; within, however, he was consumed by the fire of hatred, and he began preparing a wicked conspiracy.

In the meantime Phocas, unaware of the net prepared to ensnare him, as well as of the intrigues and conspiracy, was living in the clouds as an eagle. With his high-rising feathers he ascended in the air of virtues. On his lips were the flowing, honeyed words of King David; but he continued to sleep on a very hard couch. He avoided gilded and soft beds where bodies touch each other, and even in his sleep would not dream of it. Rather, he enjoyed those higher sweetnesses of life which were as the stars. He would escape and depart [from his wife], remaining apart like a raven at night,

966 sleepless atop a building. But his [chaste] behavior was disliked by the Empress, who wanted caresses and carnal pleasures. And that is the reason why she attached herself to Tzimisces and became tied to him by love, while the latter developed wicked thoughts about the Emperor.

And she handed over Nicephorus Phocas [to his enemy] after having surrounded him with her armed people, and led him as a lion to his couch in order to deliver him to enemies in the same way as the murderous Delilah led Samson, or as Tindareda led her companion to bed.

And who would have dared to commit something similar? Perhaps only a lioness [disturbed] feeding her cubs, or a tigress, or a badly-angered she-bear.

These hunting dogs [assassins] followed Phocas, found him lying on his simple couch and killed him without pity although he appealed to them with the words of God. And the blood of this just man was spilled onto the ground. It happened just as Cain raised his hand against Abel while he was weeping and addressing himself to God.[55]

During the reign of Nicephorus Phocas [his spiritual adviser] was Athanasius of Athos. When he was an army commander he became greatly attached to Athanasius of Athos, and on the latter's advice he built a monastery on the Holy Mountain[56] and even a cell for himself. He wanted to pass his life there but his preoccupation with the government did not permit it.[57]

ABOUT THE RUSSIAN PRINCE SVIATOSLAV

Under this Emperor Nicephorus, in the year 6475 [967],

---

55. Nicephorus Phocas was murdered at night on December 11-12, 969.

56. "Holy Mountain"—Mt. Athos.

57. Nicephorus Phocas was greatly influenced by the ascetic examples of his uncle, Michael Maleinos, Abbot of a Thessalian Monastery. The latter prevented him from becoming a monk and gave him Monk Athanasius as his spiritual guide, who became famous during his life as a *thaumaturge*, ("wonderworker"), Brehier, p. 164. The story of Theophanos and Tzimisces was originally written by the Byzantine chronicler Manassea, then became popular in various versions of the Chronograph. See, f.i., Turdeanu, E., *Le dit de l'Empereur Nicephore Phocas et de son epouse Theophano*, Saloniki, 1976, pp. 1-28; Tvorogov, 203.

Sviatoslav marched against the Bulgarians. It was Emperor **968**
Nicephorus who asked him to march against them. He did so
because they steadily attacked Constantinople. And there was a
battle between the Bulgarians and Sviatoslav, and he defeated them
and took eighty cities on the Danube, and settled in the city of
Preslav, receiving tribute from the Greeks.

In the year 6476/968. The Pechenegs came into the Russian land
for the first time while Sviatoslav was in Preslav [Bulgaria][58]. Ol'ga
with her grandsons, Iaropolk, Oleg and Vladimir, prepared for
siege in the city of Kiev. The Pechenegs besieged the city with strong
forces and an endless number of them surrounded the city so that it
was impossible to leave the city or to dispatch any information; and
the people suffered from hunger and thirst. Then people from the
other shore of the Dnieper assembled their boats and attempted
to cross to this side but they were unable to get to Kiev; nor could
anyone from the city get out to them. The people in the city became
grieved and said, "Is there someone who could go to the other shore
and tell them that if they do not come to the city by the morrow, we
will have to surrender to the Pechenegs?"

A young man told them, "I will cross the river." And at night he
left the city with a bridle and started searching among the Pechenegs
because he knew the Pecheneg tongue very well. He asked, "Has
anyone seen my horse?" And they took him for their own. When he
came to the river he took off his clothes and jumped into the river in
order to cross it. Seeing this, the Pechenegs tried to pursue him and
shot arrows but they could not harm him. The people on the other
side saw this and came to him in a boat and brought him to their
troops. He told them, "If you do not get to the city by tomorrow
morning, the people of Kiev will surrender to the Pechenegs."

Then their voevoda, Pritich, said, "Let us board our boats and
then let us bring the Princess [Ol'ga] and the princes to this side,
where we have people. If we do not do this, Sviatoslav will execute
us." When, the next day, light appeared, they boarded their boats
and trumpeted mightily on their trumpets, and the people in the city
began to shout. The Pechenegs thought that the Prince [Sviatoslav]
had arrived and they ran off from the city in all directions. And Ol'ga
went from the city to the boats with her grandsons and her people.

58. The Pechenegs have been mentioned on a previous occasion, but
their first attack against Kiev was, apparently, in 968.

969   When the prince of the Pechenegs saw this, he went to voevoda Pritich, and the Pecheneg prince inquired, "Who has come?" He was told, "People from the other side." And the Pecheneg prince asked, "Who are you?" And Pritich said, "I am his [Sviatoslav's] man. I have come to defend the city, and behind me is Prince Sviatoslav marching with a numberless multitude." He said this in order to frighten them. The Pecheneg prince told Pritich, "Be my friend," and Pritich said, "So be it." They shook hands and the Pecheneg gave Pritich his horse, his saber and his arrows. Pritich gave him his armour, his shield and his sword. And the Pechenegs retreated from the city because there was not enough water for the horses in the river Lybed'.

Then the Kievans sent their envoys to Sviatoslav in order to tell him, "Prince! You conquer and rule foreign lands but you have abandoned your own! The Pechenegs have nearly captured your mother, your children and us. If you don't come to protect us, they will conquer us. Have you no pity for your fatherland, for your mother, who is old, or for your children?" Hearing this, Sviatoslav quickly mounted his horse and rode with his troops to Kiev. He embraced his mother and his children, and regretted what had happened to them at the hands of the Pechenegs. He gathered his troops and chased the Pechenegs into the prairie; and there was peace.

In the year 6477/969. Sviatoslav told his mother and his boyars, "I do not like living in Kiev; but I want to live in Preslav on the Danube [in Bulgaria]. It is the center of my land because all goods come thither. From the Greeks—gold, brocade, wine and various fruits. From the Czechs and Hungarians—silver and horses. From Russia —furs, wax, mead and slaves."

Ol'ga told him, however, "Do you not see that I am ill? Why do you want to leave me?" She was already ill and said, "Bury me and then you may go wherever you want." Three days later Ol'ga died, and she was lamented by her son and her grandsons and all the people wept bitterly, and they carried her and buried her in the place where she had ordered. And Ol'ga had ordered not to celebrate a *trizna* for her.[59] She secretly had a presbyter [at her court] and he buried the blessed Ol'ga.

59. *Trizna*: a pagan memorial banquet after a funeral.

She was in the same way the precursor of the Christian faith [in Russia] as a star precedes the sun or dawn precedes the light of day. And she shone among the pagans as the moon at night or as a pearl shines in dung, for they [pagans] were in [spiritual] dung since they were not yet washed [from their sins] by Holy Baptism. Those who are purified by holy baptism take away their sinful clothes of the old man, Adam, and put on the clothes of a new Adam, who was Christ. But we may tell her, "Rejoice, you, the first Russian to learn of God! You began our reconciliation with Christ." She was the first among the Russians to attain the heavenly kingdom and she is praised by Russian princes and the sons of Russia as their [Christian] precursor. They do this because even after her death she intercedes with God for Russia. The souls of the just do not die, and the Lord protected blessed Ol'ga from evil and from the cunning of devils.

In the year 6478/970. Sviatoslav assigned Iaropolk to Kiev and Oleg to the land of the Drevlians. Then the Novgorodians came, asking him to give them a prince. But Iaropolk and Oleg did not want to [rule in Novgorod]. Then Dobrynia told the Novgorodians, "Ask Vladimir [to be your prince]." He said this because Vladimir was [Sviatoslav's] son from Malka, Ol'ga's stewardess, and Malka was Dobrynia's sister; thus Dobrynia was Vladimir's uncle.

As is known, Vladimir was born in Budutin, where Ol'ga had sent Malka because she was angered [about Malka's affair with Sviatoslav]. She owned that town there and before her death she bequested this town to the [Church of] the Holy Mother of God.[60] And the Novgorodians asked Sviatoslav, "Give us Vladimir," and he gave them Vladimir, who went with his uncle Dobrynia to Novgorod, while Sviatoslav left for Preslav [in Bulgaria].

FROM THE GREEK CHRONICLE: THE REIGN
OF THE GREEK EMPEROR JOHN TZIMISCES.

After Nicephorus Phocas, John Tzimisces reigned for six years and six months [969-976]. Tzimisces was a courageous and formidable ruler toward his enemy. When he was crowned and the Arabs learned of it, they took fright. The Assyrians[61] tasted his sharp

---

60. The information provided in this last paragraph cannot be found in the *Hyp., Laur.* or *Novgorodian* chronicles.

61. Actually not the Assyrians, but the Mesopotamian Arabs who had their capital in Baghdad.

970 sword and [their emirs of the dynasty of] Hamaden quickly fled from him. The Emperor brandished his sword against his enemies, and so terrorized all the barbarians living within Greek confines that he inspired them to forget their pride. He spread the Byzantine territories over innumerable enemy cities which used to attack [the empire], and he built fortresses and towns as far as the waters of the Tigris. The Cilician warriors were frightened by him, and the Arab commander trembled at his power. The Phoenicians felt his skillful hand and the Syrians fled the flashing of his lance. Edessa and the valleys of the river Euphrates saw him. The Greek horses were watered in the river Euphrates and their proud galloping warriors filled the river.

The Scythians,[62] who live on the Danube River, saw his regiments slashing to pieces and frightening his enemies, and they saw his generals killing, chasing away and defeating his foes. He was a lion attacking bulls with high ribs, catching them, tearing them apart and wounding them. And the river turned to blood; the water of the Danube became crimson and the Greeks celebrated victories on the fields of the Danube while he filled the barbarian hearts with terror. He defeated the Bulgarians and took the city of Preslav, capturing their chieftains and their tsar, and brought Tsar Boris, himself, to Constantinople. He took from him [Boris] the shining of his crown and deprived him of his jewels and of his linens and purple clothing. He honored him, [however, later] granting him high title: he promoted him to *magister*.[63]

ABOUT SVIATOSLAV.

Thereafter the proudest prince, Sviatoslav, who at that time reigned over Russia, arrived there with a large army and he captured many Bulgarians, whom he subdued. He took up residence in Dorystolon [present Silistria]. Learning of this, Tzimisces attacked him with well-trained army troops, and soundly defeated him; in this way the Bulgarians came under the dominion

---

62. There were no Scythians in Tzimisces' time. The Byzantine chroniclers, from whose works these discourses about Byzantium were taken, called all the people of the south Russian and Danubian prairies "Scythians." In this case, the chronicler gave the name "Scythian" to the Bulgarians.

63. This is another story from *The Chronograph*.

of the Greek scepter. Tzimisces was a person who loved people and **971**
was generous toward their rulers and those with high titles. By his
own will he let Sviatoslav retreat with the latter's remaining forces.
Sviatoslav went with his troops into the [land of the] Pechenegs,
spent the winter there and found there his end from the hungry
teeth of those who lived there.[64]

Such a one was Tzimisces, shepherd of his flock of sheep and
[their] guardian against beasts. He was a man who would not put his
head down to sleep but would remain awake, and who would crush
the jaws of beasts with strong claws. In time of tranquility and peace
he was gentle toward all—sweet, joyful, cheeful-looking—and from
his eyes shone joy and the image of gentleness; his hand was
generous and his heart was generous and magnanimous. [His
government] was another divine paradise from which flew four
rivers: justice, wisdom, bravery and chastity. If he had not soiled
himself with the sin of the murder [of Nicephorus Phocas] he would
have been verily a star which emanates light and provides life.
Tzimisces, however, ended his life and public duties in the natural
way, as all do—by the cloud of death, and the casket covered his eyes
rich in love. And now there remained Basil to reign together with
Constantine, both born to the purple, descendants of Romanus, who
was the son of Constantine and who reigned earlier over the Greeks.

ABOUT THE RUSSIAN PRINCES.

During the reign of this Emperor Tzimisces, in the year 6477
[969], Ol'ga passed away, and in the year 6478 [970], during the
reign of the same emperor, Sviatoslav appointed Iaropolk to Kiev,
Oleg over the Drevlians, and Vladimir to Novgorod.

In the year 6479/971. Sviatoslav arrived at Preslav but the Bulgars
prepared themselves for a siege in the city. The Bulgarians made a
sally to fight [the troops of] Sviatoslav and there was a great battle,
and the Bulgarians almost overcame them; but Sviatoslav said to his
warriors, "Perhaps we are supposed to die here; but oh! my brothers
and my host! let us behave as men!" And toward evening Sviatoslav
won the battle and stormed the city with lances, saying, "This will be
my city!" And he sent his envoys to the Greeks, telling them, "I want
to campaign against you and take your city [Constantinople], just as I

---

64. A more detailed account of this campaign can be found further
under the year 971 A.D.

971 took this one." But the Greeks told him, "We do not want to fight you; rather, accept tribute for yourself and your troops, and tell us how many there are of you, and then we will pay you according to the number of heads." So the Greeks decided, wanting to deceive the Russians because Greeks are deceitful to this day.

And Sviatoslav said, "There are twenty thousand of us." And in this way he added another ten thousand to his army.[65] And Sviatoslav marched against the Greeks, the Greeks marched against the Russians. When the Russians saw such a great multitude of warriors they were greatly afrighted; but Sviatoslav prevailed upon them, "Oh, my men! We have nowhere to go. Willing or not, we must fight them. Let us not cover the Russian land with shame but, rather, let us leave our bones here because those who died [on the battlefield] will never be covered with shame. But if we run away, then we will be covered with shame. No, we should not retreat; therefore, let us fight staunchly and I will march before you. If my head falls, then look to yourselves." And the warriors said, "Prince! Wheresoever your head should fall, there ours will likewise fall."[66] And the Russians prepared themselves for the fight and the Greeks likewise prepared themselves against them, and the two armies engaged in battle. The Russians moved to the onset and there was a fierce fight which Sviatoslav won, and the Greeks fled. Then Sviatoslav marched against the city [of Constantinople] campaigning and destroying the fortress, which stands empty to this day. The Emperor summoned his lords into the palace and told them, "What should we do? We cannot resist him." And the lords decided, "Emperor! Send them gifts. Let us test him, whether he does not like gold and brocade." And they sent him gold and brocade, and a very wise man, telling him, "Watch his eyes and his face and his expression." The envoy took the gifts and went to Sviatoslav. When Sviatoslav was told that the Greeks had come with reverence, Sviatoslav said, "Let them approach." And they were brought to him. This envoy, approaching, bowed to him and placed before him the gold and the brocade, and Sviatoslav said to his pages, without looking [at the

---

65. There were thirty-eight thousand soldiers in the Byzantine army. It was still about four times stronger than Sviatoslav's army.

66. The Greek historian, Leo the Deacon, quotes another battle harangue of Sviatoslav's which very much resembles this one in the Russian chronicles.

gifts], "Take whatsoever you want." And they took it. Seeing this, the **971** Imperial envoy returned to the Emperor, who again summoned his magnates and courtiers. They were told, "When he arrived he did not look at the gifts but just ordered his pages to take them away." One of those who had been summoned to the Emperor said, "Test him again. Send him military weaponry." And the Emperor obeyed him and sent Sviatoslav swords and other weapons. When the Imperial envoy brought them to Sviatoslav he took them, became very friendly and ordered that the Emperor be praised and kissed.

The envoy returned to the Emperor and described all that had happened. The magnates decided, "This man should be a very good fighter because he does not care for wealth but accepts and esteems weapons. Let us pay him tribute." And the Emperor sent [his envoys] who had to say the following: "Do not march to the city [of Constantinople]. Accept tribute from us, whatsoever you want." Sviatoslav drew near to Constantinople and he was given tribute. He even took tribute for those of his warriors who had been killed, saying, "Their families will have it." He took many gifts and returned to Preslav with great glory.

Seeing that he had only a small army, he said to himself, "They will deceive us and kill my troops and me." [He said this] because many people had been killed among his troops, and therefore he told them, "I will return to Russia and bring a larger army." He sent his envoys to the Emperor because the latter was in Dorystolon, and said, "I want to have lasting peace and friendship with you." Hearing this, the Emperor was very glad and with his envoys he sent gifts greater than the previous ones. Sviatoslav accepted the gifts and took counsel with his retinue, saying the following: "If we do not conclude a peace treaty with the Emperor and the Emperor learns we are so few, he will come and besiege us in this city. But the Russian land is far away and the Pechenegs are at war with us, so who will help us? Let us conclude peace with the Emperor because he has given us tribute and it will be sufficient for us. But if he does not pay tribute, then, assembling a larger army, we will again campaign from Russia against Constantinople." His troops liked this speech and sent their best men to the Emperor. In the morning the Emperor summoned them and invited the Russian envoys to speak. They said, "Our Prince says the following: 'I want to have amity with the Greek Emperor, which will be concluded for many future years.'" The

971 Emperor was glad and told his scribe to write the speeches of Sviatoslav in a charter, and Sviatoslav's envoy dictated his speech.

And the scribe began to write what the envoy said: "According to the agreement made under Sviatoslav Igorevich, Grand Prince of Russia, in the presence of his voevoda, Svenel'd, this was written by Theophilos, secretary to John Tzimisces the Greek Emperor, in Dorystolon on June 11th in the fourteenth year of the Indiction. I, Sviatoslav, Prince of Russia, according to my previous pledge, confirm this agreement by my oath. I want to have peace and perfect friendship with all the Greek emperors, with Basil and Constantine, who are the God-inspired Emperors, and with all your people. And so do all Russians want who are under me, the princes and boyars and all Russians, forever and ever. I will not plot or intend to campaign against your country, neither will I gather an army nor send any spy into your country or all lands which are under the Greek dominion. Neither will I do this in the dominion of Chersonesus or in any other cities or in the Bulgarian land. But in case someone else intends to start a war against your land, I will be against him and will fight him. And since I have given my pledge to the Greek Emperor, now, together with me, the boyars and all Russia have done the same, and we will adhere to this agreement. In case, however, some of the aforementioned should not follow this agreement, all of those with me and under my command will be accursed by the gods in whom we believe, by Perun and by Volos, the god of cattle. And we will then become as yellow as gold and be massacred with our own weapons. Let us regard this as true, as we have agreed with you and as has been written in this charter and sealed with our seals."

Sviatoslav went [by way of the Black Sea and the Dnieper] to the cataracts, and Svenel'd, his voevoda, told him, "Prince! Let us not go by boat. Let us circle 'round on horseback because the Pechenegs are camped near the cataracts." Sviatoslav, though, did not heed him and proceeded by boat; but the people of Preslav sent their [agents] to the Pechenegs, saying the following: "Prince Sviatoslav is marching against you toward Russia. He has received great wealth from the Greeks but has a very small army." When the Pechenegs learned this they occupied [the banks of the Dnieper] near the cataracts, and when Sviatoslav reached the cataracts he was unable to pass through them. And so he remained over the winter in the

Beloberezh'e.⁶⁷ But they [Sviatoslav's troops] did not have enough food and there was a great famine among them. Even a horse head was sold for as much as half a grivna, and Sviatoslav had to pass the winter there. When spring of the year 6480 [972] arrived, Sviatoslav marched toward the cataracts but he was attacked by Kuria, the Pecheneg prince, who killed Sviatoslav. He took his head and made out of his skull a gold-encrusted cup out of which he drank. Svenel'd, however, came to Kiev, to Iaropolk, and reported everything to him. And there were altogether twenty-eight years of the reign of Sviatoslav.⁶⁸

971

67. *Beloberezh'e:* the shore of the Black Sea near the Dnieper.

68. In the Byzantine chronicle we find a more detailed and realistic account of Sviatoslav's campaigns in Bulgaria, where he first went in 968 or 969 during the reign of Nicephorus Phocas, and not in 967, as mentioned in *Nik.* and *Laur.* He returned to Bulgaria in late summer, 969, landing near the Danube delta. Soon after he stormed the Bulgarian capital, Preslav, and then, moving rapidly, crossed the Balkan range and in spring, 970, captured Adrianople, some hundred miles distant from Constantinople. He did not press his advantage and proceeded no further. Tzimisces, who became emperor after Phocas' assassination, was able to counter the Russians only in the fall of 970, when his general, Bardas Scleros, inflicted a defeat on part of Sviatoslav's army. The latter recrossed the Balkans and remained in northern Bulgaria. On March 28, 971, Tzimisces sent a fleet of three hundred ships into the Black Sea and the Danube in order to attack Sviatoslav from the north. On Good Friday, 971, Preslav fell to the Greeks, and Sviatoslav retreated to Dorystolon, now Silistria, on the Danube, where Tzimisces besieged him. On July 22 Sviatoslav laid down his arms and only then—not on July 11—signed a treaty with Tzimisces. The text of the treaty in the *Prim. Chron.* and in *Nik.* was probably only a preamble to it. After meeting Tzimisces, Sviatoslav left for Russia on July 24. Leo the Deacon, a Byzantine chronicler who witnessed the meeting between Tzimisces and Sviatoslav, gives a detailed description of the Prince, which is actually the earliest exact description of a Russian ruler:

"Sviatoslav came to the meeting place on the Danube by boat, rowing just as the other oarsmen. He was of average size, had a flat nose, blue eyes, heavy eyebrows, was shaven and had a long, shaggy mustache. His head was shaven except for a tuft of hair hanging on each side, which denoted his noble lineage. His neck was very thick, his chest very wide, and the other features of his body were comely. His appearance was quite somber and fierce. In one ear was an earring adorned with a ruby and two pearls. His white shirt distinguished him from the other Russians only by its extreme cleanliness . . . After he spoke with the Emperor, all the time sitting on the bench of his boat, he recrossed the river." (Lev Diakon, *Istoriia*, SPb, 1820,

973 THE BEGINNING OF THE REIGN OF IAROPOLK

In the year 6481/973. Iaropolk began to reign in Kiev in place of his father, Sviatoslav, and he reigned over all [lands] in the same way as his father and his grandfather.

In the year 6483/975. The son of Svenel'd, named Liut, who liked hunting, left Kiev in order to hunt beasts in the forests. Prince [Oleg, who ruled over the Drevlians] saw him and asked, "Who are you?" The other answered, "I am the son of Svenel'd." Oleg came closer and killed him because Oleg was also hunting there. Since that time there was hatred between them, Iaropolk and Oleg. Svenel'd always told Iaropolk, "You should fight against your brother and take over his dominion," because he wanted to have revenge for his son.

In the year 6485/977. Iaropolk marched against Oleg, his brother, into the land of the Drevlians, and Oleg marched against him; and they prepared for battle, and the armies fought and there was a fierce massacre. Iaropolk defeated Oleg. Oleg tried to escape with his warriors into the city called Vruch.[69] There was a bridge over the moat leading to the city gate and they squeezed and pushed each other into the moat, and so they pushed Oleg from the bridge into the moat, and many people fell on him. People and horses trampled him. When Iaropolk entered Oleg's city to take over the power there, he sent people looking for his brother. They searched but could not find him. Then one Drevlian said, "Yesterday I saw him pushed from the bridge into the moat." Iaropolk sent to look for him. They pulled corpses from the moat from dawn till dusk—the entire day, so to say; and the next day at the ninth hour they found his corpse among the dead bodies in the moat, and they brought him and laid him on a carpet. Iaropolk came to his body and wept bitterly over it, exclaiming, "Oh, my dear brother, what a misfortune! Better, I were dead and you alive. And all this was wreaked by the cunning deeds of Satan." He turned toward Svenel'd, saying, "Do you see this? You wished this and you achieved it." He buried him in a place near the city called Vruch, and his grave remains there to this day. And Iaropolk seized the rule [over the Drevlians]. Iaropolk had a Greek wife who was previously a nun. She had been brought [from

---

97. See also Brehier, 174-175; Vasiliev, I, 319.) This description leads one to believe that Sviatoslav looked like a Slav, perhaps with some Finnic blood, rather than a Varangian.

69. Now Ovruch in Volynia.

Bulgaria] by his father, Sviatoslav, who married her to Iaropolk **978** because of the beauty of her face. When Vladimir heard in Novgorod that Iaropolk had killed Oleg, he became frightened and escaped beyond the [Baltic] sea. Iaropolk assigned his posadniks to Novgorod and became the only ruler in Russia, in the same way as his father and his grandfather.

In the year 6486/978. Iaropolk defeated the Pechenegs and imposed a tribute on them.[70]

In the year 6487/979. The Pecheneg Prince Ildei came to Iaropolk and petitioned to be accepted in his service. Iaropolk accepted him and gave him towns and districts and held him in great honor. The same year ambassadors came to Iaropolk from the Byzantine emperor and made a [treaty] of peace and love with him. They came to him on account of tribute in the same way as they had to his father and his grandfather. The same year an envoy came to Iaropolk from the Pope of Rome.

PORTENT.

The same year there were portents on the moon, on the sun and on the stars, and there was a great and terrifying thunder with strong winds and a tornado. There was much harm done to people, to cattle and to the animals in the forest and in the prairie.[71]

In the year 6488/980. Vladimir returned to Novgorod with the Varangians and took the city. He sent away the namestniks of Iaropolk, saying, "Go and tell my older brother, Iaropolk: 'Your younger brother, Vladimir, is marching against you. Be ready for battle.'"

When Iaropolk heard this from his younger brother, Vladimir, he became grieved and began to assemble numerous warriors because he, himself, was very brave. But his voevoda, Blud, told him, "Your younger brother, Vladimir, cannot fight against you because a tomtit cannot fight an eagle. Don't be anxious and do not fear him. Make haste to gather your troops." Blud said this deceitfully to his lord, Iaropolk, because he was flattered and corrupted by

---

70. This entry of A.D. 978 is in neither the *Laur.*, *Hyp.* nor the *Novgorodian* chronicles.

71. This entire entry under A.D. 979 is to be found neither in *Laur.* nor *Hyp.* nor *Novg.*

980 Vladimir.[72]

THE REIGN OF VLADIMIR IN NOVGOROD [AND WAR WITH IAROPOLK]

Vladimir settled in Novgorod and reigned there. He sent an envoy to Rogvold, prince of Polotsk, to tell him the following: "I want to marry your daughter." The latter asked his daughter, "Do you want to marry Vladimir?" She answered, "I don't want to remove the boots of the son of a slave; but I want to marry Iaropolk." This Rogvold came from beyond the seas and reigned in Polotsk, while Tur reigned in Turov—and from hence descend the people of Turov. The pages approached Vladimir and told him the entire speech of Rogneda, daughter of Rogvold, Prince of Polotsk. Vladimir, however, assembled many troops: Varangians, Slovens, Chud and Krivichs, and marched against Rogvold. At that time Rogneda intended to marry Iaropolk; but Vladimir came to Polotsk and killed Rogvold and his two sons, and he took his daughter, Rogneda, as his wife.[73]

From thence he marched with numerous troops against his brother, Iaropolk, who was in Kiev; but Iaropolk was unprepared to fight Vladimir. He prepared for siege in Kiev, together with his people and his voevoda, Blud. Vladimir, who camped at Dorogozhich, fortified himself between Dorogozhich and Kapich, and the moat of these fortifications remains to this day. Then Vladimir sent his [agents] to Blud, Iaropolk's voevoda, cunningly saying, "You must accept me. In case I kill my brother, Iaropolk, you will be my favorite and you will be in the place of my father, and you will be greatly honored by me. I did not start the fight among my brothers but he did, and I became frightened; therefore I marched against him." Blud answered Vladimir's envoys, "I will help you and will be your friend."

Oh, evil human deceit! One accepts honor and gifts from his own prince and then tries to destroy him. Worse than those people are [only] the devils: indeed, Blud betrayed his prince after receiving much honor from him, and he was responsible for his blood. This

---

72. This last paragraph can be found only in the *Nik. Codex.* It appears in neither *Hyp., Laur.* nor *Novg.*

73. A more detailed version of this same story can be found in *Nik.* under the year 1128.

Blud was besieged in the city together with Iaropolk but he sent to **980**
Vladimir suggesting him to attack the city with his army because he
intended to kill his own lord, Iaropolk. But he was unable to kill him,
and thinking slyly he suggested to him not to make sallies from the
city in order to fight [Vladimir]. Blud told Iaropolk, "The people of
Kiev send [tidings] continually to Vladimir, telling him, 'Storm the
city and we will turn over Iaropolk to you.' Listen to me, my Prince,
and escape from the city."

Iaropolk followed his advice, escaped from the city and fortified
himself in the fortress of Rodnia at the mouth of the river Ros'.
Thereafter Vladimir entered the city of Kiev and from thence
marched to the fortress of Rodnia and besieged Iaropolk in Rodnia.
And there was great famine there, and till now there is the saying,
"Misery as in Rodnia." Then Blud said to Iaropolk, "Do you see how
many troops your brother has? We are unable to defeat them. Make
peace with your brother." He said this deceitfully. Iaropolk replied,
"So be it." Thereafter, Blud sent [his men] to Vladimir, saying the
following, "Now my plot has been accomplished. When I bring
Iaropolk to you, command that he be killed." Hearing this, Vladimir
went to his father's castle [of Rodnia] about which we spoke before;
he entered it with his troops and his retinue. Then Blud said to
Iaropolk, "Go to your brother and tell him, 'Whatever you give me, I
will accept.'" Iaropolk went but a certain Variazhko told him,
"Don't go thither, Prince, for they will kill you. Better, flee to the
Pechenegs and bring many of their warriors." But Iaropolk did not
heed him and came to his brother, Vladimir, and when he entered
through the door two Varangians stabbed him in the breast with
their swords. Blud, meanwhile, closed the door and did not permit
anyone [of Iaropolk's people] to enter, and in such a way was Iaropolk killed. Variazhko, seeing that Iaropolk was killed, fled from
the court to the Pechenegs and for a long while fought together
with the Pechenegs against Vladimir, until the latter forced him to
pledge [his fealty] to him.

Vladimir took to wife the Greek widow of his brother, although
she was pregnant and it was Sviatopolk [later called the Accursed]
who was born from her.

From a sinful root the fruit is always evil, because his
[Sviatopolk's] mother had been a nun, and then Vladimir took her
without wedding her. He was the fruit of adultery and therefore

980 Vladimir did not like him because he was at the same time brother [actually, uncle] and father to him.

Thereafter the Varangians said to Vladimir, "The city is ours. We have taken it and want to have a tribute from them of two grivna from each man." Vladimir, however, answered them, "Wait a month until they get the kunas." They waited a month but he did not give them anything, and the Vargangians said, "You have cheated us; but now show us the way to the Greeks." And he told them, "Go!" He sent them to the Greeks but first he selected from among them good, brave and wise men and dispersed them among his cities. The others went to Greece to the Imperial City. Vladimir, however, sent his envoys to the Emperor, ahead of them, saying, "The Varangians are coming to you. You should not keep them in the City so as to prevent them from doing much evil in the City as they did here. You should, rather, send them to various places, and not let a single one into the City."

THE BEGINNING OF THE REIGN OF VLADIMIR IN KIEV

And Vladimir began to reign alone in Kiev. On the hill outside his palace he placed several idols: Perun, who was made of wood but had a silver head and a golden moustache; and he also placed other idols: Khors, Dazh'bog, Stribog, Simargl and Mokosh.[74] And the people made sacrifices to them, called them gods and would bring their sons and daughters to them to be sacrificed; and Vladimir worshipped them. All the people made sacrifices, considering them gods, and in this way they defiled the whole land and this hill with such worship. The Most Blessed God, however, does not want the [spiritual] death of sinners. On the same spot there was [subsequently] erected the Church of St. Basil, about which we will speak later. Vladimir appointed his uncle, Dobrynia, to Novgorod; and when Dobrynia came to Novgorod he put an idol of Perun above the Volkhov river, and the people of Novgorod sacrificed to him as if he were God.

Vladimir was obsessed by lust for women, and he had the following wives: Rogneda, whom he assigned to [the city] Lybed',

---

74. Perun was god of thunder and lightning; Khors and Dazh'bog—gods of sun and well-being; Stribog—god of winds. The attributes of gods Simargl and Mokosh are unclear.

where is now the town of Peredslavino; and from her were born four **981** sons, Iziaslav, Mstislav, Iaroslav, Vsevolod, and two daughters. From the Greek woman he had Sviatopolk; from the Czech woman he had Vysheslav; and from another one he had Sviatoslav and Mstislav; and from the Bulgarian woman, Boris and Gleb. In Vyzhgorod he had three hundred concubines and three hundred in Belogorod and three hundred in the fortress of Rodnia, and two hundred in the village of Berestovo, which is called Berestovo even now. He could never satisfy his lust and therefore he would bring to his place the wives of other husbands and would violate virgins. He was given to women in the same way as Solomon.

HOW MANY WOMEN DID SOLOMON HAVE?

Solomon had seven hundred wives, three hundred concubines and five hundred others. He was very wise but because he loved women he finally perished. This one, Vladimir, however, was not enlightened but later he found the way of salvation. Great is Our Lord and Great is His Power and His Wisdom is beyond limits.

In the year 6489/981. Vladimir campaigned against the Poles and conquered their cities, Peremyshl', Cherven' and other towns which are Russian. He also defeated the Viatichs and imposed a tax on every plough just as his father had done.

In the year 6490/982. The Viatichs started fighting and Vladimir marched against them, defeating them for the second time.

In the year 6491/983. Vladimir marched against the Iatvags, defeated them and took over their land.[75]

When he returned to Kiev he wanted, together with his people, to sacrifice to his idols. The elders and boyars decided, "Let us cast lots for a youth or virgin, and on whomsoever the lot falls, that one will be sacrificed to the gods." There lived [in Kiev] a Varangian who had his home there where now is the Church of the Holy Mother of God which was later built by Vladimir. This Varangian came from the Greeks with his son, Ivan, and resided in Kiev, and he secretly confessed the Christian faith. He had a young son who had a very handsome body and soul, and the lot fell on him because of the devil's cunning. The devil could not stand it, he had power over all

---

75. The Iatvags were a Lithuanian tribe then living in present southern Belorussia.

983 [the pagans], while this one was as a thorn in his heart. Therefore the accursed one tried to destroy him and incited the people against him.

Then those who were sent to him [to the Varangian] told him, "The lot has fallen on your son because our gods want to take him for themselves; and we will make a sacrifice to the gods." But the Varangian answered, "Your gods are no gods but just pieces of soulless wood. Today they exist but tomorrow morning they may rot away. They do not eat, do not drink, do not speak and are made by hands out of wood with an axe and a knife. There is just One God in the Heavens, and the Greeks celebrate services to Him and worship Him because He created the heavens, the earth, the stars, the sun, the moon, and man, and He let men live on earth. And what have your gods done? They, themselves, were made. I will not give my son to these devils."

Those who were sent to him reported this to the people, and then the people took up weapons, went to his place and surrounded his place. He was standing on the porch with his son and they told him, "Give us your son. We will sacrifice him to the gods." And he answered, "In case they are gods, then they should send one god and take my son. So why do you want him?" But the people started shouting and they cut away the foundation under the porch, and so they were killed.

At that time the people were not enlightened [in the Christian faith] and were pagan. The devil rejoiced because he was unaware that his own destruction was already nigh. He tried to destroy Christian people but he was finally chased away by the Venerable Cross into other lands. The accursed one thinks in the following manner: "My dwelling is there where the Apostles did not teach and where the Prophets did not preach." They did not know the Prophet, who said, "And I will call those mine who are not yet mine." And about the Apostles it was said, "Their sermons will go over the entire earth and will be proclaimed in all the ends of the universe." Although the Apostles were not here personally, their teaching spread over the entire universe, as well as in the churches, in the same manner as a trumpet trumpets. With their teaching we defeat the inimical evil and we trample it with our feet. But these two received the Crown of Heaven from Christ God just as the martyrs and righteous men.

In the year 6492/984. Vladimir marched against the Radimichs. **984**
He had a voevoda named Volchii Khvost ["Wolf's Tail"]. Vladimir
sent Volchii Khvost forward and the latter met the Radimichs on the
river Peshchan, and defeated them. Now the Russians vex the
Radimichs by saying, "The people of Peshchan ran away from the
Wolf's Tail!" The origin of these Radimichs was in Poland but they
came hither [to our land] and paid tribute to Russians, and to this
day they engage in carting.

In the year 6493/985. Vladimir campaigned against the Bulgars
of the Niz.[76] And he went thither by boat together with his uncle,
Dobrynia. The Torks came on horseback and on the way they
defeated the Bulgars.[77] Thereafter Dovrynia told Vladimir, "I
looked at the prisoners, and all of them had on boots. These will not
pay us any tribute [because they are too clever]. Let us look for
people wearing bark shoes." Vladimir made peace with the Bulgars
and they pledged to each other. The Bulgars said, "In case there will
be no peace preserved between us, then we may pay tribute—but
only in the case that stone starts to float and the hops sink in water.[78]
Then Vladimir returned to Kiev.

SARACENS.

In the year 6494/986. The Saracens of the Moslem faith came to
Vladimir, saying, "Prince! You are wise and intelligent but you are
unaware of our law. Believe in our law and worship Muhammed."[79]
Vladimir inquired about their faith and did not like it.

GERMANS.

Thereafter the Germans came from Rome from the Pope,
saying, "Our Great Pope says all of us are the creation of One God
and all people descend from the same Adam, and your land is the
same as our land but your faith is dark and badsmelling, while our

---

76. The *Niz* was a lowland, actually, the land on the mid-Volga.

77. Here are meant the Moslem Turkic Bulgars on the upper Volga near Kazan', who were active merchant people engaged in trade between Russia and the Moslem Middle East. The Torks were a small Turkic tribe usually allied with the Russians against other nomads.

78. *Laur.* text is slightly different.

79. In the *Hyp.* and *Laur.* chronicles not the Saracens but the Moslem Volga Bulgars are mentioned.

986 faith is light. We celebrate the church services and we worship Lord God Almighty, Jesus Christ, Who created the heavens and earth and all creatures, seen and unseen." Vladimir inquired, "And what are your Commandments?" And they said, "Prayer, alms and fasting, as much as possible. And those who eat and drink or do something else do all by the grace of God, and so we were taught by the Holy Apostles, Peter and Paul, and others." And Vladimir told them, "Return home. Our forefathers did not want to accept this."

KHAZAR JEWS.

Khazar Jews heard about these discussions and came to Vladimir, saying, "We have heard that the Moslem Bulgars came to you, and then the Christians came, and they taught you about their faiths. But the Christians believe in One Whom we crucified, and we believe only in One God—of Abraham, Isaac and Jacob." And Vladimir asked, "And what is your law?" They answered, "To be circumcised, not to eat pork, not to eat hare meat and to observe the Sabbath."[80] And Vladimir said, "Where is your land?" They answered, "In Jerusalem." He asked, "Do you live there?" The Jews responded, "God became wrathful with our forefathers and He scattered us into various lands because of our sins, and our land was given over to the Christians." And then Vladimir said, "And you try to teach other people? You, yourselves, were rejected by God and were scattered. If God liked your law and you, you would not be scattered in foreign lands. How can you think that we would accept such an evil [faith]?"

GREEKS.

Then the Greeks sent Vladimir a philosopher who said, "We have heard that the Saracens came to you, trying to convince you to accept their faith, but their faith defiles the heavens and the earth because they are accursed more than any other people, and they follow the example of Sodom and Gomorrah. On the latter God let fall burning stones and flooded them and they were drowned and perished. In the same way these Saracens must expect the day of

---

80. The Khazars, who had a state on the lower Volga, were pagan, Moslem, Christian and Jewish. Their dynasty, however, embraced the Mosaic religion.

their ruin when God comes to judge on earth, and He will destroy all those whose deeds are unlawful."   **986**

Thereafter the philosopher said, "We also have heard that people from Rome, from the Pope, came to you to teach you about their faith, but their faith is somewhat different from ours. They celebrate [Communion] with wafers which were not given by God. God ordered to celebrate [Communion] with bread, and gave it to the Apostles, taking the bread and saying, 'This is My Body broken for you.' And then He took a cup, saying, 'This is My Blood of the New Testament.' And those who do not do thus do not follow the true faith."

Then Vladimir said, "The Jews came to me saying that the Germans and the Greeks believe in One God Whom they crucified."

The philosopher answered, "Verily, we believe, and it was prophesied by God's Prophets that He should be born from an Immaculate Virgin, should be crucified, should be buried and should be resurrected on the third day, and should be taken into Heaven. But they, the Jews, killed those Prophets and others they sawed with wooden saws. And when this Prophecy was fulfilled and He came down to earth and by His Own Will accepted crucifixion, and He was resurrected and ascended into Heaven, then [God] expected that they [the Jews] should repent within forty and six years. But they did not repent, and God sent the Romans against them, and they [the Romans] went thither and destroyed their cities and scattered them throughout all lands." Then Vladimir said, "Why did God come to earth and accept such a passion?" The philosopher said, if you want to hear about it, I will start from the very beginning, why God came down to earth." Vladimir promised to listen carefully and the philosopher began to speak.

[THE SPEECH OF THE PHILOSOPHER
ABOUT THE CHRISTIAN FAITH.][81]

In the beginning on the first day God created Heaven and Earth. The second day He created the land which is among the waters. The same day He divided the waters and half of them were

---

81. The text of this speech in *Nik.* differs in many places from that found in the *Hyp., Laur.* and *I Novgorodian* chronicles. As those texts, in its general line it follows the books of the Bible but is contaminated by details taken from the *Apocrypha* and from some Byzantine chronicles, particularly

986 spread above the land and half below the land. The third day were created the seas, rivers, brooks, lakes and seas. The fourth day were created the sun, moon and stars with which God adorned the Heavens. The first of the angels who was in the rank of Archangel saw all this and he became proud and said, "I will go upon the earth and will take over the earth, and I will build my throne in the clouds of the north and then I will be equal to the Highest." But for this pride God cast him from the Heavens with all those who were under him and in his place put [the Archangel] Michael. The name of the enemy was Satanail, and he broke away from the original glory and called himself God's enemy. On the fifth day God created the whales, fish, reptiles and the feathered birds. On the sixth day God created the beasts, cattle and serpents of the earth. And then God created man, and he was created in the Image of God. On the seventh day God rested from his labor and this day was the Sabbath. And then God planted Paradise on the East in Eden and He brought thither the man whom he had created, and He instructed him to eat from all the fruit trees which were in Paradise but not to eat from one, which would provide him with the understanding of Good and Evil. And so Adam was in Paradise and saw God and the angels who glorified Him. Then God cast sleep upon Adam and Adam slept. Then God took a rib from Adam and created his helper, his wife, and He brought her to Adam and Adam said, "This is the bone of my bones, the flesh of my flesh, and she will be called my wife." And then Adam gave names to the beasts, to the birds and to the reptiles, and the angels, themselves, told him their names. And God subdued unto Adam all the animals and cattle and he possessed all of them, and they obeyed him.

The devil saw how God honored the man and became envious and assumed the appearance of a serpent, and came to Eve and told her, "Why don't you eat from the tree which is in the midst of Paradise?" And Eve said to the serpent, "God commanded us, 'You

Harmatolos' work. In the authoritative opinion of D. Likhachev, the latest and most precise commentator on the *Primary Chronicle*, although this speech was probably compiled in Russia, it resembles some Byzantine, Bulgarian and even Arab works of the same type. *Prim. Chron.* commentaries by Likhachev, II, 330-2. Likhachev believes that this speech is the earliest Russian literary work compiled in the 990's. Likhachev, D.S., *Velikoe nasledie,* Moscow, 1975, pp. 10-11.

may eat from every tree which is in Paradise but you should not eat from the one which is in the middle of Paradise. If you do, you will die the death.'" The serpent said to the woman, "You will not die the death. God knew that the day when you eat from it your eyes will be opened and you will be as God and you will know about Good and Evil." The woman saw that the fruit of the tree was good to eat and pleasant to see and she took a fruit and ate it, and gave of it to her husband and he ate, and their eyes were opened and they understood they were naked. Thereafter they sewed fig leaves together and made themselves girdles.

986

And God said to Adam, "The earth will be accursed from your deeds and you will be in grief all the days of your life." And then God said, "If you had not stretched your hand in order to take the fruit of the Tree of life, you would have lived forever." And God drove Adam from Paradise, telling him, "Now you must labor on earth because you were made from it." And Adam sat down across from Paradise and wept and shed tears, and labored on the land, and God cursed the earth. And Satan was full of joy because the earth was accursed. This was the first fall of man from the angelic life.

Adam begot Cain and Abel, and Cain was a ploughman and Abel was a shepherd. Cain brought a sacrifice to God from the fruits of the earth and God did not accept his gifts; but Abel brought his first lamb and God accepted the gift of Abel. Then Satan entered into Cain and incited Cain to kill Abel. Cain said to Abel, "Let us go together into the fields," and Abel followed him. And when they went thither Cain wanted to kill Abel but he did not know how to kill. Satan, however, told him, "Take a stone and hit him on the head," and he killed him. And God asked Cain, "Where is your brother, Abel?" And that one said, "Am I my brother's keeper?" And God said to Cain, "Your brother's blood cries out to me, and you will groan and tremble unto the end of the days of your life."

Adam and Eve wept bitterly but the devil rejoiced and said, "So it is. God created him and commanded him and I made him break away from God. And now I have made them weep." And he bewailed Abel for one year and did not know what to do with his body because he did not know how to bury him. Then on the command of God two small birds flew in. One of them died and the other made a hole for it and buried it there. When Adam and Eve saw this they dug a pit and put down Abel and buried him, lamenting. And Adam lived for two hundred thirty years and he begot Seth and two daughters. One of them became the wife of Cain and the other the wife of Seth, and from them man multiplied and his numbers grew on earth. And they did not know the One Who created them and they were filled with vice and all manner of evil and murder and envy, and the people lived as animals.

There was only one just man among these people. This was Noah, who begat three sons: Shem, Ham and Japeth. And Lord God said, "My spirit should not remain in those people because they are just flesh." And he added, "I will flood all of them from man to the cattle."

ABOUT THE ARK.

Lord God told Noah, "Build an ark out of square logs and make windows in the ark, and cover it with pitch inside and with tar outside. And so the ark will be built [to the following specifications]: three hundred cubits long, fifty cubits wide and thirty cubits high. And in this way thou wilst build the ark, and makest a roof and makest a door on the sides, and the floor should be double. And then I will bring a flood upon the earth which will destroy all creatures under heaven who have the spirit of life." The building of the ark took a hundred years, and Noah warned the people that there would be a flood on the earth: "Repent your hatred." But they only laughed at him. When Noah built the ark Lord God told him, "Get into the ark with your wife, your sons and the wives of your sons; and take with you seven male and seven female of pure animals, and two males and two females of impure animals." And Noah took them into the ark as he was told by God.

And God brought a flood upon the earth, and all creatures were flooded, while the ark floated on the water. When the water receeded, Noah, his sons and their wives left the ark and from them [human beings] multiplied on the earth. And the people made a unanimous decision, saying: "Let us build a tower as high as heaven." And they started building it and the elder was Nevrod. But God said, "The people have multiplied but their intentions are vain." And God descended to destroy the tower and divided [the human race] into seventy tongues and two. The language of Adam was not taken away, however, from Eber because he was the only one who did not participate in this madness and because he said, "If God wanted men to build such a tower He would have spoken His word, because it was He Who created the heavens, the earth and the sea, and all things visible and invisible." And for this reason [his tongue] did not change—and from him are descended the Jews.[82]

[The rest of the men] became divided into seventy and one tongues, and they scattered into [various] lands, and each of them developed his own customs; and at the instigation of the devil they worshipped the forests, wells and the rivers, but did not know God.

And from Adam to the flood were 2,240 and two years; and from the flood to the divisions of the tongues, 520 and 9 years; and thereafter the devil led men to a greater temptation, and they began to make idols: some of wood, others of copper, yet others of gold, silver or marble. And they worshipped them and would bring them their daughters and sons to be sacrificed before them; and the entire earth was defiled. The headman of the idol worship was Serug, who made idols after the names of dead men, some of whom were kings and some were heroes, some were magicians and some adulterous women. This Serug begat Terah, and Terah begat three sons: Abraham, Nahor and Haran.[83]

Terah made idols as he had learned from his father; but Abraham recovered his reason, looked at heaven and saw the sun, the moon and the stars, and he said, "Verily, there is a God and those [idols] made by my father only deceive men." And Abraham said to himself, "I will test my father's gods," and he said to his father, "Father! Why do you deceive men by making wooden idols? God is the One Who created the heaven and earth." And Abraham took fire and set fire unto the temple with the idols. Haran, Abraham's brother, seeing this and being a worshipper of the idols, tried to save them but he burned himself in the presence of his father. Prior to this happening sons had never died before their fathers but beginning with this case sons would die before their fathers.

God loved Abraham, and God said to him, "Leave this land and the house of your father and go to the land which I will show you. And I shall make of thee a great nation and all the generations on earth will bless thee."

---

82. There is no name of Nevrod (Nevrot in *Nik.*) in *Gen.* Neither is there in *Gen.* the name of Eber. This last name was taken from the *Chronicle* by Harmatolos, *Prim. Chr.*, Vol. II, p. 333.

83. Compare *Gen.* 11:22-25.

986 And Abraham did as he was told by God; and Abraham took the son of his brother because he was his nephew and his brother-in-law, because Abraham married Sarah, his brother's daughter; and he came to a large oak in the land of Canaan. And God told to Abraham, "Unto thy seed will I give this land."[84] And Abraham bowed down to God. He was seventy and five years old when he left the land of Haran. But Sarah was barren because she was ill of barrenness, and Sarah said to Abraham, "Go and have my handmaid," and she took Hagar and gave her to Abraham; and Abraham went in unto Hagar, and Hagar conceived and bore a son, and Abraham named him Ishmael. But thereafter Sarah also conceived and bore a son and named him Isaac. And God told Abraham to circumcise the youth, and Abraham circumcised him on the eighth day. And God loved Abraham and his people, and called them His people, and to distinguish them from the other tongues he called them His own people. This Isaac grew up and Abraham lived one hundred seventy and five years, and he died and was buried.

Isaac lived sixty years and begat two sons, Esau and Jacob. Esau was cunning and Jacob was righteous, and he worked for his uncle Laban for fourteen years; and [Laban] gave him [as wives] two sisters, [his daughters] Leah and Rachel, and as a dowry two handmaids. From Leah were born Reuben, Simeon, Levi, Judah, Issachar and Zebulon. And from Rachel's handmaid were born Zebulon, Gad and Asser; and from Leah's handmaid were born Dan and Naphtali; and from Rachel, Joseph and Benjamin. And from them the Jews multiplied.[85]

When Jacob went to Egypt he was one hundred and thirty years old, and with him came seventy and five persons, and he lived in Egypt seventeen years and died, and his race worked as slaves in Egypt for four hundred years. During these years the Jews prospered and multiplied, but the Egyptians burdened them with labor. And at that time there was born a child to the Jews in Egypt, and the magicians told the Egyptian king that this newborn child would intend to destroy Egypt. And at once the king commanded that all newborn Jewish children be drowned in the river; but Moses'

---

84. Compare *Gen.* 11:31 and 15:7.

85. According to *Gen.* 35:23-26, Rachel's handmaid, Bilhah, bore Dan and Naphtali; Leah's handmaid, Zilpah, bore Gad and Asher.

mother, who was afraid that he would be destroyed, took the infant, put it in a box and left it in the meadow near the river. At that time Thermuthi, Pharoah's daughter, came down to the river to bathe and, seeing the crying child, she took him up out of compassion and named him Moses, although his previous name was Nehemia. It was a beautiful child, and she nourished him, and when the child was four years old the Pharoah's daughter brought him to her father. When the Pharoah saw him he fancied him, and Moses embraced the king around his neck and knocked off the crown from the king's head, and stepped upon it. The magicians saw this and said to the king, "Oh, King! Kill this child, for if you do not kill him he will destroy all Egypt." But the king paid no attention to them and even commanded that no more Jewish children should be killed.[86]

Moses grew to manhood and became a great person in the Pharoah's house. But at that time there was another king, and the nobles hated him. Once Moses killed an Egyptian who was beating a Jew, hid him in the sand, and thereafter he fled to the Midian land, where, wandering in the desert, he learned from the Archangel Gabriel about the creation of the world, the first man, about the flood and the division of the tongues, and how many years men had lived, about the movement of the stars, the dimensions of the land and all wisdom.

And then God appeared to him in a burning bush and God said to him, "I saw the plight of My people who live in Egypt. Thou must go there so as to liberate them from the hands of the Egyptians, and lead them out of that land. Go to the Pharoah, king of Egypt, and tell him, 'Let Israel be free for three days that they may offer a sacrifice to God. And in the case the king will not grant you [this], I will destroy him through My miracles.'" When Moses and Aaron came to the king, he did not pay any attention to them, and God sent ten punishments upon Pharoah and all his people.

The first punishment: He turned the water of the river into blood; the second: toads; the third, mice; the fourth, dog's flies; fifth, the plague of the cattle; sixth, burning boils; seventh, hunger; eighth, locusts; ninth, three days of darkness; tenth, a plague among

---

86. The entire speech of the "Philosopher" and, especially, the story of Moses taken from the *Chronograph* and Harmatolos' *Chronicle*, differ from the *Bible*.

986 the people. These punishments were visited upon them because for ten months they [the Egyptians] killed Jewish children. And when the plague was visited upon the Egyptians, Pharoah told Moses and Aaron, "Go away as soon as possible!" And Moses gathered the Jews together and departed from the Egyptian land. And the Lord led them through the desert to the Red Sea; and preceding them was a pillar of fire in the night, and one of clouds in the day. When Pharoah learned that these people had fled he pursued them, and when he drove them to the sea the Jews, seeing it, murmured against Moses, "We were better off in the Egyptian land. Why have you led us to death?" And Moses called upon God, and the Lord said, "Why callest thou upon me? Smite the sea with a rod." And Moses did so, and the waters were divided for a distance of twelve days' travel; and the sons of Israel went into the sea. Seeing this, Pharoah pursued them, but the sons of Israel went on dry land amidst the sea; and when they were on the shore, the waters came together and flooded Pharoah and all his warriors.

The Lord gave his favor to Israel and they travelled for three days from the sea into the desert, and so they arrived in Marah; there the water was bitter and the people began to murmur against God, but God showed them a tree and Moses put [the wood of this tree] into the water and the water became sweet. Thereafter the people murmured against Moses and Aaron, saying, "We were better off in Egypt because there we ate meat to our fill, onions and bread." And the Lord told Moses, "I have heard the murmuring of Israel's sons," and God let them eat manna to their fill.

And then on the mountain of Sinai the Lord gave Moses the law on the tablets; and Moses came down from the mountain and found an idol in the shape of a calf, which the Israelites worshipped as a god, and he said, "Oh, Israel! Is this thy god that brought us out of Egypt?" And Moses massacred three thousand of them. Thereafter they could not find any water, and the people murmured against Moses and Aaron because they did not have any water; and God said to Moses, "Smite the stone with thy rod." And Moses said to the people, "Should I get water from this stone if I am willing to do it?" And God was wrathful against Moses because they did not glorify or magnify Lord God, and because of these people's murmurings Moses could not enter the promised land. Moses wept bitterly because of their sin toward God. Then God took Moses to the mountain of Nebo,[87] showed him the promised land and told him, **986** "Thou shalt not enter it." And Moses died on the mountain and was buried by Archangel Michael.[88]

The rule [over Israel] was then taken by Joshua, son of Nun, who led Israel into the promised land and who killed all the kings of Canaan and all their forces, and settled Israel's sons in that place. After Joshua's death they had judges: Judah and Simeon, and then fourteen other judges who forgot God and worshipped idols. To punish them God delivered them into the hands of foreigners, and when they repented God pardoned them; but once delivered, they turned back to evil. After those judges there was the priest, Eli; and then Samuel the Prophet judged Israel. But the people told Samuel the Prophet, "Give us a king to rule over us." But this request was evil to him, and God was wroth against Israel; and Samuel prayed to God about this and the Lord told him, "Follow the request of the people. It will not be you who will be rejected; neither have I to reign over them." Samuel repeated the Lord's words to the people, who were asking of him a king: "You ask for a king, but then your wealth will decrease and he will take a tenth of your villages and your vinyards and will give it to slaves and eunuchs; and you will be enslaved, and you will become slaves. Then you will cry to God, but he will not hear you." But the people did not heed him.

Now there was a man from the lineage of Benjamin, whose name was Kish, the son of Abiel, and he had a son whose name was Saul.[89] He had a large body, so strong and handsome as not one among the sons of Israel. Once the asses of Kish became lost and Kish sent his son, Saul, to search for them. He could not find them but a youth told Saul to go to the city and ask Prophet Samuel about the lost asses. When they approached the city Samuel came out to meet them; the day before Saul arrived, the Lord revealed it to Samuel, and the Lord said unto him to anoint Saul to the Kingdom. And Samuel the Prophet commanded all the people to go to [worship] the Lord in Mizpah, saying, "You have forsaken the Lord, Who saved you from all evils, now you ask for a king; therefore, take your place now according to your banners and your

87. *Deut.* 34; in *Nik.* mount of Vam.
88. Not in *Deut.* 34.
89. Abbreviation of *I Sam.* 9:1-2.

986 tribes." And Samuel brought all the tribes of Israel and again asked the Lord, "Is this the man You told me of?" And the Lord answered, "This man remained hidden in the ark," and Samuel brought Saul, placed him before the people and anointed him king. But Saul did not walk in the law of the Lord, and the Lord told Samuel to anoint David secretly to the king: "But do not let Saul know that you anointed David, son of Jesse." And Samuel the Prophet did so and anointed David King of Israel and found favor with God, doing everything according to the command and will of God. God promised David that from his lineage a Saviour would be born. Thus David began to prophesy concerning the incarnation of God: "I bore Thee from my loins before the morning star." He prophesied and reigned for forty years and died. After him reigned his son, Solomon, who built a temple to God and called it the "Holy of Holies." After Solomon, his son, Rehoboam, reigned, and under him the kingdom of the Jews became divided into two: one was [the kingdom of] Jerusalem and the other, of Samaria. In Samaria reigned Jeroboan the son of Nebot, a slave of Solomon's, an apostate; he made two golden calves and set one in Bethel and the other in the hills in Dan.[90] He told the people, "These are the gods of Israel, who delivered you from [the yoke of] Egypt." And the people worshipped them, forgetting the True God. In Jerusalem they also began to forget the True God and worshipped Baal, called the "god of war," who is Ares; and they forgot the God of their forefathers.

Then God started to send them real prophets who began exposing their lawlessness and idol-worship; but they beat the prophets who exposed them. And God was wrathful toward Israel and said, "I shall cast you from Me and I will call other people who will obey Me; and if they sin, I shall not remember their sins!"

So the Lord sent His prophets, saying to them, "Prophesy the rejection of the Jews and the calling of the Gentiles." Hosea was thus the first to prophesy, saying, "I will cause the kingdom of the house of Israel to cease, I will break the bow of Israel, and I will have no more compassion on the house of Israel; but I will cast them off and reject them, saith the Lord, and they shall be as wanderers among the nations." [*Hos.* 1:4-6; 9:17.]

90. *I Kings* 12:2-32. Here, as in other places of the "Speech of the Philosopher," the Biblical text has been drastically shortened and altered.

And Jeremiah said, "If Samuel and Moses arise, I will not have mercy on them." [*Jer.* 15:1.] And then Jeremiah said, "Thus saith the Lord: I have sworn by My Great Name that My Name shall henceforth be mentioned no more by the lips of the Jews." Likewise Ezekiel said, "Thus saith the Lord Adonai: I will scatter thee and the whole remnant of thee to all the winds, for thou hast defiled My sanctuaries with thine abominations; I will reject thee and have no more mercy upon thee." [*Ezek.* 5:10-11, paraphrased.]

And Malachi said, "I have no pleasure in you, saith Jehovah. From the east to the west My Name shall be glorified among the Gentiles. In every place incense shall be offered unto My Name, and a pure offering, for Great is My Name among the Gentiles. Wherefore I will deliver you into exile and to the scorn of all nations." [*Mal.*, 1:10-11; 2:9.] Isaiah the Great said, "Thus saith the Lord: I will stretch out my hand against thee, I will destroy thee and scatter thee, and restore thee no more." [*Isa.* 1:25.] And further, the same prophet said, "I have hated your feasts and your new moons; your Sabbaths I do not accept." [*Isa.* 1:13-14]

Amos the prophet said, "Hear the word of the Lord: I will bring tears upon you; the house of Israel has fallen and was not quick to arise." [*Amos* 5:1-2.] Malachi said, "Thus saith the Lord: I will send upon you a curse, and will curse your blessing; I will destroy it, and it shall not be among you." [*Mal.* 2:2.] Many prophesied of their [Jews'] rejection, and to such prophets God gave His commandment to prophesy the calling of other nations in their stead.

Thus Isaiah called upon them, saying, "Law shall go forth from me, and my judgment is the light of nations. My justice approaches quickly; it shall go forth and in My arm shall the Gentiles hope." [*Isa.* 51:4-6.] Jeremiah said, "Thus saith the Lord: I will establish a new covenant for the house of Judah. I will give covenants for their understanding, and write upon their hearts. I will be their God, and they shall be my people." [Jer. 21:32-34.] Isaiah said, "The old things are passed away, but I declare the new. Before their appearance, it has been revealed unto you. Sing unto the Lord a new song. Those who serve Me shall be called by a new name, which shall be blessed throughout all the earth. My house shall be called a house of prayer for all nations." [*Isa.* 42:9-10; 56:5-7.] The same Isaiah said, "The Lord will show His right arm before all nations, and all the ends of the earth shall see salvation from Our God." [*Isa.* 53:10.]

986

986 And David said, "Praise the Lord, all ye lands, praise Him, all ye people." [*Ps.* 118:1.] Since God so loved His new people, He promised to descend among them Himself, and to appear as a man in the flesh, and to suffer for the sin of Adam. Thus men began to prophesy concerning the Incarnation of God.

First, David said, "And God said unto My Lord: Sit upon My right, until I shall set Thine enemies as a footstool for Thy feet." [*Ps.* 110:1.] And once more, "The Lord said unto me: Thou art My son, this day have I begotten Thee!" [*Ps.* 2:7.] And Isaiah said, "No envoy or messenger, but God, Himself, shall come to save us." [*Isa.* 63:9.] And again, "For unto us a Child is born in Whose arm is authority, and He shall be called the great counsellor of the angels. Great is His might, and of His peace there will be no end." [*Isa.* 9:6 rephrased.] And again, "Behold, a maiden shall conceive, and shall bear a Son, and they shall call His name Emmanuel." [Isa. 7:14.]

Micah said, "But Thou, Bethlehem Ephrathah, which art little among the thousands of Jews, out of thee shall come forth a Ruler to be Prince of Israel, and His going forth is from everlasting. Therefore will He give them up till the time when the mother travails, and the rest of His brethren return to the sons of Israel." [*Mic.* 5:2-3.]

And Jeremiah also said, "This is our God, and no other shall be compared with Him. He has found the way of all wisdom, He has given it to Jacob his youth. Then He appeared on earth and lived with men." And again, "Man exists. But who shall know how God exists or how man dies?" Zechariah said, "They have not heeded My son, and I will not give ear to them, said the Lord." [*Zech.* 7:13.] Hosea said, "Thus saith the Lord: 'My flesh is from them." [*Hos.* 9:12; *Jer.* 17:9.]

Prophesies were likewise prophesied and uttered about His passion. Thus Isaiah said, "Woe unto their souls! For they have done evil unto them, saying, 'Let us kill the righteous man.'" [*Isa.* 3:9-10.] Likewise he said, "Thus saith the Lord: 'I will not resist them or speak against them. I offered my back to wounds and my countenance to blows, and I turned not my face away from them and from spitting.'" [*Isa.* 1:5-6.] Jeremiah said, "Come, let us destroy the tree with the fruit thereof, and cut him off from the land of the living." Moses said of His crucifixion, "Thy life shall hang in doubt before thee." [*Deut.* 28:66.] David said, "Why do the nations rage?"

[*Ps.* 2:1.] And Isaiah said, "He was led like a lamb to the slaughter." **986**
[*Isa.* 53:7.] And Esdras said, "Blessed be the Lord: He stretched out His hands and saved Jerusalem." They spoke also of the resurrection. David said, "Arise up, oh Lord, judge the earth for Thou shalt inherit all the nations." [*Ps.* 84:8.] And likewise, "Them the Lord awakened as one out of sleep," [*Ps.* 78:6.] and also, "Let God arise, let His enemies be scattered." [*Ps.* 68:1.] Likewise, "Arise, oh Jehovah; oh God, lift up Thy hand." [*Ps.* 10:12.] Isaiah said, "The people that walked into the land and the shadow of death, upon you light shall shine." [*Isa.*] And Zechariah said, "In the blood of Thy covenant I have set free Thy prisoners from the pit where there is no water." [*Zech.* 9:11.] Many things were prophesied concerning Him, all of which have been fulfilled.

Vladimir, however, asked the philosopher, "At what time was it fulfilled, and did it really happen? When is it still supposed to happen?"

And he answered him, saying:

All this was fulfilled when God was incarnated. As I said before, when the Jews persecuted the prophets and their kings trespassed the law, God, because of their sins, gave them over to defeat and into captivity, and to be taken to Assyria, where they labored for seventy years. Thereafter they returned to their land and had no kings but they had archpriests, until Herod, who was a foreigner and who reigned over them.

During his reign, in the year five thousand five hundred, Archangel Gabriel was sent by God to the city of Nazareth to the Virgin Mary, who was from the lineage of David, and he told her "Rejoice! Thou who art full of gladness. God is with you." And from these words the Word of God was conceived in her womb and she gave birth to a Son, and she gave Him the name, Jesus.*

Then the magi came from the east, asking, "Where has the King of the Jews been born? We have seen the star in the east and have come to worship Him." Hearing about this, King Herod was very

---

*In *Nik.* the speeches of the Greek missionaries to Vladimir closely follow the texts found in *Prim. Chron.* as preserved in *Laur.* and *Hyp.* These speeches were written on the basis of Arabic translation from Greek, with some minor changes and addenda. Still, two important features should be kept in mind: (1) the Greek original of the Scriptures slightly differed from Latin which became the foundation of the English version of the *Bible.* (2) The Church Slavonic of that time was a very new and imperfect tool.

986 troubled and, together with him, all Jerusalem; and he summoned the bookmen and the elders of the people and asked them, "Where has Christ been born?" And they told him, "In Bethlehem of the Jews." Learning this, Herod sent [his people], telling them, "Kill all the children who are in Bethlehem and who are two years old or younger." And they went and killed all the children; but Mary, fearing this, hid the child. And then Joseph and Mary with the child escaped to Egypt, where they remained till the death of Herod.

In Egypt the angel of God appeared to Joseph, saying, "Arise! Take the child and his mother and go into the land of Israel." He went thither and settled in Nazareth.

When [Christ] became thirty years old He began to perform miracles and to preach the Kingdom of Heaven. He chose twelve apostles whom He called His disciples; and He began to perform miracles, to resurrect the dead, to heal lepers, to make the lame walk, and to give sight to the blind; and He performed many other miracles in the way the prophets prophesied about Him, saying, "This will heal our sickness and will carry away our diseases."[91] And He was baptised in Jordan by John, and then He showed the way of regeneration to the new people. When He was baptised the heavens opened and the Holy Ghost descended upon Him in the form of a dove. And from heaven there was a voice, saying, "This is My Beloved Son in Whom I am well pleased." [*Mat.* 3:17.]

And He sent His disciples to preach the Heavenly Kingdom and penitence for the remission of sins. He fulfilled the prophecies and began to preach how the Son of man must suffer and be crucified and that He would rise again on the third day. While He was teaching in the temples the archpriests and bookmen became filled with envy and sought how to kill Him. They took Him captive and carried Him to Pilate. Pilate questioned Him and since they [the Jews] had turned Him over to him [Pilate] without any guilt, he wanted to release Him; but they [the Jews] told him, "If you release Him you are not the friend of Caesar," and then Pilate ordered that He should be crucified. The Jews took Him and carried Him to the place of the skull and there they crucified Him. Then darkness spread over the entire land from the sixth hour to the ninth, and at the tenth hour He gave up His ghost. The curtain of the temple was

---

91. *Isa.* 53:4: "He hath borne our sickness and carried our sorrows."

rent in twain and many graves opened up and many dead, whom He commanded to go to Paradise, arose.

Jesus was taken from the cross and was put into a tomb and the grave was sealed with seals, but the Jewish people put their guards there, saying, "His disciples may steal Him." Jesus, however, arose on the third day, and when He arose from the dead He appeared to His disciples and told them, "Go into all nations and teach all lands of the baptism in the Name of the Father, Son and Holy Ghost."

He remained with them for forty days and appeared to them after His resurrection. When forty days had passed He ordered them to go to the Mount of Olives, and there He appeared to them and He blessed them, saying, "Stay in the city of Jerusalem until I send you One Who was promised by My Father." And having said this, He ascended into Heaven, and they bowed to Him and returned to Jersualem, where they assembled in the temple. When the day of Pentecost came to an end, the Holy Spirit descended over the holy apostles and they received the promise of the Holy Spirit and they went to all parts of the universe, teaching and baptising with water and spirit in the Name of the Father, Son and Holy Ghost.

And Vladimir asked, "What was the purpose in the birth of Christ from a woman, of being crucified on wood and being baptised with water?"

The philosopher answered him:

This happened because from the very beginning the human race sinned through woman, and because the devil seduced Adam with the help of Eve and he was driven out of Paradise because God avenged Himself on the devil. And, also, He was born from a woman because Adam was driven out of Paradise because of a woman; and therefore God became Incarnate from a woman, and He showed all faithful the way to Paradise.

And He was crucified on the wood of a tree because Adam tasted [the fruit] of the tree, and therefore fell from nature; and therefore God suffered passion on wood in order to defeat the devil with the wood of a tree. Now from the Tree of Life the righteous one in Paradise will have food and gladness.

And concerning regeneration by water: this happened because in the time of Noah the sins of men multiplied and God brought a flood upon earth and let the people drown in the water; and therefore God said, "Since I destroyed people with water because of

986 their sins, now with water I will cleanse men from sin and they will be regenerated by water." It also happened because the Jewish people became cleansed in the water of the sea from the Egyptians' bad customs. And, then, it happened because water was the first to be created. It was said, "The Spirit of God hovered over the face of the water," and therefore people are now baptised through water and Spirit. The first transfiguration was performed by water, and it was Gideon who did it. When the angel of God came to him he ordered him to go fight the Midianites. [*Judges* 6:11-15.] And in order to learn the will of God he left the fleece on the threshing floor, so long as there should be dew on the earth, yet the fleece would be dry; and he put the fleece there. On the morrow he saw that over the entire earth there was dew and the fleece remained dry; and indeed, it happened thus. And he said, "I will try to find the will of Lord God once more: in case the land should be dry and the dew be on the fleece." And then it happened thus. [*Judges* 6:36-38.] This wonder was a prophetic symbol that aliens and unbelievers [non-Jews] represented the land while the Jews represented the fleece. Therefore the dew appeared on those [non-Jewish] countries, and this dew was their Holy Baptism, while the Jews remained dry [and non-baptised]. Thus the prophet prophesied that regeneration would occur by means of water.

The Apostles taught throughout the entire world about faith in God and how to worship God; and we, the Greeks, accepted their teaching, and now the entire world believes in their teaching. God determined the day in which He would come from Heaven to judge both the quick and the dead, and He will render justice according to the deeds of each: the righteous will receive the Heavenly Kingdom and ineffable beauty and gladness, and they will not die unto ages and ages. But sinners will have endless, eternal torments, inextinguishable fire, their worms will be immortal and there will be hellish darkness with no end to their torments. That will be the torment of those who do not believe in Our Lord, God, Jesus Christ; and this will happen because they will not be baptised and will be tormented in fire eternally without end.

The philosopher told all this to Vladimir and showed him a cloth on which was represented the terrifying Judgment of Christ; and he showed that on the right side were the righteous ones, going in great gladness to Paradise; and on the left side were the sinners, going to torment. Vladimir sighed and said, "Happy are those who **987** are on the right side but woe to those who are on the left side." And the philosopher said, "If you want to be on the right side of Christ with the just ones, accept our Greek faith and become baptised in the Name of the Father, Son and Holy Ghost." Vladimir took this advice to heart and said, "I will wait for awhile," because he wanted to study all religions. And Vladimir gave many gifts to this philosopher, rendered him great honor and let him go.

[PRINCE VLADIMIR'S CONVERSION TO CHRISTIANITY]

In the year 6495/987. Vladimir summoned his boyars and the city elders and told them, "The Bulgars[92] came to me and said, 'Accept our faith.' Thereafter the Germans came and they praised their Law. The Jews also came. The last to come were the Greeks, and they denied the Laws of the others and praised their own Law, and they spoke at length, telling about the beginning of the world, and what they said was very clever, and it was wonderful to listen to it, and one is pleased when he hears them because they told me about the other Light. [They said] 'Those who believe in our faith will then be resurrected after death and will not die unto the ages of ages; but if you accept another law, then you will burn forever in the other world.' What is your answer?" The boyars and elders said, "You know, Prince, no one will speak ill of his own religion but will praise it; but if you really want to learn, you have people for this. Send them to find out where what manner of religions are, and in what way they worship God." And the Prince and all the people were pleased by this speech and they selected wise and intelligent men whose number was ten. Vladimir told them, "Go to the [Moslem] Bulgars and study their faith and their service." They went thither and when they arrived there they saw their [the Bulgars'] wicked deeds and all manner of impurity and evil smells and bowing in the temple; and they returned to their land. Vladimir told them, "Go, now, to the [Catholic] Germans and look there, also, and from thence go to the Greeks in Constaninople." They went to the Germans and looked at their church and their church service, and then they went to Constantinople and came to the Emperor.

The Emperor said [to his men], "Find out why they have come."

92. Bulgars from the Volga, who were Moslem.

987 And they told of everything. Hearing these words, the Emperor was very glad and honored them greatly the same day. On the morrow the Emperor sent [his officers] to the Patriarch, saying the following: "The Russians have come to investigate our faith. Prepare the church vessels and the church clergy, and don the vestments of the bishop so they can see the glory of Our God." When the Patriarch heard this he summoned the clergy and, as usual, celebrated the holiday [church service], burning the censer, and the choir sang. There was harmony and divine beauty which were wonderfully composed. Then the Emperor came with Vladimir's envoys to the church, put them on an elevated place and showed them the beauty of the church, piety and the divine service, and the Patriarch and bishops. When they were before God in great piety and all was of wonderful beauty, [the Russian envoys], seeing this, became amazed and their hearts and souls were moved; and they loved the Greek faith and praised their church service.

Emperors Basil and Constantine let them return to their land with great honor and gifts. When they returned to their land, the Prince summoned the boyars and elders and said, "These are the men who were sent by us, and they have returned and we will hear from them what happened." And he told them, "Tell of everything before my retinue."

And they said, "First, we went to the [Moslem] Bulgars, and we saw how they bow in their temple, standing without belts. After they bow they sit down and look here and there without any sense, and there is no joy among them and everything is sad and bad-smelling; and there is no good religion among them. Then we went to the [Catholic] Germans and saw how they celebrate the service in the church, but we saw no beauty and were not impressed. Thereafter we went to the Greeks, and they led us to the church, where they celebrate the service to their God; and we were amazed and did not know whether we were in Heaven or on the earth. There is nowhere such beauty or such harmony on earth, and we can not even describe it. Verily, God is there with them. We can neither speak of it nor forget such beauty and such harmony. A man who tastes something sweet does not want thereafter to eat anything bitter; and so we cannot remain where we are, but we have to go thither."

Then the boyars told Vladimir, "In case the Greek faith were not marvelous, your grandmother Ol'ga would not have accepted it because she was the wisest of persons." And after their answer, Vladimir said, "Where should we accept baptism?" And they answered, "Wherever you would like."

In the year 6496/988. Vladimir with very strong forces marched against Chersonesus, the Greek city [in the Crimea] and the people of Chersonesus fortified themselves in the city. Vladimir set up his camp halfway between the city and the cove, about one arrow's shot from the city; but he could not be seen well from the city. Although Vladimir bestirred himself mightily, he could not succeed in the least; and he became frightened and told [his commanders], "If they do not surrender, we must remain here many years." But they did not listen to him. Then Vladimir ordered them to approach the city closer and fill the moat with earth; but the people of Chersonesus secretly made a tunnel under the city wall and took out the earth which was put there by the [Russian] warriors. And all the earth that was put in the moat by the warriors was secretly taken out by the city people and carried into the city. Vladimir was very much astounded that he could not fill [the moat].

A man from Chersonesus named Anastas wrote a letter attached to an arrow and shot the arrow to Vladimir, and there it was written, "Vladimir! I, Anastas, tell you truthfully that there are wells behind you to the east; from these wells water goes by pipes into the city. If you dig there [at the pipe] you will deprive them of water and you will take the city." Learning this from Anastas, Vladimir was so astounded that he looked at Heaven and said, "My Lord, if the city surrenders, I must become baptised and accept the Greek law." And he ordered to dig and found the water flowing through the pipes into the city, and they cut off the flow of the water and the people of the city became thirsty. They became exhausted, and surrendered.

Vladimir entered the city with his lords, comforted the minds of everyone and was good toward them, and he, himself, rejoiced with great joy and sent [his envoys] to the Greek Emperors Basil and Constantine,[93] sons of Emperor Romanus and grandsons of Constantine Porphyrogenitus and great grandsons of Leo the Wise, saying, "I took your glorious city of Chersonesus and I can do the same to your Great City [Constantinople] in which you reside. I will do this if you do not give your sister, Anna, who remains with you

---

93. Basil the Bulgar Killer, 976-1025; Constantine, 961-1025.

987 unmarried, to be my wife." Hearing this [the Emperors] felt offended and did not want to give him their sister as wife because he was not Christian, and they sent [envoys] to him, saying, "It is not fitting that a Christian should marry a pagan. If you want, then be baptised and accept our Greek Law. Then you will be able to inherit the Heavenly Kingdom and you will be of the same faith and the same mind and the same opinions as we, and all blessings will be with you."

Vladimir told these envoys, "Go and tell your Emperors Basil and Constantine that I have taken your faith to heart more than any other faith under the sun. Those I have studied and did not like. I studied your faith and loved it very much and I want to be baptised and I want to accept your Greek faith. I will do this if you give me your sister, Anna, who is unmarried, to be my wife."

And they sent [their envoys] to Vladimir to tell him, "Be baptised and then we will send you our sister." Vladimir said, "Those who will come with your sister will baptise me." The Emperors accepted his word and sent him their sister, Anna, with dignitaries and with priests, but she did not want to go. "How can I go," she said, "to the pagans? It would be better for me to die here." But her brother told her, "For your sake, God will convert the Russian land to penitence and the Greek land will escape evil punishment. Do you see how much evil the Russians have done to the Greeks? If you don't go to him now, he can do the same to us." And they forced her with difficulty to go.

She obeyed them and went with the dignitaries and priests to Vladimir in Chersonesus. According to God's will, at that time Vladimir developed sore eyes and he could not see anything because his illness was very serious. And then the Imperial Princess Anna sent him [an envoy] who told him, "If you want to be rid of your disease, be rapidly baptised." Hearing this, Vladimir said, "If it is this way, then, verily, the God of the Christians is Great, and there is no God besides Him," and he ordered that he be baptised at once. He was baptised in the Church of St. James in the city of Chersonesus inside the fortress, in the place where the people of Chersonesus have their market, and he was baptised by the Bishop of Chersonesus, together with the priests who came with the Imperial Princess. Vladimir's palace remains there to this day near the site of the church, and the palace of the Imperial Princess is behind the side of the altar.

At the very moment when he was baptised by the Bishop, he **987** recovered his sight and became healthy, just as if he had never been ill, and he praised Lord God Jesus Christ and rejoiced with great joy. Seeing this, his lords, princes and boyars also became baptised in the name of the Father, the Son and the Holy Ghost, and accepted the Greek faith; and there was great joy among them.

Some people—for instance, the Germans—who did not witness this, say that Vladimir was baptised in Kiev; others say that he was baptised in Vasiliev; and some others give yet another version; but they do not speak the truth because they do not see what they are saying; the truth is that Vladimir was baptised in Chersonesus, as it was written before, and he accepted the Greek faith and learned about religion in Chersonesus, and he demonstrated many good virtues: justice, patience, love, humility, love of man and mercifulness; and he was firm in the faith of Lord God and he burned in spirit with the Divine Faith as if it were fire, and he was feared by those who do not believe in Our Lord Jesus Christ.[94]

94. The story of Vladimir's campaign to Chersonesus, usually called "The Chersonesus Legend" (*Korsun'skaia legenda*), is correct in its main line despite several inaccuracies in details (*e.g.*, the date and place of Vladimir's baptism, *a.o.*). According to Byzantine and Arab historians of that time (Yahia of Antiochia, Kedrin, Zonar and Psell, *a.o.*), Vladimir in 989 sent a corps of Varangian mercenaries to Emperors Basil and Constantine (which is indirectly confirmed by the story of Vladimir's permitting the Varangians to go to Constantinople, mentioned under 980 in *Nik.*) to help the Emperors fight a rebel general, Bardas Phocas. As compensation for this help he was promised the hand of Princess Anna, sister to the Emperors. After quelling the mutiny, the Emperors refused to give Anna as wife to Vladimir, so the latter attacked and took Chersonesus, threatened Constantinople and, finally, received Anna as his wife. Modern scholars of early Russian history and Russian church history believe, however, that Vladimir received baptism in 987 in Kiev before his campaign to Chersonesus. In the *Prim. Chr.* as well as in *Nik.* there is indirect indication of this (see, for instance, the story of Vladimir's baptism under 988) when the chronicler says, "Some people say that Vladimir was baptised in Kiev . . . but they do not speak the truth." Probably, the story of Vladimir's baptism in Chersonesus, the so-called "Chersonesus Legend," was written in the late XI century on the basis of local Crimean legend. See Kartashev, I, 113-117; Likhachev, II, 320-346. Monk Jacob in his "Praise of Prince Vladimir" (XIth century) says that Vladimir was baptised twenty-eight years before his death, which also indicates that he was baptised in 987 ($1015 - 28 = 987$). The same Jacob says that he took Chersonesus the third year after his baptism—in 989—which

987   [THE SERMON]

When Vladimir was baptised in Chersonesus, they taught him the Christian faith, saying the following:

Now, thanks to the grace of Christ God, you are newly born and you are cleansed from your sins, and you have become the son of Light and the heir of the heavenly kingdom. Preserve carefully the internal sense of the teaching about God in your heart: your eyes should not participate in any evil sights and hearing vain words should be unpleasant for you. Your tongue should be clean from impure words and your lips should be clean when you praise Christ God. Your hands should not be soiled with evil deeds; your thoughts and all your desires should be directed toward the heavenly kingdom, and you should be meek and obedient to God: "Whatsoever therefore you eat and drink or whatsoever you do, do all to the glory of God." [*I Cor.* 10:31.] Always be quiet, meek, humble, responsible and capable of emotions. "Thou shalt love the Lord Thy God with all thy soul and all thy heart and all thy mind and strength, thou shalt love thy neighbor as thyself." [*Luke* 10:27.] You should believe in the same Creed which we received from three hundred eighteen holy fathers who gathered at the first Council,[95] and this is: "I believe in One God, Father Almighty, Maker of Heaven and earth," and you must preserve the confession of the Orthodox faith with love and wisdom, and also believe in One God Father Who was not born, One Son Who was born and One Holy Ghost Who proceeds [from the Father]. Three complete and perfect Hypostases which are One but which are divisible in number and person but not in their divinity. They have separate Hypostases without being divided and are united without being the same. God the Father Who is Everlasting, abides in fatherhood. He is unbegotten, He is without beginning but He is the beginning and the cause of all. Because He was unbegotten, He was senior to the Son and the Holy Ghost, and from Him was born the Son before all ages, and from Him proceeds the Holy Spirit, Who is beyond the ages and incorporeal. Together they are Father, Son and Holy Ghost.

means that he was baptised in 987. The appearance of missionary embassies in Kiev also seems to have been customary for the time. In any case, there were several such embassies from Rome in Kiev.

95. The first oecumenical Church Council met in Nicea in 325; it is usually called "The Council of Three Hundred Eighteen Fathers."

The Son is of one Substance with the Father, and He was before **987** all ages and He is distinguished from the Father and Spirit in that He was born. The Spirit is the Holy Ghost, He is of the same Substance as the Father and Son and is everlasting. The Father had fatherhood, the Son—sonship, and the Holy Ghost—the proceeding. The Father is not of the same Hypostasis as the Son or the Holy Spirit, nor the Son of the same as the Father or the Holy Spirit; and the Holy Spirit is not of the same as the Son or the Father because their attributes are unchangeable. There are not three Gods but One God because it is One Godhead in Three Hypostases. By the desire of the Father and Holy Spirit, the Son saved their creatures. He did not leave the nature of the Father but descended from Heaven and the Divine and Most Pure Word entered the womb of the Virgin. And He took animate, vocal and wise flesh which previously did not exist, and so came the Incarnate God Who was ineffably born while His Mother preserved Her Immaculate Virginity. Suffering neither confusion nor any change, He remained as He was, became what He was not and He assumed the aspect of a servant of Truth only in semblance but in a being similar to us although in every respect immune to sin. He was born by His own will, by His own will He became hungry, by His own will He became thirsty, by His own will he labored, by His own will He feared, by His own will He died. And it [His death] happened verily and not in semblance; and He suffered the natural, unimpeachable passions of man. He was crucified and He suffered sinless death. And He was resurrected in His own flesh and without any corruption of the flesh. He ascended into Heaven and He sits on the right hand of the Father, and He will come with glory to judge the quick and the dead. He ascended in the flesh and so will He descend once more. With this I acknowledge one baptism by water and Spirit, and I will participate in the Holy mysteries of the Communion and I believe that they are the true Flesh and Blood of Christ. I accept the entire church tradition, I will worship the honorable and sacred icons, and I will worship the Honorable Cross, the Holy Relics and the sacred vessels.

ABOUT THE COUNCILS

I believe in the Seven Councils of the Holy Fathers.

In the first, which took place in Nicea, three hundred eighteen

987 fathers participated who excommunicated Arius and who preached the Immaculate and Orthodox faith. [In the year 325.]

The Second Council took place in Constantinople with the participation of one hundred fifty holy fathers, who excommunicated Macedonius, who denied the Holy Ghost and proclaimed the Oneness of the Trinity. [In the year 381.]

The Third Council, in which two hundred holy fathers participated, took place in Ephesus and it was summoned against Nestorius, whom they excommunicated and who also proclaimed the worship of the Holy Theotokos. [In the year 431.]

The Fourth Council took place in Chalcedon and was attended by six hundred thirty holy fathers who discussed the teachings of Eutycheus and Dioscorus, whom the holy fathers excommunicated and who proclaimed that Our Lord Jesus Christ was the True God and the True Man. [In the year 451.]

The fifth council took place in Constantinople with the participation of one hundred five holy fathers, and they discussed the tenets of Origen and Evagrius, and excommunicated them. [In the year 553.]

The Sixth Council, which took place in Constantinople and which was attended by one hundred seventy holy fathers, was summoned against Sergius and Cyrus, whom the holy fathers excommunicated. [In the year 680-681.]

The Seventh Council, which took place in Nicea for the second time, was attended by three hundred fifty holy fathers, and these holy fathers excommunicated those who did not venerate the Holy Icons. [In the year 787.]

ABOUT THE LATINS.

I do not accept the tenets of the Latins because their tenets are perverse. They enter the church without bowing to the ground before the icons; but they just bow, standing. Thereafter, they trace a sign of the cross on the ground and instead of making the sign of the cross on the ground and kissing it, they just stand before them. When they prostrate to kiss it, and when they arise, they trample it. This is not the tradition received from the Apostles because the Holy Apostles taught that the cross should be kissed and the use of icons is prescribed thus. According to Basil, Luke the Evangelist painted the first icon and sent it to Rome. He [Basil] says that the honor rendered to icons derives from the honor to those whom we venerate.

The Latins also call the earth their mother. If the earth is their mother, then their father is heaven, because at the beginning God created the earth and the heavens. And so we pray: "Our Father Who art in Heaven." And if the earth is their mother, why do they spit on their mother and pollute it, in place of kissing it? Earlier, the Romans [Catholics] did not act thus and they participated in all the Councils, to which people came from Rome and from the other Sees.

To the First Council which took place in Nicea and which was against Arius, Pope Sylvester sent his bishops and his priests. From Alexandria there was Athanasius; from Constantinople, Patriarch Mitrophanus sent his bishops to represent him; and in this way they established the Articles of Faith.

At the Second Council, there was Damascus from Rome; Timotheus from the Patriarch of Alexandria; Miletius from the Patriarch of Antiochia; Cyril from Jerusalem; and there was also Gregory the Theologian.

In the Third Council the Roman Pope Coelestinus participated; from Alexandria, Cyril; from Jerusalem, Juvenalius.

The Fourth Council was attended by Leo from Rome; by Anatolius from Constantinople; and Juvenalius from Jerusalem.

The Fifth Council was attended by Vigilius of Rome; Eutychius of Constantinople; Apollinarius of Jerusalem; and Domnus of Antiochia.

The Sixth Council was attended by Agathon of Rome; by Georgius of Constantinople; Theophanus of Antiochia; and Peter the Monk from Alexandria.

The Seventh Council was attended by Hadrian of Rome, Tarasius of Constantinople, Politianus of Alexandria, Theodoret of Antiochia, and Elias of Jerusalem. And all these with their bishops assembled in order to write the Articles of Faith.

ABOUT PETER THE STAMMERER.

A short time after the seven Councils, Peter the Stammerer with others seized the See of Rome and corrupted the Faith and was rejected by the Sees of Constantinople, Alexandria, Antiochia and Jerusalem. He upset Italy, disseminating a different teaching, and he did not stand to the unanimously proclaimed Faith but taught it

987 differently; for some of these priests who celebrated the church services were married to one wife while others had up to seven wives, and there were many other differences. Guard yourselves from their teaching. They forgive sins for payment. Which can be the greater evil? God preserve thee from all those and grant thee the Heavenly Kingdom through the prayer of the Most Glorious and Immaculate Theotokos, Mary, and All the Saints. Amen.[96]

Vladimir accepted all these teachings with great joy from the Bishop of Chersonesus, honoring him with great respect and embracing him in the Name of God and giving him many gifts. He promised to observe strictly all his obligations given during Holy Baptism, and all the Commandments of Christ, and to observe with God's help all the rules which are supposed to be observed by the Orthodox. And there was great joy among the people, and the Word of God spread and the Christian people multiplied.

As was fitting, a short time after his baptism Vladimir celebrated his wedding, taking to wife the Imperial Princess Anna, sister of the Greek Emperors Basil and Constantine, and he gave vast alms to all paupers and poor, and to travellers and orphans and widows; and on his command there were placed in the streets pitchers with wine and mead and boiled food and meat, fish and all manner of vegetables and fruit. Everyone who wanted could eat without hindrance and with great joy. Thereafter Vladimir sent [his envoys] to the Greeks, to His Holiness Patriarch Photius of Constantinople and received from him the first Metropolitan of Russia, Michael of Kiev and the entire Russian land.[97]

METROPOLITAN MICHAEL OF KIEV AND ALL RUSSIA.

This Metropolitan was a Greek teacher and very wise. He was a man of strongly observed pious life. By birth he was from Syria. He was quiet and meek and peaceful, and very merciful; but sometimes

---

96. There was no Pope Peter either in the eighth century or later. Peter the Stammerer is a legendary person. *Khronograf po velikomu izlozheniiu* was the source of this item in *Prim. Chr.*; Tvorogov, pp. 144-145.

97. Metropolitan Michael is not mentioned in *Laur.* or *Hyp.* There is considerable confusion in sources about the organization of the early Russian church. It can be the vague memory of a mission sent by Photius to Russia in the 860's. It is obvious that in 989 Patriarch Photius (who ruled from 856 to 867 and from 877 to 896) could not have sent any bishops to Vladimir. See the Foreword to this volume.

he could be angry and fierce when the occasion required it. Vladimir honored him greatly and remained in agreement and in great friendship. Everyone rejoiced and the Glory of God was spread. With the blessing of his spiritual father the Metropolitan, Vladimir built a church in Chersonesus on a hill, which was actually a mount which had been piled up in the middle of the city with sand taken from other places. And this church stands there to the present day. Thereafter there came from Greece many envoys from the emperors. They came in order to honor and to bring gifts and to witness friendship. From the Pope of Rome envoys also came bringing Holy Relics to Vladimir. At the same time the Pecheneg Prince Metigai came to Vladimir, became Christian and was baptised in the name of the Father, Son and Holy Ghost. And Vladimir returned to the Greeks the city of Chersonesus, for the sake of the Imperial Princess.

989

In the year 6497/989. Vladimir, together with his spiritual father, Metropolitan Michael, went to Kiev, taking with him the relics of Saint Clement[98] and Phebus, his disciple, as well as holy crosses, holy icons and the sacred church vessels. From among the priests of Chersonesus he selected several, including Anastas, who wrote the letter which was sent on an arrow. And he took with him two copper statues, four copper horses and three copper lions. He placed Anastas under the jurisdiction of his spiritual father, Metropolitan Michael. When he came to the city of Kiev he ordered the idols be destroyed and burned in fire. His words were pronounced with authority but many received baptism with joy. Metropolitan Michael baptised Vladimir's twelve sons, who names were Vysheslav, Iziaslav, Sviatopolk, Iaroslav, Vsevolod, Sviatoslav, Mstislav, Boris, Gleb, Stanislav, Pozvizd and Sudislav. And he assigned his first son, Vysheslav, to Novgorod the Great; and Iziaslav to Polotsk; Sviatopolk to Turov; and Iaroslav to Rostov. After the death of his senior son, Vysheslav, he assigned Novgorod to his fourth son, Iaroslav. And he assigned Boris to Rostov and Gleb to Murom, and Sviatoslav to the Drevlians, and Vsevolod to the city of Vladimir. And Mstislav to Tmutarakan'.[99] And Stanislav was assigned to

---

98. St. Clement was a Christian saint from Chersonesus.

99. Tmutarakan: Russian territory in the X-XIIth centuries in the northern Caucasus near the present city of Taman', across from the Crimea.

989 Smolensk and Sudislav to Pskov. Thereafter Vladimir, after counseling with awe and great care with his spiritual father, the Metropolitan, addressed the following words to all his people: "In case any of you do not go to the river [Dnieper] to be baptised in the Name of the God Father, Son and Holy Ghost, he will be the enemy of Christ God and of us and there will be no mercy to him from us." Hearing this, the people went to be baptised with great joy. On the morrow Vladimir, together with his spiritual father, his children, his Imperial Princess wife, his boyars and his priests, went to the river Dnieper and there assembled a great multitude, a numberless quantity of people, together with even infants at the breast; and they all remained in the water up to their breasts, holding their infants in their arms while standing in the water. The priests who stood on the shore read prayers and baptised all of them in the Name of the Father, Son and Holy Ghost. And there was great joy among the people, and humility and mutual love, and everyone contemplated Christ God with faith and love; and thanks to the blessing of the Holy Spirit, they multiplied. Vladimir, seeing all this, rejoiced in heart and soul. Looking toward heaven, he wept and said, "Lord God Who created the heavens and the earth! Care for these new people of Thine and give them the opportunity to learn about Thee, the True God, as the other Christian lands have learned; and strengthen their faith, true and incorruptible. And help them, Lord, against their enemies, and give them hope in Thy Help and hope in the defeat of evil plots." He ordered that churches be built and honorable monasteries be established. He built a Church of St. Basil on the same hill on which Perun and the other devilish idols had stood. Also, in all cities and towns churches and monasteries were built. The number of priests multiplied and the Orthodox faith blossomed and shone as the sun.

Thereafter His Holiness Metropolitan Michael of Kiev and all Russia took counsel with his son, Prince Vladimir, how to strengthen the Orthodox church. They started to take little children from their mothers and fathers and to send them to school to learn literacy. There was a great number of schools of Scripture. The Metropolitan summoned all literate teachers and assigned them to preserve Orthodoxy and piety stoutly, and to avoid senseless and indecent speech. And thanks to [the work of] these numerous wisdom-loving philosophers in the Russian land, the prophecy was fulfilled, "In

that day shall the deaf hear the words of the Book and the language **990**
of the stammerer will become clear." [*Isa* 29:18; the second part of
this quotation is amended.] Those who had never heard the words of
Divine Scripture now, by the grace of Christ God, became good
philosophers, according to the words of the Prophet: "I will have
mercy on him if I am willing to do so." [*Ex.* 33:19.] "Great is the Lord
and wonderful are Thy deeds. His decisions remain concealed and
there are not words to praise Thy wonders!" "Oh, the depth of the
riches both of the wisdom and knowledge of God! How unsearchable are His judgments, and His ways past finding out! For who hath
known the mind of the Lord? or who hath been His counsellor?"
[*Rom.* 11:33-34.] Those who once were as animals and who, as
madmen, worshipped idols and spilled blood, now, thanks to the
grace of Christ, have become enlightened and live according to the
Gospel. They rise up unto Heaven, and among them are wonderful
and wisdom-loving philosophers. Glory to Thee, Jesus Christ, Son of
God, glory to Thee for everything done by Thee.

In the year 6498/990. Many Pechenegs came, who caused the
Christians much harm. Vladimir, however, marched against them
with many warriors. Many of them [the Pechenegs] were killed and
only a few escaped. Then Vladimir began to build towns and
fortresses on the Desna, Oster, Trubezh', Sula and Stugna rivers,
and there he settled the Slovens, who are also called "Novgorodians;" the Krivichs, who are also called the "people of Smolensk";
the Chud'; and the Viatichs. He waged war against the Pechenegs
and defeated them.

The same year Vladimir sent a philosopher called Mark the
Macedonian to the Volga Bulgars, who are also called the "sons of
Hagar," Ishmaelites" or "Saracens" because they are thus named
after the free Sarah or after Hagar, who was handmaid to Sarah.
They also have other names: "Moslems," "Tatars" and various other
devilish names. Arriving there, Mark said [as Vladimir had
instructed him to apprise them], "You used to come to me when I
was not yet enlightened in the Orthodox faith, and you used to
praise your perverse religion, and tried to force me to accept it. Now
I have seen the truth about this, how disgustful it is, and I have not
accepted it." [Vladimir also instructed him what to do.] "And now
you should go to them and preach them the divine word so that they
believe in Lord God and Our Saviour, Jesus Christ, and that they be

991 baptised with divine baptism and be of the same faith and the same mind as we, and receive the heavenly blessing. In case they do not want to be enlightened with divine baptism, they should not fight about it because they, themselves, taught me earlier concerning their faith, and I did not fight against them. Now they, too, should not fight us." The philosopher went to the Bulgars and preached to them at length concerning the word of God. They were quite crazy, however, with their madness so he returned to Vladimir in Kiev, [where] he was greatly honored by him and was praised by all. The same year four princes from [the Volga] Bulgars came to Vladimir in Kiev and they became enlightened with divine baptism. Vladimir honored them and was glad.[100]

The same year Metropolitan Michael of Kiev and all Russia journeyed to Novgorod the Great, together with the bishops sent him by Patriarch Photius, who gave him six bishops to help him.[101] Vladimir's uncle, Dobrynia, and Anastas accompanied them. They destroyed the idols and baptised many people. They also built churches and assigned priests to the cities and towns. The same year there was great peace everywhere. The same year from the Greek Emperors an envoy came with the assurance of friendship.[102]

In the year 6499/991. Metropolitan Michael travelled over the Russian land and to Rostov. He was accompanied by four bishops sent by Patriarch Photius, as well as by Dobrynia and Anastas. And other bishops sent by Photius were residing in Kiev. The Metropolitan with the bishops taught how to worship the Only God, Who is praised in the Trinity, and instructed and preached the understanding of God, and piety, to very many people. And he baptised an endless number of people, built many churches and

---

100. This entry under 6498/990 is missing almost in its entirety from *Laur.*, *Hyp.* and *Novg.* Only the sentence about the building of towns and fortresses on the rivers Desna, Oster, Trubezh, Sula and Stugna appears in these chronicles. In *Nik.* it is followed by a discussion of the Moslem faith, *Szazanie o khulnei vere Strachintsei, PSRL* IX, pp. 59-63. The sources of this *Skazanie* are unclear and it has no counterpart in any other Russian literary works. Since it has no bearing on Russian history and is of legendary background, it is omitted from this translation.

101. Photius: a ninth century Patriarch who, a hundred years before Vladimir's reign, sent a bishop to Russia—possibly, Bishop Michael.

102. A similar entry, without mention of Metropolitan Michael, can be found in the *Novg.* chronicle under 6497/989.

appointed presbyters and deacons; and he organized the clergy and determined the rules of piety. And there was great joy among the people and the number of believers grew, and the Name of Christ God was glorified everywhere. The same year from the Greeks came masons and builders of stone buildings to Kiev to Prince Vladimir.

The same year there was a great flood.

The same year a Pecheneg prince, Kuchiug, of those who are called Ishmaelites, came to Vladimir in Kiev and accepted the Greek faith and was baptised in the name of the Father, Son and Holy Ghost, and served Vladimir with a pure heart and defeated many pagans. Vladimir loved him and greatly honored him, and so did the Metropolitan, princes and boyars respect and love him. The same year the ambassador from the Pope in Rome came to Vladimir with assurances of friendship and respect.[103]

In the year 6500/992. Vladimir campaigned in the Suzdalian land and baptised many people there. Together with him were two bishops from Patriarch Photius. And there he laid the foundation of the city in honor of his own name, the city of Vladimir, on the river Kliazma. And he built there a wooden church to the Immaculate Theotokos, and the bishops sent by Patriarch Photius instructed the people. There was great piety and the Christian faith shone as the sun, and spread forward from day to day. Vladimir was very happy in his soul and heart, and he distributed a large amount of his wealth to the paupers and poor; and he left food and drink in the streets so that everyone who wished could eat to his fill. The same year Vladimir sent [his army] against the Pechenegs and defeated them, and they returned victoriously, bringing the joyous news to Vladimir. The same year envoys came to Vladimir from Boleslav of Poland. The same year His Holiness Metropolitan Michael passed away. He had lived a very sound life, laboring greatly for God, instructing the newly baptised people, caring for the Orthodox faith and teaching everyone concerning the wisdom of God. And Vladimir greatly lamented him and shed tears. Only with difficulty could he be consoled by the bishops sent by Patriarch Photius and by his princes and boyars. This Metropolitan was always in great friendship and was of good council with and to Vladimir.[104]

103. This entire entry under 6499/991 is not to be found in the *Laur.*, *Hyp.* and *Novg.* chronicles.

104. As mentioned above, Bishop Michael was probably the first Russian bishop, in 860-870 and not in the time of Vladimir.

993   LEONTIUS, METROPOLITAN OF KIEV AND ALL RUSSIA.

The same year Vladimir received from the blessed Patriarch Photius of Constantinople Metropolitan Leontius of Kiev and all Russia, and there was great joy among the people. The same year envoys came to Vladimir in Kiev from Heinrich of Bohemia with the assurance of friendship. The same year Leontius, Metropolitan of all Russia, consecrated Joachim of Chersonesus to be Bishop of Great Novgorod and Pskov. He came to Novgorod and destroyed the places of pagan worship as well as the idols; and he cut Perun to pieces and threw it into the river Volkhov. And a great glory to God was everywhere.[105]

METROPOLITAN LEONTIUS OF KIEV AND
ALL RUSSIA APPOINTS BISHOPS TO THE CITIES

The same year Metropolitan Leontius of Kiev and all Russia consecrated Bishop Neophit to Chernigov; and he appointed Bishop Theodore to Rostov; and Stephen to Vladimir, and Nicetas to Belgorod; and he appointed bishops to many other cities. The people rejoiced and Orthodoxy shone, and the name of Christ was glorified and the word of God grew and spread.[106]

In the year 6501/993. With the blessing of his spiritual father, Metropolitan Leontius of Kiev and all Russia, Vladimir in Kiev built a stone church of the Immaculate Theotokos. The mason masters were Greek and the church was adorned with icons, books and church vessels. All those holy crosses, venerable icons and sacred vessels which [Vladimir] had taken in Chersonesus he gave to the church of the Immaculate Conception and to his spiritual father,

---

105. Leo, Leon or Leontius, at that time was head of the Bulgarian church with its See in Ohrid. He is mentioned in several entries as one of the first heads of the Russian church. Since, apparently, the Russian church was at that time under the jurisdiction of the Archbishopric of Ohrid (West Bulgaria), it is possible that he was mentioned as the hierarchical overseer of the Russian church, or perhaps he travelled to Russia. See the Foreword to this volume and Kartashev I, 134-135.

106. This entry of 6500/992 is missing in its entirety in *Laur.* and *Hyp.* In *Novg.* under 6497/989, however, it is mentioned that the first Archbishop of Novgorod was Joachim of Chersonesus. In the same *Novg.* entry of 989 it is written that the first Russian Metropolitan was Theotemptus, but he was appointed to the Kievan See only in 1039.

Metropolitan Leontius.[107]

994

He assigned to this cathedral church of the Immaculate Theotokos one tithe from his whole realm, and one tithe from all proceedings of the court; and from the markets, the income of every tenth week in all the cities; and from all herds of cattle, one-tenth every year; and from all grain, one-tenth every year was assigned to Lord God and Our Saviour, Jesus Christ, to His Immaculate Mother Theotokos, and to His father, Metropolitan of Kiev and all Russia.

In the entire Russian land and in all principalities the bishops built cathedral churches according to the early Greek *Nomocanon*;[108] also, the church court and the entire statute of the church were given according to the previous Greek *Nomocanon*, to the Holy Church of the Immaculate Conception, and to his father, the Metropolitan. He ordered that none of them should be changed, neither by his descendants nor by his boyars nor by anyone else, and up to the end of the world no one should dare to interfere in the church and bishops' matters. He wrote an oath which he deposited in the Holy Divine church in the presence of Leontius, Metropolitan of Kiev and all Russia, of the bishops sent by Patriarch Photius and the Russian bishops, as well as in the presence of priests and monks and his Princess and boyars, saying the following: "In case anyone should criticize my statutes, which are based on the earlier Greek *Nomocanon*, he will be excommunicated." The same day there was a great feast with the Metropolitan, bishops, boyars and all his magnates, and great wealth was distributed to the poor and paupers.[109]

In the year 6502/994. Vladimir campaigned against the [Volga] Bulgars and waged war, defeating them. He returned joyfully to Kiev. The same year there was a great drought and it was very hot. The same year the envoys sent by Vladimir to the Pope of Rome

---

107. The information concerning the building of this church is to be found in the *Laur.* and *Hyp.*, chronicles under the year 989. Leontius, however, is not mentioned there. The church became known as the Tithe Church (*Desiatinnaia*). Information about the tithe appears in *Laur.* and *Hyp.* under 6504/996.

108. *Nomocanon:* Ecclesiastic codex of law.

109. The data about the building of this church, usually known under the name, "Tithe Church" (*Desiatinnaia*) in *Laur.* and *Hyp.*, is under 6497/989 and 6504/996.

995 returned to Kiev.[110]

In the year 6503/995. Vladimir returned to Kiev. Thereafter he campaigned against the Croats.[111] And when the Pechenegs heard about this they attacked him, and he went against them. They sent forward a very tall and powerful man, challenging Vladimir to send a man to fight with him. Vladimir despatched people throughout the entire Russian land, asking them to find such a man. Then a tanner came and said, "I have a son who was recently cutting the newly tanned hide of a great bull. For some reason he became angry and tore this hide in two with his own hands." Vladimir commanded that he be summoned and instructed that a large bull be burned with hot iron. The bull became enraged and charged ferociously but the youth caught him with his hands by the side and pulled out a piece of hide with the meat. Vladimir and all his magnates were very happy and commanded him to fight with the Pecheneg bogatyr'.[112] When they came together the Pecheneg began to laugh, saying, "How can this bag of bones dare to challenge me?" because the youth was middlesized. He went to the youth, roaring fiercely as a lion, and became as maddened with pride as a demon. He began shouting and howling at the youth. Relying upon God and the Immaculate Theotokos, the youth did not fear but went against him, defeated and killed the Pecheneg bogatyr'. Seeing this, the Pechenegs ran away but Vladimir chased them and killed them. He founded a city on that ford, calling the city "Pereiaslavl'" because the youth won his glory there.[113] And he made the youth a great dignitary and also honored his father with great respect, as well as his entire family. He returned to Kiev rejoicing over the glory and the victory.[114]

In the year 6504/996. Vladimir laid the foundation of Belgorod and brought many people thither from other cities. Vladimir liked this city more than any other and built a church of the Reincarnation of Christ there.[115]

110. This item is not to be found in *Laur.*, *Hyp.* or *Novg.*

111. Here are meant the White Croats then living in the Carpathians, and not the Croats of the Balkans. In *Laur.* and *Hyp.* this item appears under the year 6500/992; in *Novg.*, under 6501/993.

112. *Bogatyr':* a powerful warrior of considerable size.

113. *Pereiaslavl'* means "beyond glory."

114. The same story, though more developed, appears in *Laur.* and *Hyp.* under 6497/989.

115. This same item appears in *Laur.* and *Hyp.* under 6497/989.

In the year 6505/997. Vladimir campaigned against the Bulgars of the Volga and Kama and, defeating them, captured many.[116]

In the year 6506/998. The Pechenegs came to Vasiliev and Vladimir marched against them with a small number [of warriors] and could not fight them; he escaped and hid under the bridge, and promised that he would build a church of the Reincarnation of Christ in Vasiliev because on that day it was that holiday. He built a stone church there and adorned it with icons and various vessels.[117]

Then he went to Kiev, and when he arrived he saw that the great Tithe Church of the Immaculate Mother Theotokos was completed, and he entered it. He prayed to God and to His Immaculate Theotokos, saying the following: "Lord God! Look upon us from the heavens and care for us. Visit this vineyard which was planted by Thy right hand. This is a vineyard of new people whose hearts Thou hast turned to reason in order to learn of Thee, the True God. Protect this church which I, Thy unworthy servant, have built, in the Name of Thy Mother Who bore Thee, the Theotokos, and the Immaculate Mary. And when someone prays in it, please listen to his prayer and forgive his sins and be merciful to him for the sake of Thy Immaculate Mother." And thereafter he wept and shed tears, saying, "I am giving to Thee, Mother of God, and to Thy most holy church and to my holy father, Metropolitan of all Russia, as I promised, one-tenth of all my wealth and one-tenth from all my cities." And he wrote down and deposited this oath in the church, saying, "If anyone criticizes this he will be excommunicated." And then he said to his father Metropolitan, "You must care for and protect well this [church of] God because it is a divine place and should not be desecrated." Then he told Anastas of Chersonesus, "You will be under the jurisdiction of our father in God, our Metropolitan, whom you must obey in every respect." And then he appointed Anastas of Chersonesus to be the church guardian and to oversee the tithes and other valuables. Thereafter the same day he had a brilliant banquet with his father Metropolitan and with all boyars and dignitaries, and this banquet lasted the whole week. Everyone rejoiced. He invited people from many other lands and

116. No such entry appears in *Laur.* or *Hyp.*

117. The same item appears in *Laur.* and *Hyp.* and *Novg.* under 6504/996.

998 distributed much of his wealth to the poor and the paupers, and to aliens and to the churches and monasteries. He ordered that there be placed in the streets barrels and buckets of mead, bread, meat, fish and cheese, eggs and all manner of vegetables for the benefit of the sick, the poor and travellers. Whoever came and ate would also praise God and the blessed Prince Vladimir. [See the footnote under the year 6501/993.]

This Vladimir was very merciful and generous and loved to give gifts. He often repeated this saying: "I cannot get troops with silver and gold but with troops I can get silver and gold." And Vladimir very much loved his warriors. He counselled with them about the divine dominion of Russia, about the administration of the land, and he lived in peace and friendship with the neighboring lands and kings: with Boleslav of Poland, Stefan of Hungary, and Heinrich of Bohemia.[118] Vladimir very much loved the reading of Divine Scripture and enjoyed their sweetness. He was always in awe of God, was quiet and meek, and would shed tears, and he was kind and friendly to all people.

ROBBERS.

The devil, who hates good, brought evil to man; and brother would fight brother, and one man would injure another, and robbery increased in the Russian land. Then the bishops and elders assembled and told the Metropolitan, "Your [spiritual] son, Prince Vladimir, is very meek and peaceful and therefore the robbers are wasting the land; what do you think of this?" The Metropolitan told them, "Go and advise him that he should act against evil people and that the robbers should be punished according to divine law, but after inquiry and investigation. It is written in Scripture, 'Be merciful with reason toward some people but protect others through wrath. For such is the will of God.' The Apostle said, that 'with well-doing ye should put to silence the ignorance of foolish men.' [*I Pet.* 2.15] For the rulers are not terror to good work but to evil. And wouldst thou have no fear of the power? Do that which is good and thou shalt have praise for the same." [Approx. *Rom.* 13.3] Then the bishops went to Vladimir and told him, "Your father Metropolitan Leontius of all Russia has sent us to you in order to say

---

118. The same item appears in *Laur.* and *Hyp.* under 6504/996.

the following: 'Robbers have multiplied in our land. Why do you not intervene against them or execute them?" But Vladimir responded, "I do so out of awe for Lord God. Who am I, who have sinned and trespassed divine law more than any other man under the sun?" And the bishops told him, "You are appointed by Christ God in order to restrain and punish evildoers and to be merciful toward the good. You should execute evildoers according to Divine Law after inquiry and investigation, and be merciful toward the good because authority must protect with fear and mercy those who obey. Otherwise, authority does not exist." Vladimir said, "I will do as is said by our [spiritual] father and Your Holiness, and instruct that it be done according to Divine Law." From that time Vladimir, after inquiry and great instruction, stood out against evil and wicked people because Vladimir was very patient and reasonable of mind.[119]

999

In the year 6507/999. The Pechenegs attacked Belgorod. At that time Vladimir was not in Kiev but in Novgorod and the people of Belgorod wanted to surrender because they were starving. One of them, however, had the idea of digging two wells. In each well he put a large barrel; and one barrel he filled with uncooked meal, the other with cooked meal [*kissel'*]. Then he invited some Pechenegs to the city and showed them the wells, saying, "This food comes out of the earth unceasingly." They ladled some of it and cooked it. They ate it and gave some to the Pechenegs, who also ate it and took some to the others. They marvelled and went away.[120]

In the year 6508/1000. Volodar' with Polovetss attacked Kiev, having forgotten all the good deeds of his lord, Prince Vladimir; he did this because he had been instructed by the devil. At that time Vladimir was in Preslav on the Danube, and there was great panic in Kiev. Then Alexander Popovich came out at night to meet them and he killed Volodar' and his brother, and slew a great many of the Polovetss. Others he chased into the prairie. Hearing of this, Vladimir rejoiced greatly and put a golden circlet on his head and made him a dignitary in his palace. The same year Ragdai the Brave, who used to fight alone against 300 warriors, passed away. Vladimir

119. A similar item appears in *Laur.* and *Hyp.* under 6504/996.

120. This is a shorter version of entries in *Laur.* and *Hyp.* under 6505/997.

1001 shed tears for him and, together with his [spiritual] father Leontius, buried him. This year there was a great flood. The same year envoys came from the Pope of Rome and from the King of Bohemia and Hungary.[1]

BOGATYRS.

In the year 6509/1001. Alexander Popovich and Ian Usmoshvets, who killed the Pecheneg bogatyr', killed a great many Pechenegs and captured their Prince Rodman with his three sons, whom he brought to Vladimir in Kiev.[2] Vladimir organized a great feast and distributed large alms to the churches, monasteries, to the poor and paupers, and he ordered that there be placed in the streets for the poor and the lame large barrels and buckets filled with mead, kvas, beer and wine, as well as with meat, fish and all manner of fruit. Whosoever wished could eat it.

The same year Vladimir sent his mercantile envoys to Rome and Jerusalem, Egypt and Babylon to see those lands and their customs.[3]

In the year 6510/1002. Manfred the Strong died. [Malfreda died in *Laur.*] The same year the Princess Rogneda, mother of Iaroslav, died.[4] The same year a son named Ian was born to Prince Sviatoslav. The same year there were many falling stars. The same year there was much rain.[5]

In the year 6511/1003. Iziaslav, son of Vladimir and father of Briacheslav, passed away.[6] This prince was very quiet, meek, well-behaved and merciful. He very much loved and respected the clergy and monks. He liked reading Divine Scripture and disliked

---

1. There is no such story in *Laur.* or *Hyp.* It is unclear who Volodar' was. He could have been a Russian or a Pecheneg prince. The Polovetss were still unknown in south Russia in Vladimir's time. Probably the chronicler meant Pechenegs. Alexander, or Alesha Popovich, mentioned in this entry, is a hero of the Russian oral heroic folk epos. It was definitely a mistake to mention him under this year 1000, because Alesha Popovich was a Riazan' hero of the XIIIth century during the Tatar invasion. Ragdai is known only from the oral epic folk tales: however, in them he is always mentioned as one of the knights of Vladimir's court.

2. This part of the entry is also based on the folk epics.

3. This item is not to be found in the *Laur.*, *Hyp.* or *Novg.* chronicles.

4. The same item appears in *Laur.* and *Hyp.* under the year 6508/1000.

5. This part of the entry is unavailable in *Hyp.* and *Laur.*

6. The same item is under 6509/1001 in *Laur.* and *Hyp.*

vain laughter. He had the gift of tears and was always kind and very patient. The same year there was a great harvest of all manner of fruits.[7]

In the year 6512/1004. The Pechenegs marched against Belgorod and Vladimir sent against them Alexander Popovich and Ian Usmoshvets with great forces.[8] Hearing of this, the Pechenegs retreated to the prairies. The same year Metropolitan Leontius imprisoned the monk, Adrian, who was a eunuch. He had been criticizing Church Law, the bishops, presbyters and monks; but soon after he came to his senses, repented and learned the Truth. Many people marvelled at his meekness, humility and his tenderness. The same year Heinrich Dobriankov the Brave was poisoned and died, poisoned by his servants. The same year Temir, the Pecheneg prince, was killed by his relatives.[9]

In the year 6516/1008. Metropolitan John[10] built a stone church in Kiev dedicated to the Holy Apostles Peter and Paul; and in the city of Pereiaslavl' he built a stone church dedicated to the Elevation of the Holy Cross. The same year there were many locusts. The same year the well-known robber, Mogut, was cleverly caught. When he appeared before Vladimir he wept profusely and shed many tears from his eyes, and told him the following: "Oh, Vladimir! In the presence of my intercessors, Lord God and His Immaculate Mother Theotokos, I pledge that I will never do any evil toward God and to people but I will repent all the remaining days of my life." Hearing this, Vladimir became meek in heart and soul, and sent him to his [spiritual] father, Metropolitan John, under the stipulation that he should never leave the latter's house. Mogut kept his promise and lived a strict, severe life. He demonstrated much meekness and humility, and when he foresaw his death he died in peace before God.[11]

---

7. This last part of the item is found only in *Nik.*

8. This part of the entry is probably of epic origin.

9. This entire entry under 6512/1004 can be found only in *Nik.* It is of interest because the case of monk Adrian was the first instance of the appearance of heretical teaching in Russia.

10. Archbishop John of Ohrid (Western Bulgaria) was also, probably, head of the Russian Church. (See Foreword to this volume.)

11. This item has no counterpart in *Laur., Hyp.* or *Novg.*

1011   Vladimir was very merciful and loved the poor, continually saying, "Blessed are the merciful because they will be fogiven."[12] "Mercy glorieth against punishment! For judgment is without mercy to him that showed no mercy." [*James* 2; 13; order of sentences changed.] "Blessed is he that considereth the poor: the Lord will deliver him in the day of evil. The Lord will preserve him and keep him alive and he shall be blessed upon the earth. And deliver not Thou him unto the will of his enemies." [*Ps.* 41.1-3.] And so he accumulated a wealth which cannot be destroyed either by worms or by moths, and even a robber cannot take it away or steal it. Through alms and faith our sins are cleansed. And also the Prophet Daniel said, "Remember your sins and break off thy sins by righteousness and thine iniquities by showing mercy to the poor." [*Dan.* 4:27] And speaking thus, he would shed tears, and he always lived peacefully and meekly in great humility, love and mercifulness. The people rejoiced and glorified the Name of Christ.[13]

In the year 6519/1011. The wife of Vladimir, the Imperial Princess Anna, passed away.

In the year 6522/1014. When Iaroslav was in Novgorod he was unwilling to send to his father in Kiev two thousand grivnas, which was the tax due [Vladimir] from Novgorod. He distributed one thousand grivnas in Novgorod, in the same way as Vysheslav had done before; and so did Iaroslav, himself, because he did not want to give it to his father, as was mentioned earlier. His father, Vladimir, wanted to march against him and ordered that the troops assemble, roads be prepared and bridges built, having the intention of going against Iaroslav, his son; but he became ill.

In the year 6523/1015. When his son, Iaroslav, heard that his father intended to campaign against him he sent beyond the sea and brought the Varangian [mercenaries] because he feared his father; but God did not grant the devil any joy. Vladimir fell gravely ill, and at that time Boris was with him. Since the Pechenegs had started raiding Russia, he sent Boris against them because he was badly ill. From this illness he passed away on the fifteenth day of the month of June.

12. A rephrasing of *Matt.* 5:7.

13. This short homily in the last paragraph is an addition to the *Laur.* text of *Pr. Chron.* by the compiler of *Nik.*, probably Metropolitan Daniel.

THE PASSING OF PIOUS GRAND PRINCE VLADIMIR **1015**

Vladimir died in Berestovo and Sviatopolk, who was in Kiev, kept it secret. At night they removed the wooden floor between the buildings, wrapped the body in rugs and lowered it to the ground. They put him [Vladimir] onto a sledge and brought him into the church of the Holy Theotokos which Vladimir had built and personally adorned with gold, silver and expensive gems. The people learned of this and an endless number of them went thither and lamented him: the boyars, because they considered him the guardian of their land, the poor lamented him as their nourisher and lord. His body was placed in a marble sarcophagus and was buried, while all wept.

He was like the new Constantine of great Rome because he [Constantine], himself, became baptised, and baptised his people, and so did this [Prince Vladimir] in the same way as that other had done. Although earlier he was obsessed with evil lust, later he repented without cease, following the words of the Apostle: "When sins abound, then grace also may abound." [*Rom.* 5:20, rephrasing.] He committed many sins when he was unenlightened but all of them were remitted through repentance and alms. Solomon said, "Our sins are cleansed through alms and faith." And, also, the Prophet Daniel said, "Break off thy sins by righteousness and thine iniquities by showing mercy to the poor." [*Dan.* 4:27.] And he [Solomon] says, "He that hath pity upon the poor lendeth unto God." [*Prov.* 19: 17.] Also, the Prophet David said, "Blessed is he that considereth the poor and the paupers, and God will deliver him in the day of evil; God will preserve him and keep him alive, and he shall be blessed upon earth; and deliver not Thou him unto the will of his enemies." [*Ps.* 41: 1-3.] Also, the other voice of the Prophet says in the Name of God, "As I shall find you, so shall I judge you." [*Wis.* 11:17.] And in another place it says, "God says, 'Thou shalt live. I do not wish the death of the wicked but that he turn from his wicked way of life.'" [*Ez.* 33:11, rephrased.] Many were righteous and virtuous, but became lazy and perished. And it also says, "The more powerful thou art, the more thou hast to atone." And God says, "Even the Saints must be in awe of Him."

Everything about this Prince Vladimir was illustrious: how much good he did for the Russian land! He Christianized her, he most eagerly confessed the Christian faith, and he shone as the sun

1015 with his good deeds in the same way as did [Emperor] Constantine, who [for his deeds] became equal to the Apostle. Lord Christ! Grant us another prince such as this one, who will observe God's Commandments and will preserve the Russian dominion and will keep us in peace, in meekness, in love and mercifulness. Grant us a healthy life, victory over the enemy, and grant us the possibility to remember and glorify spiritually holy Prince Vladimir; and to recall him with joy, and all the Orthodox princes who lived dutifully according to Thy will and who observed the words of Thy truth. And grant us to win divine love for each other and to do everything for Thy Sake so that in the present the just one will not be hungry and will inherit the promised eternity. And let us receive it thanks to Our Lord Jesus Christ's grace and love for men, Whose is the glory and the power, together with the Father and the Holy Ghost, now and ever and unto the ages of ages.[14]

The same year there were terrifying portents in the sky.[15]

ABOUT THE HUNGARIANS.

When the Hungarians, who are also called Pannonians, saw that the pagans living in Russia had accepted holy baptism, then, as if it were an act of God, two Hungarian princes also became enlightened, went to Constantinople and accepted holy baptism together with

---

14. This *Encomium* to Vladimir is in *Prim. Chron.*; but the compiler of *Nik.* added some quotations from the *Bible*..

15. The text of this entry follows closely the entry in *Laur.* and *Hyp.* for 6523/1015. Russian medieval sources all are unanimous that Vladimir's conversion to Christianity produced a great alteration in his mind and morals, and that he became a devout and pious Christian. *Prim. Chron.* in *Laur.* and *Hyp.*; the famous sermon by Metropolitan Hilarion, *On Law and Grace* (see S. Zenkovsky, *Medieval Russia's Epics, Chronicles* and *Tales*; and Monk James in *Pamiat' i pokhvala Vladimiru* (SP, 1893, V. Sreznevskii, ed.). It is of interest to note here, also, that the Norwegian King Olaf Tryggwison (d. 1000) spent many years in Kiev at the court of Vladimir, visited Byzantium, became strongly influenced by Christian ideals and, upon his return to Norway in 993-995, received baptism and Christianized his nation. After his conversion he likewise became a true believer of exemplary Christian life. There could well have been some mutual spiritual interchange between him and Vladimir. About Olaf Tryggwison, see N. de Baumgarten, *Olaf Tryggwison, roi de Norvege et ses relations avec St. Vladimir de Russie* in *Orientalie Christiana*, XXV (1921), 1-37; also, P. A. Munch, *De Norske Folks Historie*, d. II b. 2, Christiania, 1854, pp. 593-595.

those who were their subjects. The Greek bishops, however, could not go to their land because of a barbarian attack on Constantinople, and therefore they could not teach them or provide them with the Divine Scripture because they did not have books in their language. Soon thereafter one of their princes named Stefan passed to God, after having performed many good deeds. When the Latins learned that the Greeks had failed to Christianize Hungary they came from Rome and cleverly taught the Hungarians, persuaded them to join their wrong teaching; also, their neighboring pagan people, the Uns [*sic*!], the Pids [*sic*!], the Germans and the Poles, and others closer to Rome, joined their wrong teaching. The island of Brittany, although Christianized long ago, also joined this wrong teaching, as was written hereinbefore.[16]

1015

[MARTYRDOM AND ENCOMIUM OF ST. BORIS AND ST. GLEB]

In the year 6523/1015. Sviatopolk reigned now in Kiev. After his father's death Sviatopolk took over the power in Kiev. He summoned the people of Kiev and began distributing benefices among them. They accepted them but their hearts were not with him because their brothers at that time were [campaigning] with Boris. Not encountering the Pechenegs, Boris returned from the campaign because he received the news, "Your father has died," and he wept greatly for his father because he was his father's most beloved son among all the other sons. He came and camped at the river Al'ta and his father's retinue told him, "We are your father's retinue. Go and assume your father's throne in Kiev." He answered, however, "I will not raise my hand against my elder brother. Since my father has died, he will be to me in the place of my father." When the warriors heard this they abandoned him and Boris remained with his personal guard.

Sviatopolk, who became filled with lawlessness, came to the mind of Cain and sent his people to Boris to tell him, "I want to be in friendship with you and I will add to what our father gave you." He flattered him, while plotting how to destroy him. At night Sviatopolk came secretly to Vyshgorod and summoned Putsha, together with the boyars of Vyshgorod, saying, "Do you accept me with all your

---

16. This paragraph is not to be found in *Laur.*, *Hyp.* or *Novg.*

1015 heart?" And Putsha, together with the boyars of Vyshgorod, said, "We are ready to lay down our heads for you," and he told them, "Tell no one but go and kill my brother, Boris," and they all forthwith promised him to do this. Solomon said about such, "Soon blood will be unjustly shed because they promise blood and gather evil. Their way ends in evil for they lose their souls because of dishonor." [Paraphrase of *Prov.* 1:16-19.] So Sviatopolk's men came to the river Al'ta at night and approached [Boris' camp] and heard that blessed Boris was singing morning prayer because he had already received the news that they wanted to kill him. Rising, he started chanting, saying the following: "Glory to God in the highest. Oh, Lord! Why hast Thou increased this number of those who come against me? Many are those that rise up against me." [*Psalms* 3:1-3, paraphrased.] And then he said, "Lord, hear my prayer and enter not into judgment with Thy servant for in Thy sight no man living is righteous before Thee. For the enemy hath persecuted my soul." [*Psalms* 140:1-3, paraphrased.] Finishing the six psalms, he began to chant from the Psalter, saying, "Many bulls have compassed me and a company of evildoers besets me. Oh, Lord, My God! In Thee do I take refuge! Save me from all them that pursue me, and deliver me!" [*Psalms* 22:12-16; part of 7:1.] And finishing reading morning prayers, he looked at the Icon of the Lord and said, "My Lord Jesus Christ, Who in this Image has appeared on earth for our salvation and Who voluntarily suffered Thy hands to be nailed on the cross, Thou didst accept Thy passion for our sins. So help me now to accept my passion, for I accept it not from those who are my enemies but from the hand of my own brother. Oh, Lord, hold it not against him as a sin!" He finished his prayer and lay down upon his couch.

THE MURDER OF BORIS.

And now, surrounding the tent, they attacked him like savage beasts, throwing lances through and stabbing Boris. They also stabbed his servant, who cast himself upon his body. He was a Hungarian guard named George, whom Prince Boris liked very much and he had given him a large golden necklace to wear when he attended him. They also killed many of Boris' servants and guards. Being in a hurry, they could not take George's necklace from his neck, so they cut his head off in order to take it. For this reason his body was not recognized among the other corpses. Those accursed ones, having killed Boris, wrapped his body with a tent and put it on a cart and drove him, although he was still breathing. When the accursed Sviatopolk saw that he was still breathing, he sent two Varangians to finish him, and those came and saw that he was still alive. One of them pulled out his sword and stabbed his heart, and thus did God-loving Boris die, on the 24th of July when the Holy Martyr Christina is remembered. And so he received the crown from Christ God and he is now numbered with the martyrs, prophets, Apostles and all saints, and he dwells in the lap of Abraham, viewing unspeakable joys and chanting with the angels and rejoicing amongst the assembly of the saints.

1015

BURIAL OF BORIS.

Bringing it from thence to Vyshgorod, they buried his body in the Church of St. Basil. These accursed and thrice anathemized murderers were from the household of Putsha, and they came to Sviatopolk boasting as if they had done a good deed, not comprehending what a lawless sin they had committed. The names of these low trespassing murderers are Putsha, Talets, Elovit and Liashko; and their father is Satan, and they all perished without being remembered and they are tormented with inextinguishable fire for ages and ages. Such are the servants of the devil; devils are sent to commit evil, while angels are sent to perform good. Angels commit no evil to man but think always about his well-being, help Christians, even intercede for them to prevent them from all evil, from the nets of the devil and from the wicked enemy. Devils always ensnare with evil and try to teach one when they see that he is honored by God. They envy him and have evil intentions. God says, "Who would seduce Ahab?" And the devil said, "I will do it." In the same way an evil man tries to do evil and he does it no worse than the devil. Devils still fear God, but an evil man does not fear God and is not ashamed before people. The devils also fear the Cross, but an evil man does not fear even the Cross. And so did these accursed murderers commit their wicked assassination.

THE MURDER OF GLEB.

Accursed Sviatopolk still thought and said, "Thus have I killed Boris, but how shall I kill Gleb?" And accepting Cain's mind, he sent [his people] with flattery to tell Gleb the following: "Hurry and

1015 come. Your father is calling you. He is gravely ill." Gleb quickly mounted his horse and went with a small retinue because he was always obedient to his father. When he came as far as the Volga his horse stumbled in a moat in the middle of a field and it hurt its foot slightly. Then he came to Smolensk, and from Smolensk he went further at dawn, stopping at Smiadyn' in a boat. At that time Iaroslav received tidings from Peredslava, his sister, concerning his father's death, and Iaroslav sent to Gleb, saying the following: "Do not go. Our father has died and our brother, Boris, has been killed by Sviatopolk."

Hearing this, Gleb wept greatly and shed tears, and bewailed his father and brother and prayed tearfully, saying, "Woe is me, oh Lord! It would be better for me to die with my brother than to live in this quickly passing world. If I were with my brother, I would be able to see thy angelic face, and I would have died with thee. What have I to do now? I, who have always loved thee and am now deprived of thy love? Why have I remained alone? Where are thy words which thou usest to speak to me, my beloved brother? No more will I hear thy gentle advice. If thou hast received God's permission, then pray to God for me so that I should receive the same death. It is better to die with thee than live alone in this deceitful world."

And so he prayed tearfully, sighing, weeping, shedding tears, moaning, and appealing frequently to God. Suddenly those wicked servants sent by Sviatopolk came to murder Gleb. Holy Gleb was advancing in his boat and they met him at the mouth of the river Smiadyn'. Then these accursed ones surrounded him with their boats, captured Gleb's boat and drew their arms. Gleb's servants became terrified, and then one of the men sent, whose name was Goriaser, ordered that Gleb be killed hastily. Gleb's cook, named Torchin,[17] pulled out a knife and stabbed his master, Gleb. And it was on the fifth day of the month of September of the year 6524,[18] a Monday, when the Holy Prophet Zacharia is remembered. And they sacrificed to God an innocent lamb amidst the fragrance of incense, a veritable victim, and he received a crown from God. He entered the heavenly dwellings and saw his longed for brother and rejoiced

---

17. Apparently Torchin was a Tork from the nomadic Turkic tribe of Torks. "*In*" is a common ending for a name derived from nationality.

18. 6523 in *Laur.* and *Vozn.* But Sept. 5, 6524 was still 1015 according to Old Russian March Calendar. See *Introduction* to this vol.

with him in ineffable joy, and received an imperishable crown through their brotherly love. "How good and how pleasant it is for brethren to dwell together in unity." [*Psalms* 133:1.] The accursed murderers returned, as David says: "The impious ones returned. Let the sinners return to hell. When they came to Sviatopolk, they told him, "We have done what you ordered." He heard it and became overfilled with pride because he did not know that the Prophet David says, "Why dost thou boast, thou proud man, of thy mischief, o mighty man? Thy tongue deviseth very wickedness all the day long." [Paraphrase, *Psalm* 52:1-2.]

After Gleb's murder his body was cast in the wilderness onto the shore of the river, between two tree trunks, and his body remained there a long time, unknown and unattended. Later, however, a pillar of fire appeared and would burn day and night, and merchants passing that place would hear angelic singing, as would those hunting or those grazing their cattle. Although they heard this and saw it, no one thought of looking for the body of the Saint, for everyone knew only that he was killed in the vicinity of Smolensk, but no one was aware where he was buried. When they recalled seeing the light burning in the wilderness, however, they sent men with venerable crosses looking for the body of the Saint. They found it where they had seen [the light]. And they went and brought it and dug [a grave].

THE BURIAL OF GLEB AND BORIS.

They buried the body of St. Gleb in the same place, in the vicinity of the Church of St. Basil, where the body of his brother, St. Boris, rests. This was done beautifully and reverently with the chanting of psalms and hymns, and they became united in body and spirit, and dwell in eternal bliss, in indescribable light, within the Kingdom of the Lord of Heaven; and

> They bestow a salutary gift upon the Russian land,
> They provide care to pilgrims coming.
> They make the lame to walk,
> They give sight to the blind,
> They cure the sick,
> They liberate those in irons,
> They open prisons,
> They bestow consolation upon the afflicted,

1015

1015   They save those who are assaulted,
They intercede on behalf of the Russian
   land,
They shine eternally as beacons.
They pray the Lord constantly on behalf of
   men.[19]

ENCOMIUM TO THE SAINTLY PASSION MARTYRS BORIS AND GLEB.

We should also render you praise, passion martyrs in Christ of the Russian land, and pray diligently, saying:

Rejoice, passion martyrs in Christ of the Russian land, you provide a cure for those who come to you with faith and love.

Rejoice, heavenly dwellers, corporeal angels similar to the image and spirit of the saints.

Rejoice, Boris and Gleb, wise in God. Like a brook, you provide water for the life-giving fount and from you flows cure for faithful men.

Rejoice, you who defeated the evil snake and who are as the morning light and stars which shine upon the Russian land and drive away darkness, and who are of steadfast faith.

Rejoice, brothers! You are together in brilliant dwellings in the Heavenly City, in undiminishing glory, which you have won through your deeds.

Rejoice, shining stars, which rise in the morning!

You Christ-loving brothers, passion-martyrs, are our intercessors!

You help submit the infidels under the feet of our princes who pray to our true Lord Christ God!

You intercede for our unity and good health!

You liberate them [the princes] from fratricidal feuds and the wickedness of the devil!

You deserve worship because we venerate your reverend triumph for ages unto ages. Amen.

19. This glorification of Saints Boris and Gleb and the following *Encomium* in the XIth century original is written in short, rhythmic sentences with grammatical rhyme, which is hard to render into English. In order to preserve the solemn cadence, this translation is couched in anaphoric lines which to some extent correspond to the repetitive pattern of the original text. It is the earliest instance of a rhythmic structure in Russian literature.

[WAR BETWEEN SVIATOPOLK AND IAROSLAV]   **1015**

THE MURDER OF SVIATOSLAV.

The accursed Sviatopolk also killed Sviatoslav, sending his own man after him when he escaped to the Hungarian land, to the Hungarian mountains, because he was instructed by Satan to commit fratricide.

Sviatopolk [began to think]: "When I shall have killed all my brothers, then I will be alone to assume power over the Russian land." And he thought in this way because of his great pride, without knowing that God gives power to whomsoever He wishes. The Most High crowns kings and princes and gives power to him whom He wants. When a land lives according to God's Will, God bestows upon it righteous kings and princes who love justice and truth, and He establishes the ruler and judge to judge righteously. When there are righteous princes on earth, many sins are then remitted. If they are wicked and evil, then God brings upon that land more evil because such a prince is the head of the land. Isaiah says, "From the sole of the foot even unto the head, there is no soundness in it." [*Isa.* 1:6.] This means that they sinned beginning with the king down to the common man. "Woe to such a city and such land whose ruler is young, likes drinking wine amidst [music of harps], surrounded with young counselors. Such rulers are given to men by God as punishment for their sins, and He takes away the elders and wise men." It happens as Isaiah says: "God doth take away from Jerusalem the meek [mighty, in *Isa.*] giant, the valiant and just judge, and the humble elder, and the wise and the obedient, and I will give children to be their princes and an abuser to rule them." [Paraphrase of *Isa.* 3:1-4.]

THE RULE OF SVIATOPOLK.

Sviatopolk the Accursed began to rule in Kiev. He summoned the people and began to endow them with *koroznos*.[20] To the others he gave kunas, and in this way he distributed a great many.

ABOUT PRINCE IAROSLAV.

At that time Iaroslav was in Novgorod and was unaware of his

---

20. *Korozno*: A valuable Russian mantle made of felt used by the rich or noble. It was a popular article of export from Russia and was highly prized.

1015 father's death, but he hired many Varangians because he feared war. The Varangians in Iaroslav's service were very numerous and they used violence upon the Novgorodians and their wives. The Novgorodians assembled and said, "We cannot abide such violence." They came together at night and killed the Varangians in the yard of Paramon. Iaroslav became angry and marched to Rakom,[21] where he settled in his court. He sent his men to the Novgorodians to say the following: "I can resurrect them no more." And he summoned a thousand of the best men who had slain the Varangians, flattered them and then massacred them. The others fled the city. The same night he received news from his sister, Peredslava, from Kiev: "Your father has died. Your brother, Sviatopolk, has taken over Kiev. He has killed Boris and Gleb and you must be on your guard." Hearing this, Iaroslav became very sad about his father, his brothers and their retinues, and the next day he summoned the remaining Novgorodians. Iaroslav held a *veche*[22] on the square and told them, "Oh, my beloved warriors! Yesterday I killed many of you, being in a state of madness, but now I will pay for it with my gold; I need you now." And he wiped his tears and said to the *veche*, "Brothers! My father has died. Sviatopolk has taken over Kiev. He has killed my brothers. I want to march against him. Help me fight!" And the Novgorodians said, "Prince! Although our brethren have been killed, we still will campaign with you." And then Iaroslav gathered one thousand Varangians and forty thousand other warriors and marched against Sviatopolk; and addressing himself to God, he said, "I did not start murdering brothers, but he did; God must be the avenger for the blood of my brothers, Boris and Gleb, because their blood was spilled without any fault on their part. And then he might do the same to me! So judge me, God, according to justice, and the wrath of the sinner must come to an end."[23]

And he marched against Sviatopolk. When Sviatopolk heard that Iaroslav had begun to campaign, he armed a numberless multitude of warriors—Russians and Pechenegs—and marched

21. Rakom was Iaroslav's suburban residence.

22. *Veche*: a town meeting. Local self-government, which lasted until the late XVth century. It was one of the main features of Novgorod's government.

23. In the *Laur.*, *Hyp.* and *Novg.* chronicles, the narrative here continues under the year 1016.

toward Liubech, remaining on one side of the Dnieper while Iaroslav was on the other. The same year Iaroslav advanced against Sviatopolk and they camped across from each other on both sides of the Dnieper. Neither of them ventured to start—neither one against the other, and so they remained encamped for three months across from each other, not daring to come together [for battle]. One of Sviatopolk's voevodas, named Volchij Khvost, rode along the shore, challenging the Novgorodians, saying, "Why have you come with this lame fellow, you carpenters? We will have you build houses for us!" Hearing this, the Novgorodians told Iaroslav, "Tomorrow we will cross the river against them. If anyone does not come with us, we will cut him to pieces ourselves." At that time the freeze had begun. Sviatopolk was camped between two lakes, and he and his retinue drank the whole night while the river Dnieper began to freeze.

1015

[In Sviatopolk's army] there was a man who had Sviatopolk's confidence but [since he was Iaroslav's supporter] Iaroslav sent his own guardsman to him that night to ask him: "Oh, you! What would you advise us to do? Our troops are very numerous but not enough mead was made." The man answered him, "Tell Iaroslav the following: 'If you don't have enough mead and you have too many troops, you can get some of it toward evening.'" Iaroslav understood that in the evening he should give the order for battle. On the morrow at dawn Iaroslav displayed his troops and crossed to the other side of the river with his army. He disembarked onto the shore and ordered that the boats be pushed off from shore, and the same night[24] they marched against them [Sviatopolk's troops] in order to fight. Then Iaroslav told his troops, "Mark yourselves. Put a cloth on your heads." And the armies came together and there was a cruel massacre, and because of the lakes the Pechenegs' [horsemen] could not come to help. [Iaroslav's army] pushed Sviatopolk's warriors to the lake and they went onto the ice and the ice broke under them, and Iaroslav began to overcome [Sviatopolk's army]. Seeing this, Sviatopolk fled and Iaroslav won [the battle], while Sviatopolk escaped to Poland.

THE RULE OF IAROSLAV IN KIEV.

Iaroslav ascended the throne of his father and grandfather in

24. Actually, while it was still dark.

1017 Kiev. At that time Iaroslav was twenty-eight years old.[25]

In the year 6525/1017. When Iaroslav came to Kiev they [Sviatopolk's men] burned the fortress and many churches, the number of the latter being seven hundred; and therefore Iaroslav grew very sad.

The same year Iaroslav laid the foundation of a [new] fortress of Kiev, which was bigger than the former; he built the Golden Gate; he laid the foundation of the Church of St. Sophia; and he built many churches and distributed so much of his wealth to the poor that it was impossible to count it. Because Iaroslav, in the way of his father, was Christ-loving and poor-loving, and he always had his mind filled with Divine Scripture. The same year the Pechenegs came to Kiev and succeeded in slashing their way into the city, and only toward evening was Iaroslav able to overcome and defeat the Pechenegs; and they fled.[26]

In the year 6526/1018. Together with the [Polish King Boleslav], Sviatopolk started campaigning with great forces and marched with the Poles against Iaroslav; but Iaroslav assembled many warriors: Russians, Varangians and Slovens [Novgorodians] and he marched against Boleslav and Sviatopolk.[27] He marched into Volynia and the two armies camped on both sides of the river Bug. In Iaroslav's army was his former guardian, a voevoda named Blud[28] and he began to challenge Boleslav, saying the following: "What are you? We will pierce your fat belly with a pike!" [He said this] because Boleslav was very fat and heavy in body, and he was almost unable to ride a horse; but he was very clever. Then Boleslav told his army, "If you do not respond to this challenge [I will fight] and perish alone!" He mounted his horse, went into the river and was followed by his warriors. Iaroslav did not have time to align his army and so Boleslav defeated Iaroslav. Voevoda Blud was killed and a great many [of Iaroslav's] troops were defeated and taken prisoner by hand;

---

25. The first half of the sentence is the same as in *Laur., Hyp.* and *Novg.*

26. This entire paragraph is not to be found in *Laur., Hyp.* or *Novg.* chronicles.

27. This is an interesting distinction made by the chronicler between Varangians and Russians, under whom he means the population of the Kiev region, the former Polians, and the Slovens or Novgorodians. Sviatopolk was married to the sister of the Polish King Boleslav the Brave.

28. In *Nik.,* Blud; "Bud" in *Laur.*

Boleslav distributed these prisoners among the Poles, while he, himself, occupied Kiev with Sviatopolk, who ascended to Vladimir's throne. Then Boleslav took to his bed Peredslava, daughter of Vladimir, Iaroslav's sister.

[While] Iaroslav escaped with four men to Novgorod, Boleslav commanded, "Distribute my troops among the cities for their supplies," and so it was done. Iaroslav wanted to escape beyond the sea but posadnik Konstantin, son of Dobrynia, together with the Novgorodians, hacked Iaroslav's boat to pieces, saying, "We want to fight with you against Boleslav and Sviatopolk." And they began to collect a tax from every man: four kunas from every man, and from the elders, ten grivnas, and from the boyars, eighteen grivnas; also, they brought the Varangians and gave them their pay, and thus was Iaroslav enabled to assemble many warriors.

While Boleslav was in Kiev crazy Sviatopolk said to his men, "Since the Poles are dispersed in various cities, kill them." And they were killed. But Boleslav escaped from Kiev after ravishing Peredslava, and he took with him the wealth of many boyars of Iaroslav and of his sister. He appointed [priest] Anastas [of Chersonesus] as tithe man over his properties because he believed his flattery. Then he took a great many captives and led them away, and occupied the cities of Cherven' Russia.[29] Then he went to his land. Sviatopolk began to rule in Kiev but Iaroslav came against him and Sviatopolk escaped to the Pechengs.

In the year 6527/1019. Sviatopolk came with a great many Pechenegs. But Iaroslav also gathered many warriors and marched against him to the river Al'ta, and camped on the same spot where Boris had been killed. There, raising his hands to heaven, he said, "The blood of my brothers cries out to Thee, oh, Lord! Revenge the blood of these just ones in the same way as Thou didst avenge the blood of Abel, when Thou punished Cain with moaning and trembling. Punish this one in the same way." And after praying, he said, "Oh, my brethren! Although you have departed from earth in body, you can still help me with your prayers against this wicked and proud murderer." After this, they [the two armies] marched against

---

29. Cherven'-Russia: a borderland between Poland and Russia at that time, in the northwestern part of Volynia and in Galicia. The name originated from the city of Cherven'.

1019 each other and the entire plain of Al'ta[30] was covered by this multitude of troops. It was a Friday and the sun began to rise; both armies came together and there was a cruel massacre such as never was before in Russia; and the warriors slaughtered each other, fighting hand to hand, and they clashed three times, and along the valley the blood flowed. Many faithful, however, saw angels helping Iaroslav, and that evening Iaroslav defeated Sviatopolk, and the latter fled.

When he fled he was seized by fear, and all his bones became soft and he could not ride. His men were obliged to carry him on a litter, and they brought him to Berest'e, running with him as he said, "Run with me, they are catching up to us!" Sviatopolk's men sent their scouts ahead asking, "Who is following him?" because they saw no one; but they ran with him and he remained lying and ill, exclaiming, "Oh, they are catching up with us! Run!" He could not endure staying on the same spot, so, chased by the wrath of God, he ran through the Polish land and crossed the wilderness between Bohemia and Poland, and there he ended his wicked life. This was right for him because this was true justice that came upon him, and after he departed from this world he received the torments due an accursed. It was shown by the deadly wounds which were inflicted upon him, and he was chased unmercifully unto death, and after death he was most unmercifully tormented, being bound to the depths of Hell. His grave is in the wilderness, and to the present day a foul odor emanates from it because the earth settled and devoured him. God inflicted this [punishment] as warning to the Russian princes, for in the case they should commit [the same crime] about which they have heard, they shall incur the same punishement. It may even be a stronger one, if they should commit wicked fratricide, since they [now] are aware of this past case.

Vengeance was exacted on Cain sevenfold for slaying Abel, [*Gen.* 4:15.] but on Lemech, seventyfold because Cain slew without knowledge of the revenge exacted by God. Lemech, however, knew of the punishment exacted upon his forefather, yet he committed murder. Lemech said to his wives, "For I have slain a man for wounding me and the young man for bruising me." Lemech said to them, "There will be seventy revenges exacted upon me because of

---

30. In *Nik.,* "the plain of Let."

it," he said, "since I committed it being aware." [Paraphrase of *Gen.* 4:18-24.] This Lemech killed two brothers of Enoch and took their wives. This Sviatopolk was cursed and thrice accursed because he was a new Lemech. It happened because he was born of adultery, just like Abimelech, who killed his brothers, the seventy sons of Gideon.[31] And so it was.[32]

[THE REIGN OF IAROSLAV THE WISE]

[6527/*1019, cont.*] Iaroslav began to reign in Kiev, and he and his retinue wiped the sweat from their brows, having achieved victory and having greatly bestirred themselves on behalf of his brothers.

ABOUT THE SEARCH FOR THE BODIES OF THE HOLY PASSION MARTYRS

The same year he began to search for their holy bodies: how and where were they buried? And he was told that St. Boris was buried in Vyshgorod but no one knew where the body of St. Gleb was; everyone knew only that he was slain near Smolensk but no one was aware where he was buried. Iaroslav began diligently searching for him and gathered many people but no one knew where the body of St. Gleb was buried. [Finally] they started recalling to each other, "People say that in the wilderness near Smolensk it is possible to see an indescribably powerful light and burning candles, and to hear angelic chanting. This has been heard by passing merchants, by hunters hunting, and by shepherds grazing their sheep." Hearing this, Iaroslav greatly rejoiced and said, "There is the body of my brother, St. Gleb," and he sent priests, monks and boyars with crosses, candles and censers to search there for it. They found the holy body, which was in no way damaged and had not become black, as usually happens with the corpses of the dead; but it was whole and shone brightly, and was fragrant. And he was buried in Vyshgorod after they dug a grave in the place where blessed Boris was buried, in the same way as it was said before.[33]

In the year 6528/1020. Iaroslav began to share kunas with his

---

31. Abimelech, who killed his brothers, was the son of Jerubbaal, and not Gideon. *Judges* 9.1, 5.

32. This text follows *Laur.* very closely.

33. Not in *Laur.*, *Hyp.* or *Novg.*, but in *Vita B.G.* and in *Mosc. late XV.*

1021 warriors. The elders each received ten grivnas; the *smerds*[34] each received two grivnas; the Novgorodians, each ten grivnas. And he let them go home, and he gave them the law and wrote a code of law, saying, "You will live according to this charter. Follow it as I have written it for you." [Posadnik] Konstantin at that time was in Novgorod, and Iaroslav became wroth with him and imprisoned him for three years in Rostov; thereafter he ordered him to be killed in Murom on the river Oka. The same year the Pechenegs came, doing much evil, and returned home.[35]

The same year a son was born to Iaroslav and he was given the name, Vladimir.

In the year 6529/1021. Briacheslav, son of Iziaslav, grandson of Vladimir[36] came with warriors from Polotsk to Novgorod and captured Novgorod, and he captured many Novgorodians, their wives, children and possessions and their cattle, and many prisoners, and he returned to Polotsk. When he arrived at the river Sudoma, Iaroslav received word of it and gathered many warriors; and on the same day marched from Kiev and caught up with him. He defeated Briacheslav and let the Novgorodians return to Novgorod. He liberated all the people captured by him [by Briacheslav] who were from the region of Novgorod and sent them to Novgorod, while Briacheslav escaped to Polotsk.

When he came to Kiev Iaroslav summoned Briacheslav and gave him two towns, Sviach' and Vitebsk. And he told him, "Be of the same mind as I," and Briacheslav campaigned together with Iaroslav [against the enemy] for the remaining years of his life.[37]

In the year 6530/1022. Iaroslav arrived in Brest.

The same year Mistislav, son of Vladimir, was reigning in Tmutarakan' and Mstislav marched against the Cherkess.[38] When the Cherkessian Prince Rededia heard of this he went against him and both armies faced each other. Then Rededia told Mstislav, "Why should we mutually destroy our troops? Let us just fight

34. *Smerd:* peasants.
35. This part of the entry is not in *Laur.*, *Hyp.* or *Novg.* chronicles.
36. For Iziaslav's descendants, see the year 1128.
37. This last paragraph is not to be found in *Laur.*, *Hyp.* or *Novg.* chronicles.
38. Cherkess—the native population of Northeastern Caucasus.

against each other. In case you overwhelm me, you will have my possessions and my wife and my children and my land. And if I win, then I will take everything that is yours." They came together, fighting fiercely, and when they fought Mstislav began to weaken because Rededia was tall and strong. And Mstislav said, "Immaculate Theotokos, help me! If I overwhelm him I will build a church in your honor!" Having thus spoken, he struck the other to the ground and pulled out a knife and slashed Rededia to death. Mstislav marched into his land, took his possessions, his wife and children, and imposed a tribute on the Cherkess. When he returned to Tmutarakan', he laid the foundation of the Church of the Holy Theotokos, and he built it and it remains there until now.

1023

In the year 6531/1023. Mstislav marched with Khazar and Cherkess troops against Iaroslav.

In the year 6532/1024. When Iaroslav was in Novgorod, Mstislav came from Tmutarakan' to Kiev, but Kiev did not accept him; and then he left and ascended to the throne in Chernigov.

ABOUT THE MAGICIANS

The same year there was an uprising of false magicians in Suzdal', and they slew the elders and women, and did this at the instigation of the devil and because of the devil's actions. They claimed that they [the old people] would hide supplies and grain and starvation would come. There was a great mutiny and such a great famine throughout the entire land that men would give away their women so the *cheliadin* would feed them.[39]

All the people had to go up to the Volga to the Bulgars and bring back wheat and rye from them, and this way they survived. When Iaroslav heard of the magicians he came to Suzdal' and caught these murderers and punished those who killed the old women; and he sacked their houses and executed others, and organized administration in the land, saying the following: "God brings starvation, plague or drought or other punishment upon the land, according to the sins of men, and people can do nothing about it.

---

39. *Cheliadin*: a social group of dependent but rather wealthy men; *smerd*: a peasant. Both terms cover a wide range of social strata. *Smerd* usually denotes "peasant" or a person of lower rural or urban class. *Cheliadin* is likewise a dependent person, maybe a slave, member of a lord's household, or even a person with specific legal status in the court of a prince.

1025 Christ God is the Only One in Heaven, and He has power over everything."

Iaroslav returned, came to Novgorod and sent beyond the sea for the Varangian Prince Iakun [Haakon] and his Varangians. And Iakun arrived with his Varangian [mercenaries]. This Iakun was very handsome and had a mantle embroidered with gold. Iaroslav and Iakun marched against Mstislav in Chernigov. Hearing of this, Mstislav came to meet them and there was a fierce battle on the river Listvena. It was fall when they met there. In the evening Mstislav prepared his troops for battle, and put the Severs in the center against the Varangians while he, himself, remained with his army on both wings. At night it was very dark and thunder rolled, and there was lightning and rain, and Mstislav told his troops, "Let us march against them. There will be great bounty for us." So Mstislav and Iaroslav moved against each other and the Severs were at the head of the troops against the Varangians. The latter were very busy slaying the Severs but then Mstislav attacked them with his own army and started slaying the Varangians. It was a bad and horrifying massacre. When lightning flashed the weapons shone, and in the lightning flashes the swords saw their path; and so they killed each other, and there was a great thunderstorm and a mighty battle. When Iaroslav saw that he was going to be defeated he escaped with the Varangian Prince Iakun. Iakun abandoned his gold-embroidered mantle and so Mstislav defeated Iaroslav and Iakun. Iaroslav came to Novgorod while Iakun went beyond the sea and died there. When on the morrow it became light, Mstislav saw his Severs and Iaroslav's Varangians lying [dead on the battlefield] and said, "Who would not be happy about this? Here the Severs lie and there, the Varangians, but my own army has remained unscathed." And then Mstislav sent his men to Iaroslav, saying, "Come and assume your throne in Kiev because you are my senior brother, while I will have this side [of the Dnieper]."[40] And Iaroslav could not then do anything but accept the peace; and the people of Iaroslav were in Kiev while Iaroslav Vladimirovich, himself, slew the magicians in Suzdal', and his brother, Mstislav the Bold, ruled in Chernigov.

In the year 6533/1025. There was born another son to Iaroslav

---

40. Iaroslav became the ruler of Russia west of the Dnieper and Mstislav of the land east of the same river.

and he received the name of Iziaslav.

In the year 6534/1026. Iaroslav assembled many warriors and went to Kiev and made peace with his brother, Mstislav, in the town of Gorodets, and the Dnieper divided the Russian land. Iaroslav took over this side and Mstislav, the other. And they lived in peace and fraternal love. Feuds and rebellions came to an end and there was great peace in the land.[41]

In the year 6535/1027. A third son was born to Iaroslav and he named him Sviatoslav.

[PORTENT]

In the year 6536/1028. There appeared a serpent in the skies which could be seen over the entire land.[42]

In the year 6537/1029. Iaroslav campaigned against the Iasy.[43] This year there was peace throughout the entire Russian land.

In the year 6538/1030. There was born a fourth son to Iaroslav and he was named Vsevolod. The same year Iaroslav marched against the city of Bielzy.[44] He fought against the Chud' and defeated them, and founded the fortress of Jur'ev.[45] Then he came to Novgorod and assembled three hundred children of the elders and the priests, and ordered them to be taught how to read the Scriptures.

THE PASSING OF BISHOP JOACHIM.

The same year the Novgorodian Bishop Joachim passed away and was succeeded by his pupil, Ephraim, who continues to teach up to now.

The same year Boleslav the Great [the Brave] of Poland passed away and there was a great disturbance in the Polish land. Rebels

---

41. In *Laur.* and *Hyp.* the last paragraph is under the year 6535/1027.

42. Apparently it was a comet; in *Laur.* and *Hyp.* this item appears under 6536/1028.

43. *Iasy*, or *Alans*, now *Ossets*, inhabited at that time the land between the Volga, Don and Caucasus. Now they inhabit only the valleys of the Caucasian range. They belong to the Iranian linguistic family. This item is not to be found in *Laur.* and *Hyp.*

44. Bielzy: a city on the river Soroki, an affluent of the Western Bug.

45. *Chud'*: present Estonians. The city of Iur'ev is also known under the names of Dorpat, Derpt or Tartu.

1031 killed the bishops, the priests of the churches and all their boyars.

In the year 6539/1031. Iaroslav and Mstislav assembled a large number of warriors and marched against the Poles. They took back the cities of Cherven' Russia, and campaigned in the Polish land and brought back many Polish prisoners, whom they distributed [among their troops]. And Iaroslav founded settlements along the river Ros', where they remain to the present day.[46]

In the year 6540/1032. Iaroslav started building fortresses along the river Ros'. The same year Uleb marched from Novgorod against the Iron Gate.[47] But very few of them returned because most perished there.

THE DEATH OF MSTISLAV.

In the year 6541/1033.[48] Prince Mstislav, son of Great Vladimir, went hunting and during the hunt he became ill and died; and he was buried in Chernigov in the Cathedral of the Holy Saviour, whose foundation he, himself, had laid. At this time construction of the cathedral had progressed so far that [the top of the wall] could be reached with the hand of a man standing on a horse. This Mstislav was imposing of stature, had red hair and a fair face,[49] large eyes and heavy brows; and he was very merciful toward the poor and had great passions toward everyone; and he was brave in war and greatly loved his troops, refusing them neither his wealth nor drink nor food.

After his death all the power in Russia remained in Iaroslav's hands and he was the only ruler of the entire Russian land. The same year Iaroslav went to Novgorod and assigned his son, Vladimir, to rule Novgorod. He appointed [Luke] Zhidiata to bishop [of

---

46. Harold Sigurdsson, King of Norway (1046-1066), who, as ally of William the Conqueror, invaded England and, on September 25, 1066, was killed in the battle of Stamford Bridge—fought as Iaroslav's ally against the Poles (1031) and, later, married Iaroslav's daughter, Elizabeth. *King Harald Saga*, trans. by M. Magnuson, Penguin Books, Harmondworth, 1966, pp. 46-48, 64, 151-152.

47. The exact location of the Iron Gate is unknown. Apparently it was a region on the river Sysola about fifty miles from Ust'sysolsk in the Vologda region. This region at that time was inhabited by Ugro-Finnic tribes. Likhachev, II, 373.

48. In *Laur.* and *Hyp.*, 6452/1034.

49. In *Laur.*, "red (fair) face" in place of "red hair and face."

Novgorod] and [Luke] Zhidiata was consecrated by the bishops. **1034**
And he [Iaroslav] had a charter written for the people of Novgorod, saying, "You will pay tribute according to this charter."⁵⁰

The same year a son was born to Iaroslav and he was named Viacheslav.

Iaroslav was in Novgorod when he received tidings that the Pechenegs had besieged Kiev. Iaroslav gathered numerous warriors, Varangians and Slovens [Novgorodians] and in the spring he came to Kiev and entered the city with his many warriors. Seeing that the Pechenegs were in endless number, Iaroslav made a sally from the city and prepared his retinue for battle. He put the Varangians in the middle and on the right side were the levies from Kiev, and on the other the levies from Novgorod. When he displayed his troops before Kiev, the Pechenegs attacked and the two armies met on the place where now stands Holy Sophia, the Metropolitan Cathedral of Russia. At that time it was a field outside the city. There was a terrible battle and Iaroslav won it with difficulty only toward evening. The Pechenegs escaped in disarray, not seeing whither they fled. Many of them drowned, some in the river of Sitomlia and others in other rivers. The remainder of them disappeared, and so they remain to this day. The same year Iaroslav became wroth with his junior brother, Sudislav, and put him in a cell in Pskov till the end of his life. This Sudislav was caluminated before Iaroslav.[51]

In the year 6542/1034.
In the year 6543/1035.
In the year 6544/1036.
In the year 6545/1037. The fortress around Kiev was completed and it had a Golden Gate. The same year they consecrated the Church of Holy Sophia in Kiev.

ESTABLISHMENT OF THE METROPOLIA.

Iaroslav established the Metropolia and extended [the building of churches]. Over the Golden Gate he constructed two churches: a

---

50. Luke Zhidiata, the first known Russian sermon writer, was Bishop of Novgorod for many years. The word, "Zhidiata," is an abbreviation of "Zhidislav." He died *c.* 1061. Likhachev II, 374.

51. In 1036 in *Laur.* He was released in 1058.

1037 Church of the Annunciation and the Church of St. George[52] and he built many other churches and organized monasteries. Under this Iaroslav the Christian faith spread and blossomed and the number of monks increased. He loved the wisdom-loving priests and respected Scripture. Iaroslav assembled many scribes who translated many books from Greek into the Slav language. Thus many books were written and obtained for the teaching of the faithful, so that they could enjoy the Divine Teaching. One selects the earth and another sows seeds, then yet another harvests and eats abundant food. And so it was. His father, Vladimir, looked and prepared the ground—we want to say, he enlightened us with baptism; but this one spread the Word of the Scripture in the hearts of faithful people, and we harvest now, accepting the learning of the Scripture. There is always great benefit in book learning: from books we are shown and taught the way to repentance; we obtain wisdom and learn temperance from the word of the books. They are like rivers which provide [water] for the Universe, and they [books] are the sources of wisdom. There is an unfathomable depth in books because with them we console our grief and because they are a bridle for our self-restraint. Wisdom is great and it was praised by Solomon, who said, "I, wisdom, have made prudence my dwelling and found out knowledge and discretion. The fear of the Lord is to hate evil; counsel is mine, and sound knowledge; I am understanding; I have might. By me, kings reign and princes decree justice. My dignitaries are respected and my judges keep the land. I love them that love me, and those that seek me diligently shall find me." [*Prov.* 8:12-13, 14-17.] Just search in the books of wisdom diligently and you will find great solace for your soul, because he who often reads Holy Scripture speaks with God and with the Holy Fathers. The soul of a person who respects the teaching of the Prophets, the teaching of the Gospel and the Apostles, the lives of the holy Fathers—receives great benefit.

Iaroslav loved books greatly, and having caused many of them to be written, he deposited them in the Church of Holy Sophia, which he, himself, built. And he adorned it with gold and silver and

---

52. Iaroslav's Christian name was Iurii (George). In order to be protected against witchcraft, the Christian name of the princes was kept secret.

church vessels, and in it are celebrated the daily services. And he **1038** built churches in the cities and towns and he respected priests, giving them contributions from his wealth and instructing them to teach people, because they are entrusted by God to teach and instruct the people and to give them an answer. And so the priests taught people piety and church attendance, and the number of priests and of good Christian people increased. And Iaroslav rejoiced, seeing so many holy churches and so many people who were verily Christians; and the devil grieved because he was defeated by these new Christian people.

In the year 6546/1038. In the spring Iaroslav went to Kiev.[53]

In the winter he campaigned against the Iatvags but was unable to submit them.

METROPOLITAN THEOTEMPTUS

In the year 6547/1039. The Church of the Holy Theotokos was consecrated by Metropolitan Theotemptus. The church was built by Great Vladimir, father of Iaroslav.[54]

THE REIGN OF THE GREEK EMPEROR CONSTANTINE, BROTHER OF BASIL, WHO REIGNED FOR TWO YEARS IN CONSTANTINOPLE.[55]

All-devouring hell does not pity anyone and it seized Basil [976-1025] with the jaws of death. The Greek dominion began to disintegrate like [a pile of] wheat. The former [Basil] passed away in old age after many years of life and the imperial dominion passed to his brother, Constantine [1025-1028 as sole emperor]. But now came the fulfillment of the proverb about the cup and glasses served with the same fingers, because the lives of these two brothers were completely different. They were very dissimilar in many respects. Basil did not care for the pleasures of life and devoted his life to the problems of war, and he greatly respected good horsemen, men at arms and shield bearers, and they all were prepared for war.

---

53. Not in *Laur.*, *Hyp.* or *Novg.* chronicles.

54. Metropolitan Theotemptus is the first historical Metropolitan of the jurisdiction of the Patriarch of Constantinople to be mentioned in the chronicles.

55. This entire story of Constantine and Romanus is in neither *Laur.*, *Hyp.* nor *Novg.* chronicles.

1039 However, as much as his brother liked, that much did Constantine dislike viewing armaments, armour, boots, and the clashing of weapons. He would not suffer them even in dreams while sleeping, and he disliked both the sound of warriors' trumpets and the exclamations of his men and the voices of war-loving soldiers. His regular exercizes were meals and the flesh of the banquet, and he greatly enjoyed shameless and lusty women who loved singing, pipes and the cymbals. Although he was a man who had lived many years and had white hair, being very old, and was fearful and always trembling, he was a man of bad thoughts who held evil counsel, blinded many people and accepted as sweetness those who lied, spread evil and caluminated. He had two daughters and thought primarily about them. Hearing from someone that the power after him might come into the hands of Romanus Argiropulos, one of his councilors, he forced this man to give up his betrothed wife and marry Zoe, his daughter born to the purple. And having done this, he passed out of this life, having little enjoyed his autocratic power.[56]

THE REIGN OF THE GREEK EMPEROR ROMANUS ARGIROPULOS, OR "THE SILVER DEALER" [1028-1034]

After Constantine, Romanus ascended to the Imperial throne and he reigned five years and eight months. He was a most wise and pious man who loved to learn about Divine matters and who enjoyed books and would attend night vespers and the hours. He built a most beautiful church consecrated to the Virgin Theotokos which was called "The Magnificent." His young Empress [Zoë], however, who bloomed with youth and burned with the passions of the flesh, seeing that Romanus lived apart and would not even remember that he was bound to his wife nor would he live with her, though still very young [she] became filled with wicked and evil ideas. There was a handsome-looking young man with a nice face whose name was Michael and whose origin was Paphlagonia. This Michael lived very happily in the Imperial palaces when the lascivious eyes of the

---

56. Constantine reigned from 1025 to 1028. Three days before his death he summoned to his deathbed Romanus Argiropulos, an important court dignitary, and placed before him the choice of either divorcing his wife at once and marrying Constantine's daughter, Zoe, or being blinded on the spot. Faced with such a choice, the pious Romanus preferred to marry Zoe and to become Emperor. Brehier, 198-199.

Empress fell on him, and when she was able to see his good features **1040** she became inflamed. Michael was young, attractive, joyful, white of face with rosy cheeks and full of drops of the dew of passion; and she most willingly became involved with him and most diligently took the blessed flowers of Michael's face. When Emperor Romanus once was relaxing and enjoying a tranquil time in the Imperial bath, some men who loved wickedness murderously assaulted and strangled him, winding [their hands] around his neck like a serpent in such a way that he did not even know how and from whence he was attacked. People say that this was done at Empress Zoë's desire but since we do not know anything about it, we can not speak of it.[57]

In the year 6548/1040. Iaroslav campaigned against the Lithuanians.

In the year 6549/1041. Iaroslav campaigned against the Mazovians, going forward in boats. [Mazovians—Poles from Mazovia, a region on the middle Visla, Bug and Narev.]

In the year 6550/1042. Iaroslav's son, Vladimir, marched against the Iam' tribe, defeated them and took many Iam' prisoners. All the horses of Vladimir's warriors died and had to be skinned alive while they were still slightly breathing. Such was the plague on the horses. The same year Iaroslav sent an army against Constantinople.[58]

IAROSLAV SENT HIS SON, VLADIMIR, TO
CAMPAIGN AGAINST CONSTANTINOPLE.

In the year 6551/1043. Iaroslav sent his son, Vladimir, against the Greeks and gave him a multitude of warriors, and he gave the command to Vyshata, father of Ian. Vladimir went against Constantinople in boats and after passing the cataracts [on the Dnieper and reaching the Black Sea] he came to the delta of the Danube; and the Russians said to Vladimir, "Let us camp here," but the Varangians said, "Let us attack the Imperial City." Vladimir followed the Varangians' advice, and from the Danube they went by sea with the warriors toward Constantinople. Seeing them, the Greeks went to the sea and began to dip shrouds from saints' relics

---

57. Romanus was strangled at the order of his wife, who was eighteen when she married him. Some hours afterwards she married her lover, Michael the Paphlagonian, and proclaimed him Emperor.

58. *Iam'*: now Karelian Finnic tribe which then lived north of Novgorod.

1044 into the water, and because of Divine wrath a storm arose at sea and there was a great and powerful thunder and a great storm, and the boats and ships began to break up, and the Varangians retreated. Prince Vladimir's ship was destroyed by the wind. Only with difficulty was Ivan Tvorimirich able to take Prince Vladimir and Iaroslav's voevodas on board his ship. All the rest of Vladimir's troops were washed ashore, their number being six thousand; and they remained there on the shore, quite naked. They wanted to return to Russia but none of the Prince's retinue would march with them. Voevoda Vyshata, seeing that the retinue was staying, said, "I will not go back to Iaroslav," and he went from the ship to the warriors. Vyshata said, "I shall go with them. As long as I am alive, I will be with them, and if I perish, I will perish with the retinue." They started to return to Russia, but the Greeks learned that the sea had destroyed the Russian [fleet].

THE GREEK EMPEROR MONOMACHUS.

And Emperor Monomachus sent fourteen ships against the Russians. Seeing with the retinue that they were advancing against them, Vladimir returned and they destroyed the Greek ships and went back to Russia, having gotten everyone to their ships. Vyshata, however, was taken by the Greeks with those who were washed ashore and they were brought to Constantinople. They [the Greeks] blinded many Russians. After three peaceful years Vyshata was permitted to return to Russia to Iaroslav.

The same year Iaroslav gave his daughter in marriage to Casimir [King of Poland]. The same year Moislav[59] offended Casimir and Iaroslav twice campaigned by boat against the Mazovians; and he told Casimir, "Since your father, Boleslav, captured many of my men, give them back to me as a dowry." Casimir gathered eight hundred Russian men who had been captured, not counting their wives and children, and gave them as a dowry to Iaroslav, his brother-in-law. This Casimir let his sister marry Iziaslav, Iaroslav's son.

In the year 6552/1044. [On the order of Iaroslav, people] dug out the remains of two princes, Iaropolk and Oleg, the brothers of Vladimir, sons of Sviatoslav, and ordered that the rite of baptism be

---

59. Prince Moislav ruled over the Mazovians, a Polish tribe in northern Poland.

performed over their remains; and they were buried in the Church of the Holy Theotokos which was built by the pious Prince Vladimir, who Christianized the Russian land.

The same year Iaroslav campaigned against the Lithuanians. The same spring he laid the foundation of the stone walls in the city of Novgorod and built them.[60]

The same year Briacheslav of Polotsk, son of Iziaslav, grandson of Vladimir and father of Vseslav, died. His son, Vseslav, ascended to the throne of his father.[61] This one was born from his mother because of magic by the mother who bore him and he had a hole from an ulcer in his head. The magicians told his mother, "This is an ulcer. Put a [magical] bandage around it and he has to wear it till the end of his life." And Vseslav wore it till the day of his death and therefore he was merciless in bloodletting.

FOUNDING OF THE CHURCH OF HOLY SOPHIA.

In the year 6553/1045. Vladimir Iaroslavich laid in Novgorod the foundation of the Church of Holy Sophia.

In the year 6554/1046.

In the year 6555/1047. Iaroslav campaigned for the third time against the Mazovians and defeated them, and he killed their Prince Moislav and conquered this land for Casimir.

In the year 6556/1048.

In the year 6557/1049. On Saturday, the fourth day of the month of March, the Church of Holy Sophia in Novgorod burned. It was very beautifully constructed and adorned, having thirteen domes. It stood at the end of Piskuplia [Bishop's?] Street over the Volkhov where now Sadko[62] built the church of Holy Boris and Gleb.[63] The same year the Princess [Irina], wife of Iaroslav, passed away.

In the year 6558/1050. The Church of Holy Sophia in Novgorod was consecrated on the Day of the Elevation of the Venerable Cross in the presence of Iaroslav and his son, Vladimir, and the consecration was performed by Bishop Luke Zhidiata.[64]

60. This sentence is not in *Laur.*, *Hyp.* or *Novg.*

61. Regarding Iziaslav and Vseslav, see the entries under 980 and 1128.

62. Sadko: a legendary and, apparently, historical hero of many epic legends.

63. This item is in *Novg.* but not in *Laur.* or *Hyp.*

64. This item appears in *Novg.*, but not in *Laur.* or *Hyp.*

1051 ELECTION OF THE METROPOLITAN OF RUSSIA BY THE RUSSIAN BISHOPS.

In the year 6559/1051. Iaroslav, Vladimir's son, Sviatoslav's grandson, was at war with the Greeks and there was enmity between them. Therefore Iaroslav took counsel with his Russian bishops and they made a decision according to the Holy Canons and according to the statutes of the Apostles. The first rule of the Holy Apostles is: two or three bishops may consecrate another bishop. According to this holy rule and to the statute of the Divine Apostles, the Russian bishops assembled and appointed Hilarion, a Russian, to be Metropolitan of Kiev and entire Russia. They did this without breaking away from the Orthodox patriarchs or from the piety of the Greek faith; and they did this not because of pride but in order to avoid the enmity and evil which raged at that time.[65]

BEGINNING OF THE CAVE MONASTERY AND THE NARRATIVE, WHY THE MONASTERY WAS CALLED THE MONASTERY OF "THE CAVE"

[*6559/1051, cont.*] Let us tell why the monastery was called the "Cave" monastery. Pious Prince Iaroslav liked Berestovo[66] very much and the Church of the Holy Apostles Peter and Paul, which was there, as well as the clergy of many priests who gathered there. And he supplied them with all that was necessary. Among these participants there was a priest named Hilarion, a pious, book-loving person who strictly observed the fasts. He used to go from Berestovo to the Dniper and to the "Ancient Monsastery," where the "Caves" is [now located.][67] At that time there was a vast forest there. He dug a small cave there about four yards long and, coming from Berestovo, he would sing the hours there and would pray to God there alone. Then God put into the heart of the Prince the thought of appointing him metropolitan in the Holy Sophia of Kiev and of all the Russian land. And so this little cave remained empty because no one lived there. A few days later a certain man who [at that time] still was a

---

65. Only the second sentence of this entry is in *Laur., Hyp.* and *Novg.* The commentaries were probably written by the compiler of *Nik.*

66. *Berestovo* was the preferred suburban residence of Vladimir and of Iaroslav, located on the hills overlooking the Dnieper river. Now it is within the walls of the Cave Monastery.

67. There are two sections in the Monastery of the Caves, the "Ancient Monastery" and the "New Monastery."

layman and who was from the city of Liubech', received from God **1051**
the thought to go abroad; and he went to the Holy Mountain [Mount
Athos] and saw the monasteries there and visited them, and he very
much liked the ways of the monks. He came to one of the
monasteries there and asked the abbot to give him holy orders. He
agreed, and tonsured him, giving him the name of Anthony; and he
instructed him and taught him the monastic rules. Then he told him,
"Now return to Russia and you will have the blessing of the Holy
Mountain on you." Then he added, "From you there will be many
monks," and he blessed him and let him depart, saying, "Go in
peace."

Anthony arrived in Kiev and pondered where to live, and he
went to the monasteries but did not like it there because God did not
want it. He started wandering in the wilderness and hills looking for
the place which would be shown him by God. He came to the hill
where Hilarion had dug his small cave and he liked that place. He
settled there and began to pray to God tearfully, saying, "Lord, let
me settle in this place and the blessing of the Holy Mountain should
be on this place, as well as the blessing of my abbot who tonsured
me." And he began living there, praying to God, eating dry
bread—and that, only every second day; he drank a very small
amount of water; and he dug the cave, not allowing himself to rest
either day or night but remained in labor in his waking hours, and in
prayer. Good people learned of this and began coming to him,
bringing him what he needed. Great Anthony became known and
those who would come to him would ask his blessing. When,
thereafter, Grand Prince Iaroslav passed away and his son, Iziaslav,
took over the power and settled in Kiev, Anthony was already
illustrious throughout the Russian land. Learning of his way of life,
Iziaslav came to him with his retinue, asking his blessing and his holy
prayers.

Great Anthony became known by all and was venerated, and the
brethren started coming to him and he would accept and tonsure
them; and so the brethren gathered around him, twelve in number.
They dug a larger cave, a church and a cell, which are there to the
present day in a cave under the "Ancient Monastery." Anthony told
the brethren who gathered there, "It was the Lord, brethren, who
brought you together, as well as the blessing of the Holy Mountain
and of the abbot who tonsured me. And I tonsure you. And God's

1051 blessing should be the first on you, and the second will be that from the Holy Mountain." He told them also, "Live here and I will appoint you an abbot because I want to go to another hill and remain there, as I have become accustomed to solitude."

He appointed them Barlaam as abbot and he went to another hill and dug a cave, which is under the "New Monastery." And there he ended his life, having passed it in piety and without having left the cave for forty years. His relics remain there to the present day. The brethren with the abbot continued to live there [in the "Ancient Monastery"] and the number of brethren in the Cave increased, and they thought of building a monastery there outside the caves. Then the abbot and the brethren came to Anthony and told him, "Father, the number of brethren . . . [68] is increasing through fasting, prayer and waking." But Anthony had neither gold nor silver because he accumulated only tears and fasting, as it is said. Then Barlaam left for the monastery of St. Demetrius, and the brethren took counsel and went to elder Anthony. They told him, "We seek an abbot," and he asked, "Who is greater among you than Theodosius? He is obedient, he is meek and he is humble, and he should be your abbot." The brethren were very happy, bowed to the elder and set Theodosius to be the abbot of the brethren, their number being twenty. Theodosius accepted [leadership of] the monastery, caring for all rules of abstinence, fasting greatly and praying tearfully. And around him monks began to congregate, and over a hundred brethren gathered.

ABOUT THE RULES OF STUDION.[69]

And they began to look for the monastic rules, and among them was Michael, a monk from the Monastery of Studion, who had come from Byzantium with Metropolitan George. With his help they started looking for the monastic rules of the Studion monastery. Theodosius found them in his place and copied all the rules of the holy and blessed monks, great fathers, and he decided for the monastery how to sing the monastic service; how to bow; and how to read Scripture; how to stand in church; and all the rules of the

---

68. Here there is an omission in all available *mss*.

69. Studion: the famous monastery in Constantinople which received its name from its fifth-century organizer, Consul Studion. Its rules were particularly severe.

church; and how to sit in the refectory; and what to eat on what days; **1052**
and all this [he did] according to the rules. Theodosius wrote all this
and gave [the rules] to his monastery, and from this monastery came
the rules of all the monasteries [of Russia]. This is the reason why the
Monastery of the Caves was honored—because [its rules are] the
oldest of all. Theodosius lived in the monastery, observing a pious
life and the monastic rules and accepting everyone who came to him.
And so I came to him, a wretched and undeserving servant, and he
accepted me in the monastery forty years ago. At the seventeenth
year from my birth I was tonsured a monk, and all this have I written
and set down—in what year the monastery began and why it is called
the Monastery of the Caves; but about the life of Theodosius, we will
speak in another place.[70]

[6559/1051, cont.] The same year three Greek singers with their families came to Kiev.

In the year 6560/1052. Iaroslav's eldest son, Vladimir, passed away in Novgorod on the fourth day of the month of October, a Sunday, and he was buried in the Cathedral of Holy Sophia which he, himself, built.

In the year 6561/1053. To Vsevolod Iaroslavich, Vladimir's grandson, was born a son: Vladimir, called Monomakh, after his mother, the Greek Imperial Princess.

In the year 6562/1054. In the fourth year of the reign of the Greek Emperor Michael the Paphlagonian.[71]

THE PASSING OF IAROSLAV.

Great Prince Iaroslav of Russia died. He was the son of Great Vladimir. While still alive he instructed his sons, saying, "I am leaving this world, my sons. Love each other because you are brethren from one father and mother. If you love one another, then God will be with you and will submit the enemy under your hands and you will live peacefully. In case, however, you live hatefully in feuds and dissension, then you will destroy yourselves and you will

---

70. This *Nikonian* version of the foundation of the Monastery of the Caves is shorter than those of *Laur.* and *Hyp.*, and is missing from *Novg.*

71. Wrong chronology. Michael the Paphlagonian reigned from 1034 to 1041. Iaroslav died in the reign of Constantine IX Monomachus, 1042-1055. The unfortunate Russian raid of 1043, however, was correctly indicated as having occurred during Monomachus' reign.

1054 destroy the land of your fathers and grandfathers which they obtained through their great labor. But remain peaceful, brother obeying brother. And I leave my place on the throne of Kiev to my senior son, Iziaslav, your brother; obey him just as you obeyed me, and he should lead you in my place. And I give the principality of Chernigov to Sviatoslav, and the principality of Pereiaslavl' to Vsevolod, and the principality of Vladimir to Igor', and the principality of Smolensk to Viacheslav." And so he divided the cities among them and commanded them not to overstep the limits of the brothers or to drive anyone away. And he called to Iziaslav, "In the case someone wishes to offend your brother, you must help so that he will not be offended." And so he instructed his children to abide in brotherly love. He, himself, however, was ill, and when he came to Vyshgorod he fell gravely ill, while Iziaslav was in Kiev and Sviatoslav was in the city of Vladimir. Only Vsevolod was with his father because he was loved by his father more than any one of his brothers; and therefore Iaroslav had been constantly with him. So came the end of the life of Iaroslav, and he transmitted his blessed soul to the Lord on the 20th day of the month of February, on the Saturday of the first week of Lent, when the memory of the Holy Martyr Theodore Tyron is celebrated. Vsevolod covered the body of his father, put it on a sledge[72] and he brought him to Kiev. The priests sang the usual chants and all the people and Vsevolod wept over him. When they had carried him thither, they laid him in a marble sarcophagus in the Church of Holy Sophia. And he lived altogether seventy years and six.

Iziaslav went to Novgorod and assigned Ostromir to Novgorod, and Ostromir marched with the Novgorodians against the Chud', and the Chud' killed him as well as many Novgorodians, during this campaign. Then Iziaslav also went against the Chud' and took the section of Kedipiv, which means "the hand of the sun."[73]

[*PSRL*, Vol. IX, pages 85-86 and 86-91 deal with Byzantine history and they are omitted. *Ed.*]

---

72. At that time in Russia it was the custom to take the body of the deceased to the burial place in a sledge.

73. This last paragraph is absent in the *Laur.*, *Hyp.* and *Novg.* chronicles. According to an inscription in the *Gospel of Ostromir* from 1057, it appears that Ostromir was still alive that year. The discrepancy may result from incorrect reading or incorrect dating.

THE REIGN OF IZIASLAV IN KIEV.   **1055**

In the year 6563/1055. Iziaslav ascended to the throne of Kiev and Sviatoslav became the prince of Chernigov, Vsevolod—of Pereiaslavl', Igor'—of Vladimir [in Volynia], and Viacheslav—of Smolensk. The same year Vsevolod campaigned against the Torks and defeated them. The same year the Polovetss appeared under [Khan] Bolush' and Vsevolod concluded peace with him, and they returned from whence they had come.[74]

The same year [the Bishop's] servant, Dudik, calumniated Bishop Luke Zhidiata, blaming the latter for indecent speech, and he [the Bishop] left Novgorod and went to Kiev. He was found guilty by Metropolitan Ephraim on the basis of Dudik's accusations as well as those of his wicked enemies, Koz'ma and Dem'ian.[75]

The same year Prince Iziaslav Iaroslavich began to reign in Kiev, and at that time Theodosius, abbot of the Kiev monastery, was there.

In the year 6564/1056. Viacheslav, son of Iaroslav, died in Smolensk, and Igor' was moved from Vladimir [in Volynia to Smolensk].

In the year 6565/1057. Iziaslav defeated the [Lithuanian tribe of] Galindians.

The same year Bishop Luke Zhidiata resumed his rule in his See of Novgorod, and his servant, Dudik, suffered. His nose and both hands were cut off and he fled to the Germans. His wicked advisers, Koz'ma and Dem'ian, also received their due for their crimes.[76]

In the year 6566/1058. Iziaslav, Sviatoslav and Vsevolod released their uncle Sudislav from the prison in Pskov in which he had been confined for twenty-four years, and they took from him his pledge of fealty on the Cross. When he left prison he took holy orders and was brought to Kiev, where he became renowned for his virtuous life.

In the year 6567/1059. Iaroslav's son, Igor', passed away. Bishop Luke passed away. The same year, while travelling from Kiev the Bishop of Novgorod, Luke Zhidiata, died in Kopys. This happened on the 15th of the month of October. The same month he was buried by his clergy, after having been bishop for twenty-three years.

74. Bolush' in *Laur.* Bulush' in *Nik.*
75. This paragraph is not in *Laur.* or *Hyp.* but a part of it is in *Novg.*
76. This last paragraph is not in *Laur.* or in *Hyp.*, but is in *Novg.*

1060   The same year Iziaslav, Vsevolod and Vseslav, assembling a numberless host, went by horse and boat against the Torks. When the Torks learned of this, they took fright and fled, and they flee to this day, and they died in flight, chased by the wrath of God. Some of them died from cold, others of starvation, and yet others from the plague, [punished] by Divine Justice.

Thus does God deliver Christians from the pagans.

The same year Iziaslav campaigned against the Susola[77] and they promised to pay a tribute of two thousand grivna. Having promised this, they chased away the tribute collector and in spring they campaigned against the city of Jur'ev, burning towns and causing much evil. They campaigned as far as Pskov. The people of Pskov and Novgorod went against them and there was a battle, and one thousand Russians were killed.[78]

In the year 6568/1060. For the first time the Polovetss invaded the Russian land and waged war. Vsevolod [of Pereiaslavl'] marched against them on February 2 and they fought each other, and Vsevolod was defeated; but after the battle they withdrew. This was the first evil caused by this godless pagan enemy. At that time their khan was a certain Iskal.

CONSECRATION OF BISHOP STEPHEN.

The same year Stephen was consecrated Bishop of Novgorod.[79]

In the year 6569/1061 there was peace.

In the year 6570/1062 there was peace.

In the year 6571/1063. There was peace. Sudislav, son of Great Vladimir, brother of Iaroslav, passed away in the holy orders of monk and *schema*[80] and he was buried in the church of the Monastery of St. George. The same year in Novgorod the river Volkhov flowed backwards for five days. This was a bad portent because four years thereafter Vseslav burned Novgorod and took many people prisoner.

In the year 6572/1064. [Prince] Rostislav, son of Vladimir, grandson of Iaroslav, great grandson of Great Vladimir, fled with

---

77. Apparently Susola was a Finno-Ugric tribe in northwestern Russia.
78. This paragraph is not in *Laur.*, or in *Hyp.*, but is in *Novg.*
79. This paragraph is not in *Laur.*, *Hyp.*, or *Novg.*
80. *Schema*: taking holy orders of the second, extremely severe, degree which forbids speech.

Vyshata, son of Ostromir, voevoda of Novgorod, from Novgorod to Tmutarakan'[81]. And when they arrived in Tmutarakan' they chased from thence Gleb, the son of Sviatoslav, grandson of Iaroslav, great-grandson of Great Vladimir, and they seized his principality.

In the year 6573/1065. Sviatoslav Iaroslavovich marched against Rostislav Vladimirovich. Rostislav, however, gave up the city [of Tmutarakan']: he was not afraid of him but he was unwilling to take up arms against his uncle. Sviatoslav came to Tmutarakan' and assigned his son, Gleb, there, and returned. Rostislav, however, came again and chased Gleb away and he, himself, settled in Tmutarakan', and Gleb went to his father. The same year Vseslav [Prince of Polotsk] began to fight.[82]

ABOUT THE HORRIFYING PORTENT.

The same year in the western part of the skies there was a portent. A very large star with blood-colored rays rose in the evening after sunset and remained in the sky for seven days. This portent boded no good; thereafter there were many infernal feuds and many raids against the Russian land by the pagans [nomads] because this blood-colored star forecast bloodshed. The same year in Kiev the fishermen who were fishing caught a monstrous-looking child in their net; I and many people asembled there till evening to look upon it; and we wondered at it. Then it was thrown back into the water. On its face it had the shameful parts about which it cannot be spoken because of the shame. The same year there was a change of the sun and there was no light, and it looked like the moon. Ignorant people claimed that it had been eaten. Such manner of portents do not presage anything good. We mean it this way because in the olden time, during the reign of Antioch, for forty days in Jerusalem there appeared armed horsemen in the air, riding horseback in golden clothes, and troops appeared, brandishing weapons. Thereupon,

---

81. Rostislav Vladimirovich did not receive any principality because his father died before the death of Iaroslav the Wise, Rostislav's grandfather. Since Tmutarakan' belonged to the Chernigov domain, Sviatoslav put his son, Igor', there.

82. Concerning Prince Vseslav, called "the Magician," see the legend under the year 1128; his attack was a major cause of the renewal of feuds among Vladimir's descendants.

1066 after this portent there was the conquest of Jerusalem by Antioch.[83] Also, during the reign of Emperor Nero there appeared over Jerusalem a star which shone like a lance. Thereupon the Romans came to conquer the city. Something similar occurred under Emperor Justinian.[84] A star began to shine in the west releasing rays, and this star was called "a shiner." It shone for twenty days, and thereafter stars fell from dusk to dawn. These falling stars produced the appearance of the sun, which shone without rays. Thereafter there were revolts and plagues and deaths; and so it happened under Emperor Mauricius.[85] A woman gave birth to a child without eyes and without hands, but on his back was a fish tail. And there also was born a dog with six feet. And in Africa, two children were born, one having four legs and the other, two heads. After all these portents, during the reign of Emperor Constantine, son of Leo[86], the Iconoclasts began their heresy.[87] There was a movement of the stars in the skies and they fell to the ground, and those who saw it considered this a sign of the end. At that same time there was a strong movement of the air. And then in Syria there was an earthquake, and the earth broke apart, forming a gap of two miles. From it, strangely enough, issued a mule which spoke with a human voice.[88]

In the year 6574/1066. Rostislav ruled in Tmutarakan' and received tribute from the Cherkess and from other lands. The Greeks became afraid of him and sent him a certain Catepano[89] with a treacherous plot. When he came to Rostislav, he won his confidence and was received by Rostislav, Catepano told him, "Your health, Prince! I want to drink to you." And he drank half the cup and gave the other half to the Prince; but he touched the cup with his fingers and under his nails he had a poison which he administered to the Prince, and the latter died within eight days. As soon as the Prince had drunk it, Catepano left for Chersonesus, and

---

83. Antioch, king of Syria of the dynasty of Seleucides, who persecuted the Jews, 174-163 B.C.

84. Justinian, Byzantine Emperor, 521-565 A.D.

85. Mauricius, Byzantine Emperor, 582-602 A.D.

86. Constantine, Byzantine Emperor, 741-775 A.D.

87. *Iconoclasts:* heretics who denied the veneration of Icons.

88. Same in *Laur.*

89. *Catepano*, governor of a province, a high administrator.

announced there that on a certain day Rostislav would die. And so it happened; but the people of Chersonesus stoned Catepano to death. Rostislav was a good warrior, a man of handsome stature who had an attractive face and was merciful toward the poor. He died on the third day of the month of February, and was buried there in the Church of Holy Theotokos [in Tmutarakan'].

In the year 6575/1067. Vseslav [the Magician], Prince of Polotsk, son of Briacheslav, grandson of Iziaslav, great-grandson of Great Vladimir, started a feud, occupied Novgorod up to the Narev suburb, burned the city and sacked everything in the Cathedral of Holy Sophia, including the censers and the bells, and retreated.[90] Although it was a cold winter, three of Iaroslav's sons—Iziaslav, Sviatoslav and Vsevolod—joined forces and went against Vseslav. They arrived in the city of Minsk and the people of Minsk prepared the city for a siege; but the brothers stormed the city and slaughtered men, women and children. Thereafter, on March 3 they came to the river Nemiga. There was a heavy snow and they marched against each other. There was a terrible battle, and Iziaslav, Sviatoslav and Vsevolod won this battle. Vseslav fled.

Later, on the tenth day of June, Iziaslav, Sviatoslav and Vsevolod gave a pledge on the cross to Vseslav, telling him, "Come to us. We will cause you no harm." Relying on their pledge on the cross, he went to them by boat, crossing the Dnieper. Iziaslav entered the town first and there they captured Vseslav, breaking their pledge on the cross. This happened at Orsha near Smolensk. They brought Vseslav to Kiev and jailed him, with two of his sons.

In the year 6576/1068. A great multitude of aliens, called "Polovetss," attacked the Russian land. Iziaslav, Sviatoslav and Vsevolod marched against them to the river Al'ta. At night they began to fight. Because of our sins, God brings grief upon us, being wroth with us.[91]

It happened because we do not heed Him, and have fratricidal feuds and dissensions as a result of the devil's deeds. And this happens with the permission of God, because of our sins. God does not wish man evil, but only good; but the devil enjoys evil murderers

---

90. For the origin of this feud between the descendants of Iziaslav and Iaroslav, see the entry under the year 1128.

91. In *Laur.*, this reads: "And the Russian princes fled, and the Polovetss won the battle."

1068 and bloodshed, and he promotes dissension and envy and hatred among brothers, and calumny.

HOMILY ON DIVINE PUNISHMENT

When someone commits a sin on earth, God punishes him with death or starvation or invasion by pagans or drought or infestation of caterpillars or with other punishments. If you repent, however, and adhere to the way God commands, then it will be as the words of the Prophet: "Turn ye unto Me with all your heart and with fasting and weeping." [*Joel* 2:12.] But if we return to evil and remain as swine in the excrement of sin, so will we remain there. Another Prophet tells us, "I knew that thou art obstinate and thy neck is an iron sinew." [*Isa.* 48:4.] If we act thus, we shall all be forgiven our sins; but if we return to iniquity we will perish in our wallowing as swine in the mire of evil. Says the Lord: "And I also have withheld the rain from you ... and I caused it to rain upon one city and caused it not to rain upon another city ... and it withered ... I have smitten you with blasting and mildew yet have ye not returned unto Me ... [Therefore] I have smitten your vineyards and your fig trees and your olive trees ... But I could not drive out your iniquity. I sent among you pestilence and painful death, and carried away your horses, but even so, you have not returned unto Me, but said, 'Let us be manly.'" [*Amos* 4:7-10. Sentence order is slightly changed.]

"When will you be sated with your iniquities? For you have turned aside from My way," says the Lord, "and have committed many transgressions ... I will be swift witness against sorcerers, my adversaries, and against adulterers, against false swearers, and against those that oppress the hireling in his wages, the widow, the fatherless, and against those who incline justice to wrong ... Why have you not restrained yourselves and your sins, but have violated My commandments and have not kept them? Return unto Me and I will return unto you ... I will open upon you the windows of Heaven and pour out a blessing upon you that there will not be enough room to receive it ... and neither shall your vine cast its fruit before the time in the fields. Ye have spoken blasphemy against Me, saying, 'It is vain to serve God!' " [*Malachi* 3:5-14, paraphrased and abbreviated.] "With their lips do they honor Me but they have removed their hearts far from Me." [*Isa.* 29:13.]

For this reason we do not receive what we ask, since the Lord said, "Then they will call upon Me but I will not answer, they will seek me diligently but they shall not find me." [*Prov.* 1:28.] "Ye have not desired to walk in My path; therefore Heaven is closed, or else opens only for a fell purpose, sending down hail instead of rain, or destroying the harvest with frost and tormenting the earth with drought because of our iniquities," says the Lord. But if you repent yourselves of your sins, "then I cause the rain to come down for you, the former rains and the latter rains; and the floors [of the] granaries shall be full of wheat, and the vats shall overflow with new wine and oil. And I will restore to you the years that the locust hath eaten, the cankerworms and the caterpillars have consumed—My great army which I sent among you," said the Lord Almighty. [*Joel* 2:23-25, abbreviated and slightly changed.] Hearing these words, let us apply ourselves to good, seek justice and free the oppressed. Let us do penance, not returning evil or slander for slander but let us rather bind ourselves with love to the Lord Our God. Let us wash away all our transgressions with fasting, with lamentation and with tears, not call ourselves Christians as long as we live as pagans.

1068

Do we not live as the pagans so long as we attach superstitious significance to encounters? For he turns back who meets a monk, boar or swine. Is that not pagan? It is part and parcel of the devil's teaching to retain such delusions. Other people attach special significance to sneezing, which is healthy for the head. By these and other similar customs the devil deceives us; and he alienated us from God by all manner of craft, through trumpets and clowns, through harps and pagan festivals. For we behold the playground worn bare by the footsteps of a great multitude, who jostle each other while they make a spectacle of the thing invented by the devil.

Churches still stand, but when the hour of prayer is come, few worshippers are found in the church; for this reason we shall suffer at the hand of God all sorts of chastisement, and then invasion by [our foes'] armies, and at the command of God we shall endure punishment for our sins.[92]

[End of the Homily.]

92. This *Homily about Divine Punishment* as it reads in *Laur.* and slightly amended in *Nik.* is ascribed by some scholars to St. Theodosius of the Monastery of the Cave; but it is hardly his style or manner of presenting the theme. Part of it was taken from the *Homily about the Drought and God's Punishment* from the popular homiletic anthology, *Zlatostrui*. It was most

1068 [KIEVAN REVOLT AGAINST IZIASLAV]

Let us now return to our narrative. Iziaslav and Vsevolod fled [from the Polovetss] to Kiev, and Sviatoslav to Chernigov; and they summoned a *veche* in the market square. The people of Kiev told the prince, "These Polovetss' raids have spread over our land. Prince! Give us weapons and horses, and we will go fight them." But Iziaslav did not heed them. Then the people began to revolt against the voevoda Kosniachek. From the *veche* they went up the hill, came to the court of Kosniachek and, not finding him, went to the court of Briacheslav [the son of Iziaslav of Polotsk, father of Vseslav], saying, "Let us go and pull out our friend [Vseslav] from the dungeon." They divided into two groups: half went to the dungeon and the other to the bridge, and thus they arrived at the prince's court. Iziaslav was holding council with his retinue in the gallery [of the palace] and they [the people] began to argue with the prince. They were standing in the yard while the Prince was watching from the window, and his retinue was standing next to him. And Tuky, brother of Chudin, said to Sviatoslav, "Prince! Do you see that the people have become angry? Send someone [to the dungeon] to guard Vseslav [Prince of Polotsk]." While he was speaking to him, the second part of the people came from the dungeon after having opened it, and the retinue told the prince, "This is verily baleful. Send for Vseslav, draw him to the window by deceit, and then we will strike him with a sword." But the prince paid no heed. Then the people started shouting and went to the dungeon where Vseslav was jailed. Seeing this, Iziaslav escaped from his court with Vsevolod, while the people burst into the dungeon to free Vseslav. This happened on the fifteenth of September. They put him in the midst of the prince's court and they sacked the prince's court, taking an endless amount of gold and silver in coin and bullion.[93]

[IZIASLAV FLEES TO POLAND.]

Since the Polovetss were fighting around the city of Chernigov, Sviatoslav gathered some troops and marched against them toward

---

probably composed after the defeat on the Al'ta river in 1068 because in its final part there is definite censure of the Russian princes for their feuding and their defeat by the Polovetss.

93. Or, gold, silver and furs. The terminology is unclear.

Snovsk.[94] The Polovetss saw him marching against them and they aligned themselves against him for battle. Seeing their multitude, Sviatoslav said to his troops, "Let us do our duty, brethren. We have no place to escape to." And they attacked them on horseback, and Sviatoslav with 3,000 troops defeated them, although there were 12,000 Polovetss. Their khan was taken alive by hand. All this happened on the first of November and victorious Sviatoslav returned to his city [of Chernigov].

[VSESLAV, PRINCE OF KIEV.]

Vseslav, meanwhile, took over the power in Kiev. And here God demonstrated the power of the Cross because [Iziaslav and his brothers] pledged to him on the Cross and then captured him, and that is the reason why God brought the pagans upon them. And it is obvious that Vseslav was liberated by the Venerable Cross. [On September 14th] the day of the Elevation of the Cross Vseslav sighed and said, "Oh, Venerable Cross! Thou hast liberated me from the dungeon because I believed in Thee."

God demonstrated the power of the Cross to show the Russian land that it should not trespass an oath on the Venerable Cross. If anyone trespasses it, he will be punished by severe punishment, and in the future age he will have eternal torment. This is because the power of the Cross is truly great.

And Vseslav remained seven months on the throne of Kiev.

THE DEATH OF BISHOP STEPHEN.

The same year Stephen, Bishop of Novgorod, went to Kiev and there the servant strangled him.[95]

In the year 6577/1069. Iziaslav, together with the [Polish] King Boleslav, marched against Vseslav; Vseslav advanced against them, and so Vseslav arrived in Belgorod. At night Vseslav stealthily abandoned his Kievan levies in Belgorod and fled to Polotsk. When, in the morning, the people saw that the Prince had escaped they returned to Kiev, summoned the *veche*, and sent to Sviatoslav and to Vsevolod, saying, "We have committed evil toward you in casting out

---

94. Snovsk: Now Sednev, a town near Chernigov at the conjunction of the Desna and Snov' rivers.

95. This last item is not in *Laur.*

1069 our prince, and now from the Polish land you are bringing an army against us. Come to the city of your father and rule over us. If you do not want to do so, we, contrary to our will, will burn the city and go to the Greek land."

Sviatoslav told them, "We will send a message to my brother. If he marches against you with the Poles in order to destroy you, we will go against him with our army because we do not want to have the city of our fathers destroyed. But in case he comes peacefully, he must come with only a small troop." And so he consoled the people of Kiev. Then Sviatoslav and Vsevolod sent to Iziaslav, saying, "Vsevolod has fled. Do not bring the Poles to Kiev because your enemy is not there. But in case you want to demonstrate your wrath and destroy Kiev, you must know that we care for the throne of our father."

[IZIASLAV'S FIRST RETURN TO KIEV.]

Hearing this, Iziaslav left the bulk of the Polish army and departed, together with Boleslav, taking only a small Polish troop. Iziaslav sent his younger son, Mstislav, ahead of him to Kiev. Mstislav arrived [in Kiev] and executed those who had liberated Vseslav from the dungeon—altogether seventy people; and he blinded some others, while some were punished without having any fault because he did not investigate them. When Iziaslav came to the city the people went out to meet him, bowing and accepting him in Kiev. Iziaslav assumed his throne on the second day of the month of May. Then he sent the Poles for supplies to the other cities, where they were stealthily slain. And then Boleslav with [the remaining] Poles returned to his land.

Iziaslav transferred the market to the hill,[96] chased Vseslav from Polotsk and put his own son, Mstislav, in Polotsk in his place; but he died there very soon. Then [Iziaslav] put in the latter's place the latter's brother, Sviatopolk.

Prince Gleb, together with the Novgorodian levies, defeated the retreating Vseslav on the Gzena on the 23rd of the month of October, and many of the Vozians [Vozans in *Novg. Syn.*] were slaughtered. In the morning they found in the chambers of the Holy Sophia the cross of [Prince] Vladimir which Vseslav had taken when

---

96. Some chronicles read "because the lower city burned out."

he came thither with his army.⁹⁷

1070

In the year 6578/1070. A son was born to Vsevolod and he was named Rostislav. The same year the foundation of the Church of St. Michael was laid in Vsevolod's monastery.

In the year 6579/1071. The Polovetss raided around Rostovets and Neiatin. The same year Vseslav [the Magician] drove Sviatopolk from Polotsk. The same year Iaropolk defeated Vseslav near Volochisk.⁹⁸

ABOUT THE DIVINERS.

At that time there came a diviner who was possessed by the devil. He came to Kiev announcing the following to the people: "In five years hence the Dnieper will reverse its course and the lands will move from one place to another. The Greek land will be where the Russian [one] now is, and the Russian [land] will be where the Greek [one] is; and other lands will change their places." Those who were ignoramuses listened to him but the faithful laughed, saying, "The devil toys with you, inviting your perdition." And so it happened. One night he disappeared and nothing more was heard of him. The devils incite people to evil and then ridicule them; they lead them to a deadly abyss after they teach them what to say. And now we will tell you of the devils' machinations and desires.

Once during a bad harvest in the region of Rostov two diviners appeared who came from Iaroslavl', announcing, "We are aware who is hoarding supplies." And they went along the Volga, and came to a township where they pointed to the wealthy women, saying, "This one hoards rye; that one hoards honey; that one, fish; and that one, fur." And the people brought them their sisters, mothers and wives. And they [the diviners], being possessed by devils, cut behind their shoulders and pulled out either rye or fish or squirrels, and they killed many women and took away their possessions from them. Then they came to Belozero, and some other three hundred people were with them.

ABOUT THE DIVINERS.

At that time it occurred that Ian Vyshatich, who collected taxes for [Prince] Sviatoslav [Iaroslavovich], came to Belozero, where

---

97. This last paragraph is not in *Laur.* or *Hyp.*, but in *Novg. Syn.*
98. "Holochisk," in Laur. and *Hyp.*

1071 people told him that two diviners had killed many women along the Volga and Sheksna rivers, and had now come thither. Ascertaining whose peasants these diviners were, and learning that they were the peasants of his prince, he [Ian] sent [his agents] to their [the diviners'] people, since they were in the vicinity, saying, "Bring these diviners hither because they are my and my prince's peasants." But they did not heed him. Then Ian decided to go to them unarmed, but his guards told him, "Do not go unarmed because they may hurt you." Then he ordered his guards, of whom there were twelve, to take weapons, and he went to them [to the diviners' people] in the forest. The latter, however, prepared to fight. Three men marched against Ian, and advanced with an axe. Coming to Ian, they told him, "Do you see? You are going to be killed. Do not go." Ian ordered his guard to fight them, and he approached those who remained apart. They tried to attack Ian and one of them raised his axe, but Ian turned the axe away and hit him with the butt. He ordered his guards to cut them down, but they [the diviners and their escorts] escaped to the forest after killing Ian's priest. Then Ian marched to the city and told the people of Belozero, "If you do not catch these diviners, I will not leave [and will continue to levy tribute] for a whole year." Then the people of Belozero went after them and brought them to Ian.

And he asked them, "Why have you killed so many people?" They answered, "Because they were hoarding supplies. If we exterminate them, there will be enough supplies. If you want, we will remove from their bodies rye, fish or other supplies." But Ian said, "This is a sheer lie. God has created man from earth and he consists of bone, muscle, and blood, and there is nothing else in him. No one else knows of this other than God." They, however, responded, "We know how man was created." And Ian asked them, "How?"

And they said, "God was bathing in a steambath and was all covered with sweat. He took an old cloth to wipe away his sweat, and threw it from Heaven onto the earth. Then Satan began arguing with God as to which of them should create man, and the devil created man but God put a soul in him. When man dies the body goes to the earth but his soul goes to God." Ian told them, "You have really been seduced by the devil. In what god do you believe?" And they answered, "In the Antichrist." And he asked them, "Where is he?" And they said, "He dwells in the abyss." Ian told them, "What manner of God would dwell in an abyss? He is the devil. God is in Heaven and He sits upon His throne, glorified by the angels, who attend Him with awe but dare not look upon Him. But this [particular] angel was driven out from Heaven because of his pride, and you call him 'Antichrist,' and he remains in the abyss, as you have told. He waits there for God to descend from Heaven and bind him up and put him in the eternal fire together with his servants and with those who believe in him. But here [on earth] you have to receive torments from me, and after death you will receive them there [in the abyss]." The diviners answered him, however, "Our gods tell us that you cannot do us any harm." But he [Ian] responded, "Your gods lie to you." They said, "We have to appear before Prince Sviatoslav in Kiev and you cannot do anything to us."

1071

Then Ian ordered that they be beaten and that their beards be pulled out. When they had been beaten and their beards had been pulled out, Ian asked them, "What do your gods tell you now?" And they answered, "That we have to appear before Prince Sviatoslav." Then Ian ordered that a piece of wood be put in their mouths and be attached to the thwart, and that they go before him in boats. He followed after them. When they camped at the mouth of the Sheksna, Ian asked them, "What else do your gods tell you?" They said, "Our gods tell us that we will remain alive because of you." Ian told them, "They spoke correctly." And they said, "If you let us go, there will be good fortune for you; but if you destroy us, you will have much grief and misfortune." But Ian rejoined, "If I let you go, there will be punishment for me from God." And then Ian asked the boatsmen, "Who among your relatives were killed by these?" They replied, "My mother," and another said, "My sister, my wife." Then Ian told them, "Take revenge for your relatives." And they took them and beat them and hung them on an oak so that they would receive their deserved revenge from God. When Ian went home a bear climbed up the tree and gnawed them. They knew and talked about others, but were unaware of their own death. For if they had been aware of their fate, they would not have come to the place where they were caught; and after they were caught, why did they say, "We will not die;" also, the other one [Ian] had already decided to put them to death? And such was the devil's bewitchment: devils do not know human thought and are not aware of the mystery. God, alone, knows human thought but the devils know nothing because they are weak

1071 and lack perception. And now let us speak of their appearance, inabilities and their soothsaying.

ABOUT THE DIVINERS.

At that time and in those years it chanced that a Novgorodian came to the people of Chud'. And he went to a diviner for some sorcery. The latter, as was his custom, began calling the devils into his house. The Novgorodian was sitting on the threshhold of that house while the diviner was lying in a trance because the devil had taken possession of him. The diviners, however, arose and told the Novgorodian, "The gods do not dare to come in because you have on something which they fear." And he [the Novgorodian] remembered that he had on a cross, and therefore he put the cross outside that house. Then the diviner again began to summon the devils. The devils, again putting him [the diviner] into a trance, told why the other had come. Then the Novgorodian asked the diviner, "Why were the devils afraid of That One Whose Cross we wear?" He [the diviner] replied, "It is the Symbol of the Heavenly God of Whom our gods are afraid." And he [the Novgorodian] asked, "What kind of gods are yours? Where do they live?" And he [the diviner] replied, "Our gods live in the abyss and have black looks and are winged and some have tails. They rise up under Heaven in order to listen to your God. Your Gods [the Trinity] are in Heaven and when one of your men dies he is brought up into Heaven. When one of our men dies, we take him to our gods in the abyss." And so it is. Sinners remain in hell in expectation of eternal torment. The righteous dwell together with the angels in Heavenly dwellings. Devils have certain power and their own appearance, but they have limitations; they seduce people because they command them to speak of their apparitions which they see, and those people are not firm in the faith: some of them see apparitions while asleep and some, while unconscious; and so they are bewitched because of the devils' instigation. This instigation of the devil occurs particularly often through women because ages ago the devil seduced woman, and she seduced man; therefore in the present generation women quite often practice witchcraft and poisoning and other devilish deeds. But men, also, are seduced by the devils because of their unbelief, as happened already in earlier generations in the time of the Apostles.

ABOUT SIMON THE MAGICIAN.

1071

In the time [of the Apostles] there lived Simon the Magician, who practiced witchcraft. He could make dogs speak as people do; once he changed himself into an old man; another time into a young man; and he could change the appearance of other people, doing so while they were bewitched [*Acts*]. Thus did Jannes and Jambres perform witchcraft against Moses but soon thereafter were unable to go against Moses. [II *Tim.* 3:8 and 7:11.] So, also, would Kunop bring devils' bewitchment upon people so that they thought they were walking on water; and he performed other devilish bewitchments, enticing them to see apparitions, for his own and others' destruction.

A DIVINER APPEARED.

In the time of Prince Gleb such a diviner appeared in Novgorod. He spoke with the people, claiming that he was God. He seduced many of them, nearly the entire city, preaching that he could foresee the future. He blasphemed the Christian faith, saying, "I will cross the river Volkhov, if you command me to do so, and I will do it in the presence of all the people." And there were great riots and rumors throughout the city, and all the people believed in him and wanted to kill Bishop Theodore. But the Bishop took up a cross, donned his vestments, and, standing amongst the people, said, "Those who want to believe in the diviner must go to him. Those who do not believe must approach the cross." And so the people became divided in twain. Prince Gleb and his retinue came to the cross and stood by the bishop, but all the other people went to the diviner. And there was a great disturbance among them. Prince Gleb, hiding an axe under his cloak, approached the diviner and asked him, "Do you know what will happen in the morning and what in the evening?" The other responded, "I know everything ahead of time." Then Gleb asked, "Do you know what happened to you today?" "I will perform great miracles," said the diviner. But Gleb pulled out his axe, struck the diviner, who fell dead, and all the people dispersed. Thus he perished in body and soul, having given himself to the devil.[99]

---

99. We do not know the reason why these various stories about diviners and divination were recorded under the year 1071. It is possible that they

1072 TRANSFER OF THE RELICS OF THE HOLY
PASSION MARTYRS BORIS AND GLEB TOOK
PLACE.

In the year 6580/1072. The grandsons of Great Vladimir, sons of Iaroslav, the three brother princes—Iziaslav, Sviatoslav and Vsevolod—together with their spiritual father, George, Metropolitan of Kiev and all Russia, Bishop Peter of Pereiaslavl', Bishop Stephen of Belgorod, Bishop Michael of Jur'ev and Bishop John of Kholm, as well as Theodosius, Abbot of the Cave [Monastery], Nicholas, Abbot of Pereiaslavl' [Monastery] and with the entire Sacred Council, transferred the relics of the Holy Martyrs from Vyshgorod to the new church which was built by Prince Iziaslav and which stands there until now. First they took [the relics of] St. Boris, which were in a wooden casket, and Iziaslav, Sviatoslav and Vsevolod carried them on their shoulders. They were preceded by a candle-bearer and a monk, behind whom were deacons with censers, thereafter the priests and the bishops with the Metropolitan. And so they all preceded the casket, which they carried into the new church. When they opened the venerable casket, the church became filled with fragrance, and those assisting glorified God. The Metropolitan was seized by awe because he had had some doubts, and he fell on the ground before the casket, beseeching forgiveness. They venerated and kissed the relics and put them into a stone sarcophagus. Thereafter they took [the relics of] Gleb, which were in a stone coffin, put them on a sledge and drove them [to the church]; but when the coffin came to the door it became immovable. Then His Holiness, Metropolitan George, together with the bishops and the entire Sacred Council, said some prayers and the princes and the people exclaimed, "God have mercy upon us!" And so they moved it and buried it [in the new church] on the second day of the month of May. After celebrating the liturgy they established a holiday, and all the princes, together with their spiritual father, Metropolitan

were told to the chronicler by Ian Vyshatich, who certainly contributed a considerable amount of the oral tradition to the chronicler. This Ian Vyshatich—"son of Vyshata"—was a member of an aristocratic family which served several generations of Kievan and Novgorodian princes. Of particular interest is the second long story, whose hero is Ian Vyshatich, himself. This story shows that the dualistic teaching of the Bogomils—known in the West as "Cathars" ("the Pure") or "Albigensians"—had also penetrated Russia in the eleventh century.

George of Kiev and all Russia, with the bishops and the entire Sacred **1073**
Council, fairly celebrated this holiday. At that time Chudin ruled
over Vyshgorod and Lazar' was the priest of the church. When the
celebration came to an end everyone went home.

[IZIASLAV'S SECOND FLIGHT TO POLAND]

In the year 6581/1073. The devil incited a feud among the
brothers, the sons of Iaroslav, the grandsons of Great Vladimir. In
this feud Sviatoslav and Vsevolod were together against their older
brother, Grand Prince Iziaslav of Kiev. They united their forces and
went together against him toward Kiev, and he, unable to resist
them, left for Poland. He had two sons, Iaropolk and Sviatopolk, but
his younger son, Mstislav, had died [earlier] in Polotsk. Sviatoslav
and Vsevolod entered Kiev on March twenty-second and Sviatoslav
ascended to the throne of Kiev although his father had given him the
principality of Chernigov as patrimony. His sons were Gleb and
Oleg.[100] Vsevolod's patrimony was Periaslavl' and his sons were
Vladimir Monomakh and Rostislav. It was Sviatoslav who instigated
the driving out of his brother. He desired more power and he
flattered Vsevolod, saying, "Since Iziaslav has made an alliance with
Vseslav [the Magician of Polotsk] and is plotting against us, we must
drive him out or else he will drive us out." And so he incited
Vsevolod against Iziaslav.

Iziaslav escaped to Poland with his possessions and his wife,
relying on his great wealth. He said, "With this [wealth] I will be able
to find an army to help me." But the Poles took away all his wealth
and showed him the way out of their land.

[SVIATOSLAV, PRINCE OF KIEV]

Sviatoslav ascended to the throne of Kiev, having driven out his
brother and having trespassed the commandments of God and the
will of his father.

It is a very great sin to trespass the will of one's father: the first
who did so were the sons of Ham, who invaded the land of Shem;
four hundred years later they received revenge from God. From the
land of Shem were the Jews, who massacred the tribe of Canaanites,
and so took back their lot and their land. And, also, Esau trespassed

---

100. Neither *Laur.*, *Hyp.* nor *Novg.* mentions Iziaslav's sons here.

1074 the commandment of his father and he was killed. It is not good to encroach upon the patrimony of another.

The same year the church of the Cave [Monastery] was founded by Bishop Michael of Iur'ev and Abbot Theodosius of the Cave [Monastery]. It happened in this way because at that time Metropolitan George of Kiev and all Russia was in the Greek land. It happened during the rule of Sviatoslav in Kiev. The same year Anthony, [formerly] abbot of the Cave [Monastery], passed away after having indicated and blessed the place for the [future construction of the] Church of the Holy Theotokos.

[DEATH OF ST. THEODOSIUS; THE
CALOYERS OF THE MONASTERY OF THE
CAVES]

In the year 6582/1074. Theodosius, Abbot of the Caves, passed away and was buried in the same cave which he had built. This happened in the second year of the reign [of the Byzantine Emperor] Romanus Diogenus.[101] Let us speak here shortly of his assumption. On the eve of Sunday of Quinquagesima, when the Lenten period was approaching, Theodosius, as was his habit, summoned and embraced all the brethren, and instructed them how to pass the time of Lent. [They were all to spend it] in nightly and daily prayer, and to keep themselves from evil thoughts and from devilish incitement. "The devils," he said, "bring seeds of evil desire [into the minds] of monks and in this way their holy prayers become impaired. If such thoughts come into your mind you must fight them with the Sign of the Cross, saying, 'Our Lord Jesus Christ, Our God, have mercy upon us.' And you must abstain from excessive eating and drinking because it leads to the development of evil thoughts which result in sin. In such way," said he, "you must resist the devils' plots and their cunning. You must avoid lateness and much sleep. You must be zealous in church singing and in observing the traditions of the Holy Fathers, and reading the Books. And above all you must have on your lips the Psalms of David, as befits monks; and in this way you will chase away devilish despondence. The most important is to love those who are younger than you and to obey and follow the elders. The elders should love and instruct the young and be an example of abstinence, vigil and humility. And so

---

101. Error: Romanus Diogenus reigned 1067-1071.

you should instruct the younger and console them, and thus pass **1074**
Lent." He also said, "God gave us the forty days [of Lent] to cleanse
our souls. It is the yearly tithe of time to be given to God. Every year
there are 365 days, and out of them every tenth day must be devoted
as a Divine tithe. This Lent lasts for forty days, after which the
cleansed soul fairly celebrates the Resurrection of the Lord and
rejoices about God. The time of Lent cleanses man's mind. From the
very beginning there was a symbol of Lent. At the beginning Adam
was not supposed to eat the fruit from a certain tree. Moses also
observed Lent for forty days before he received the Covenant on the
Mount of Sinai and saw the glory of God. Samuel was born by his
mother during Lent. The Ninevites were saved from the wrath of
God by Lent. Daniel observed Lent and later was blessed with great
visions. Elijah observed Lent and was taken into heaven and dwelt
there, receiving Celestial Sustenance. The three youths quenched
the raging of the fire through their fasting. [*Dan.* 3:22-26.] Our Lord
fasted for forty days and so He showed us the time of fast. The
Apostles uprooted devilish teaching through fasting. Through
fasting our [Great Church] Fathers became the Beacons of the world
and they shine even after death, having demonstrated their great
work. They exhibited great labors and continence as, for instance,
the great Anthony, Euthemius, Sabbas and other Fathers. And so let
us follow their examples, my brethren."

After having instructed the brethren, he embraced each one,
calling them by name, and then he would leave the monastery,
taking a few small loaves with him. Then he would go to his cave and
would lock the door to it, and would cover the door with dirt and
speak to no one. If he needed some utensil, he spoke through the
small window [but only] on Saturday or on Sunday. All the other
days he spent in fasting and prayers and in strict abstinence. On
Friday, the eve of St. Lazarus' day, he returned to the monastery
because on that day the period of the forty days of fasting ended—it
begins on the Monday of St. Theodore and ends on Friday, the eve
of St. Lazarus' day; however, the fast of Holy Week is established on
account of the Lord's Passion.

This time Theodosius came, as usual, to embrace the brethren
and celebrate Holy Week with them. But when the great day of the
Resurrection of Our Lord Jesus Christ came, which is customarily
solemnly celebrated, he suddenly fell ill. He was ill and bedridden

1074 for five days. In the evening he ordered that he be carried out into the yard, and the brethren put him on a sledge and placed him across from the church.[102] Then he instructed that all the brethren be summoned; and they rang the bell and assembled.

He told them, "My brethren, fathers and children! I am leaving you because during Lent while I was in my cave the Lord revealed to me that I must leave the world. Whom do you want as abbot? I will give him my blessing." They answered, "You are father to us all. Whomsoever you appoint will be our father and our abbot, and we will obey him as we have obeyed you." Then our father, Theodosius, said, "Leave me now and nominate the one whom you want—with the exception of two brethren, Nicholas and Ignatius. But you may nominate whomsoever you want from among the others, beginning with the elder and ending with the younger." They listened to him and went into the church. After consulting, they sent him two brethren, who spoke the following: "Whomsoever God wants and whosoever shall be in agreement with your sacred prayers and whomsoever you would like, him would we like, too." But Theodosius answered, "If you want me to appoint an abbot, I will do so not according to my wish but according to the intentions of God." And he named Jacob the priest; but the brethren did not like him [Jacob], and said, "He was not tonsured here." Indeed, Jacob had come from Letech [on the river Al'ta] together with his brother, Paul [already being a monk]. And they asked him to appoint Stephen, the choirmaster, who was Theodosius' pupil, and said, "This one has grown up under your guidance. Give us him." Then Theodosius said, "I suggested Jacob according to God's intentions but you want to do according to your own will." He agreed with them, however, and appointed Stephen to be abbot, and he gave his blessing to Stephen, saying, "I turn the monastery over to you. Rule it with care and adhere to the same rule which I introduced, and do not change the tradition or the charter of the monastery, but do everything according to the monastic rules and the customs." After this, the brethren took him up and carried him into his cell and laid him on his cot.

SVIATOSLAV COMES WITH HIS SON, GLEB.

When the sixth day came of the illness of great Theodosius, he

102. This was an old Russian custom: to put a dying man, or the dead, on a sledge.

grew worse; and then Prince Sviatoslav with his son, Gleb, came to see him. While the prince was sitting in his cell, Theodosius told him, "Now I am leaving this world and I entrust this monastery to your care in the event there should be any trouble in it. I appoint Stephen to be abbot. Do not allow anyone to harm him." The prince embraced him, promised to care for the monastery, and departed.

1074

When the seventh day arrived, Theodosius became quite wearied, and he summoned Stephen and the brethren, telling them, "Upon my departure from this world, should I find favor with God and be accepted by Him, then after my departure this monastery will grow larger and grace will remain with it. Then you will know that God has accepted me. If, however, after my death the number of caloyers in this monastery decreases and there appears great scarcity in the monastery's supplies, then you will know that I did not please God." When he had thus spoken, the brethren wept and said, "Father! Pray to God for us. We know that your work will not be disregarded by God." The brethren remained with him throughout the night; when the eighth day came, it was the second Saturday after Easter, and at the second hour of that day he gave up his soul into God's hands. This was on the third day of the month of May, the eleventh year of the Indiction. He was lamented by all the brethren.

Theodosius willed that he should be buried in his cave, in which he had worked and labored. They did as he said: "Bury my body at night;" and so they did. When evening came the brethren took up his body and laid it in the cave in which he had accomplished his many labors, and they thanked Our Lord God, Jesus Christ, and accompanied him with all honor, chants and candles. Thereafter Stephen took over the monastery and the blessed flock which Theodosius had assembled: they have been caloyers who [to the present day] shine in Russia as stars. Some of them adhered strictly to fasting, others to vigil, others to genuflection; others would fast every other or every third day. Some ate only bread and water, some—only boiled vegetables; and the junior ones obeyed the senior, not venturing to speak in their presence; and they did all this with great discipline and obedience. And the senior ones had great love for the younger; they instructed them and consoled them as if they were their beloved children. In case a brother should commit some sin, they would console him with Divine Scripture; then they would share the penitence with him for three or four days because

1074 there was such a great love among them. Indeed, such was the love among the brethren, and such was their great abstinence. When a brother would leave the monastery, all the brethren would grieve about it and would send after him and would summon him to return to the monastery, and then all of them would go to intercede with the abbot and would ask him to accept this brother into the monastery with joy. Such was the love among them and such was their abstinence and fasting. And I would like to mention some of the wonderful men among them.

Such, first of all, was Damian the Presbyter, who adhered so strictly to fasting and abstinence that he ate nothing but bread and water until his death. And when someone would bring a sick child or person ill with some illness, they would come to the monastery to blessed Theodosius, who would order Damian to read a prayer on behalf of the sick one; he would pray and anoint him, and all those who came to him in faith were cured. When Damian fell ill and was lying on his sickbed awaiting his end, the Angel of God came to him in the semblance of Theodosius, promising him the Kingdom of Heaven for his labor. Thereafter Theodosius came to him with the brethren and remained sitting in his cell. The sick man looked at the abbot and said, "Don't forget, Abbot, what you promised me." And Great Theodosius understood that the other had had a vision and told him, "Surely, brother Damian! As I promised, so it will be." And he, Damian, closed his eyes and transmitted his soul into God's hands. The abbot and brethren buried his body.

And there was also another brother, Jeremiah, who even remembered the Christianization of the Russian land. He had a God-given gift: he could foresee the future. When he saw someone with wicked thoughts, he would reprove him secretly and instruct him to beware of Satan. Also, in case some brother intended to leave the monastery, he would know of it and would tell him about his thoughts and console him. Whatever he told anyone would happen.

There was also another brother, named Matthew, and he was clairvoyant. Once while standing in church in his customary place he turned his eyes toward the brethren standing on either side [of the altar] and noticed that a devil was walking about in the semblance of a Pole, carrying under his garment the flowers called *lepoks*.[103]

---

103. *"Lepok,"* from *"lepi,"* "handsome," "attractive," "good."

Walking around the brethren, he would take a *lepok* from under his coat and would throw it at someone; and when the flower stuck to one of the singing brethren, that one would become absent-minded and would thereupon leave the church under some pretext, and would go to his cell to sleep and not return to church until the end of the service. Then he would throw the flower at some other, but the flower would not stick to him and then this brother would remain faithfully throughout the service until they finished singing matins, and only then go to his cell. Seeing this, this elder informed the brethren.

1074

On another occasion this elder saw the following: as usual, before dawn when this elder attended matins, the brethren would go to their cells and this elder was the last to leave the church. Once when he was going to his cell he sat down under the bell to rest because his cell was quite far from the church. Then he noticed a crowd moving from the gate: raising his eyes, he saw a man riding on a pig and others walking alongside of him. The elder asked them, "Whither are you going?" And this devil riding on the pig answered, "We are going for Michael Tolbekovich." The elder made the sign of the cross and returned to his cell, but when day dawned the elder understood what the matter was and told the custodian, "Go and inquire whether Michael is in in his cell," and he was told, "Yesterday after matins he jumped over the fence." And then the elder told the abbot and brethren of his vision. This elder was alive when Theodosius died, and when Stephen became abbot, and he was also alive when Nikon became abbot after Stephen. Once, when he was attending matins, he raised his eyes to look at Abbot Nikon but he saw an ass standing in the abbot's customary place; thereupon he understood that the abbot had not yet arisen. This elder had many other visions and he died at a very advanced age in this monastery.

There was also another caloyer, by the name of Isaac. When he lived in the lay world he was wealthy because he was a merchant, a native of Toropets. He decided to become a monk, and distributed his wealth among the needy and among the monasteries, and he went to great Anthony in his cave and prayed him to be tonsured a monk. He was received by Anthony, who put the monastic vestments upon him and gave him the name, Isaac; but his lay name was Chern'. This Isaac led a very strict ascetic way of life. He wore a hair shirt, and ordered that a goat be brought for him. Then he skinned

1074 the goat, put its skin over the hair shirt, and the raw goatskin dried out on him. He locked himself up in a cave in one of the passages, in a very small cell four ells long, and prayed there tearfully to God. His food consisted of small Communion loaves, and that only every second day; and he drank a very small amount of water. Great Anthony, himself, used to carry food to him, passing it to him through a window so small that only his hand could pass through it; and in such a way the other would receive it, And thus he did for seven years, not going out into the light. He did not sleep on his ribs but would only sleep briefly seated.

One day as usual, from dusk to midnight he knelt and sang Psalms. Tiring of this, he sat down. While seated, as was his habit, he extinguished his candle, and suddenly a blinding light shone as bright as the sun, and two beautiful young men appeared to him with faces shining as the sun. They told him, "Isaac! We are angels and now Christ is coming to you. Fall down before Him." He did not understand that this was a devilish plot, and the idea of making the sign of the cross [to protect himself against devils] did not occur to him. He stepped out and bowed to this devilish apparition as if it were Christ. The devil exclaimed, "Now you are ours, Isaac!" And they led him to his cell, set him down there and seated themselves next to him. The entire cell and the monastery were filled with them. One of the devils, whom they called Christ, said, "Take the flute and drums and harps and play nicely, and Isaac will dance." They began playing drums, harps and flutes, and played to him. When he was completely exhausted they left him half-alive and departed, having dishonored him. When, in the morning, light came and it was time to eat bread, Anthony came, as usual, to his little window, saying, "God bless you, Father Isaac," but there was no answer and Anthony said, "Oh, he has probably passed away," and he sent to the monastery to fetch Theodosius and the brethren. They dug out where the entrance was walled and entered and picked him up, believing him dead. They brought him and laid him before the cave, and then they saw that he was alive. Then Abbot Theodosius said, "This is the result of a devilish plot," and they laid him on a cot and Anthony cared for him.

At that time Iziaslav came from Poland, and Iziaslav became wroth with Anthony because of Prince Vseslav [the Magician of Polotsk], and he sent Sviatoslav to arrest Anthony and to take him to

Chernigov.[104] Arriving in Chernigov, [Anthony] took a liking for the Boldin Mountains and dug a cave there and settled there. Now, the Monastery of the Holy Theotokos is located there on the Boldin Mountains, where it remains to the present day. When Theodosius learned that Anthony had left for Chernigov, he went with the brethren to take Isaac, and he brought him to his own cell, where he cared for him. The latter [Isaac] was so weak in body that he was unable to turn from one side to the other, nor was he able to get up or sit; but he would only lie on one side, and urinated on his cot, and from this urinating many worms infested his hip. Theodosius, himself, washed him with his own hands and kept him clean for two years. Theodosius prayed to God for him and read prayers over him day and night. Only in the third year did he [Isaac] begin to speak and hear, and started getting up and walking like an infant. He did not, however, care to go to church and they [the brethren] were obliged to take him to church. Therefore Theodosius told him to go with the brethren to the refectory, and he would set him apart from the brethren and would put bread before him; but the latter would not take it, so [monks] would place it in his hand. Then Theodosius said, "Put the bread before him but do not put it into his hand. He has to eat for himself." The latter, however, did not eat for a whole week; but slowly, watching the others, he began to eat bread, and so he learned how to eat and in this way Theodosius delivered him from the plot of the devil.

1074

Then Isaac [again] adopted a strict ascetic life. When Theodosius passed away and Stephen took his place, Isaac said, "Devil, you betrayed me once when I just sat in the same place; but now I will not lock myself in a cell and will have victory over you staying in the monastery." Again he donned the hair shirt, and over the hair shirt he put a coat of very rough cloth, and he began to act strangely [as a fool in Christ]. He also began to help the cooks prepare food for the brethren. He would go to matins ahead of everyone, planting himself there immovably. When winter and cruel cold came, he had shoes so worn that his feet would freeze to the floor, but he would not move his feet until matins were over. After matins he would go to the kitchen and prepare the fire, water and wood before the other cooks arrived. One of the cooks, who had the

104. About Vseslav's rule in Kiev, see the year 1068.

1074 same name of Isaac, used to ridicule Isaac, saying, "Over there is a black crow. Go and catch it." [Though there was no crow] Isaac would bow before him to the ground, would go to that place, get the crow and bring it, in the presence of all the cooks. They took fright and told the abbot and the brethren, and they began to respect him. He, however, not wanting any glory, began to behave strangely [in the manner of fools in Christ], behaving so unpleasantly toward the abbot, brethren and lay people that some of them would hurt him. Then he started going into the world, continuing to make himself a fool in Christ. He settled in the same cave in which he had been before because by that time Anthony had already passed away. In his cell he would assemble some youths and they would don monastic habits. Therefore he would receive blows from Abbot Nikon and from the parents of these youths. He endured all, accepting beatings, nakedness and the cold, by day and by night.

Once at night he set a fire in a stove in a hut near the cave but the fire began issuing from the crevices because the stove was old and cracked. Having nothing with which to fill the cracks in the stove, he stepped on the chinks with his naked feet, and thus remained standing on the flame until the fire burned out in the stove, and then he got down.

Many other things were told of him and I, myself, witnessed some of them. And so he achieved victory over the devils and cared about them no more than about flies. He would tell them, "You, devils, tempted me once in my cave because I did not know about your plots and your wickedness; but now I have My Lord Jesus Christ, God, and I rely upon the prayer of Father Theodosius, and hope in this way to defeat you." The devils showed him much malevolence, saying, "You are ours because you bowed before our head and before us;" but he reposted, "Your head is Antichrist and you are devils," and he would make the sign of the cross over his face and then they would disappear. Once they came to him at night, terrifying him during his sleep, and it seems that there were many people with hoes and spades saying, "We will destroy this cave and bury you here." The others told him, "Run away, Isaac, they want to bury you!" But he answered them, "If you were people, you would have come during the day; but you are the darkness and you come in darkness, and darkness will have you." Then he made the sign of the cross and they disappeared.

Other [devils] came to frighten him, in the guise of bears or lions; snakes would crawl to him, or some other reptile, but they could do nothing to him and would admit to him, "Oh, Isaac, you defeated us." And he said, "You defeated me by appearing in the Image of Jesus Christ and the angels, but you are unworthy of such appearance. Now you appear in the guise of animals, cattle, serpents and reptiles because you are like them." Therefore there was no more maliciousness done him by the devils. He, himself, told us, "My fight with them lasted three years," and thereafter he began to live strictly, observing abstinence, fasting and vigil, and thus he lived until the end of his life. He fell ill in his cave and was brought to the monastery, and before eight days he passed away to God. Abbot John and the brethren covered his body and buried him.

Such were the caloyers of the monastery of Theodosius, and they shine after their death like the stars, and they pray to God for the present brethren and for their brethren in the lay world, and for those who contribute to the monastery. To the present day they live a virtuous life, remaining together in community, celebrating the services, praying, remaining obedient, and do so for the glory of Almighty God, preserved by the prayers of Theodosius. Amen.[105]

In the year 6583/1075. Abbot Stephen started building the Church of the Cave Monastery on the foundations built by Theodosius, and it was continued by Stephen and was completed within three years, on the eleventh day of the month of July.

The same year there came ambassadors from Germany to Sviatoslav. Being very proud, Sviatoslav showed them his wealth and they viewed an endless amount of gold, silver and brocades.[106] He said, "All this is nothing because it remains dead [without use]. Much better than these are warriors because such [men] can get

---

105. At least some of these stories from *Prim. Chr., Laur.* and *Nik.* were written by Nestor, for they share several features and common details with Nestor's "Life of St. Theodosius."

106. In the annals of Lambert von Herzfeld (year 1075) it is mentioned that Burghard, Ambassador of Emperor Heinrich IV of Germany, brought to the Emperor from Russia, from Prince Sviatoslav, such an amount of gold, silver and valuable clothing that no one could remember such a vast amount ever before having been brought to Germany. Sviatoslav gave these valuables to the Emperor in order to thank him for not having provided assistance to Sviatoslav's brother, Iziaslav. Lambertus von Herzenfeldensis, *Monumentae Germaniae Historiae,* Annales, Vol. III, p. 230.

1076 everything, and more than this." So, similarly, did Hesikiah boast, the King of Judea, in the presence of the envoy of Nebuchadnezzar, King of Assyria, and his wealth was taken to Babylon and after his death all his possessions disintegrated. [II *Kings* 18:13-26, rephrased.]

In the year 6584/1076. Vladimir, son of Vsevolod, and Oleg, son of Sviatoslav, campaigned aginst the Czechs in order to help the Poles.

THE DEATH OF SVIATOSLAV, SON OF IAROSLAV.

The same year, on the twenty-seventh day of the month of December, Sviatoslav, son of Iaroslav, passed away after his sores were cut away. He was buried in the [Cathedral of] St. Savior in Chernigov. In the month of January, Vsevolod, son of Iaroslav, grandson of Great Vladimir, ascended to his throne.

[THIRD REIGN OF IZIASLAV IN KIEV]

In the year 6585/1077. Iziaslav marched together with the Poles and Vsevolod campaigned against him. Boris commenced to reign in Chernigov on the fourth day of the month of May but he ruled for only eight days and escaped to Tmutarakan' to [Prince] Roman. Vsevolod marched to Volynia to meet his brother, Iziaslav, and they made peace. Iziaslav came and reascended the throne of Kiev on the fifteenth day of July. Sviatoslav's son, Oleg, remained with Vsevolod in Chernigov.

[OLEG'S SEDITION. DEATH AND *ENCOMIUM* OF PRINCE IZIASLAV]

In the year 6586/1078. In the month of April [Prince] Oleg [Sviatoslavovich] escaped from Vsevolod to Tmutarakan'.

The same year Gleb Sviatoslavovich, grandson of Iaroslav, great-grandson of Great Vladimir, was killed in Zavoloch'e.[107] He was merciful toward the poor, loved pilgrims, cared for the church, was a man of warm faith, quiet, loved people, was meek, merciful and patient. He was buried in [the Cathedral of] St. Saviour in Chernigov.

---

107. *Zavoloch'e:* "Land beyond the portages;" this was the name of the vast region between the Volga and the northern Dvina rivers, inhabited by Finnic tribes.

When Iziaslav was ruling in Kiev and Vladimir Monomakh in **1078** Smolensk, Oleg [son of late Prince Sviatoslav] and Boris [son of late Prince Viacheslav] led the pagans into the Russian land, and together with the Polovetss they marched against Vsevolod [who ruled in Chernigov]. Vsevolod went toward the river Sozhitsa to meet them but the Polovetss defeated the Russians and many of the latter were killed: [among them] Ivan Zhiroslavich, Tuky, Chudin's brother, Porei, and many others. This happened on the twenty-fifth of August. Then Oleg and Boris occupied Chernigov, while Vsevolod joined his brother, Iziaslav, in Kiev. They embraced each other and held council: Vsevolod reported to his brother concerning the events and what had happened to him.

But Iziaslav told him, "Brother, do not grieve! Are you not aware how much harm I, myself, experienced? First, did you not, my own brothers, banish me and take away all my wealth? Then, when I was banished for the second time, also by my brothers, did it happen by my own fault? Did I not wander in foreign lands and was I not deprived of all my possessions without having done anything wrong? And now you, my brother, should not grieve. In the case we shall have our share in the Russian land, it will be the possession of both of us. If we lose, we will lose together; but I am ready to lay down my life for you. I do not like to see any harm done to my brothers, but I enjoy it when they fare well."

And so he consoled his brother [Vsevolod] and commanded his troops to assemble. There was an endless number of warriors, and Iziaslav with his son, Iaropolk, and Vsevolod with his son, Vladimir [Monomakh], marched against Chernigov. Oleg and Boris were not in the city at that time and the people of Chernigov made preparations for a siege and closed the city. Since the people of Chernigov did not want to open [the gates of] the city, [the attack began]. Vladimir [Monomakh] stormed the eastern gate at the river Strizhen' and occupied the outer city, burning it while its inhabitants escaped to the inner city.

When Iziaslav and Vsevolod learned that Oleg and Boris were approaching, they marched against them in order to prevent them [from joining the defenders of Chernigov], and moved [their troops] against Oleg. Thereupon Oleg told Boris, "Let us not march against them for we cannot resist four princes; but let us go and petition our uncles [Iziaslav and Vsevolod for peace]." But Boris

1078 answered him, "See, I am ready [to fight], and I will go against all of them." He boasted greatly, not realizing that God opposes the proud and provides the humble with His help, and therefore the proud should not boast of his strength. And so Boris marched against them; they were in the field near the town of Nezhatin.

DEATH OF BORIS.

They clashed and there was terrible carnage. First Boris, son of Vjacheslav, was killed—who had boasted greatly.

DEATH OF IZIASLAV.

And then [Grand Prince] Iziaslav, son of Iaroslav, grandson of Vladimir, dismounted, when suddenly someone approached and struck him in the shoulder with a lance; and so [Prince] Iziaslav was slain, son of Iaroslav!

The battle continued but [finally] Oleg fled with some troops and escaped with difficulty; he went to Tmutarakan'.

Iziaslav was killed the third day of the month of October. His body was transported in a boat which went as far as Gorodets [town on the Dnieper in the vicinity of Kiev]. The entire city of Kiev went to meet their prince; his body was placed on a sledge and taken into the city: priests and monks bore it, chanting hymns; but the chanting could not be heard because the city of Kiev bewailed his death [so loudly]. Behind his body Iaropolk, weeping, marched with troops: "Oh, Father! Oh, my Father! How much grief have you experienced in this world; so many misfortunes befell you from people, and even from your own brothers. This time, albeit you were not killed by your brothers, you have, however, laid down your life for your brother!" They brought his body into the Church of the Holy Theotokos and placed it in a marble sarcophagus.

[ENCOMIUM]

Iziaslav was a man of fair features and imposing stature; he had a peaceful cast of mind, hated a lie and loved the truth. He did not care for flattery, had just ideas and would not render evil for evil. He endured so much harm in Kiev: he was driven out [from his throne], his household was sacked, but he did not require revenge for all these wrongs. Although some people claimed, "He executed, he killed," these were not his misdeeds but those of his son [Iaropolk]. As it was said, his brothers banished him and he was obliged to wander in foreign lands, and when he again sat on his throne [in Kiev] Vsevolod came to him, eager [for help]; but he did not tell him [Vsevolod], "I suffered very much at your hands, yet did not return evil for evil." Rather, he consoled him, saying, "Since you, brother, once demonstrated your love for me, restored me to my throne and called me your senior, I will not remind you of your earlier wickedness because you are my brother and I am yours, and I will lay down my life for you!" And so he did. He did not tell him, "How much malice you did to me, and now, in your turn, malice has befallen you!" And he did not tell him, "It is not my concern!" But he took his brother's grief upon himself and proved his great love, thus following the Apostle's words, "Encourage the fainthearted." [I *Thess.* 5:14.]

1078

Truly, if he committed any sin in this world it will be forgiven him because he laid down his life for his brother, not seeking greater power or vaster wealth, but solely for the sake of his brother's offense. The Lord said of these, "Greater love hath no man than this: that a man lay down his life for his friends." [*John* 15:13.] And Solomon also said, "A friend loveth at all times and a brother is born in adversity." [*Prov.* 17:17.] For as [Apostle] John said, "God is love; and he that abideth in love, abideth in God and God abideth in him. Herein is love made perfect with us. That we may have boldness in the day of judgment because as He is, even so are we in this world. There is no fear in love; but perfect love casteth our fear away because fear hath punishment, and he that feareth is not perfect in love ... If a man says, 'I love God,' and hateth his brother, he is a liar, for he that loveth not his brother whom he hath seen cannot love God, Whom he hath not seen. And this Commandment we have from Him: that he who loveth God, loveth his brother, also." [I *John* 4:16-21.] Through love everything may be fulfilled: God came down to earth because of love, and He was crucified for us sinners, He took away our sins being nailed to the Cross. And He gave us the Cross to drive away devilish hatred. Out of love the martyrs shed their blood. Out of love this Prince [Iziaslav] also shed his blood on behalf of his brother, thus fulfilling the Commandment of the Lord.

This Prince Iziaslav, son of Iaroslav, grandson of Great Vladimir, ruled in Kiev for twenty-nine years. His sons were Mstislav, Sviatopolk and Iaropolk.[108]

[End of Encomium]

108. It may be of interest to point out here that the author of the *Primary*

1079 THE REIGN OF VSEVOLOD IAROSLAVOVICH IN KIEV

Vsevolod ruled in Kiev on the throne of his father, Iaroslav, and of his brother, Iziaslav, thus assuming power in all of Russia. And he assigned his son, Vladimir [Monomakh] to Chernigov, and he assigned [his nephew] Iaropolk Iziaslavovich, to Vladimir [in Volynia], adding the region of Turov to his patrimony.

The same year German was consecrated Bishop of Novgorod the Great.[109]

In the year 6587/1079. Roman, together with the Polovetss, raided the [region] around Kiev;[110] however, [Prince] Vsevolod [of Kiev] took a position near Pereiaslavl' and concluded a peace treaty with the Polovetss. Thereafter, Roman retreated with the Polovetss and they killed him on the second day of the month of August, and the bones of this son of Sviatoslav, grandson of Iaroslav, still lie there [in the prairie].

Oleg [Sviatoslavovich] was captured [by the Greeks in Tmutarakan'] and imprisoned beyond the seas in Constantinople.[111]

Vsevolod appointed Ratibor as his posadnik in Tmutarakan'.

In the year 6588/1080. The Torks of Pereiaslavl' started fighting the Russians. Vsevolod sent [against them] his son, Vladimir [Monomakh], and Vladimir defeated the Torks.

In the year 6589/1081. Davyd Igorevich and Volodar' Rostislavich escaped on the 18th day of the month of May and went to Tmutarakan'. They went thither, arrested Ratibor and took over power in Tmutarakan'.

In the year 6590/1082. The Polovets khan Osen' died.

In the year 6591/1083. Oleg returned from Byzantium to Tmutarakan'.[112] He captured Davyd Igorevich and Volodar' Rostislavich and took over power there. He put to death the Khazars

---

Chronicle, 800 years before L. Tolstoy, in this earliest Russian book stressed the essence of Christ's teaching, "God is Love." Later medieval writers also often quoted this verse of Apostle John's. Tolstoy, however, cared little for Old Russian writing and, probably, never read or heard of Prince Iziaslav.

109. In the *Lists of Novg.* not in *Novg.*, *Laur.* or *Hyp.*

110. Toward Voin, in *Laur.*

111. See the year 6586/1078 and 6591/1083, and the footnote.

112. Oleg, well known from *Igor's Lay* as Oleg Gorislavovich, was the main instigator of the feuds and plots among the princes of Russia. Probably, he was deported by the Greeks from Tmutarakan' to

who instigated the murder of his brother as well as his own arrest, **1084**
and released Davyd and Volodar'.[113]

In the year 6592/1084. On Easter Day Iaroslav visited Vsevolod [in Kiev].

At that time both Rostislavichs [Volodar' and Vasil'ko] escaped from Iaropolk and thereafter drove Iaropolk out of the city of Vladimir [in Volynia]. Then Vsevolod dispatched his son, Vladimir [Monomakh] against them. Vladimir [Monomakh] chased both Rostislavichs from the city of Vladimir and set up Iaropolk [as prince] there. The same year Davyd captured merchants in Olesh'e who were trading with Byzantium, and took their goods. Vsevolod sent [his men-at-arms] to get him, brought him to Kiev and set him up as Prince of Dorogobuzh.[114]

In the year 6593/1085. Heeding the counsel of wicked advisors, Iaropolk [in Volynia], son of Iziaslav, grandson of Iaroslav, great grandson of Great Vladimir, wanted to campaign against Vsevolod. Learning of this, Vsevolod sent his son, Vladimir [Monomakh], against him, and Iaropolk fled to Poland, leaving his mother and troops in Lutsk. When Vladimir arrived in Lutsk the inhabitants of the city of Lutsk surrendered, whereupon Vladimir appointed Davyd [Igorevich] to be prince of Vladimir [in Volynia] in the place of Iaropolk. Then he brought the latter's mother, wife and troops to Kiev and confiscated his possessions.

[IAROPOLK'S DEATH AND *ENCOMIUM*]

In the year 6594/1086. Iaropolk returned from Poland and made peace with Vladimir [Monomakh, Prince of Kiev], son of Vsevolod,

Constantinople, and then to the island of Rhodos not only because of the complaints of the Khazars, who lived in the northern Caucasus near Tmutarakan', but also of the Kievan Prince Vsevolod. He spent two years on Rhodos and then returned to Tmutarakan' with his Greek wife, Theophania Muzalon.

113. In *PSRL* IX, pp. 110-114, appear items on Byzantine history under Emperor Romanus Diogenus (1068-1074), Michael Ducas (1074-1078), Nicephorus Botaniates (1078-1081) and Alexis Comnenus (1081-1118); none of this information is related to Russian history and is therefore omitted.

114. According to *Laur., Hyp.* and *Nik.*, the reference here is to "Greeks," but the *Voznesenskii* chronicle—which used an earlier source than the aforementioned works—indicates that the merchants were not Greeks but "Grechniki," which means merchants who traded with Byzantium.

1086 grandson of Iaroslav, great grandson of Great Vladimir. Vladimir and Iaropolk were cousins, the children of brothers [Iziaslav and Vsevolod]. And so Vladimir returned to Chernigov while Iaropolk again became prince of Vladimir [in Volynia]. He remained there only some days and then left the city of Vladimir and went to Zvenigorod. He did not arrive in Zvenigorod because [on his way] he was struck down by the accursed Neradets, who was taught by the devil and by evil people: on the twenty-second day of the month of November while lying on a cot, he [Iaropolk] was pierced with a sabre by the accursed [Neradets], who came riding up on a horse. Iaropolk arose, pulled out the sabre and cried out loudly, "Oh! You, malefactor, you have caught me; but let not Merciful Christ Our Savior take revenge upon you!" Accursed Neradets escaped to [Prince] Riurik [Rostislavich] in Peremysl', while Iaropolk's guards —Radorii, Voikin and others—put Iaropolk's body on their horses before them and bore it, first, to the city of Vladimir [Volynia] and from thence to Kiev.

To meet his body with ecclesiastic honor, there came with crosses, censers and candles the blessed Metropolitan John with his [spiritual] son, pious Prince Vsevolod, the latter's children, Rostislav and Vladimir, the entire sacred council, monks and a multitude of people. And they all wept loudly and shed many tears over his body and accompanied it with psalms to the Church of St. Demetrius, and they buried his body honorably in the sarcophagus in the church of the Holy Apostle Peter, which he, himself, had begun building earlier in the month of December. Iaropolk suffered many misfortunes at his brothers' [and cousins'] hands without having been at fault, himself. He was banished by them, offended, robbed, constantly caused grief and woe, and finally died a bitter death. But he rendered himself worthy of eternal life and joy: he suffered without any guilt. So was this blessed Prince Iaropolk: quiet, meek, mild, full of love [for his brethren], generous; he was not rancorous or vengeful toward those who sinned against him; he was patient, had the gift of tears, was sweet and enjoyed everyone's company. He was very well read, remaining aloof from drinking and revelry. He gave a tithe of all his properties to Lord God, to the Most Pure Theotokos, and to His Holiness [the Metropolitan]. This tithe consisted of a tenth of his cattle and harvest every year. He greatly respected the bishops, priests and monks. He would adorn the churches, he supplied the poor and paupers with food, gave clothing to the naked and to pilgrims. Even saddened and grieved because of his brethren's [behavior], he would always pray to God, saying, "My Lord God! Take me under Thy protection, have mercy upon me, accept my prayer and do not let me take vengeance against those who have caused me evil; and grant me death at the hand of persons alien to me in the same way as Thou gavest it to my brethren, Boris and Gleb, so that my blood may wash away my sins, so that I may escape evil snares and devilish temptations, and vain worldly life with its confusions. And grant me eternal peace and joy." And the Most Merciful did not deny his prayers. He received those blessings "which eye saw not, and ear heard not, and which entered not into the heart of man, whatsoever things God prepared for them that love Him." [I *Cor.* 2:9.]

1087

In the year 6595/1087.

In the year 6596/1088. John, Metropolitan of Kiev and all Russia, consecrated the church of St. Archangel Michael in the monastery [founded by] Vsevolod. At that time Lazarus was the abbot of this monastery.

The same year Sviatopolk left Novgorod to be Prince of Turov [in Volynia]. The same year Abbot Nikon passed away. The same year the Kama and Volga Bulgars captured Murom.[115]

In the year 6597/1089. Metropolitan John of Kiev and all Russia, together with Bishop Luke of Belgorod, Bishop Isaac of Rostov[116] and John of Chernigov consecrated the church of the Assumption of the Holy Theotokos in Theodosius' monastery of the Caves. This happened during the rule of pious Prince Vsevolod Iaroslavich, his children, Vladimir Monomakh and Rostislav, while Ian was the *tysiatskii* of Kiev, and John was the abbot [of the Monastery of the Caves.]

The same year, during the reign of Emperor Alexis Comnenus [1081-1118], the rule of Patriarch Nicholas [of Constantinople], as well as the rule of Vsevolod, Grand Prince of Kiev, and the rule of his son, Vladimir [Monomakh] of Chernigov, and the rule of Metropolitan John of Kiev and all Russia, the relics of St. Nicholas the Miraclemaker were transferred from Myra [in Lycia, in Asia

---

115. In *Laur.*, these items are under the year 1088.
116. Isaiah, in *Laur.* and *Hyp.*; no data in *Novg.*

1090 Minor] to the city of Bari [in southern Italy].[117]

DEATH OF METROPOLITAN JOHN OF KIEV AND ALL RUSSIA.

The same year John, Metropolitan of Kiev and all Russia, passed away. This John was well versed in books and learning, he was merciful to the poor and to widows, was kind toward the rich and to paupers, was quiet, meek, gentle, reticent yet eloquent; he used to console the grieving by quoting Holy Scripture. There was no such [outstanding metropolitan] in Russia before him, and there never will be in the future.[118]

In the year 6598/1090. Ianka [Ann, daughter of Prince Vsevolod of Kiev] went to Constantinople, to Byzantium, and brought from thence John the Castrate, Metropolitan of Kiev and all Russia, about whom people wondered, "This new John has arrived: will he be the same [good Metropolitan as John I] or not?" He stayed one year in Kiev and then died.[119]

EPHRAIM, METROPOLITAN OF KIEV AND ALL RUSSIA.

In the year 6599/1091. Ephraim, Metropolitan of Kiev and all Russia, consecrated the church of St. Michael [in Pereiaslav'l], which he built, himself. [This church] was very large because the Metropolitan See was previously in Pereiaslavl', and many metropolitans of Kiev and all Russia lived there, and the bishops were also consecrated there. He enlarged and adorned this church with all manner of embellishments and church vessels.[120]

This Ephraim was [also] a castrate; he was greatly virtuous, was tall of stature and very lean. He constructed a large number of buildings; he completed building the church of St. Michael and laid the foundation for a church in the name of Holy Martyr Theodore, over the city gate; and of another church of St. Apostle Andrew, near the church of St. Theodore on the Gate; [he also built] a bath.[121]

---

117. This last passage is not present in the *Laur. Hyp.* or *Novg.* chronicles.

118. In *Laur.*, these same items appear under the year 1089.

119. In *Laur.*, this item appears under the year 1089. This John was a man of little learning and simple speech, though candid.

120. This is the only mention in ancient sources that the Metropolia was once located in Pereiaslavl'.

121. A stone bathhouse, as never existed in Russia before: *Laur.* chronicle.

[He also built] homes for the infirm and hospitals, and everyone who came thither was treated without payment; and he did the same in his city of Militino, and in the other cities of his metropolia, as well in his districts, sub-districts and towns; and nothing similar had ever been in Russia.[122] In Pereiaslavl' he laid the foundation of a stone wall starting at the church of St. Theodore, and many other buildings, and he built it, beautifully embellishing the city.

The same year Theodore, the Greek Metropolitan, came from the Pope of Rome bringing many relics of saints. The same year there was a very good harvest.[123]

[TRANSFER OF THE RELICS OF ST. THEODOSIUS AND *ENCOMIUM*.]

In the year 6600/1092.

In the year 6601/1093. The abbot of the Monastery of the Caves took counsel with the monks and decided, "It is not meet to leave the body of our father Theodosius outside the limits of the monastery and of his church because it was he who laid the foundation of this church and brought the caloyers together." And so he instructed that a place be prepared where his relics could be laid.

Three days later, on the day of the Dormition of the Holy Theotokos, the abbot ordered that they dig in the place where the relics of our father Theodosius lay. I, myself, was witness to his decision, and what I am going to relate to you is not hearsay but the account of an eyewitness.

The abbot came to me and said, "Let us go to the cave of Theodosius." I and the abbot, without saying anything to anyone, went thither in order to find a place to dig. We determined the spot where the digging was to be done, and marked it. It was close to the entrance. Then the abbot told me, "Do not speak of this to anyone, but take with you whomsoever you want to help you." The same day[124] I prepared some spades for digging, and on Tuesday, secretly from all, I took with me two brethren and went to the cave. We sang psalms and began digging. I became weary from work and let it be done by another brother, and so we dug until midnight but could not

---

122. This last sentence is not in *Laur.*, *Hyp.* or *Novg.*

123. The last two sentences are not in *Laur.*, *Hyp.* or *Novg.* In *Laur.* the items dealing with Metropolitan Ephraim appear under the year 1090.

124. In *Nik.*, on the seventh day; in *Laur.* and *Hyp.*, it reads "the same day."

1093 reach [the burial place] and became grieved, thinking that we were digging in the wrong direction. Then I took the spade and began to dig diligently, while my friend slept before the cave. Suddenly he said, "It's ringing!" I had just reached [the burial place of] the relics when he said, "It's started ringing!" and I therefore answered him, "I've reached it!" When I did so, I was seized by awe and started to pray, "God have mercy upon us!"

At that time the abbot had still kept secret the transfer [of the relics]. Two brethren who were sitting in the monastery and looking at the cave [of Theodosius] [suddenly] saw three shining pillars above the cave, like the arches of a rainbow. These pillars of light were over the cave of our blessed Father Theodosius; they remained there awhile longer, then moved and stood by the church where, subsequently, were laid [the relics of] our Father Theodosius, teacher and preceptor of the human flock of the Russian land.

At the same time Stephen, who succeeded him as abbot [of the Cave Monastery] and presently is bishop, looked across the field from his monastery and saw a bright light shining above the cave [of Theodosius], and he thought that the transfer of Theodosius' relics had already begun. [He had been told the previous day about the intention to transfer the relics.] Regretting that they had begun the transfer without him, he mounted a horse and rode rapidly [to the cave], taking with him Clement, whom he had appointed abbot in his own place. Approaching, he glimpsed a multitude of candles above the cave. Coming closer to the cave and seeing no one about, he entered it and saw us sitting near the relics.

When I began to dig around the relics in order to clean them, I sent for the abbot [to tell him] the following, "Come, we will remove [the relics] from [the place of burial]," and the abbot with two other brethren came up. We dug some more around them, stepped back and then we saw that the relics did not fall apart but that only the hair on the head stuck together. Then we put the relics on a vestment and placed them before the cave.

The next day there assembled Bishops Ephraim of Pereiaslavl', Stephen of Vladimir [in Volynia], John of Chernigov, the abbots of all monasteries with their monks, and pious people, and they took up the relics of Theodosius, proceeded with incense and candles to his own church and buried him there in the right aisle. This occurred on the fourteenth of the month of August, a Thursday, in the first hour of the day, in the fourteenth year of the Indiction. And we solemnly celebrated this day. **1093**

Now I will speak shortly of how the prophesy of Theodosius was fulfilled. When Theodosius was still alive and was abbot of the Monastery, and was ruling the flock entrusted to him by God, he cared not only for the souls of his caloyers but also for those of lay people, paying attention to the condition of their souls and bearing in mind their salvation. He paid particular attention to his spiritual children, providing them with consolation and instruction and giving them his blessing when visiting them.

Once he came to the house of Ian and his companion-spouse, Maria—whom Theodosius loved greatly because their life was in accord with the Lord's Commandments and they lived in mutual love. So when once he came to them and was instructing them concerning alms, the poor, and the Heavenly Kingdom which the righteous will receive, as well as concerning the torments of sinners and the hour of death, he spoke of the burial of the body. Ian's wife asked him, "Who knows where I shall be buried?" But Theodosius replied, "Verily, in whatsoever place I shall be buried, there you will be buried in the same place!" And this happened: the abbot died eighteen years ago, but it then occurred that the same year, on the sixteenth day of the month of August [two days after Theodosius' relics were transferred] Maria, wife of Ian, died. The caloyers came, chanted the burial hymns, took up her body and buried it in the church of the Holy Theotokos across from the burial place of St. Theodosius, in the left aisle of the church. Theodosius was buried there on the fourteenth, and she on the sixteenth [of August].[125] Thus was fulfilled the prophesy of our Father Theodosius, a good shepherd who cared for his human flock most devotedly. He did this with humility and meekness, paying strict attention to them, watching over them and praying for them, as well as for all Christian people and the Russian land. And, now, after thy departure from this life, pray thee for the faithful, for all thy pupils who look upon

125. It is very probable that this lady, Maria, was the wife of Ian Vyshatich, who had been mentioned on several occasions in the *Prim. Chr.* and in *Nik.*, and who apparently supplied the chronicler with a number of important items of information. Ian Vyshatich was a high civil and military official in the service of the Kievan princes in the second part of the eleventh century, and apparently extended his patronage to the Kievan Cave Monastery.

thy hearse and remember thy instruction and asceticism, and who glorify God.

ENCOMIUM OF ST. THEODOSIUS

I, thy sinful servant and pupil, wonder with what manner of words I may praise thy righteous life and thy asceticism; nonetheless, I furnish here a few words of praise.

Rejoice, our father and preceptor, Theodosius!
Thou hast forsaken this vain world,
Thou hast given thy love to silence,
Thou hast served God in the quietude of monastic life,
Thou hast received all the beneficial Divine gifts,
Thou hast ascended through fasting,
Thou hast despised carnal passions and pleasures,
Thou hast rejected the attractions and desires of this age,
Thou hast followed the way of silence of the sublime fathers,
Thou hast ascended through thy meekness,
Thou hast beatified thyself and rejoiced through the letters of the Scriptures.
Rejoice!
Thou hast strengthened thyself with hope,
Thou hast received eternal blessings,
Thou hast mortified carnal temptations, the source of lawlessness and chaos,

Thou, reverend father, hast escaped devilish crafts and plots,
Thou, father, hast won repose among the righteous,
Thou hast won recompense for thy labors,
Thou hast become the heir of the Fathers,
Thou hast followed their teaching, traditions, ascetism and rules.

Thou hast imitated the virtues and life of Great Theodosius,
Thou hast followed his way of life and ascetism,
Thou hast followed his rules in all thy labors,
Thou hast offered the liturgical prayers to God,
Thou hast born the prayerful censer of its fragrant incense,
Thou hast defeated worldly passions and the prince of this world,
Thou hast defeated the devil and won victory in the world over his crafts,

Thou hast withstood his arrows and his proud intentions, **1093**
Thou hast strengthened thyself with the power of the cross and with Divine succor.

Pray, venerable father, that I might escape devilish snares, and guard me from evil by thy prayers.[126]

PORTENTS.

[*In the year 1093.*] The same year there was a portent: the sun seemed about to disappear, and there remained just a small part of it, which looked like a young moon. This happened at the second hour of the twenty-first day of the month of May.

The same year when Vsevolod was hunting near Vyshgorod and when the snares were laid and [the beaters] were shouting, a tremendous snake dropped from the sky and struck the earth. All the people heard how it hit the earth, and they took fright.

The same year a soothsayer came to Rostov but he soon perished.[127]

PORTENT.

In the year 6602/1094. A most unusual occurrence took place in the city of Polotsk. At night was heard a moaning in the street, as if devils were looking for people. Those who left their homes in order to see [what was happening] were struck down invisibly by devils with a disease from which they died, and no one dared to leave his house. Thereafter they [the devils] started appearing on horseback in the daytime: no one could see them, but their horses' hooves were visible. Thus were struck all the people of Polock and their region. People said of them, "The ghosts of their dead have struck down the people of Polotsk." This portent began in the city of Drutsk.

The same summer there was another portent in the sky: a large circle appeared in the middle of the sky.

---

126. This "Transfer of the Relics of St. Theodosius and *Encomium*" was probably written by Nestor. It is ascribed to him in the *Paterikon of the Kievan Monastery of the Cave,* and its stylistic manner, particularly the first person narrative, recall Nestor's "Life of St. Theodosius." Likhachev, II, 416; cf. "The Life" in *Uspenskii sbornik XII—XIIIvv.*, Moscow, 1971, pp. 11-135. The authorship of the *Encomium,* also written in the eleventh century, is less certain.

127. In *Laur., Hyp.* and *Novg.* these entries are under the year 1091.

1094   The same year there was a drought and the earth seemed to burn, and many forests and marshes started burning by themselves. There were many other portents in [various] places.

The Polovetss vigorously attacked from different sides and took three cities: Pesochen, Perevoloka and Priluki. Many towns were pillaged and the Polovetss campaigned on both banks [of the Dnieper river].

The same year Vasil'ko Rostislavovich, together with the Polovetss, fought against the Poles.

The same year [Prince] Riurik, the son of Rostislav, died.

The same year many people died from various diseases, and those who sold coffins would say, "From St. Philip's Day to Shrovetide we sold seven thousand [coffins]."

All this occurred because of our sins—our sins and misdoings multiplied, and God brought these calamities upon us. He summoned us to repent and to abstain from sin, envy, other evildoings, and from the snares of the devil.[128]

THE DEATH OF PRINCE VSEVOLOD.

In the same year 6602 [in the year 6601 in *Laur.* and *Hyp.*], in the first year of the Indiction, Grand Prince Vsevolod, son of Iaroslav, grandson of Vladimir, died on the thirteenth day of the month of April, and was buried on the fourteenth. This was Maundy Thursday of Holy Week; and he was laid in a sarcophagus in the great Church of Holy Sophia. This pious Prince Vsevolod was a God-loving man from childhood. He loved justice, cared for the needy, honored the bishops and priests, and much loved the monks, contributing to their needs. He abstained from drunkenness, from gluttony, from carnal pleasures, and for these reasons he was beloved by his father [Prince Iaroslav the Wise]. And his father used to tell him, "My son! There is a blessing upon you because I hear of your meekness; and I enjoy this because in this way you console me in my old age. I hope you will ascend to the throne [of Kiev] after your [senior] brothers, in a righteous way and not by the way of violence. And when God leads you out of this [earthly] life, I want you to be buried in the same place where I shall be buried, in the vicinity of my grave, because I love you more than [I do] your brothers."

128. *Laur.*, *Hyp.* and *Novg.* list these same items under the year 1092.

This prophetic speech of his father was fulfilled as he spoke it, **1094** when he [Vsevolod] ascended to the throne [of Kiev] after the passing of his [senior] brothers. After the death of his brother [Iziaslav] he ruled in Kiev but he had more trouble there than he had when he had been in Pereiaslavl'. In Kiev he had [constant] trouble, which was caused by his brothers' sons. They importuned him, desiring more power. And from them he had much unpleasantness and grief, and because of them he became afflicted by illness, complicated by old age. He began to prefer the advice of younger people, and would hold council with them. These [younger advisers] started to envy and to dislike his retinue; then they interfered with his justice, while the clerks would sack and sell [into slavery] the common people. The Prince, however, was unaware of all this, being ill.

When he became direly ill he sent for his son, Vladimir Monomakh, who ruled over Chernigov. When Vladimir arrived and saw him so ill, he lamented. When his [Vsevolod's] time came, he passed away quietly and meekly in the presence of Vladimir Monomakh and his younger son, Rostislav, rejoining his father [in the other world]. He was prince in Kiev for fifteen years, one year in Pereiaslavl', and also in Chernigov fifteen years.

Vladimir Monomakh and his brother, Rostislav, prepared his body for the funeral. Then the bishops, abbots, caloyers, priests, boyars and common people took his body, singing the ritual hymns, and buried his body in [the Cathedral of] Holy Sophia, as I mentioned earlier.

Thereafter, Vladimir Monomakh began to ponder, saying, "In case I ascend to the throne of my father, I will have a feud with Sviatopolk[129] because his father was on the throne [of Kiev] before [my father]." Considering this, he sent to Turov for Sviatopolk, while he, himself, returned to Chernigov; and Rostislav returned to Pereiaslavl'.

THE REIGN OF SVIATOPOLK [THE SECOND] IN KIEV [1094-1114]

On April 24th, the next Sunday after Easter, Sviatopolk came [from Turov] to Kiev; the people of Kiev met him outside the city to

---

129. That is, Sviatopolk of Turov, the son of Iziaslav, late prince in Kiev, 1054-1078.

1094 greet him, and accepted him joyfully. He ascended to the throne of his father and his uncle [his father's brother]. The same year when the Polovetss learned that Vsevolod had died, they sent their envoys to Sviatopolk offering him peace. Sviatopolk, however, without consulting his senior commanders, those of his late father and of his father's brother, following only the advice of those officers who had come to Kiev with him, arrested the envoys and put them in prison. As soon as the Polovetss heard of this, they started raiding. A large number of Polovetss came and besieged the city of the Torks. Thereupon Sviatopolk released the Polovetsian envoys and asked for peace, but the Polovetss did not want peace any longer, and they marched forward, foraging in the Russian land. Then Sviatopolk gathered his troops, intending to march against them.

Sensible persons [in his court] told him, "Do not fight them because you have a small army;" but he responded, "I have seven hundred of my guard and twenty thousand who will be able to do battle with them."[130] Then other unwise [persons in his court] started saying, "Let us go, Prince!" The sensible ones, however, insisted: "Even if you had eighty thousand[131] under arms, even then such a number would not be too much. Our land has become impoverished because of war, and from taxes and fines. Better, ask your cousin, Vladimir [Monomakh of Chernigov] to help you!" And Sviatopolk heeded their advice and asked Vladimir to help him.

Vladimir assembled his troops and asked his brother, Rostislav, Prince of Pereiaslavl', to come to Sviatopolk's aid.

When Vladimir Monomakh came to Kiev they assembled in the [Vydubetskii monastery of] St. Michael, but again began feuding and quarreling. Finally they agreed on a truce [among them] and pledged on the cross to help each other. Sensible men [of the court] told them, "Why do you remember your grievances now? You do so while the pagans [Polovetss] are ravaging the Russian land. You may settle your claims later; but now, decide what to do about the Polovetss: to make peace with them, or to fight them!" Vladimir [Monomakh] was for peace [with the Polovetss] but Sviatopolk was for war; and so Sviatopolk, Vladimir Monomakh and the latter's brother, Rostislav, marched forward toward Trepol'ie and came to

---

130. In *Laur.*, this reads: "seven hundred guards;" in *Hyp.*, "eight hundred guards." There is no mention of twenty thousand.

131. In *Laur.*, *Hyp.* and *Novg.*, "eight thousand."

the river Stugna. There Sviatopolk, Vladimir and Rostislav **1094** summoned their retinues for council; they intended to cross the river. They began to deliberate and Vladimir said, "Since we are covered by the river from their attack, let us conclude peace with them." And this opinion was supported by [the senior men] Ian and the others. But those from Kiev [Sviatopolk's men] did not agree, and said, "We want to fight. Let us cross to the other side of the river!"

The others liked this advice and crossed the river Stugna, which at that time was full of water. Sviatopolk, Vladimir Monomakh and his brother, Rostislav, mustered their army for battle and began to advance. Sviatopolk was with the right wing, Vladimir Monomakh with the left, while Rostislav was in the middle. They passed Trepol'e and crossed the redoubt.

The Polovetss also marched against them, having their bowmen in the front line. Our men took position between the redoubts and raised their banners. But the [Polovetsian] bowmen came from behind the redoubt, advanced toward the redoubt and placed their own banners on it. Then they attacked Sviatopolk and defeated his troops. Sviatopolk resisted staunchly but his soldiers fled, fearing the enemy; and then Sviatopolk fled, also. Thereupon the Polovetss fell upon Vladimir Monomakh and a fierce battle ensued there. [Finally] Vladimir and Rostislav also fled. They came to the river Stugna and Vladimir, with Rostislav, began to ford it; but Rostislav began to drown before the eyes of Vladimir, who wanted to save his brother but also nearly drowned, himself. And so [Prince] Rostislav, Vsevolod's son, Iaroslav's grandson, Great Vladimir's great grandson, drowned. Vladimir Monomakh succeeded in crossing the river Stugna with a small number of warriors: many [soldiers] from his regiment had fallen and his boyars were slain. When he arrived at the other bank of the Dnieper, he bewailed his brother and his soldiers and came to Chernigov greatly grieving.

[In the meantime] Sviatopolk fled to Trepol'e and prepared the city for siege; but he remained there only till evening, and went the same night to Kiev. The Polovetss saw that they had gained the victory and spread out across the [Russian] land, ravaging, while some of them returned to Torchesk. This misfortune occurred on the day of the Ascension of Our Lord Jesus Christ, the twenty-sixth of the month of May.

1094 People searched for Rostislav's body in the river, found it and brought it to Kiev. His mother lamented him and all the people bewailed him greatly because he was so young.[132] The bishops and priests and caloyers assembled to sing the usual [burial] chants, and they buried him near his father in the Cathedral of Holy Sophia in Kiev.

The Polovetss continued the siege of the city of Torchesk but the Torks withstood them and slew many enemy from the city walls. Then the Polovetss began to press them and cut off the water supply, so the people [in the city] suffered greatly from thirst and hunger. Therefore the Torks sent [envoys] to Sviatopolk, to tell him, "We will surrender if you will not supply us with provisions." Sviatopolk sent them supplies but it was impossible to bring them into the city. A great many [Polovetsian] warriors besieged the city for nine weeks, and then they divided themselves into two parties: one remained besieging the city, the other made off for Kiev and went as far as the region between Kiev and Vyshgorod. Sviatopolk marched [against them] toward [the town of] Zhelan'ia, and the two armies clashed and a battle ensued. Our men fled from the enemy, the wounded fell before them, and most [of the Russians] were slain. [The number of slain was] even greater than in the Trepol'e battle. Sviatopolk returned to Kiev with only two men, while the Polovetss returned to Torchesk. This evil was on the twenty-third of July. The next day, on the twenty-fourth, was the holiday when the Holy Martyrs Boris and Gleb are remembered, and there was great lamentation in the city [of Kiev] on that day. All this occurred because of our sins.

[HOMILY]

God permitted pagans to defeat us, not because He wanted to show His mercy [to pagans] but in order to punish us because we were inclined toward evil deeds. He punished us with the invasion of pagans, and they were His weapon, in order to provide us with opportunity to ponder our evil ways. ON HOLIDAYS. The reason why God visited us with this grief on holidays was the following: the first misfortune befell us at Trepol'e on the Day of the Ascension of Our Lord Jesus Christ; the second, however, was on the holiday of Boris and Gleb, which is the new holiday of the Russian land. On a

---

132. Prince Rostislav's drowning in the Stugna is referred to in *Prince Igor's Lay*.

similar occasion the prophet said, "And I will turn your feasts into **1094** mourning and all your songs into lamentation." [*Amos,* 8:10.] Thus there occurred great lamentation in our land, our towns and cities became deserted because the people fled from our enemies.

As the prophet says, "Ye shall be smitten before your enemies; they that hate you will rule over you, and ye shall flee when none pursueth thee. And I will break the pride of your power ... and your strength shall be spent in vain ... Your land shall be despoiled and I will bring a sword upon you ... and your cities shall be wasted ... and I will walk contrary to you in wrath ... because you walk contrary to me ..." And so says Lord God of Israel. [*Lev.* 26:17-33; the sentence order is changed and there are many omissions.]

For the wicked sons of Ishmael burnt our towns and barns, and set fire to many churches. Let no one wonder at it: "Where there is a multitude of sins, there are also testimonies of retribution."

For this reason the world shall perish!
For this reason wrath shall spread!
For this reason our land has been tormented!
Some [of us] have been taken into slavery!
Some have been slain;
Some died a bitter death.
Some trembled, seeing the massacre!
Some of us died of starvation and thirst!
There is One Commandment;
There is one punishment.
But many were those who were hurt
And manifold were grief and terrible torments.

Yet it is meet and just for us to be punished, because [Divine] punishment is [sent] to strengthen our faith. We deserve to be rendered into the hands of this alien tribe, the most lawless on earth. Let us, therefore, proclaim loudly, "Righteous art Thou, oh Lord, and righteous are Thy judgments." Let us say likewise as the thief [on the cross] said, "We get just recompense for our deeds." [*Luke* 23:41.] Let us exclaim with Job, "It hath been as the Lord appointed, blessed is the name of the Lord forever." [*Job* 1:21, rephrased.]

Yes! Thanks to the incursions and torments inflicted by pagans, we now better understand Our Lord Christ, Whom we have angered:

We have been glorified by Him, but we did not glorify Him;

1094
    We have been honored [by Him], but we have not honored [Him];

We have been hallowed [by Him], but we have not understood.

We have been redeemed [by Him], but we have not requited [Him] with good;

We have been reborn [through Him],[133] but we have not honored [Him as Our Father];

We have sinned and therefore we have been punished.

We have wronged, and now we suffer.

And what is so strange and terrifying among [us], a Christian nation? It is the spreading of fear, of hesitation and of many misfortunes. Our cities are ravaged, our towns are devastated. Let us walk through meadows where herds of horses, our sheep, our cattle used to graze and we will find them empty. Our fields are overgrown and have become the dwelling place of [savage] beasts. But we still hope for the mercy of God. Our Blessed Lord has punished us with beneficial intent: "He hath not dealt with us after our sins, nor rewarded us after our iniquities." [*Ps.* 103:10.] It is meet that Our Blessed Lord Christ not punish us according to the multitude of our sins. This is what the Lord has done unto us:

He created us,

He redeemed the fallen,

He forgave the crime of Adam,

He granted us cleansing [purification],

He shed His blood for us.

Since He saw us living unjustly, He sent war and grief upon us, and yet, despite our deeds, we may win the life to come and obtain mercy, because our souls, being chastised in this life, may find mercy in the age to come and escape torment. Lord God does not take revenge twice for the same trespass. Oh! Ineffable [Divine] love for man! He brings us back to Himself even against our own wills! Ah, His endless love for us [prevails] although we went astray from His Commandment! Now, however, we have to suffer His chastisement against our will and, suffering it against our will, let us accept it with resignation.

    Where was our meekness? Now there are only tears everywhere!

---

133. This is a reference to the Christianization of Russia.

Where were our sighs? Now our lamentation spreads through the streets because of the innocent slain by the lawless. The Polovetss ravaged widely and then returned to Torchesk, where the people were exhausted by starvation and surrendered to the [Polovetsian] warriors. The Polovetss occupied the city, set fire to it, divided [the captive] people among themselves, and led them away to their land.

1094

Many Christians suffered: they were grieved and tormented. They froze in the winter, their faces became emaciated from hunger and thirst, their bodies became black, their [new] country was strange to them. Their tongues were inflamed, they were naked and barefoot, their feet were hurt by thorns. Tearfully they inquired of each other, "I was from such and such a city..." while others [would say], "I am from such and such a village." In such way they inquired of each other with tears, speaking of their families, sighing and lifting their eyes toward the Most High, Who knows all fates.

But let us not dare to say, "God hates us!" We should not speak in such a way!

Whom does God love so much as us?

Whom did He honor, glorify and exalt so much as us?

None!

We have so much incurred His wrath because we have been honored by Him more than any other nation; but we have sinned worse than any other people! We have been enlightened by Him[134] more than any other land, and although we were aware of the Lord's will, we scorned it and therefore we have been chastised more severely than any other nation. I, myself, am sinful. I anger God greatly and often, and every day sin many times.[135]

---

134. Here, again, Russia's Christianization is meant.

135. In these last paragraphs of the *Homily* is found the earliest indication of the later idea that by granting Christianity to Russia, God selected that country for a special role and mission in history: "We have been honored by Him more than any other nation and therefore must be better Christians than any other people." According to Tatishchev, this text ends with the word, "Amen." Therefore Tatishchev, and, later in the nineteen twenties, Shakhmatov considered that the earliest, initial version of the *Primary Chronicle* ended here. (*Nachal'nyi Kievskii svod*.) Tatishchev, V.N., *Istoriia rossiiskaia*, Vol. II, pp. 101 and 252 (M.-L., 1963). Likhachev, II, 420, and other modern investigators of the *Povst' vremennykh let (Primary Chronicle)* believe that *Nachal'nyi svod* was concluded in 1097, with the

1095 [1094 cont., also 6602/1094 in *Laur*. but 6601/1093 in *Hyp*.] The same year, on the first day of the month of October, Rostislav, Mstislav's son, Iziaslav's grandson, Iaroslav's great grandson, Great Vladimir's gr. gr. grandson, passed away. He was buried on the sixteenth day of November [in Kiev] in the Tithe Church of the Holy Theotokos.[136] The same year [Prince] Oleg came to Chernigov with Polovetsian troops from Tmutarakan', and Vladimir Monomakh prepared the city for siege. Oleg, however, approached the city and burnt the churches and monasteries near it. Then Vladimir [Monomakh] made peace with Oleg, left the city and went to his father's former principality of Pereiaslavl'. Meanwhile, the Polovetss ravaged around Chernigov but Oleg would not interfere with them because he, himself, had led them thither to wage war.

THE LOCUSTS.

The same year, on August sixteenth,[137] locusts infested the Russian land and destroyed all the grass and a vast amount of grain. Nothing similar was ever heard of since the earliest days of the Russian land, but our eyes witnessed this [chastisement] for our sins.

BISHOP STEPHEN'S DEATH.

The same year Stephen, Bishop of Vladimir, died. This happened in the sixth hour of the night on the twenty-seventh day of the month of April. He was earlier abbot of the Monastery of the Caves.

In the year 6603/1095. The Polovetss, together with [the so-called] son of Diogenes, attacked and ravaged the Byzantine land.[138] But the Emperor captured "Diogenes' son" and ordered him to be blinded.

---

description of the convention of the princes in Liubech, with the idea of providing this early chronicle with a definite ideology of the unity of the Russian land and the uniqueness of the Russian mission. The *Nik.* text follows closely the text of *Laur*.; the rhythmic organization of certain paragraphs is also found in *Laur*.

136. This first part of the annual entry is found in *Laur*. under the year 1093.

137. In *Laur.*, August 26.

138. This so-called "son of Diogenus" was apparently (according to Anna Comnena, *Aleksiada*, M. 1965, p. 226 ff.) an imposter claiming to

The same year the Polovetsian [Khans] Itlar and Kytan[139] asked **1095** Vladimir [Monomakh] for peace; Itlar came to the city of Pereiaslavl', while Kytan and his troops took up a position between the ramparts. Vladimir gave his son, Sviatoslav, as a hostage to Kytan, while Itlar remained in the city with choice troops.

The same year Slaviata came from Kiev, as Sviatopolk's envoy to Vladimir, and Ratibor's detachment began discussing with Vladimir how to slay Itlar's troops. Vladimir was unwilling to do this and asked, "How can I do it? I gave them an oath." But the soldiers answered, saying to Vladimir, "Prince! There is no sin in it. Despite all their oaths, they constantly raid your [principality] and ravage the Russian land unceasingly, spilling Christian blood." And Vladimir agreed with them. The same night Vladimir sent Slaviata to the ramparts with some troops and with the Torks. First of all, they kidnapped Sviatoslav secretly [who had been hostage with the Polovetss]; then they killed Kytan and slew his troops. This was a Saturday evening, and that night Itlar and his soldiers stayed in Ratibor's house, unaware of what had happened to Kytan. The next morning, Sunday, when it was time for matins, Ratibor sent armed soldiers with the order to heat the house [in which Itlar was staying]. Then Vladimir sent his guard, Bandiuka, to Itlar's soldiers, and Bandiuka told Itlar: "Prince Vladimir invites you, saying, 'You must first get dressed in the heated house, then have repast at Ratibor's, and thereafter come to me.'" And Itlar answered, "It will be done thus." When they entered the heated house, [Vladimir's soldiers] locked them up. Then they climbed on the roof of the house, made a hole in it, and Ol'beg Ratiborich took his bow, set an arrow in it and shot Itlar through the heart; and his soldiers were also slain. Thus badly ended the life of [Khan] Itlar. This happened on the first Sunday of Lent, the twenty-fourth day of February.[140]

be the son of the Byzantine emperor, Romanus Diogenus, 1067-1071. But since he was Vladimir Monomakh's son-in-law, it is difficult to presume that Vladimir Monomakh—himself related to the Byzantine dynasty—would let his daughter marry an imposter. See *Ist. Zap.*, Vol. 22, 1947, pp. 96-98. Emperor Alexis Comnenus, 1081-1118; Anna Comnena was his daughter.

139. "Kylan" in *Laur.*, "Kytan" in *Nik.*

140. It is interesting to note that in the principality of Pereiaslavl', located on the frontier prairie, a considerable role was played by the Torks, another Turkic tribe which was allied with the Russians. The names "Diandiuka" and "Ol'beg" are Turkic, and the Torks participated in the massacre of Kytan and his Polovetss.

1095   Sviatopolk and Vladimir Monomakh sent for Oleg [in Chernigov], ordering him to march, together with them, against the Polovetss. Oleg promised to campaign with them but did not take the same route. Sviatopolk and Vladimir went to the Polovetsian encampments, occupied them, captured cattle, horses, camels and slaves, and brought them to their lands. They both became angry with Oleg because he did not join them in this raid against the pagans.

Then Sviatopolk and Vladimir sent to Oleg, saying, "You did not campaign with us against the pagans, who devastate the Russian land; and you support Itlar's people. Either kill them or give them to us because they are our enemies and enemies of the Russian land!" But Oleg did not heed them and hatred arose among them.

DEATH OF BISHOP GERMAN.

The same year Bishop German came from Novgorod to Kiev, and there he died during the rule of Ephraim, Metropolitan of Kiev and all Russia.[141]

The same year the Polovetss marched against the city of Iur'ev, besieged it for the entire summer and nearly took it; Sviatopolk, however, pacified them. Nonetheless, the Polovetss crossed the river Ros', while the people of Iur'ev fled to Kiev. Then Sviatopolk ordered that a fortress be built on Vitichev hill[142] and named it after himself: *Sviatopolchii grad* [Sviatopolk's City]. He also ordered Bishop Marin of Iur'ev to settle there, together with people of Zasakov and of other cities, while the Polovetss burned the abandoned city of Iur'ev.

The same year [Prince] Davyd Sviatoslavich gave up Novgorod for Smolensk, and then the Novgorodians sent their envoys to Rostov in order to get Mstislav Vladimirovich [son of Monomakh] to rule as prince in Novgorod. [He agreed and] they took him to Novgorod, saying to Davyd, "Do not come to us anymore!" And Davyd returned to Smolensk while Mstislav began to rule in Novgorod.[143]

The same year Iziaslav, Vladimir's son, went from Kursk to

---

141. This item appears only in *Nik*.
142. On the river Stugna, a tributary of the Dnieper.
143. Apparently Davyd tried to return to Novgorod.

Murom, and the people of Murom accepted him [as their prince]; and there he arrested Oleg's posadnik.

The same year on the twenty-eighth day of the month of July locusts infested Russia, covering the earth, and it was terrifying to see. They moved toward the northern lands, eating the grass and millet.

In the year 6604/1096. Metropolitan Ephraim of Kiev and all Russia consecrated Nicetas Bishop of Novgorod.

[STRUGGLE BETWEEN VLADIMIR MONOMAKH AND OLEG]

The same year Sviatopolk and Vladimir sent to Oleg, saying the following: "Come to Kiev. Let us set the Russian land aright in the presence of bishops, abbots and the [foremost] men of our fathers, as well as the burghers, so that we can defend the Russian land from the pagans." Inspired by violence and for the sake of proud words, Oleg said, "It does not behoove me to be judged by bishops, abbots or the boyars, who are our servants."[144] Heeding the suggestions of evil advisors, he did not want to go to his brothers,[145] Sviatopolk and Vladimir, who told him, "If you don't go against the pagans [Polovetsians] or come to our councils, it means that you conspire against us and want to aid the pagans; and then there will be a feud between us." So then Sviatopolk and Vladimir marched to Chernigov against Oleg; but on the third day of the month of May, Saturday, Oleg escaped from Chernigov to Starodub. Sviatopolk and Vladimir besieged that city but those of the city fought very fiercely. And those [men of Sviatopolk's and Vladimir's] attacked the city and many were wounded on both sides. A fierce fight took place between them but after they had besieged the city thirty-three days, the people of the city became wearied. Then Oleg came out of the city, desiring peace, and they made peace with him, saying the following: "Go to your brother, Davyd, and then come to Kiev, where the throne of our fathers and grandfathers is, because Kiev is the senior city in all our land and it behooves us to assemble there and bring order." Oleg promised to do this and pledged on the cross.

---

144. The word, "boyars," cannot be found in corresponding texts of earlier chronicles. Apparently, the compiler of *Nik.* put it in to reflect the later mentality of the sixteenth century, according to which the boyars were the monarch's servants.

145. Actually, to his cousins.

1096 The same year [Khan] Boniak with Polovetss came to Kiev on Sunday evening, campaigned around Kiev and burned the court of the prince in Berestovo. The same year Prince Kuria fought with the Polovetss at Pereiaslavl' and on the twenty-fourth day of the month of May burned [the town of] Ustié. Oleg [meanwhile] left Starodub and marched to Smolensk but he was not received by the people of Smolensk. And then he went to Riazan'. Sviatopolk and Vladimir [meanwhile] returned home.

The same year, on the thirtieth day of the month of May, Tugr-Khan, father-in-law of Sviatopolk, came to Pereiaslavl' and camped near the city, but the people of Pereiaslavl' fortified themselves inside the city. Sviatopolk and Vladimir, however, marched against him on this side of the Dnieper, came to Zarub, crossed [the river], and the Polovetss did not notice them because God protected them; and they prepared themselves for battle and marched to the city. The inhabitants of the city saw them and went joyfully to meet them, while the Polovetss camped on the other shore of the Trubezh, preparing for battle. Sviatopolk and Vladimir crossed the Trubezh toward the Polovetss, and Vladimir wanted to array his troops in battle formation; but they disobeyed him and attacked the enemy on horseback. Seeing this, the Polovetss fled and our men sent warriors after them, cutting the enemy to pieces.

On that day, the nineteenth of the month of July, God provided the Russians great salvation, and the strangers were defeated; their prince, Tugr-Khan, was killed, and with him his son and other princes; and many of our enemies were killed. The next day Sviatopolk took the dead Tugr-Khan, who was his father-in-law and his enemy, brought him to Kiev, and buried him in Berestovo between the road which leads to Berestovo and another road leading to the monastery.

[BONIAK ATTACKS KIEV]

On the twentieth day of the same month, a Friday—unexpectedly—the godless, mangy [Khan] Boniak stealthily, like a beast, came for the second time to Kiev, and the Polovetss almost entered the city and set fire to the forests in the marshy land of the suburb, [then] turned to the monastery and burned Stephen's monastery and the villages. They came to the Cave Monastery while we were in our cells resting after matins and started shouting near the monastery, putting two banners before the monastery gate while we escaped from the back of the monastery, and some others ran to the church lofts. The godless sons of Ishmael burst the gate to the monastery, went to the cells, breaking the doors, and took away all they found in the cells. Thereupon they burned the House of Our Lady, the Holy Mother of God; and coming to the church, they set fire at the southern door, while others did the same at the northern door; and they entered near the chapel where the tomb of Theodosius was, taking the icons, burning the doors and offending God and our faith. God permitted this to happen because their sins and lawlessness did not end there; and [they] said, "Where is their [the Russians'] God? Why does He not help and save them?" And they spoke other offensive words, making fun of the holy icons because they did not know that God punishes His servants through the evils of war because they must be as gold, which is proved in the forge: Christians have to enter the Kingdom of Heaven through many griefs and misfortunes; but those pagan offenders who in this world have joy and wealth will in the other world receive torture by the devil, and they are predestined to eternal fire. Then they burned the beautiful [*Krasnyi*] palace which was built by pious Prince Vsevolod on the hill called Vydubets; it was all burned by the accursed Polovetss. And therefore we, heeding the Prophet [actually king] David, exclaim, "' O My Lord God, make them like unto whirling dust and as the stubble before the wind. Destroy them with Thy storm, like as the fire that burneth up the forest. Make their faces ashamed.'" [*Ps.* 83:13-16; some words omitted.] They have defiled Thy Holy House, the monastery of Thy Mother and the corpses of Thy servants. These godless sons of Ishmael, who were released for the punishment of the Christians, killed several of our brethren with their arms.

1096

[THE BACKGROUND OF THE POLOVETSS]

They came out from the desert of the Jews[146] between the east and the north; seven tribes of them came out: the Torkmens and the Pechenegs, the Torks and the Polovetss. Methodius [of Patar][147]

---

146. In the original text, in the chronicle by Harmatolos, and in *Hyp.* and *Laur.*, "Yathrib desert."

147. Methodius of Patar: this reference deals with the *Revelation of Methodius of Patar*, the work of anonymous writers, probably from the fourth century A.D., incorrectly ascribed to Methodius, bishop of the cities of Patar

1096 witnesses that eight tribes of them escaped when they were massacred by Gideon. [*Judges*, Chapter 6:11.] He massacred four [tribes of] them, and the eight fled to the desert. Others claim that they are the sons of Ammon, but that is not true. The sons of Moab [*Gen.* 19:37.] are the Khvalis[148] while the sons of Ammon are the Bulgars; but the Saracens, the sons of Ishmael, claim that they are the children of Sarah and call themselves "Saracens," which means, "We are those of Sarah." Thus the Khvalis and the Bulgars descend from the daughters of Lot, who conceived them from their own father. [*Gen.* 19:36.] And therefore their tribe is impure. And Ishmael [*Gen.* 16:15] begat twelve sons,[149] from whom descended the Torkmens, the Pechenegs and the Torks and the Kumans—that is, the Polovetss, who come out of the desert. And after these tribes at the end of ages there will come out the impure people who were walled in the mountains by Alexander [the Great] of Makedon.

[THE WALLED PEOPLE OF THE NORTHERN URALS]

And I want to tell what I heard four years ago from Iuriata Rogovich of Novgorod, who told me the following: "I sent my man to Pechora[150] to the peoples who pay tribute to Novgorod; and my man went to them and from there to the Iugra;[151] and the language of the Iugra people is dumb[152] and they are neighbors of the Samoeds in the northern country. The Iugra people told my man, 'It is a real wonder that we did not hear of it in previous years, but heard it three

---

and Lycia in Asia Minor in the third-fourth centuries A.D. This *Revelation*, originally written in Syrian and later translated into Greek, treats the origin of the world, describing the background of various peoples and world history to the end of the world, expected in the year 7,000[1492] from the creation of the world. This *Revelation* was known in Russia in two Church Slavonic translations done in Bulgaria. According to the knowledge available to the chroniclers, all eastern nomadic people originated from the Biblical Ishmael, son of Abraham and his slave, Hagar.

148. *Khvalis* were apparently people living at the Khvalis, now the Caspian, Sea—probably Khazars.

149. This information is taken from Harmatolos.

150. Pechora: a region along the Pechora river in the extreme northeast of European Russia.

151. *Iugra*: Finno-Ugric tribes, also called "Voguls" or "Mansi," in the northern Urals and northwestern Siberia, related to the Hungarians.

152. "*Nem:*" "dumb" or "foreign."

years ago—that there are mountains [the Urals] which go to the gulf of the sea [the Arctic Ocean], and they are as high as the sky. And inside these mountains [one hears] shouting and [voices] speaking, and [these people] are [trying to] break through the mountain because they want to get out. And there is a little window cut into the mountain and they speak through it; but we do not understand their language, and they point to iron, waving their hands and asking for iron; and if someone gives them a knife or an axe, they quickly give furs in exchange. But the way to the mountains is impassable because of the snow and the forest. Therefore we can not always get there. They are farther away to the North."

But I said to Iuriata, "They are the people walled in by Alexander, King of Makedon, as related by Methodius of Patar: 'I went to the Eastern land, to the sea, called the Land of the Son, and I saw there the impure tribes of Japhet, and I became aware of their impurity. They eat all manner of impure [food] and do not bury their dead. And they eat the female *izvorogi*[153] and all manner of impure animals. Alexander saw this and took fright that they may corrupt the land, and chased them into the high mountains of the northern land."

Following God's commandment, the northern mountains encircled them, and they did so save for a space of six arm-lengths. Then there were erected gates of copper and they were covered with *sunklit*, a compound which can neither be burned by fire nor destroyed by iron. In the latter days, according to the commandment of God, eight tribes will come out from the Yathrib desert, and after them those evil tribes will come out of the northern mountains, where they are now locked up.[154]

But let us now return to our original narrative.

[NEW CONFLICT BETWEEN MSTISLAV
MONOMASHICH AND OLEG SVIATOSLAVICH]

[6608/1096] Although Oleg promised his brother, Davyd, to come to him in Smolensk and then, together, to go to Kiev to

153. *Izvorogi:* a fetus after miscarriage.

154. According to Methodius of Patar, *sunklit* (in Greek, *asyghytos*) is a legendary indestructible compound. In *Laur.*, the famous *Instruction* by Vladimir Monomakh is inserted in the middle of this story concerning the origin of the Polovetss and the northern tribes.

1096 conclude a treaty [with the other princes], he did not want to do this. He went to Smolensk and, assembling his troops, made off to Murom, where Iziaslav Vladimirich was ruling at that time [Iziaslav was the second son of Monomakh]. When Iziaslav received word of Oleg's advance he sent for troops from Suzdal' and Rostov' and for the people of Belozero, and he gathered many warriors together. Then Oleg dispatched [his envoys] to Iziaslav to tell him, "Go to Rostov, the domain of your father; but this city [of Murom] is my father's domain. When I take Murom, I will conclude a treaty with your father because it was he who chased me away from my father's city. Or are you, also, unwilling to give me my bread—[provide land]?"

Iziaslav, however, paid no heed, relying on the great number of his troops. Oleg, though, relied upon justice because Oleg was right in all respects; and he marched toward his city [of Murom]. Iziaslav drew up [his troops] for battle before the city, and then Oleg with his army made a thrust at them. The two [armies] clashed in fierce battle [during which] Iziaslav, son of Vladimir Monomakh, grandson of Vsevolod, great grandson of Iaroslav and great-great grandson of Vladimir the Great, was killed. This occurred on the sixth day of the month of September. Those remaining of [Iziaslav's] warriors fled, and Oleg entered the city, whose citizens received him. Iziaslav's body was taken up and laid in the Monastery of Saint Savior, and from thence [later] was transported to Novgorod and buried in the left aisle of [the Cathedral of] Holy Sophia.

Having taken the city [of Murom], Oleg put into irons those who came from the cities of Rostov, Belozero and Suzdal'; and then he hurried to Suzdal', whose citizens surrendered to him. Oleg pacified this city: some were arrested, some were deported, while their possessions were confiscated. Then he marched to Rostov, whose people submitted to him. And so he took over all the lands of Murom and Rostov, assigned his posadniks and began to collect taxes.

Then Mstislav [Vladimir's son and Iziaslav's brother] sent his envoys from Novgorod to tell Oleg, "Depart from Suzdal' and go to Murom, and do not occupy a domain which is not yours; meanwhile, I will send my men to my father [Vladimir Monomakh] and will reconcile the two of you. It is no wonder that my brother was killed: in battle, both tsars and their men are often slain."

Oleg, however, did not want to heed his words because he

intended to seize Novogord, also; therefore Oleg sent his brother, **1096** Iaroslav, with an avant guard, while he, himself, remained [with his troops] in the field near Rostov. Mstislav consulted his Novgorodians and sent Dobrynia Raguplovich with his advance troops.[155] First of all, Dobrynia began arresting [Oleg's] tax collectors. When Iaroslav—who was in the avant guard on the river, Medveditsa—learned that the tax collectors had been arrested, he fled by night, went to Oleg and told him that Mstislav was approaching and that the warriors of the avant guard had been captured. Thereupon Oleg retreated toward Rostov, while Mstislav reached the Volga, where he learned that Oleg had retreated toward Rostov, and he pursued Oleg.

Meanwhile, Oleg arrived in Suzdal'. Learning that Mstislav was pursuing him, he ordered that the city be burned. [After the conflagration] there remained only the monastery[156] belonging to the Metropolitan, and the church of St. Demetrius, which had been given [to the monastery] by Metropolitan Ephraim, together with several townships.

METROPOLITAN EPHRAIM

This outstanding man, Ephraim, Metropolitan of Kiev and all Russia, was a person of many virtues and holy life. During and after his life, thanks to the power of Christ, he performed many miracles.[157]

[STRUGGLE IN SUZDALIA BETWEEN MSTISLAV AND OLEG]

[From Suzdal'] Oleg fled to Murom, and when Mstislav arrived in Suzdal' he settled there and dispatched [his men] to Oleg to proffer peace and tell him, "I am junior to you; therefore, send your [envoys] to my father and return those of my warriors whom you have captured. Thereafter, I will obey you in every respect." Oleg dispatched [envoys] to him, pretending that he wanted peace, and Mstislav believed him and let his warriors go to outlying towns. Then the week of St. Theodore arrived, during Lent; and when it was the Saturday of St. Theodore and Mstislav was dining, he [Mstislav] learned that Oleg was on the river Kliazma and was approaching

155. In *Laur.*, it reads "Rugailovich."
156. In *Laur.*, this reads "Monastery of the Caves."
157. This last paragraph is not in *Laur.*

1096 stealthily, and had already drawn very near.[158] Mstislav, however, trusting Oleg, did not send outposts; but God knows how to protect the pious from wickedness: Oleg halted at the Kliazma, expecting that Mstislav would attempt to escape. [The latter, however, did not] and the same day his troops began to rally around him, while on the next day the levies of Novgorod, Rostov and Belozero arrived. Then Mstislav drew up his troops for battle before the city, but neither Oleg nor Mstislav attacked; and so they remained for four days, the one facing the other. And Mstislav received the news, "Your father has sent you your brother, Viacheslav, with the Polovetss." Viacheslav came on Thursday after St. Theodore's week, while on Friday Oleg reached the city [of Suzdal'] and prepared for battle. Mstislav, in the meanwhile, advanced to meet him with his levies from Novgorod and Rostov. Then Mstislav entrusted Vladimir's standard to a Polovets warrior named Kunui and gave him some foot troops and placed him on the right wing, where Kunui drew up his foot troops and displayed Vladimir Monomakh's standard.

When Oleg saw Vladimir's standard, he took fright. Fear seized him and his warriors. [Still] they marched against each other: Oleg against Mstislav and Iaroslav against Viacheslav. With the Novgorodian levies, Mstislav crossed the burned city and confronted the enemy at the river Koloksha. The fighting was intense and Mstislav began to overcome him. When Oleg saw that Vladimir's standard was advancing and was moving into his rear, Oleg took fright and fled, and so Mstislav won.

Oleg escaped to Murom, leaving Iaroslav [his brother] there to prepare for a siege, and he, himself, went to Riazan'. Mstislav marched toward Murom, made peace [with its citizens] and moved his levies from Rostov and Suzdal' toward Riazan' in pursuit of Oleg. Oleg escaped from Riazan'; then Mstislav arrived there and made peace [with the populace] of Riazan', releasing those of his men who had been imprisoned by Oleg. Then Mstislav sent [his envoy] to Oleg to say, "Do not flee again, but send a petition to your brethren[159] asking them not to deprive you of Russian land. I, myself, will send to my father to intercede on your behalf." Oleg promised to do this. Then Mstislav returned to Suzdal', from whence he went to his city

158. The first week of Lent is devoted to the grand martyr, St. Theodore of Tyre.

159. Actually, cousins.

of Novgorod. This happened, thanks to the prayers of the venerable Nicetas, Bishop of Novgorod. All this occurred in the year 6604 [1096] at the end of the half of the fourth Indiction.

1097

[VASILII'S STORY OF THE BLINDING OF VASIL'KO
AND THE ENSUING FEUDS[160]]
[PRINCES' CONVENTION IN LIUBECH]

In the year 6605/1097. [Princes] Sviatopolk Iziaslavich and Vladimir Monomakh Vsevolodich and Davyd Igorevich, all grandsons of Iaroslav, as well as Vasil'ko Rostislavich, great grandson of Iaroslav, and Davyd Sviatoslavich with his brother, Oleg [of Chernigov]—both grandsons of Iaroslav—met in the city of Liubech in order to establish peace. They told each other, "Why do we destroy the Russian land and feud among ourselves whilst the Polovetss ravage our land and rejoice that we wage war among ourselves? From henceforth, let us unite with pure hearts and let us protect the Russian land. Each of us should possess the domain of his father: that is, Sviatopolk Iziaslavich—Kiev; Vladimir Monomakh Vsevolodich and Sviatoslav's sons: Davyd, Oleg and Iaroslav—[the principalities given them] by Vsevolod; Davyd [Igorevich]—the city of Vladimir [in Volynia]; Rostislav's sons: Volodar—[the principality of] Peremysl' [in Galicia]; and Vasil'ko—Terebovl' [also in Galicia]. And they pledged on the cross to the following: "In case any of us should attempt [to appropriate someone else's domain], then all of us and the Venerable Cross will be against him." And they all assented, "Yes! The Venerable Cross and the entire Russian land will be against such a one." And they took leave and parted.

[PRINCE DAVYD OF VLADIMIR IN VOLYNIA PLOTS AGAINST PRINCE
VASIL'KO OF TEREBOVL']

Sviatopolk came to Kiev with Davyd and there all rejoiced. Only the devil was aggrieved at this good agreement. Satan penetrated there into the hearts of some men and they began to plot, telling Davyd Igorevich, "Vladimir [Monomakh] made an agreement with

---

160. Vasilii's story of the blinding of Vasil'ko and the ensuing feuds forms one single annual entry under the year 1097 in the *Primary Chronicle.* Actually, it embraces some four years: 1097-1100. In *Nik.* it appears with some minor changes and is divided into several smaller narratives, each covering a phase of the events. This translator has added in brackets some additional headings for several phases of the feuds.

1097 Vasil'ko against Sviatopolk and you." Believing these false words, Davyd started to incite Sviatopolk against Vasil'ko, saying, "It is he who killed your brother, Iaropolk. Now he is plotting against you and me. He is the same person who made an agreement with Vladimir. Care for your own head!" Sviatopolk became perplexed in mind and said, hesitantly, "What is this, truth or falsehood?" Then Sviatopolk told Davyd, "If you speak the truth, God will be your Witness. But if you speak from envy, God will hold you responsible." Sviatopolk however, became anxious for his brother and pondered whether it be true, and accepted Davyd's words as the truth. Thus did Davyd win Sviatopolk, and they began to plot against Vasil'ko. Neither Vasil'ko nor Vladimir, however, knew aught of this.

Then Davyd told Sviatopolk, "In case we do not gain power over Vasil'ko, then neither you will reign in Kiev nor I, in Vladimir [in Volynia]." And Sviatopolk agreed with him.

Vasil'ko approached on the fourth day of the month of November, and crossed the river Dnieper toward the Vydubetskii [Monastery, near Kiev] to make a pilgrimage to St. Michael's. He supped there and pitched camp at Rudnitsa. In the evening he returned to camp. When morning dawned someone from Sviatopolk came, saying, "Do not depart from hence because it will soon be my namesday." Vasil'ko, however, refused, saying, "I cannot delay because there may be unrest at home." Then Davyd sent for him. "Do not depart, brother. Do not disobey your senior brother." But Vasil'ko did not want to obey. Then Davyd told Sviatopolk, "Do you see? He does not obey you but wants to be independent from you. If he leaves for his land, you will see—he may occupy your cities of Turov and Pinsk and other of your cities, and then you will remember me. Better, invite him and seize him, and then give him to me." Sviatopolk agreed and sent for Vasil'ko, saying, "If you do not want to stay till my namesday, then please come now to embrace me and we will be together with Davyd." Unaware of the plot prepared against him by Davyd, Vasil'ko promised to come [to Kiev]. He mounted his horse and rode. [In Kiev] he was met by [Sviatopolk's] steward, who told him, "Do not come, Prince. They want to seize you." But he did not believe him and responded, "Why should they seize me? Only yesterday they pledged on the Cross, saying, 'If someone should fight another, then the venerable Cross and all of us will be against him.'" He pondered, made the sign of the Cross, and said, "The Lord's will be done."

1097

He went to the Prince's court with a few guards and was met by Sviatopolk; and they entered the house. Then Davyd came and sat down, while Sviatopolk spoke, "Remain, brother, till my holiday," and Vasil'ko answered, "I cannot remain, brother, for I have already ordered my camp to go forward." Meanwhile, Davyd remained seated as if dumb. Then Sviatopolk said, "At least stay for breakfast, brother," and Vasil'ko promised to breakfast. Then Sviatopolk said, "Please sit here and in the meanwhile I will go and order them to prepare breakfast," and he departed, while Davyd remained with Vasil'ko. Vasil'ko began to talk to Davyd, but Davyd would not listen or answer because he was afraid, having that plot in his mind. After staying awhile, Davyd said, "Where is my brother?" and he was told, "He is on the porch." Then Davyd arose and said, "I will go after him, but you, brother, stay here." And he arose and left. As soon as Davyd was gone, Vasil'ko was seized: this occurred on November the fifth. And he was put in double irons and guards were attached to him overnight.

On the morrow Sviatopolk summoned the boyars and the people of Kiev, and told them what he had been told by Davyd Igorevich: "He killed my brother, Iaropolk, and now is plotting with Vladimir Monomakh and wants to kill me and to take my cities." The boyars and people responded, "Prince, care for your head. If what Davyd says is true, Vasil'ko must be punished; but if Davyd has not spoken the truth, then Davyd must receive punishment from God and answer to Him." When the abbots learned of this they interceded with Sviatopolk on behalf of Vasil'ko, but at that time the Metropolitan was in the city of Sinelitsa. Sviatopolk told them, "All this was done by Davyd." Learning of this, Davyd began to persuade Sviatopolk to blind [Vasil'ko]. "If you don't do it, and you let him go, neither you nor I will be Prince." Sviatopolk wanted to release him but Davyd did not because he feared him.

The same night they took him by cart to Belgorod, a small town ten versts[161] from Kiev. He was brought in irons in the cart, and there he was taken out of the cart and carried into a small house. When he was sitting there, Vasil'ko noticed a Torchin sharpening his knife.[162] He understood that they wanted to blind him. He appealed

---

161. Ten *versts* are the equivalent of six miles.

162. The Torks were a Turkic tribe on the southern Russian frontier.

1097 to God, crying and wailing.

THE BLINDING OF VASIL'KO ROSTISLAVICH, GRANDSON OF VSEVOLOD, GREAT GRANDSON OF IAROSLAV

Then the people sent by Sviatopolk and Davyd entered [the house]. They were Snovid Izechevich [a Tork], the stableboy of Sviatopolk; and Dmitrii, Davyd's stableboy. They spread out a rug. When they had spread it, they seized Vasil'ko and tried to throw him onto the floor but he resisted stoutly and they were unable to put him on the floor. Then other people came and they threw him onto the floor and bound him and took a board from the stove and put the board upon his chest. On one side of the board sat Snovid Izechevich, on the other, Dmitrii; but they could not keep Vasil'ko still. Then two others came and they took another board from the stove and they sat on the board, and so they pressed his shoulders so strongly that his chest cracked. Then another Tork, named Berendei, who was a shepherd with Sviatopolk, came with a knife and tried to strike him in the eyes but he missed, wounding him in the face. This wound is still to be seen on Vasil'ko's face. Thereafter he hit him in the eyes, took out his eye, then struck the other eye and took it out, also. Meanwhile, Vasil'ko lay as if dead. Then they left him on the rug, put him into the cart and carried him like a corpse to Vladimir [in Volynia]. When they rode past the bridge near Zdvizhden' they halted at the market place, pulled his shirt from him, for it was covered with blood, and gave it to someone to be washed. When it had been washed, they put it on him while the others were at dinner. Seeing him, some people began to lament as if he were dead. Hearing the wails, Vasil'ko asked, "Where am I?" And they answered him, "You are in the town of Zdvizhden'." Then he asked for water, which they gave him; and he drank some water and consciousness returned to him, and he came back to his senses, touched his shirt and asked, "Why did you take it off? It would be better for me to accept death in a bloodied shirt, and so I should appear before God." When they finished dinner they came to him, put him into the cart and went further on this November road for at that time it was the month of November. They arrived with him in the city of Vladimir, on the sixth day, and Davyd also arrived with him as if he had hunted and caught a beast. They put him in the household of Vakei and thirty men to guard him, as well as two of the guards of the Prince [Sviatopolk], Ulan and Kolcha.[163]

VLADIMIR (MONOMAKH) VSEVOLODICH SUMMONS DAVYD SVIATOSLAVICH AND OLEG SVIATOSLAVICH.

When Vladimir heard that Vasil'ko had been taken prisoner and blinded, he was horrified, wept greatly and said, "Nothing similar to this evil has ever happened in the Russian land, neither in the time of our grandfathers nor in the time of our fathers." Then he sent for Davyd Sviatoslavich and Oleg Sviatoslavich, saying, "Come to Gorodets and we will try to rectify this evil which has happened in the Russian land among us brethren. It is as if we have been struck by a knife. If we do not rectify this, a still greater evil will arise against us. Brother will massacre brother and the Russian land will perish, while our enemies, the Polovetss, will appear and take over the Russian land."

When Davyd Sviatoslavich and Oleg Sviatoslavich heard this, they were seized by grief, wept and said, "Nothing similar has ever occurred in our clan."[164] And then they assembled their troops and went to Vladimir Monomakh, who at that time was in the forests with his soldiers.[165] Vladimir, Davyd and Oleg sent their men to [Kiev to] Sviatopolk, saying, "What manner of evil have you caused the Russian land? Why did you thrust this knife into us? Why have you blinded your brother? What was his fault? You should have exposed him before us and we would have done justice. Now, disclose his fault to us and why you have done this."

Sviatopolk responded, "I was told by Davyd Igorevich, 'Vasil'ko killed brother Iaropolk and now wants to kill you and seize your cities of Turov, Pinsk, Brest and Pogorina; and he intends to join Vladimir and then Vladimir would rule in Kiev, and Vasil'ko in the city of Vladimir in Volynia.' And I had to care for my own head and I did not blind him; but it was Davyd who took him to his city." The men of Vladimir—Davyd and Oleg—decided, "Do not try to excuse yourself under the pretext that Davyd blinded him. He was not

---

163. Apparently both were also Torks.

164. Prince Davyd Igorevich, who initiated the blinding of Vasil'ko, was from the Volynian line of princes, being the son of Igor' and grandson of Iaroslav. Davyd, son of Sviatoslav, also a grandson of Iaroslav, was prince of Smolensk.

165. In *Nik.* this reads, "*v bogu.*" Apparently this is a spelling error and it should read, "*v boru*," as in *Laur.* "*Bor*" is an evergreen forest.

1097 blinded in Davyd's city but in yours." Thereupon they went to their camps. On the morrow they wanted to cross the Dnieper and march against Sviatopolk, and the latter wanted to flee from Kiev; but the Kievans did not let him go. The while, Metropolitan Nicephorus told Sviatopolk, "You must repent the evil you have done, and pray to be at peace with your brethren. God willing, I will go to your brethren to ask them for peace and friendship. And Princess Anna, widow of Prince Vsevolod, will try to do the same, with me." All agreed to this. Then the Metropolitan and the Princess Dowager of Prince Vsevolod went to Vladimir, saying, "We pray you, Prince, as well as your brethren, not to destroy the Russian land. If you begin war among yourselves, the pagans will rejoice and take our land, which was won by your fathers and your grandfathers with great labor and courage. They defended the Russian land and sought more lands, but you—you want to destroy the Russian land, and for this, in the present and in the future, you will be fiercely tormented without mercy. Make peace among yourselves. Care for the Russian land together. Fight and wage war against the pagans." When Vladimir heard this, he wept bitterly and said, "Indeed, our fathers and grandfathers cared for the Russian land but we are ready to destroy it."

And he accepted their petition, receiving the Metropolitan as if he were his own father; and he also honored Princess Anna, widow of Vsevolod, whom he respected as much as his own mother for the sake of his own father, because he greatly loved his father; and during his life, as well as after his death, he never disobeyed his counsel. He also respected the Metropolitan and the bishops, never disregarding their advice. He had such love in Christ for the Metropolitan, bishops and abbots, and so regarded all monastic people and those [travellers and poor] who would come to him that he would feed them and give them to drink and supply them with provisions just as a mother cares for her children. When he would see someone drunk, misbehaving, or committing some other misdeed, he would never judge him but would exercise his love and respect for him. Now let us return to our original narrative.

After the Metropolitan and dowager of Prince Vsevolod had visited Vladimir, they returned to Kiev and repeated all these speeches to Sviatopolk and to the Kievans, saying that peace was possible. Then they [the princes] dispatched envoys among themselves and came to some decision. Vladimir with his brothers told Sviatopolk, "Since it was Davyd's wickedness, as you have told us, you, Sviatopolk, must campaign against Davyd, and you have either to take him prisoner or drive him away." Sviatopolk agreed, and they pledged on the cross among themselves, concluding peace.

1097

At that time Vasil'ko was in Vladimir in the above-mentioned place. When Lent was approaching and I, sinner, was, myself, in Vladimir, once at night Prince Davyd Igorevich sent for me. I came to him and saw that he was with his court. He had me sit down and said, "Last night Vasil'ko told Ulan and Kolsha, 'I have heard that Vladimir and Sviatopolk are marching against Davyd. It would be good if Davyd agreed that I send my men to Vladimir, asking him to return because I know what to tell him; and then he will not advance.' And now, Vasilii,[166] I am sending you to Vasil'ko, your namesake, together with these guards, to tell him, 'In the case you want to dispatch your men and Vladimir retreats, I will give you any city you would like to have: either the city of Vsevolozhsk or Trebovl' or Peredivl'.'"[167]

So I went to Vasil'ko and repeated all Davyd had said. Vasil'ko said, "I have never said so, but I still rely upon God and will dispatch my men [to Vladimir] that they should not shed blood on my behalf; but I wonder that Davyd is ready to give me my own city: Terebovl' is my own domain, it is now and will be." And so it happened, because soon he received his domain. Then he told me, "Go to Davyd and tell him, 'Send me Kul'mei because I want to send him to Vladimir.'" But Davyd did not heed this and sent me back to say, "Kul'mei is not here." Then Vasil'ko told me, "Stay here with me awhile."

Then he told his servant to leave, sat down close by me and told me, "I have heard that Davyd wants to render me over to the Poles. He has not had enough of my blood and wants more of it, by delivering me to the Poles, because I have done them much harm. I wanted to do so and avenge the Russian land. If now he extradites me to the Poles, I do not fear death but I will tell you truly that God has sent me all this for my pride. [Before I fought the Poles] I received the news that the Berendeis, the Pechenegs and the Torks were coming to join me, and I said to myself, 'If I should have the Berendeis, Pechenegs and Torks, then I can tell my brothers,

---

166. Priest Vasilii was the author of the story of the blinding of Vasil'ko.
167. Peremil' and Shepol' in *Laur.*; Terebovl' and Peredivl, error in *Nik*.

1097 Volodar' and Davyd, "Give me your junior guard and you, yourselves, rejoice and revel.'" And I thought to myself that the next winter I would fall upon the Polish land and take revenge for the Russian land, and would then take the Bulgarians of the Danube and resettle them in my land. And I intended thereafter to ask Sviatopolk and Vladimir to give me troops against the Polovetss. I thought that either I would find my glory or I would lay down my life for the Russian land. I had no bad intention in my heart either toward Sviatopolk or toward Davyd, and I swear before God and His Coming Last Judgment that I had no evil intention against my brethren. It is only for my pride and boasting that God deposed me and humbled me."

Thereafter, the same spring when the Easter holiday approached, Davyd marched to occupy the domain of Vasil'ko. He was met near the city of Buzhsk by Volodar', Vasil'ko's brother; but Davyd did not venture to fight Volodar', Vasil'ko's brother, and prepared himself for a siege in Buzhsk, where Volodar' besieged him; and Volodar' told Davyd, "Why have you done this evil and do not now repent it? You should remember how much harm you have caused." Then Davyd calumniated Sviatopolk, saying, "I did not do this. It was done by Sviatopolk; this evil was not committed in my city. I, myself, feared that they would seize me and do the same to me. Therefore, I had against my will to join the conspiracy and go with Sviatopolk." But Volodar' said, "God witness it. Release my brother at once and I will make peace with you." Davyd was happy [at this proposal] and sent for Vasil'ko, whom he brought and turned over to Volodar'. Peace was concluded and they parted; and Vasil'ko resumed his reign in Trebovol', while Davyd returned to Vladimir.

[VASIL'KO AND VOLODAR' WAR AGAINST DAVYD IGOREVICH.]

In the spring Volodar' and Vasil'ko marched against Davyd. They came to the city of Vsevolozhsk, while Davyd prepared himself for siege in Vladimir. They camped near Vsevolod's city and then stormed it, burned it, and people fled the fire; but Vasil'ko ordered that they all be slain, and he took revenge on innocent people and shed much innocent blood. Thereafter, they marched to the city of Vladimir [in Volynia] and Davyd prepared himself for siege in Vladimir, while the others encircled and laid siege to the city. They sent a message to the people of Vladimir, saying, "We do not come against either your city or against you, but against our enemies, Turiak, Lazar' and Vasil', because they are our enemies and they inspired Davyd, and Davyd heeded them and committed this evil. If you want to fight for them, we are prepared; but if you do not, turn over our enemies to us." Hearing this, the citizens summoned a *veche* and told Davyd's people, "Extradite these men for we will not fight for them. We may fight for you, but not for them. If you do not do so, we will open the gates of the city, and then you must think of yourselves." So, against his will, [Davyd] had to turn them over; but he said, "They are not here because I sent them to Lutsk." Then they went to Lutsk but Turiak had fled to Kiev, while Vasil' and Lazar' had returned to Turiisk. When the people learned that they were in Turiisk, they summoned the populace against Davyd, saying, "Extradite those whom they want. If you do not do so, we will surrender." Then Davyd sent for Vasil' and Lazar', to get them, and he turned them over. They made peace on a Sunday and the next day they hung Vasil' and Lazar'; and then Vasil'ko's people shot at them with arrows and marched away from the city.

1098

And thus was exacted the second revenge; but it was not a just one for vengeance should be had by God, and they should have relied upon God for revenge, as the prophet says: "I will render vengeance to mine adversaries and will recompense them that hate Me." [*Deut.* 32:41.] And then, "Vengeance belongeth unto Me," says the Lord. [*Rom.* 12:19.] And the Apostle says, "Avenge not yourselves, beloved." [*Rom.* 12:19; the verse continues: "and give not place unto wrath."]

When they [Vasil'ko and Volodar'] retreated from the city, [the citizens] took them [Lazar' and Vasil'] from the gallows and buried them.

In the year 6606/1098.

[SVIATOPOLK'S CAMPAIGN IN VOLYNIA]

In the year 6607/1099. [Vasilii's story, continued.] [6605/1097 in *Laur.*] Sviatopolk Iziaslavovich [Grand Prince of Kiev], who promised to cast out Davyd, marched to the city of Brest toward the Poles, calling the latter to his aid. When Davyd Igorevich learned of this he went [himself] to [King] Vladislav [of Poland] requesting help. The Poles promised to help and received fifty grivnas of gold from him, and told him, "March to Brest with us. Sviatopolk is

1099 summoning us to council and we will bring about peace between you and Sviatopolk." Davyd listened to them and marched, together with Vladislav, to Brest; but Sviatopolk prepared for siege in the city, while the Poles camped on the Bug river. Sviatopolk began to negotiate with the Poles and gave them large gifts [so as to win them over] against Davyd. Then [King] Vladislav told Davyd, "Sviatoslav pays me no heed. Return." So Davyd returned to the city of Vladimir while Sviatopolk made an agreement with the Poles and advanced toward Pinsk, sending thither his troops. Arriving at Dorogobuzh, he waited upon his remaining warriors and then marched against Davyd, who was in Vladimir; and there Davyd prepared himself for siege. He relied upon aid from the Poles because they had told him, "As soon as the Russian princes, your brethren, come against you, we will be your helpers." But they lied because they had received gold from both Davyd and Sviatopolk. Sviatopolk besieged the city for seven weeks. Then Davyd asked him, "Let me leave the city." Sviatopolk promised him and they made a pledge on the cross. [Davyd] left the city of Vladimir and went to the city of Cherven'. So Sviatopolk entered Vladimir on Holy Saturday, while Davyd fled to the Poles. As soon as Sviatoslav drove out Davyd, he began to plot against Volodar' and Vasil'ko, saying to himself, "This is the domain of my father and brother," and he marched against them. When Volodar' and Vasil'ko learned of this, they marched to meet him, taking with them the venerable cross on which he had pledged to them, [saying], "I went against Davyd and want to have peace and friendship with you." But Sviatopolk broke his pledge on the cross, relying on his large army. They came together in the field near Rozhnia, and the two armies prepared for battle. Then Vasil'ko raised the cross, exclaiming, "You have pledged on this! First, you took my sight, and now you want to take my soul. This cross should decide about us!" The two armies clashed but many pious folk saw a cross high in the clouds over Vasil'ko. It was a fierce battle and many were slain in both armies. Seeing how cruel the battle was, Sviatopolk escaped to the city of Vladimir. Having defeated Sviatopolk, Volodar' and Vasil'ko remained on the field, saying, "We should stay on our border." And they did not advance further.

    Sviatopolk fled to Vladimir with two sons, Mstislav and Iaroslav, and two sons of Iaropolk, Iaroslav and Sviatosha, as well as the son of Davyd Sviatoslavich and the remaining troops. Sviatopolk assigned to the city of Vladimir his son, Mstislav, who had been borne to him by a concubine; and he sent Iaroslav to Hungary, asking the Hungarians to fight Volodar' and Vasil'ko; while he, himself, returned to Kiev. Sviatopolk's son, Iaroslav, went to Hungary [and after his negotiations] King Koloman and two bishops advanced as far as Peremyshl' on the river Vagra, while Volodar' prepared himself for siege in the city.

1099

At that time Davyd returned from Poland, leaving his wife, the princess, with his brother, Volodar'; and he, himself, went to the Polovetss. He was met by the Polovets Prince Boniak. Thereafter Davyd Igorevich returned and advanced against the Hungarians. As they advanced, they camped overnight, and when it was midnight Boniak arose, rode a ways off from the troops and began howling like a wolf. A wolf answered him, and then many wolves began howling. Then Boniak returned [to the camp] and told Davyd, "Tomorrow we will defeat the Hungarians."

In the morning Boniak prepared his warriors for battle; Davyd had one hundred warriors while Boniak had three hundred ninety Polovetss. Boniak divided them into three troops and attacked the Hungarians. He sent Altonapa into the avant-guard, giving him fifty men. Then he put Davyd under the standard in the main troops and gave him three hundred men. The remainder he divided into two parts, fifty men on each side.

The Hungarians took up their positions for battle, looking very handsome in their armour, [which shone] like moving water because there were one hundred and twenty thousand Hungarians.[168] And their regiments took up positions far apart, the one from the other. Altonapa rode to the first outpost and shot arrows at them, then fled from them. The Hungarians followed him and when, pursuing Altonapa, they passed Boniak, the latter struck their rear and killed them while Altonapa turned around and did not permit the Hungarians to retreat. In this manner a great multitude of them were slain, and most of their troops were forced to remain in one place. Boniak divided his troops and, surrounding the Hungarians, forced them to retreat in one single group, and slew them as a falcon slays a magpie. The Hungarians fled and many of them were drowned in the Vagra river, others in the river San; and so they were pursued for two days [while Davyd and Boniaks's troops] slew them.

---

168. Obviously, according to the medieval manner, the chronicler exaggerated the number of Hungarians.

1099 Their Bishop Tupan was killed, as well as many magnates. People say that forty thousand of them perished.[169]

Iaroslav escaped to Poland, going to Brest, while Davyd occupied the cities of Sutesk and Cherven'; then he unexpectedly appeared in the city of Vladimir to fight Mstislav. Mstislav prepared himself in the city for siege, with his avant guard, in which were the levies of Brest, Pinsk and Vygoshev. Davyd besieged the city and stormed it intermittently. On one occasion he stormed it near the towers, while others fighting round the city shot arrows at each other which fell as rain on the city. Mstislav was about to shoot but as he stood on the wall an arrow suddenly struck him in the chest, having passed through the logs. He was taken down and died that same night. [His soldiers] hid his death for three days but announced it on the fourth day, in the veche. Then the citizens decided, "Our Prince is killed; but if we, ourselves, surrender to Davyd, he will destroy us all." So they sent to Sviatopolk to say, "Your son has been killed and we are exhausted from famine. If you do not come, the people are ready to surrender because they cannot withstand the famine."

Sviatopolk sent [to rescue the city of Vladimir] his voevoda, Putiata, who, with his troops, went to Lutsk to Prince Sviatosha, the son of Prince Davyd Sviatoslavovich [of Chernigov]. There were Davyd's men, and an agreement was made between Sviatosha and Davyd which they strengthened with a pledge on the cross; and Sviatosha told Davyd, "If Sviatopolk campaigns against you, I will inform you of it." But Sviatosha did not do this; he arrested Davyd's men and marched against Davyd. Sviatosha and Putiata came on the fifth day of August [to the vicinity of the city of Vladimir] where Davyd's troops were besieging the city. It was midday and Davyd was sleeping. They attacked him and started fighting. The citizens jumped from the walls and also commenced slaying Davyd's warriors. And so Davyd and his nephew, Mstislav, fled. Sviatosha and Putiata took over the city and assigned Sviatopolk's posadnik, Vasilii, there; and thereafter Sviatosha went to Lutsk, while Putiata went to Kiev. Davyd, however, fled to the Polovetss, where he was met by Boniak. Then Davyd and Boniak marched against Sviatosha and the city of Lutsk. They besieged Sviatosha in the city but made peace. Sviatosha left the city and went to his father in Chernigov,

---

169. The Hungarian sources admit that their losses were very considerable; Likhachev, II, 464.

while Davyd took over Lutsk, from whence he marched to Vladimir. **1099**
Posadnik Vasilii fled from the city and Davyd took over Vladimir
and began to reign there. [Here ends Vasilii's story of the feud
involving Vasil'ko's blinding.]

In the year 6608/1100. On the tenth day of the month of June,
Mstislav [son of Vladimir Monomakh] left Davyd Igorevich and
went over the sea. The same year on the thirtieth day of the month
of June the kinsmen Sviatopolk Iziaslavich [of Kiev], Vladimir
Monomakh Vsevolodich, Davyd and Oleg Sviatoslavich [of Chernigov and Smolensk] met in the town of Uvetichi and came to an
agreement of peace among themselves.

The same year on the second day of the month of July in the
same town of Uvetichi, all the above-mentioned princely kinsmen—
Sviatopolk of Kiev, Vladimir Monomakh, Davyd and Oleg Sviatoslavich—assembled and sent for Davyd Igorevich [Prince of Vladimir in Volynia], promising him friendship and the throne of the
city of Vladimir in Volynia. Davyd Igorevich came to them and
said, "Why did you invite me? What manner of grievance have you
against me?" Vladimir Vsevolodich Monomakh answered, "You
yourself, sent us a message: 'Brethren! I want to come to you and to
complain of the offense done me.' Since you have come, sit down
together with your kinsmen on the same rug. About what do you
complain and of whom do you complain?" Davyd answered nothing.
Then the kinsmen mounted their horses. Sviatopolk was with his
troops. Davyd [Sviatoslavich] and Oleg [Sviatoslavich] stood a
distance apart, each with his own [troops]. Davyd Igorevich
remained aside and they did not permit him in their council,
discussing Davyd's case separately. They conferred and sent their
man to Davyd [Igorevich]. Sviatopolk sent Putiata; Vladimir sent
Urogost and Ratibor; Davyd and Oleg [the sons of Sviatoslav], a
Tork. The envoys went to Davyd Igorevich and told him, "Your
kinsmen have decided they do not want to give you the throne of
Vladimir because [by blinding Vasil'ko] you threw a knife at us, and
this has never been [before] in the Russian land. We do not want to
imprison you nor do we want to cause you any evil; but here is what
we will give you. Go and rule in the fortress of Buzhsk and you will
also receive Duben and Chartorisk from Sviatopolk, while Vladimir
gives you 200 grivnas; and between them, Davyd and Oleg [sons of
Sviatoslav] also give you 200 grivnas." At the same time they sent

1101 envoys to Volodar' and Vasil'ko, saying, "Take your brother, Vasil'ko, to yourselves and share together the same domain, Peremyshl'. If you like it, remain there. If not, Vasil'ko may come to us and we will care for him here. Also, give us back our slaves and peasants." But neither Volodar' nor Vasil'ko accepted this. Davyd settled in Buzhsk and later Sviatopolk also gave Dorogobuzh to this Davyd Igorevich, and he died there. He gave the city of Vladimir to his son, Iaroslavets [Iaroslav], who was born to him by a concubine.

THE REIGN OF EMPEROR JOHN PORPHYROGENITUS [OF BYZANTIUM]

After Emperor Alexis Comnenus, his son, John Porphyrogenitus, reigned for four and twenty years, seven months and twenty-three days. He was Orthodox.[1]

In the year 6609/1101. Vseslav, Prince of Polotsk, died in the ninth hour of the day on the fourteenth day of the month of April.

The same year, at the third hour of the second day of the month of May, Prince Vladimir Monomakh Vsevolodich laid the foundation in Smolensk of a stone church of the Holy Theotokos, the seat of a bishopric.

The same year Iaroslav Iaropolchich [grandson of Grand Prince Iziaslav of Kiev] started fighting in Brest. Sviatopolk [the Grand Prince of Kiev] caught him there in the city, put him in irons and brought him to Kiev; but the Metropolitan interceded on his behalf with Sviatopolk; and Grand Prince Sviatopolk, heeding his [spiritual] father, the Metropolitan, released him from irons and freed him after he gave an oath on the cross and on the relics of the Holy Passion Martyrs Boris and Gleb. The same year all [the princes], the kinsmen Sviatopolk, Vladimir, Davyd, Oleg and Iaroslav [the latter's brother], met in Zolocha. All the Polovets rulers sent their envoys to these kinsmen requesting peace, and the Russian princes decided, "If you want peace, let us assemble at Sakov." The Polovetss agreed, and they all met together in Sakov, where they made peace with the Polovets rulers. They exchanged hostages and returned home; this happened on the fifteenth of the month of September.

In the year 6610/1102. Iaroslav Iaropolchich[2] escaped from Kiev

---

1. This item, specific to *Nik.*, is incorrectly dated. Emperor John Comnenus reigned from 1118 to 1143.

2. Iaroslav Iaropolchich was under arrest in Kiev after his rebellion in Brest. See 6609.

on the first day of the month of October. At the end of that same month, Iaroslav Sviatopolchich [Prince of Vladimir] lured Iaroslav Iaropolchich and caught him on the Nura and brought him back to Kiev to his father, Sviatopolk, who put him in irons.

1102

[NOVGORODIANS WANT MSTISLAV TO BE THEIR PRINCE]

The same year on December twentieth Mstislav Vladimirovich came to Kiev with the Novgorodians because Sviatopolk had an agreement with Vladimir [Monomakh] that Novgorod should be the domain of Sviatopolk's sons and that he had assigned his son [Mstislav] to the principality of Vladimir [in Volynia]. The men of Vladimir Monomakh said to Sviatopolk, "Vladimir Monomakh has sent us his son, Mstislav, with the Novgorodians, and they are now at your place; and they [the Novgorodians] want to have his son [Mstislav] and will return [with him] to Novgorod." And Grand Prince Sviatoslav told them, "Above us are God and justice. I agreed with Vladimir Monomakh to the following: Novgorod will remain my domain, and therefore my son will go to Novgorod." The Novgorodians told Sviatopolk, "Prince! We have been sent to you because our citizens of Novgorod have decided, 'We do not want either Sviatopolk or his son. In case your son has two heads [so that he may lose one], then you may send him to us. But this one [Mstislav] was given us [by his grandfather, Grand Prince] Vsevolod, and we have nurtured him for our prince, while you forsook us.'" Sviatopolk had a lengthy argument with them because they did not want his son, and they returned to Novgorod, taking with them [their Prince] Mstislav Vladimirich [son of Monomakh].

PORTENTS.

The same year, beginning with the twenty-ninth of the month of January, there were apparitions in the skies for three days and they seemed as a bright dawn from the east, south, north and west. There was such light all night as if a full moon were shining. The same year on the fifth day of the month of February there was a portent on the moon. On the seventh day of the same month there was a portent on the sun. The sun was covered with three arcs, and there were other arcs, one above the other. Seeing these portents, the pious caloyers prayed to God with tears and sighs so that God should turn these portents to good.

1103   The following year God put a good idea into the minds of the Russian princes. They decided to march against the Polovets land, and this happened; but we will speak of it in the next annual entry.

The same year on the eleventh day of the month of August, Iaroslav Iaropolchich passed away. The same day a son, Andrei, was born to Vladimir Monomakh.

The same year the daughter of Iaropolk, Sbyslava, was given as wife to [King] Boleslav of Poland. This happened on the sixteenth day of the month of November.

In the year 6611/1103. Prince Mstislav, son of Vladimir Monomakh, laid the foundation of a stone church of the Annunciation of the Immaculate Theotokos in the *Gorodishche* [in Novgorod].[3]

[JOINT CAMPAIGN OF THE RUSSIAN PRINCES AGAINST THE POLOVETSS]

The same year God put it into the hearts of the Russian princes—Sviatopolk Iziaslavich, Grand Prince of Kiev, and Vladimir Monomakh—to take counsel in Dolobsk. Sviatopolk came with his troops and Vladimir, with his own; and they held council in the same tent. The commanders of Sviatopolk's troops, having conferred, said, "It is inappropriate to act now, in spring. If we march with our peasants, we will destroy them and their harvest." Vladimir, however, replied, "I wonder, my friends! You want to care for the horses used for ploughing, but why do you not consider the fact that as soon as a peasant begins to plough, a Polovets will come and shoot him with an arrow, take his horse, enter his village, take his wife, his children, and all his wealth? You are worried about the horses, but you are not concerned about [the peasants] themselves." And Sviatopolk's commanders could find no argument with this. Then Sviatopolk arose and said, "Well, I am already prepared." Then Vladimir said, "Brother, you do a great deed for the Russian land." And they sent for Oleg and Davyd [Sviatoslavichs], saying, "Let us march together against the Polovetss, and either we will live or we will lay down our lives for the Russian land." Davyd [Sviatoslavich] listened to them but [his brother] Oleg did not want to participate and excused himself: "I do not feel well."

3. *Gorodishche*: residence of the Novgorod princes; located south of Novgorod; Karger, M.K., *Novgorod Velikii*, Leningrad-Moscow, 1966, p. 11.

Vladimir embraced his cousin [Sviatopolk] and marched to Pereiaslavl'. Sviatopolk followed him. After them came [the princes] Davyd Sviatoslavich, and Davyd Vseslavich as well as Mstislav Davydovich—grandson of Igor'; Viacheslav Iaropolchich, grandson of Iziaslav; and Iaropolk, son of Vladimir Monomakh. They all advanced against the Polovets in boats, and when they reached the cataracts they stopped at a place called Protolchi, on the island of Khortitsa [both below the cataracts of the Dnieper]. Then they mounted their horses. The footmen left the boats and marched through the prairies for four days. They arrived at Suten'.[4]

1103

When the Polovetss learned that the Russians were marching against them, an endless number of them assembled and they began to deliberate. [Khan] Urusoba spoke: "Let us petition for peace with the Russians. They will fight us fiercely because we have caused much evil to the Russian land." But those younger than Urusoba said, "Perhaps you fear the Russians; but we do not. We will slay them all and then march into their land; and who may protect them against us?" The Russian princes and warriors prayed to God and gave their pledges to God and His Immaculate Mother. Some prayed for the memory of those who had died; some distributed alms to the poor; and some gave grants to monasteries. After praying, they marched. The Polovetss sent Altonapa, who was famous for his courage, with the avant guard, and the Russians ambushed Altonapa's avant guard, encircled him and slew him and those who were with him. Not one remained alive because they all were slain.

Then the Polovets armies advanced like wild boars. It was impossible to see them all; but the Russians advanced against them and Great God put terrifying fear into the minds of the Polovetss. Great fright seized them and they trembled at the sight of the Russian warriors. They were as if asleep, and their horses' legs were without strength. But our men advanced against them joyously, either on horseback or on foot. Seeing the Russians attacking, the Polovetss did not wait but fled before the Russian armies. We pursued them and slew them. This was the fourth day of the month of April, when this great salvation [from the pagans] was granted us by God, and He gave us a great victory over our enemies.

4. Suten': Apparently the present river, Molochnaia.

1104 In the [Polovets] armies twelve khans were killed: Urusoba, Kchii, Altonapa, Pukitan, Pukuman, Aisup, Kurotkach, Negrep, Surbor and others of their khans. Having defeated their enemies, the kinsmen [the Russian princes] sat down and [the Polovets] Khan Belduzia was brought to Sviatopolk. Belduzia promised him a great amount of gold, silver, horses and cattle, and gave an oath not to fight against the Russians for the rest of his life. Sviatopolk did not accept it and sent him to his kinsman, Vladimir Monomakh. Vladimir questioned him, asking, "Why have you broken your oath?" The other wept and promised a large ransom for himself. Vladimir conferred with Grand Prince Sviatopolk and ordered that the Polovets Prince Belduzia be slain, after telling him, "You and all your khans gave an oath [not to raid Russia] but you broke it and spilled much innocent Christian blood. This injury and this blood remains on your hands." And so was the Polovets Khan Belduzia slain. Thereafter the kinsmen [the Russian princes] assembled and Vladimir Monomakh said, "On this day when we have witnessed an act of God, we should rejoice and be happy because the Lord has delivered us from our enemies, whom He has submitted to us; and He has destroyed the serpent's head and given booty to the Russian people." And then they took cattle, sheep, oxen, horses, camels and the train with great booty and with slaves, and also caught the Pechenegs and the Torks with their train. The Russians returned with a vast number of prisoners and much booty, with glory and great victory.

The same year on the first day of August, Locusts descended [upon the Russian land].

On the eighteenth day of the same month, Sviatopolk advanced [into the prairie] and built the fortress of Iur'ev, which had previously been burned by the Polovetss.

The same year on the fourth day of the month of March, Iaroslav [son of Vladimir Monomakh] fought the Mordva tribes, and Iaroslav was defeated.[5]

In the year 6612/1104. On the twentieth day of the month of July the daughter of Volodar' married the [Byzantine] prince, son of [Emperor] Alexis, in Constantinople. The same year, on the twenty-first day of the month of August, Peredslava, daughter of Sviatopolk, married the Hungarian Crown Prince.

5. The Mordva were a Finnic tribe living on the Oka river in a region southeast of present Moscow.

THE ARRIVAL OF METROPOLITAN NICEPHORUS.

1105

The same year on the sixth day of the month of December, Metropolitan Nicephorus came to Russia [from Constantinople].

On the thirteenth day of the same month, Viacheslav Iaropolchich passed away.

The sixteenth day of the same month Nicephorus was enthroned as Metropolitan of Kiev and all Russia.

Toward the end of this year, Sviatopolk sent [his commander] Putiata against the city of Minsk; Vladimir sent his son, Iaropolk; while Oleg [of Chernigov], together with Davyd Vseslavich, himself marched against [Prince] Gleb [of Minsk] but they did not succeed in the least and returned.

The same year a son, named Briacheslav, was born to Sviatopolk.

PORTENT.

The same year there was a portent. The sun was surrounded by a circle, in the middle of which was a cross. In the middle of the cross was another sun, and on both sides of the circle there were again two suns. Above the suns beside the circle there was an arc with horns pointed toward the north. The same portent occurred in the same manner on the third day of the month of February on the moon. It also occurred at night on the moon.

METROPOLITAN NICEPHORUS CONSECRATED THREE BISHOPS TO THE CITIES.

In the year 6613/1105. Metropolitan Nicephorus consecrated Amphilochius to be bishop of the city of Vladimir [in Volynia] on the twenty-seventh day of the month of August. The same year he consecrated Lazar' to be bishop of the city of Pereiaslavl', on the twelfth day of the month of November. The same year, on the tenth day of the month of December, he consecrated Menas to be bishop of Polotsk.

In the year 6614/1106. The Polovetss ravaged around Zarezhsk and therefore Sviatopolk sent against them Ian Vyshatich and his brother, Putiata;[6] they chased [the Polovetss] away and took back those who had been captured. The same year the good elder, Ian

---

6. *Laur.*: Ian and Ivan Zakharich (a Kozarin).

1107 [Vyshatich], who lived ninety years, passed away.⁷ He lived according to the rule of God, died at an advanced age and was not worse than the first righteous ones. From him I heard many things. He was a good man, meek and humble, and kept apart from all evil deeds. His place of burial is in the Monastery of the Caves in the aisle, and there his body has remained since his burial, which took place on the fourteenth day of the month of June.

On the seventeenth day of the month of February of the same year, Prince Sviatosha, son of Davyd, grandson of [Grand Prince] Sviatoslav, was tonsured. He received the monastic name of Nicholas.

The same year the Lithuanian tribe of Zimegola defeated the princes, children of [late Prince] Vseslav [of Polotsk] and slew nine thousand of their troops.

The same year in the month of December Princess Eupraksia, daughter of the late Prince [Vsevolod] of Kiev, took the veil.⁸

In the year 6615/1107. On the fifth day of February the earth shook.

The same year Boniak, Sharukan the Old and many other khans raided [the Russian land], camping at the city of Lubny. Then the [princes], kinsmen, Sviatopolk, Vladimir, Oleg, Sviatoslav, Mstislav, Viacheslav and Iaropolk, assembled. They marched against the Polovetss toward Lubny, and in the sixth hour of the day they forded the river Sula and shouted at them. The Polovetss were so frightened that they could not even display their banners, and they fled, taking their horses, while others fled on foot. Our men began slaying them, and captured others alive, pursuing them as far as the river Khorol. They killed [Khan] Taaz, brother of Boniak; they

---

7. Ian Vyshatich and his father, Vyshata, apparently contributed a large amount of information to this chronicler. Vyshata, son of the Novgorodian posadnik, Ostromir, to whom the oldest preserved Russian book, the *Gospel of Ostromir*, belonged, was a descendant of Dobrynia, St. Vladimir's uncle. Their family was the most influential with the Kievan princes.

8. Princess Eupraksia was the divorced wife of Emperor Henry IV of the Holy Roman Empire of the German nation. Because of the emperor's perversions, she obtained a divorce from Pope Gregory VII. After a stay in Germany, Italy and Hungary, Eupraksia returned to Russia. Her divorce from the emperor was one of the great ecclesiastical and social events of history at that time. This item appears in *Nik.* and *Hyp.*, but not in *Laur.* or *Novg.*

captured alive [Khan] Sugr and his brother; only Sharukan escaped with difficulty. He fled from his camp, which was taken by the Russian warriors. This happened on the twelfth day of the month of August, and [the Russians] returned home after a great victory. Sviatopolk arrived in the Monastery of the Caves for matins on the holiday of the Assumption of the Holy Theotokos, and his kinsmen-princes embraced each other with great joy, saying, "Our enemies, the Polovetss, have been defeated, thanks to the prayers of the Immaculate Theotokos and Our Holy Father, Theodosius." It was Sviatopolk's habit to come to venerate the relics of Theodosius when he was going to campaign, or on any journey, and he would then ask the abbot to pray for him and his soldiers. Only then would he commence upon his travel or campaign.

The same year the dowager princess [widow of Prince Iziaslav], mother of Sviatopolk, passed away on the fourth day of the month of January. The same year Princes Vladimir, Davyd and Oleg went to [Khan] Aiepa and to the other [Khan] Aiepa and made peace with them. And Vladimir married his son, Jurii, to Aiepa's daughter, the granddaughter of Asen', while Oleg married his son to [the other Khan] Aiepa's daughter, the granddaughter of Girgen. And this happened on the twelfth day of the month of January. The same year, on the seventh day of the month of May, the wife of Prince Vladimir passed away.

In the year 6616/1108. On the ninth of the month of March, Grand Prince Sviatopolk [of Kiev], son of Iziaslav, grandson of Iaroslav, great grandson of Great Vladimir, built a stone church of St. Archangel Michael with fifteen domes and covered them with gold.[9] And he embellished it beautifully.

THE DEATH OF BISHOP NICETAS.

The same year on the first day of January Bishop Nicetas of Novgorod passed away and was buried in the chapel of St. Joachim and Anna [of the cathedral] of the Holy Sophia. The same spring, thanks to the labor of Bishop Nicetas, they started painting frescoes in the [cathedral] of Holy Sophia.

THE CONSECRATION OF BISHOP JOHN.

The same year John was consecrated Bishop of Novgorod.

---

9. In *Hyp.* and *Laur.* no number of domes is given.

1109   The same year Abbot Theoktistus completed building the refectory of the [Kievan] Monastery of the Caves, of which the foundation had been laid at the command of Prince Gleb, who contributed to it. The same year the rivers Dnieper, Desna and Pripet' flooded. The same year God put it into the heart of Theoktistus, Abbot of the Caves [Monastery], that Abbot Theodosius should be listed in the *Synodikon*, and he spoke of this to Prince Sviatopolk. The prince was very glad, promised to do it and commanded the metropolitan to enter [the name of St. Theodosius] in the *Synodikon*.[10] He [Prince Sviatopolk] ordered the same for all dioceses and all bishops, and they included the name of St. Theodosius with joy in all *Synodikons*. And he commanded that he be remembered during the services [in all churches].

The same year on the eleventh day of the month of July, Catherine, daughter of the late prince [Vsevolod], passed away.

The same year they completed building the [church of the] Holy Theotokos on the Hill, of which the foundation was laid by Stephen, Abbot of the Caves.

In the year 6617/1109. In Kiev on the top of the church of St. Archangel Michael of the Golden Cupola, an unknown bird appeared which was remarkable for its majesty, and it shone with all colors and sang unceasingly. A tremendous sweet beauty arose from it and it remained on top of this church for six days, then flew away and no one ever saw it again.

The same year on the tenth day of the month of July [the former Empress of Germany], Eupraksia [the divorced wife of Emperor Henry IV], daughter of Vsevolod, who had accepted monastic orders, passed away and was buried in the Monastery of the Caves near the southern entrance. Above her [burial place] a chapel was built.

The same year on the second day of the month of December Prince Dmitrii Igorevich occupied the Polovets camps on the river Don.

In the year 6618/1110. In spring Prince Sviatopolk, with Princes Vladimir and Davyd, campaigned against the Polovetsian land. They went as far as Voin and returned home.[11]

   10. *Synodikon*: the list of particularly venerated deceased persons whose names are mentioned during church services. This was the first step toward the canonization of St. Theodosius.

   11. Voin: a town on the east bank of the Dnieper river, some eight miles

PORTENT.

1111

The same year on the eleventh day of the month of February there was a portent in the Cave Monastery. A fiery pillar appeared which extended from the ground to the sky, and lightning flashed over all the land. In the skies there was thunder in the first hour of the night, and the entire world saw it. This pillar first stood over the stone refectory so that it was impossible to see the cross. Remaining there for a time, it moved above the church, and halted over the tomb of Theodosius. Then it rose, turned toward the east and thereafter became invisible. It was not a fiery pillar but an angelic appearance, for angels appear either as a fiery pillar or as fire, according to David: "Who maketh winds His messengers, flames of fire his ministers?" [*Ps.* 104:4.] And they are sent forth by the order of God, as it is according to the Will of the Lord and Creator of all things. For the angel appears in a blessed location and in the house of prayer, and demonstrates a small portion of the apparition which can still be seen by man. A man is unable to view the nature of angels in the same way as great Moses was unable to see the angelic nature. For in that day ... led ...[12] This apparition indicated that some event was to happen, and so it did in another year. "Shall not the angel lead the way against aliens and adversaries, as is said: 'For My angel shall go before thee and thy angel will be with thee?'"[13]

In the year 6619/1111.

In the year 6620/1112. The Russian princes Sviatopolk Iziaslavovich [of Kiev], Vladimir Monomakh Vsevolodich, Sviatoslav, Iaropolk, Mstislav, David Sviatoslovich with his son, Rostislav; Vsevolod Ol'govich, and Davyd Igorevich came to the city of Rukan.[14] The people of the city came out, bowed to the Russian

south of Pereiaslavl'.

12. Here, in *Nik.*, this sentence is unfinished. *Hyp.* reads, "In those intense days a pillar of cloud led the children of Israel by day and a pillar of fire by night."

13. A rendition of Gen. 13:21-22 and *Ex.* 23:23. In *Laur.* and *Troits.* this entry ends with the following statement: "I, Sylvester, Abbot of the Monastery of St. Michael, wrote these chronicles relying upon the grace of God. It was written during the reign of Prince Vladimir (Monomakh) when awe reigned in Kiev, and at that time I was abbot of St. Michael. This was in the year of 6624 (1116), in the ninth year of the Indiction. Those who read these books, remember me in your prayers."

14. In *Hyp.* we read, "... to the city of Khan Sharukan."

1113 princes and brought fish and wine. On the morrow the Russians went to the city of Sugrov and burned it, and the Russians engaged the Polovetss in battle on the river Degei, on the twenty-fourth of March. The Russian princes defeated the Polovetss and paised God on that day. Then the Monday of Holy Week arrived and the aliens again assembled their troops and advanced like huge wild boars, multitude upon multitude, and the Russian armies retreated. Then God sent an angel to help the Russian princes and the Polovetsian regiments clashed with the Russian regiments. It was like thunder and a fierce fight ensued betweeen them, with many casualties on both sides. Then Vladimir Monomakh went ahead with his regiments. Seeing them, the Polovetss took fright and fell before Vladimir's regiments, being invisibly defeated by the angel. Many people saw the heads falling, invisibly severed. And on this day, March twenty-seventh, they [the Russians] defeated them on the river Salnitsa and took their wealth and captured some. And we asked them, "How is it possible that you, with such strength, could not resist us? Why were you forced to flee?" And they said, "How could we fight you when others were riding above you in shining and terrifying armour, helping you? They were the angels which were sent by God to help the Christians!" It was God Who put into the heart of Vladimir Monomakh the idea of uniting his kinsmen against the aliens. And an apparition was seen in the Monastery of the Caves. There was a fiery pillar above the stone refectory which then moved to the church, and from the church to Gorodets. It happened this way. At that time Vladimir Monomakh was in Radostyn'.[15]

CONFLAGRATIONS.

At that time there were conflagrations in the lower city in Kiev, in Chernigov, in Smolensk and in Novgorod.

In the year 6621/1113. Mstislav with Novgorodian levies defeated the Chud' in the *bor*.[16] The same year Mstislav laid the foundation for the church of St. Nicholas the Wondermaker on the princes' estate [in Novgorod].

---

15. Radostyn': a location near Gorodets in the vicinity of Kiev. This same item appears in greater detail in *Hyp.* under the year 6619/1111.

16. *Bor* denotes a primeval evergreen forest.

The same year Iaroslav, son of Sviatopolk, campaigned for the **1114** second time against the Iatvags,[17] defeating them. Davyd Igorevich [Prince of the city of Vladimir in Volynia] passed away on the twenty-fifth of May.

The same year Ianka [Ann], daughter of Vsevolod, passed away, on the third day of the month of November.

CONSECRATION OF BISHOP THEOKTISTUS.

The same year on the eleventh day of the month of January, Nicephorus, Metropolitan of Kiev and all Russia, consecrated Theoktistus Bishop of Chernigov.[18]

In the year 6622/1114. PORTENT. There was a portent on the sun in the first hour of the day and all could see it. Very little of the sun remained, only as much as the lower horns of the moon. This occurred on the nineteenth day of the month of March.

THE PASSING OF GRAND PRINCE SVIATOPOLK [OF KIEV].

The same year on the sixteenth day of the month of April the pious Grand Prince Mikhailo Iziaslavich, called Sviatopolk, passed away.[19] This was in the twenty-third year of the reign [of Emperor John Porphyrogenitus].[20] And he was Grand Prince for twenty-one years.

The same year Roman Vseslavich died in Riazan' and Mstislav, grandson of Igor', also died.

CONSECRATION OF BISHOP DANIEL.

The same year on the sixth day of the month of November Nicephorus, Metropolitan of Kiev and all Russia, consecrated Daniel Bishop of Iur'ev.

The same year Sviatoslav Vladimirich, son of Monomakh, died

---

17. *Iatvags*: a Lithuanian tribe in present Belorussia.

18. This entry, except the sentence concerning Iaroslav's campaign against the Iatvags, the death of Anna and the consecration of Theoktistus, is not to be found in *Laur.*; it follows *Novg. Syn.*

19. As mentioned before, in the XI—XII centuries the Russian princes used to conceal their Christian names in order to prevent any witchcraft against them. They were known under their customary Slavic dynastic names: i.e., Sviatopolk, Iaroslav, Vladimir, etc.

20. This remark is in error because John II Porphyrogenitus reigned from 1118 to 1143.

1114 on the seventeenth day of the month of January.

CONSECRATION OF BISHOP CYRIL.

The same year on the sixth day of March Nicephorus, Metropolitan of Kiev and all Russia, consecrated Cyril bishop.

THE REIGN OF THE BYZANTINE EMPEROR, MANUEL PORPHYROGENITUS.

After Emperor John [in Byzantium] his son, Manuel Porphyrogenitus, reigned. He reigned for thirty-eight years and was Orthodox.[21]

THE REIGN IN KIEV OF GRAND PRINCE VLADIMIR VSEVOLODICH MONOMAKH, IAROSLAV'S GRANDSON.

After the passing of Grand Prince Sviatopolk Iziaslavich of Kiev, Grand Prince Vladimir Monomakh Vsevolodich, grandson of Iaroslav, great-grandson of Great Vladimir, came to Kiev and was received by the people of Kiev with great honor. On Sunday, the twentieth day of the month of March, he ascended to the throne of his father, Vsevolod, becoming the Grand Prince of Kiev. And the people rejoiced and all manner of disturbances quieted.

The same year Vladimir began to discuss with the boyars a possible campaign against Constantinople, and the boyars answered him, "The heart of the Tsar is in the hands of God and we are in your hands." The Grand Prince assembled his army and sent his voevodas against Constantinople into Thrace. They captured a great many people and returned home in good health. At that time the Emperor of Constantinople was Constantine Monomachus who waged war against the Persians and against the Latins. Therefore Emperor Constantine sent Metropolitan Neophitus of Ephesus to Grand Prince Vladimir, and with him came two bishops—the Bishop of Mytilene [?] and the Bishop of Miletus [?], as well as the military governor of Antiochia, Augustus [Co-Emperor] of Alexandria,[22] Abbot Eustace of Jerusalem, and with them he [the Emperor] sent to the Grand Prince a cross made from the life-giving wood.[23] Also, [he

---

21. Again, this item on Byzantine history, found only in *Nik.*, provides erroneous chronology: Manuel I reigned from 1143 to 1180.

22. In the twelfth century Alexandria in Egypt was in the hands of the Moslems and not of the Byzantine emperor.

23. The wood of the cross on which Christ was crucified.

sent] the imperial crown which he used to wear on his own head and which is now called the "Hat of Monomachus" and a silver box which was used by Augustus, Emperor of Rome, when he revelled [sic!], and golden chains and innumerable other imperial gifts. Metropolitan Neophitus came with the two bishops to Grand Prince Vladimir and began to petition him, the Grand Prince, in the name of the Emperor: "We ask Your Majesty for peace and friendship, so that there should be no disturbance in the Divine Church, and that all Orthodoxy remain at peace under the power of our empire, as well as Your Great Autocratic Majesty of Great Russia. And beginning now, you will be called 'God Crowned' Tsar henceforth." And from then on Grand Prince Vladimir Vsevolodich was called "Monomakh" and "Tsar of Great Russia," and for the remaining time he was in peace and love with Emperor Constantine. Since that time all grand princes of Russia have been crowned with this imperial crown when they ascend to the throne of the grand principality.[24]

In the year 6623/1115. On the first of the month of May, a Saturday, a stone church was consecrated in Vyshgorod. On the second day of the same month, all Russian princes and kinsmen transferred the relics of the Holy Passion Martyrs Boris and Gleb into this stone church, and Vladimir Monomakh ordered that expensive cloth and furs be thrown down[25] so that the people who were tired could easily enter the church. And on the fourth day [the relics] were placed in the sarcophagus. The same year on the eighteenth day of the month of March Prince Oleg Sviatoslavich [of Chernigov] passed away. The same day Voigost' laid the foundation of a church of St. Theodore of Tyron between two streets in the city of Novgorod.

    24. *Hyp.*, under 1116, speaks briefly of Prince Viacheslav's and Foma Ratiborovich's campaign on the Danube, probably against Thrace or Bulgaria, at that time dominated by Byzantium. The parts of the same items dealing with gifts from the then Byzantine emperor—who was Alexis I Comnenus and not Constantine Monomachus (reigned 1042-1053)—are later apocryphal discussions by a fifteenth or sixteenth-century Muscovite publicist endeavoring to embellish Russian history and the importance of the Muscovite rulers. After this story on pages 144-149 of *Nik.*, Vol. IX of *PSRL*, comes the description of the argument between Bishop Hilarion of Meglyn and the Armenian heretics over the Divine Nature of Christ. It is primarily a discussion and denial of Manichean teachings. Since this item does not pertain to Russian history, its translation has been omitted here.

    25. Onto the ground, probably because of the mud.

1116   The same year Vladimir Monomakh built a bridge over the Dnieper.

The same year Vladimir marched to the city of Minsk. On the eighteenth day of the month of January his children occupied the city of Drutsk, while he, himself, remained at Minsk.[26]

In the year 6624/1116. I, the sinful monk Sylvester, Abbot of St. Michael's, have written these books which in the Greek language are called *chronograph*, while in the Russian language they are called *vremennik* or *letopisets*. I did so during the rule of His Holiness and Divine Church guidance of our lord Nicephorus, Metropolitan of Kiev and all Russia; and also during the reign of the pious and Orthodox Kievan Grand Prince Vladimir Monomakh, son of Vsevolod, grandson of Iaroslav, great-grandson of great and holy Vladimir, equal to the Apostles, named in holy baptism "Basil," and who baptised the entire Russian land. I wrote this because of my love for Lord God and the Immaculate Theotokos, and His Saints, as well as on behalf of my fatherland, the Russian land. And I did so for the salvation and use of all. I beg all those who read this book to pray for me in their prayers, so that, thanks to the prayers of the Immaculate Theotokos and all saints, I will hear the sweet and joyful voice of Lord God on the Day of the Last Judgment and will be forgiven from endless torments and receive the blessed promises of God. Amen.[27]

6624/1116. The same year Mstislav Volodimirich marched with the Novgorodian levy against the Chud' and on the day of the Forty Martyrs he took the town of Medvezhiia Golova ["Bear's Head"].

The same year Mstislav laid the foundation of a new city wall in Novgorod which was larger than the previous one. Pavel, posadnik of Novgorod, laid the foundation in Ladoga of a stone fortress.[28]

In the year 6625/1117. Iaropolk Volodimirich built a fortress and gave it to the people of Drutsk, whom he subjugated.

The same year Bishop Minas of Polotsk died, on the twentieth of the month of July.

---

26. This entry is close to *Laur.*

27. See the entry under the year 1110 for the original text. Sylvester completed writing his version of the *Primary Chronicle* in 1116, but brought it only to the year 1110. Thus, the entries of the years 1111-1116 are not his. In any case, the texts of these entries in *Nik.* are a combination of texts from *Laur., Hyp.* and *Novg.*, and were most probably taken from a now unknown South Russian chronicle.

28. Text resembles *Laur.*

The same year Leon Diogenevich,[29] Vladimir's son-in-law, **1117** marched against Emperor Alexis and several cities on the Danube surrendered to him. On the fifteenth of the month of August, in the city of Derestol on the Danube, however, two Saracens sent by the Emperor cunningly killed him.[30]

The same year Iaropolk campaigned in the Polovetsian land up to the river Koldon and took many prisoners, occupying three Polovets cities: Galin, Cheshuev and Sugrov.[31] He brought with him many Alans and captured a wife for himself there, an Alan woman.[32]

The same year Oleg Sviatoslavich [Prince of Chernigov] passed away.[33]

The same year [Grand Prince] Vladimir Vsevolodich [Monomakh] laid the foundation of a stone church of the Holy Martyrs Boris and Gleb on the river Al'ta, where they were killed.[34]

The same year Vladimir Monomakh took Prince Mstislav from Novgorod and assigned him to Belgorod, while Vsevolod Mstislavich became Prince of Novgorod.[35]

The same year there was a portent in Novgorod near [the Novgorodian cathedral of] Holy Sophia. This happened because of a thunderstorm on the fourteenth of the month of May. At the tenth hour, when vespers were being sung, one of the deacons was struck by lightning and the whole choir and all the people attending fell down; but all arose alive. In the evening there was also a portent on the moon.

The same year Abbot Anthony laid the foundation in Novgorod of a stone church [to St. George] in the Monastery of the Holy Theotokos.

The same year Dobrynia, posadnik of Novgorod, passed

---

29. Leon Diogenevich was a pretender to the Byzantine throne. See the beginning of the entry under 1095.

30. Text close to *Laur.* and *Hyp.*

31. These names have been corrected according to *Laur.*

32. *Alans*: in Old Russian, *Iasy*, now called *Ossetians*. They were a nomadic Iranian tribe which then roamed in the prairies north of the Black Sea, Caspian Sea and even in Central Asia. Text close to *Laur.*

33. In *Laur.* these items are under the year 1116; the death of Oleg, under 1115; in *Nik.* it was already mentioned under 1115.

34. Actually, only Boris was killed on the Al'ta. 1117 in *Laur.*

35. 1117 in *Laur.*

1118 away.³⁶

In the year 6626/1118. Vladimir [Monomakh] campaigned against Iaroslav [or Iaroslavets] Sviatopolchich and marched toward the city of Vladimir [in Volynia]. He made peace with him and then left. Vladimir was very wroth at him because Iaroslavets quarreled with his wife, who was Vladimir's granddaughter and the daughter of Mstislav.³⁷

DEATH OF BISHOP LAZAR'.

The same year on the sixteenth of the month of September Bishop Lazar' of Pereiaslavl' died.

CONSECRATION OF BISHOP SYLVESTER.

Nicephorus, Metropolitan of Kiev and all Russia, consecrated Sylvester in his place as Bishop on the first day of the month of January.³⁸

The same year Vladimir Monomakh wed his son, Andrei, to the granddaughter of Tugr Khan, a Polovetsian ruler.³⁹

In the year 6627/1119. Iaroslavets Sviatopolchich sent his wife away. She was the daughter of Mstislav, and granddaughter of Vladimir; therefore, Vladimir Monomakh marched against him toward the city of Vladimir [in Volynia]; but he [Iaroslavets] fled to Hungary and all his warriors abandoned him.⁴⁰ Vladimir [Monomakh] sent his son, Roman, to the city of Vladimir [in

---

36. These last items follow *Novg.*

37. Close to *Laur.*; but neither *Laur.* nor *Hyp.* mentions Iaroslavets' wife.

38. Close to *Laur.*, 1118.

39. In *Hyp.*, 1117. The original version of *The Primary Chronicle* was, most probably, written by Monk Nestor of the Kievan Monastery of the Cave. In 1116 Abbot Sylvester of the Vydubetskii Monastery brought it up to the year 1110. In the reign of Mstislav the Great an unknown chronicler extended it to the year 1118. The further text of *Nik.* is based on various chronicles, of which the main sources were the no-longer extant chronicle of Pereiaslavl', which used the Ultra March Calendar, and on the chronicle of Suzdal'. *Nik.*'s chroniclers had at their disposal later *mss.* works in which the contents of these chronicles, as well as various other sources, were incorporated.

40. Monomakh's granddaughter was Iaroslavets's third wife. Previously, he was married to a Hungarian; subsequently, to a Polish princess.

Volynia] to be prince there; but the latter died on the fifteenth of the month of January. Then Vladimir Monomakh sent his other son, Andrei, as prince to the city of Vladimir.

The same year Gleb Vseslavich passed away. The same year Abbot Cyriacus and Prince Vsevolod Mstislavich laid the foundation of a stone church of the Holy Martyr George in the monastery in Great Novgorod. The same year Abbot Anthony's church was completed in the Monastery of the Holy Theotokos in Novgorod.[41]

In the year 6628/1120.[42] Iaroslav campaigned on the river Don against the Polovetss but he did not find them and returned home. His brother, Jurii Dolgorukii[43] campaigned against the Bulgars [of the Volga], took many prisoners and defeated their troops.

The same year the Torks and Berendeis fled from the Russian land. They became confused and perished there.

The same year Boris came from Kiev to be posadnik in Novgorod.

DEATH OF METROPOLITAN NICEPHORUS.

In the year 6629/1121. Metropolitan Nicephorus of Kiev and all Russia died in the month of April.

PORTENT.

In the year 6630/1122. On the tenth of the month of March there was a portent on the sun and on the twentieth of the same month there was a portent on the moon.

The same year the wife of Prince Mstislavl' died, on the twelfth of the month of January.

DEATH OF BISHOP DANIEL.

The same year on the ninth of the month of September Bishop Daniel of Jur'ev died.

METROPOLITAN NICETAS.

The same year Nicetas came from Constantinople to be Metropolitan of Kiev and all Russia.

---

41. A slightly different and shorter text is in *Laur.* and *Hyp.* under 6626/1118.

42. 6626/1118 in *Laur.* and *Hyp.*, but texts differ.

43. Dologorukii: "Long-armed," so called because of his acquisitive proclivities.

1123 DEATH OF BISHOP AMPHILOPHEUS.

The same year Amphilopheus, Bishop of Vladimir, died, and the earth trembled somewhat.

The same year the Poles took prisoner [Prince] Volodar', Vasil'ko's brother. The same year Mstislav Volodimirich married in Novgorod the daughter of Dmitri Zavidovich.[44]

THE DEATH OF BISHOP SYLVESTER.

In the year 6631/1123. The blessed Syvlester, Bishop of Pereiaslavl', died on Maundy Thursday, on the twelfth of the month of April.

The same year Prince Davyd Mstislavich died in Chernigov. After him his brother, Iaroslav, became Prince of Chernigov.

CONSECRATION OF BISHOP SIMEON.

The same year Nicetas, Metropolitan of Kiev and all Russia, consecrated Simeon to be Bishop of Vladimir in Volynia.

The same year Theoktistus, Bishop of Chernigov, died, on the sixth day of the month of August.

[IAROSLAVETS CAMPAIGNS AGAINST THE CITY OF VLADIMIR. HIS DEATH.]

The same year Prince Iaroslavets, son of Sviatopolk, grandson of Iaroslav, great-grandson of Great Vladimir, marched to the city of Vladimir in Volynia against Prince Andrei, son of Vladimir Monomakh, grandson of Vsevolod, great-grandson of Iaroslav, great-great-grandson of Great Vladimir. He came with a multitude of warriors, with Hungarians, with Poles, with Czechs, with the levies of Pinsk, and with Princes Volodar' and Vasil'ko, sons of Rostislav. This multitude of warriors besieged Prince Andrei in the city of Vladimir, but Prince Andrei Volodimirovich prepared the city of Vladimir for the siege and fought them fiercely. His father, Vladimir Monomakh, gathered troops in Kiev but did not have time to send them quickly from Kiev.

Prince Iaroslavets, however, rode around the city of Vladimir and loudly threatened Prince Andrei and the citizens, saying, "On the morrow I will take your city and torture all of you mercilessly." And so, on the morrow when the sun rose many warriors began

---

44. Text close to *Hyp*.

preparing [to attack the city]; but Prince Iaroslavets, not waiting for his troops, alone with but two soldiers, went to the city. Some citizens, however, had left the city secretly at night and had hidden themselves along the route on which Iaroslavets was supposed to go. When Prince Iaroslavets passed them, they leaped up unexpectedly and struck him with a lance. His troops hurried up to him, took him, already dying, and bore him to camp, to his tent, where he died.

All his innumerable soldiers—the Hungarians, Czechs, Poles, the levy of Pinsk, and the Princes Volodar' and Vasil'ko, sons of Rostislav—lamented lengthily over him. Then they sent to the city of Vladimir, to Prince Andrei Volodimirich Monomashich, saying, "Your kinsman, Prince Iaroslavets, sought to seize the throne in his city of Vladimir and brought us with him as aid. But now he is lying dead and we have no one to fight for." Prince Andrei Volodimirich, hearing this, greatly rejoiced and made peace with them; and he rendered them great honor, giving them many gifts. They buried Prince Iaroslavets in the city of Vladimir, which he had wanted to conquer and in which he wanted to live; but, unexpectedly, he was laid there dead. As it is said, "Not by one's own will, nor for one's deeds, but only by God's mercy—and to God all things are possible, but to man, nothing." Prince Andrei Volodimirich, son of Monomakh, settled firmly as Prince in the city of Vladimir, while Prince Iaroslavets's troops disbanded, each going to his own place.

1123

A CHURCH COLLAPSES.

The same year on the tenth day of the month of May, a Saturday, before vespers, the stone church of St. Michael in Pereiaslavl' collapsed. It was built and adorned by blessed Ephraim, Metropolitan of Kiev and all Russia, who lived in his city of Pereiaslavl'.

The same year Vsevolod Mstislavich marched with the Novgorodian levy from Novgorod against the Iam'[45] and defeated them; but his march was an evil one. They had to pay a fur for a piece of bread.

The same year Vsevolod Mstislavich married, in Novgorod.

The same year His Holiness, Nicetas, Metropolitan of Kiev and all Russia, imprisoned an evil heretic named Dmitrii in the jail of his

---

45. *Iam'*—a Finnic tribe.

1124 town of Sinelitsa.⁴⁶

CONFLAGRATION.

In the year 6632/1124. There was a great conflagration in Kiev and nearly the entire city burned for two days; and also the Podol burned.⁴⁷ Nearly seven hundred churches burned, and this happened on the twenty-third and twenty-fourth days of the month of June, on the holiday of the birth of St. John the Baptist.

PORTENT.

The same year there was a portent on the sun; and this happened on the eleventh day of August at the ninth hour of the day, before vespers. The sun grew smaller, becoming as small as the moon, and grew smaller until noon, then disappeared entirely. There was darkness and great fear; and the stars and moon disappeared; but thereafter the sun grew rapidly and again became full, and all were happy.

The same year Prince Volodar' Rostislavich and his brother, Vasil'ko Rostislavich, died, on the twenty-eighth of the month of February.

The same year the dowager princess of Prince Iaropolk died.

THE PASSING OF GRAND PRINCE VLADIMIR MONOMAKH.

In the year 6633/1125. On the nineteenth of the month of May the pious Grand Prince Vladimir Monomakh, son of Vsevolod, grandson of Iaroslav, great grandson of Great Vladimir, passed away. He ruled Kiev for thirteen years and he lived altogether for seventy and three years from his birth. He was blessed with high morals and became glorious through his victories for the Russian land over the pagan Polovetss. And all lands feared his name and in all countries he was spoken of with awe. [It was thus] because he loved the Lord God with all his soul. We also claim that we love God, but we do nothing for Him. Let us try to preserve His Commandments and so we will demonstrate our love for God. The

---

46. This is the second earliest mention of the spread of a heresy in Russia, the first being in 6512. Most probably, Dmitrii was associated with the dualistic sect of the Bogomils, who were very strong in the Balkans, particularly in Bulgaria and Bosnia.

47. *Podol*: the lower part of the city, near the Dnieper.

Lord said, "One who loves Me will preserve My Commandments." **1125**
This wonderful Vladimir Monomakh endeavored to preserve the
Commandments of God and always had the fear of God in his heart,
as well as His Word, because He said, "They will recognize you as My
pupils because you love each other." "Love your enemies, do good
to those who hate you, and pray for them that despitefully use
you." [*Luke* 6:27-28.] Therefore Lord God brought under his
[Monomakh's] hand all his enemies because he was never proud or
boastful but relied upon God, and God submitted all his enemies
under his foot; he preserved the Commandments of God, did good
to his enemies, and would release them with gifts. He was merciful
beyond all measure because he remembered the Word of God, Who
said, "Blessed are the merciful, and they will be saved. Blessed are
those who think of the poor and the paupers, and in an evil day they
will find salvation from God." [*Matt.* 5:1-11, rephrased.] He also did
not spare his wealth, and distributed it to those who asked for it; and
he built and adorned churches and monasteries, and he greatly
respected the clergy and the monks, and always gave them sufficient
for their needs. And he greatly respected his kinfolk, the Holy
Martyrs Roman and Davyd.[48] He erected a beautiful church on the
Al'ta river and named it after them because the blood of St. Boris was
shed there. He greatly pitied [people] and he received this gift from
God. When he attended church he hearkened to the singing and the
reading, he would keep firmly in mind [the meaning] of the chants
and the readings, and he would become meek and would shed tears.
That is why God did everything he asked, and he lived out his years
in well-being. He passed away on the river Al'ta in his beloved
church, which he created through his many efforts. All his sons—
Mstislav, Iziaslav, Sviatoslav, Iaropolk, Viacheslav, Roman, Iurii,
Andrei—amid his boyars carried him to Kiev, and he was buried
in [the Cathedral of] Holy Sophia next to his father.[49]

THE REIGN OF MSTISLAV [THE GREAT]

After him the throne of the Grand Principality was taken by his
eldest son, Mstislav. When he was still young he fought on [the river]
Koloksha against Oleg Sviatoslavich, who was his uncle and the

---

48. Roman and Davyd: the Christian names of Monomakh's great
uncles, the Holy Martyrs Boris and Gleb.

49. This praise follows rather closely the text of *Laur.*

1125 grandson of Iaroslav. [This happened] because [Oleg's father] Sviatoslav was the senior brother of Mstislav's grandfather, Vsevolod, [and therefore] Oleg, himself, wanted [at that time] to be Grand Prince [in Kiev]. But Mstislav defeated him and chased him to Tmutarakan' and from thence he went to Riazan'.[50]

[IAROPOLK DEFEATS THE POLOVETSS]

Iaropolk, Vladimir Monomakh's son and Mstislav's brother, received [the principality of] Pereiaslavl'. When the Polovetss learned that Prince Vladimir Monomakh had died they came rapidly raiding, together with the accursed Torks—and with those, wanted to fight the Russian land. But God prevented their intentions and they did not succeed in the least [in joining the Torks]. When Iaropolk received news [of the raid] he chased the Torks into [their] city the same night. Thus, when the Polovetss reappeared, Prince Iaropolk, strengthened with divine help and not waiting for any other assistance either from his brothers or from anyone else, only with [his] people of Pereiaslavl', caught them at Stenia. But [still] the Polovetss came again while he advanced, prepared for the fight against them. Then pious Prince Iaropolk, calling on the Name of God and remembering [the deeds of] his father, dared [to accept battle], with his retinue, and defeated the pagans, with the help of the venerable cross. And very many [Polovetss] were killed and others drowned in the river. And thus Prince Iaropolk returned [home to Pereiaslavl'], praising and glorifying God for His divine help.[51]

THE STORM OF HAIL.

The same year there was in Novgorod a great storm of hail which destroyed houses and drove herds of cattle into [the river] Volkhov, and some of them drowned and others were caught hardly alive. The same year in the Monastery of St. Anthony in Novgorod they finished painting the Icon of the Most Pure Mother of God. The same year on the nineteenth of the month of May the Novgorodians installed Prince Vsevolod Mstislavich [on the throne

---

50. Tmutarakan': an extreme southeastern Russian settlement in the eleventh century which was in the northwestern Caucasus near the delta of the Kuban' river, where the city of Taman' is now located.

51. This paragraph is very close to *Laur*.

of Novgorod].⁵²

In the year 6634/1126. On the fourth day of the month of October, Nicetas, Metropolitan of Kiev and all Russia, consecrated Mark, abbot [of the Monastery] of St. John, to be bishop of Pereiaslavl'.

METROPOLITAN NICETAS DIES.

The same year on the ninth of the month of March, Nicetas, Metropolitan of Kiev and all Russia, passed away. The same year the [dowager] princess [widow of] Vladimir Monomakh passed away on the eleventh day of the month of June. The same year on the first day of the month of August at the eighth hour of the night there occurred an earthquake. The same year Miroslav Goriatinich was assigned as posadnik of Novgorod.

In the year 6635/1127. Prince Briacheslav, younger son of Sviatopolk, passed away on the twenty-eighth of the month of March and was buried on April fifth. The same year [Prince] Davyd⁵³ Ol'govich chased away his uncle, [Prince] Iaroslav Sviatoslavich, from Chernigov, and he massacred his retinue and sacked [the city]. Mstislav, however, joined by Iaropolk, decided to campaign against Vsevolod [Davyd's brother] on behalf of Iaroslav [Sviatoslavich]. But Vsevolod sent for the Polovetss, and seventeen thousand of them came with [Khans] Seluk and Tas. And they were camped at the oak forest of Ratimir beyond [the river] Vyr'. Their envoys were dispatched to Vsevolod but they were not permitted to pass through and returned; Iziaslav, son of Iaropolk, came to Veresk, found their [the Polovetss'] envoys on the river Knia, and brought them to Iaropolk. Since the Polovetss had no news for a long while from the [Princes Vsevolod and Davyd] Ol'govichs they became anxious and retreated, fleeing.

Mstislav, pressing Vsevolod more and more, told him, "You brought the Polovetss but you did not succeed in the least." And the latter [Vsevolod Ol'govich] again petitioned and sent the boyars and gave gifts, and so they remained all summer and winter. Iaroslav [Sviatoslavovich] came from Murom, greeted Mstislav and said, "You pledged on the cross [to support me]. Let us go against

---

52. Follows *Novg. Syn.*
53. In both *Laur.* and *Hyp.* we find "Vsevolod Ol'govich."

1127 Vsevolod." Vsevolod, however, began to pray Mstislav not to keep his pledge on the cross.

At that time the abbot of [the monastery of] St. Andrew was Gregory; he was liked very much by Vladimir [Monomakh] and was respected by Mstislav and the other people. And he wanted to prevent war on the behalf of Iaroslav [Sviatoslavich] and said [to Mstislav], "It will be a great sin if you break your pledge on the cross; but it is better to break it than to spill the blood of Christians." And he gathered the council of the clergy together because the Metropolitan was not then there, and he said to Mstislav, "Your sin will be upon us." Mstislav acted according to their will and broke his oath on the cross which he had given to Iaroslav, and therefore he lamented thereafter throughout all the days of his life, while Iaroslav [Sviatoslavovich] retreated to Murom.

[MSTISLAV'S CAMPAIGN AGAINST THE KRIVICHS AND POLOTSK]

The same year Prince Mstislav Vladimirich, son of Monomakh, sent his brothers against the Krivichs[54] and they went by four routes: [two brothers of Mstislav and Prince] Viacheslav went from Turov and [Prince] Andrei went from the city of Vladimir; Vsevolodko[55] from Grodno and Viacheslav and Viacheslav Iaroslavich[56] from Klechesk. And he ordered them to go against [the city of] Iziaslavl'. And he ordered Vsevolod Ol'govich to go with his brothers toward Borisovo by the route of Strezhevo. And he sent [his voevoda] Ivan Voiteshich at the same time with the Torks. And he sent his [own] son, Iziaslav [Mstislavich] with a regiment from Kursk against the city of Logozhesk. He sent his other son, Rostislav, with the levy of

54. The *Krivichs*, a Russian tribe living then in the vicinity of the cities of Polotsk and Vitebsk in present northeastern Belorussia, were ruled by the descendants of their own tribal prince, Rogvold, whose daughter, Rogneda, became a concubine of Vladimir (980-1015), Christianizer of Russia, and who bore him a son, Iziaslav, who, in his turn, became the prince of Polotsk. There was hereditary hatred between the clan of Iziaslav, especially his grandson, Vseslav, called the "Magician," and both branches of the clan of Iaroslav the Wise, the Ol'govichs and the Monomakhovichs, although both Iziaslav and Iaroslav were children of the same Rogneda. For background, see the legend in this chronicle under the year 1128.

55. Vsevolodko Davydovich, grandson of Igor', Iaroslav the Wise's son and husband of Agathea, Monomakh's daughter.

56. Either a son of Iaroslav Sviatopolkovich or the son of Iaroslav Iaropolkovich.

Smolensk against Drutsk. And he told them that they must all attack **1127** [the city of Iziaslavl'] on the same day, the fourteenth of the month of August. Iziaslav [Mstislavich] hurried and arrived one day before his brothers, took the people from the city [of Logozhesk] because they surrendered to him, being afraid, while the people [of the city] of Iziaslavl' began fighting with Viacheslav and Andrei. For two days Iziaslav did not hurry from Logozhesk and [then] went to [the city of] Iziaslavl' to meet his uncles, taking with him his brother-in-law, Briacheslav.[57] The latter was marching to [join] his father [Davyd Vseslavich] but when he was halfway there he took fright and, unable to move either hither or thither, he decided to surrender into the hands of his brother-in-law [Iziaslav], bringing with him the people whom he had taken from [the city of] Logozhesk. When the people of [the city of] Iziaslavl' saw their prince [Briacheslav] with the people of Logozhesk, who were taken over without having done malice, they said to [Prince] Viacheslav, "Give us your oath before Lord God that you will not sack us." It was in the evening when Vorotislav, the tysiackii of Prince Andrei, and Ivanko, the tysiackii of Prince Viacheslav, sent their warriors into the city. And when dawn came they saw all [of their own] warriors had [gotten into the city and] sacked it during the night. Only the valuables of Mstislav's daughter [the wife of Prince Briacheslav] remained preserved with great difficulty because [the soldiers of Vorotislav and Ivanko] fought [to protect them]. And so they [Mstislav's troops] returned with a large number of captives. Thereafter the people of Novgorod came with Vsevolod Mstislavich to the town of Nelogozh. And also the people of Polotsk, assembling, chased Davyd with his sons and went to [Prince] Mstislav [of Kiev], taking Rogvold with them; there they asked Mstislav to appoint him [Rogvold] prince of Polotsk. Mstislav did this according to their will, and they took Rogvold and brought him [as their prince] to Polotsk.

The same year Prince Iziaslav Sviatopolkovich died on the thirteenth day of the month of December, and was buried the fourteenth.[58]

The same year [Prince] Vsevolod Mstislavovich laid the foundation in the Petriatin estate in Novgorod of the stone church of

---

57. Briacheslav: prince of Vitebsk in the Polotsk land, son of Prince Davyd Vseslavovich, Prince of Polotsk, and a daughter of Mstislav.

58. This first part of the entry is as in *Laur.*

1128 St. John, in honor of the name of his son. The same year in Novgorod there was a very heavy snow which covered the ground, the water and the houses, and it lasted two nights and four days. The water was very high in the river Volkhov, and the snow remained till the day of St. Jacob. In the fall the frost destroyed all the rye and there was a famine, and during the winter one *os'minka* [one-eighth of a measure of grain] of rye was sold for half a grivna.[59]

In the year 6636/1128. Prince Boris of Polotsk passed away. The same year there was a very high flood and people drowned, and the water carried away the rye and the buildings. The same year Prince Mstislav laid the foundation of the stone church of St. Theodore. The same year the [monks] of Pechersk [the Kievan Cave Monastery] took over the church of St. Demetrius and renamed it [the church of] St. Peter. And it was a great sin and injustice.[60]

THE LEGEND OF POLOTSK
[ABOUT THE DESCENDANTS OF ROGVOLD, ROGNEDA, IZIASLAV AND VSESLAV]

There is a story which is told by those who knew the olden time. When Rogvol'd ruled the land of Polotsk and Vladimir was still a youth and pagan in Novgorod, he had a voevoda by the name of Dobrynia, who was very brave and a very handsome man. This one sent [his envoy] to Rogvol'd asking the hand of the latter's daughter, by the name of Rogneda, for Vladimir. He [Rogvol'd] asked his daughter, "Do you want to marry Vladimir?" and she answered, "I don't want to take off the shoes of a slave's son, but I want to marry Iaropolk."[61] This Rogvol'd came from beyond the seas and he had his principality in Polotsk. When Vladimir heard this he became angry at these words, to wit, "I don't want to marry the son of a slave." And Dobrynia [also] became very offended and full of wrath, and he took his warriors, marched against Polotsk and defeated Rogvol'd. Rogvol'd escaped to the fortress and [Dobrynia's] army stormed the fortress and took it, as well as Prince Rogvol'd and his wife and his daughter. And Dobrynia spoke much offense to him and to his daughter, betrothed her to the son of a slave [Vladimir],

59. Close to *Novg. Syn.*
60. As in *Laur.*
61. According to legend, Vladimir was the son of Prince Sviatoslav and Malusha, a servant of Sviatoslav's mother, Ol'ga while his brother, Iaropolk, a fiance of Rogneda's, was apparently the son of a noblewoman.

and ordered Vladimir to be with her in the presence of her father and her mother. And thereafter he killed her father. And Vladimir took her as his wife. And so, having done, Vladimir gave her the name, "Goreslava." And she bore him a son, named Iziaslav.

1128

Vladimir, however, took many other wives and became mean with her. Once he came to her and fell asleep. [At night] she wanted to kill him with a knife but he awoke and caught her by the hand. She told him, "I am badly offended because for my sake you killed my father, mother and brothers, and you conquered his land. And now you don't love either me or my child." [Vladimir] ordered her to dress and to prepare the entire royal garb and accessories as if he were to marry her, and told her to sit down on the bed in a bright room. And he came to strike her [with his sword]. But she did the following: she gave a sword to her son, Iziaslav, into his bare hands, saying, "When your father comes, go forward and say to him: 'Father, do you want to live on this earth or do you believe that you are immortal? Oh, Father! Take this sword and put it into my chest because I don't want to see the bitter tears of my mother.'" Vladimir told him, "Oh, my child, who put you here?" And he shed tears and threw down his sword and called the boyars and told them of this. And they said, "Don't kill your son because of her but establish a principality for her and give it to her with her son." Vladimir built a city and gave it to them, naming it Iziaslavl'. And since that time the grandsons of Rogvol'd raise their swords against the grandsons of Iaroslav.[62]

The same year there was a great famine in Novgorod and one os'minka of rye was [to be had] for a grivna. And the people ate linden leaves and birch bark, and others ground and mixed it with chaff and straw, and some ate eels, moss and horsemeat. And people fell dead one next to the other from starvation, and there were corpses lying in the markets and in the streets and everywhere along the roads. And [the people] hired hirelings to carry the dead from the city; and there was such a stench that it was impossible to go out. There was grief and misfortune for everyone! Mothers and fathers would give their children away to merchants for nothing, but those would let them die; and others would go to foreign lands. And thus, because of our sins, our land was laid waste.[63]

62. As in *Laur.*
63. As in *Novg. Syn.*

1129 The same year Cyriakos, abbot of Saint George, passed away in Novgorod.[64] The same year Ivan, son of Vsevolod, died in Novgorod.[65]

In the year 6637/1129. Iaroslav Sviatoslavich, grandson of Iaroslav, great grandson of Great Vladimir, died in Murom. The same year Mikhalko Viacheslavich died in Riazan'. The same year Prince Mstislav put the princes of Polotsk with their wives and children in prison in Constantinople.[66] The same year Danilo came from Kiev to Novgorod to be posadnik.[67]

In the year 6638/1130. Mstislav sent his children, Vsevolod, Iziaslav and Rostislav, with their retinues and with the Novgorodian levies, against the Chud'[68] and they defeated them and imposed a tribute.[69] The same year [Bishop] John gave up his bishopric after having remained there for twenty years.

CONSECRATION OF BISHOP NIPHONT.

The same year His Holiness, Michael, Metropolitan of Kiev and all Russia, consecrated Niphont, a holy and God-abiding man, to be Bishop of Novgorod. The same year the stone Church of St. John was completed. And Petrilo was given the office of posadnik in Novgorod.[70]

In the year 6639/1131. Mstislav, son of Vladimir Monomakh, with all the forces of Novgorod and with the people of the Nizovskaia land,[71] marched against Lithuania; they campaigned there long and, capturing many people, returned home with great joy. The same year the princes of Riazan', of Pronsk and of Murom defeated and killed many Polovetss. The same year Mstislav

---

64. As in *Novg. Syn.*

65. As in *Novg. Kom.*

66. Mstislav had family contacts with the Byzantine court, his grandmother being a Byzantine princess from the house of Monomachus.

67. As in *Laur.*; the last sentence as in *Novg. Syn.*

68. *Chud'* was a Finno-Ugric tribe in northern Russia, north and northeast of Novgorod.

69. As in *Laur.*

70. As in *Novg. Syn.*, except second sentence, which is as in *Novg. Kom.*

71. *Niz, Nizovskaia zemlia*: lands on the upper Volga and its tributaries, the kernel of Suzdalian and Muscovite Russia.

Vladimirovich laid the foundation of the Church of the Holy **1132**
Mother of God of Pirogosht.[72]

[PASSING OF GRAND PRINCE MSTISLAV OF KIEV]

In the year 6640/1132. Mstislav, son of Vladimir Monomakh, grandson of Vsevolod, great grandson of Iaroslav and the great, great grandson of Great Vladimir, passed away on the fourteenth of the month of April after having been Prince in Kiev for six years. His sons were Vsevolod, Iziaslav, Rostislav and Sviatopolk.[73]

72. This church is mentioned also in the concluding lines of *Prince Igor's Lay.* As in *Laur.* and *Hyp.*; however, the source of the Riazan' item is unknown.

73. First part of the item is in *Laur.* and *Hyp.*, but abbreviated.